Modern
English Reader

Charlton Laird

Hilliard Distinguished Professor
University of Nevada

Robert M. Gorrell

Vice-President
University of Nevada

William Lutz

Director of Freshman English
Rutgers University, Camden

Ronald E. Freeman

Professor of English
University of California, Los Angeles

Modern English Reader

SECOND EDITION

PRENTICE-HALL, INC., ENGLEWOOD CLIFFS, NEW JERSEY 07632

Library of Congress Cataloging in Publication Data

Main entry under title:

Modern English reader.

    Compiled in 1970 by R. M. Gorrell, C. Laird, and
R. E. Freeman.
      Includes index.
      1. English language—Rhetoric. 2. College readers.
I. Laird, Charlton Grant, date-   II. Gorrell,
Robert M., comp. Modern English reader.
[PE1408.M585 1977]   808'.0427   76-30499
ISBN 0-13-594176-8

Modern English Reader, 2nd ed., Laird / Gorrell / Lutz / Freeman

Printed in the United States of America

10 9 8 7 6 5 4 3 2

PRENTICE-HALL INTERNATIONAL, INC., *London*
PRENTICE-HALL OF AUSTRALIA PTY. LIMITED, *Sydney*
PRENTICE-HALL OF CANADA, LTD., *Toronto*
PRENTICE-HALL OF INDIA PRIVATE LIMITED, *New Delhi*
PRENTICE-HALL OF JAPAN, INC., *Tokyo*
PRENTICE-HALL OF SOUTHEAST ASIA PTD. LTD., *Singapore*
WHITEHALL BOOKS LIMITED, *Wellington, New Zealand*

Acknowledgments

GOODMAN ACE, "You Could Have Knocked Me Down with a Fender," *Saturday Review,* May 18, 1974. Copyright © 1974. Reprinted by permission of the author and the Saturday Review.

SHANA ALEXANDER, "Will Power Change Women?" from *Newsweek,* Apr. 1, 1974. Copyright © 1974 by Shana Alexander. Reprinted by permission of Shana Alexander.

CLEVELAND AMORY, from "Curmudgeon at Large," *Saturday Review,* Feb. 21, 1976. Copyright © 1972. Reprinted by permission of the author and the Saturday Review.

ROBERT E. ANNIN, from *Ocean Shipping: Elements of Practical Steamship Operation* (New York: Century, 1920).

RICHARD ATCHESON, "It's Easy to Spend at Le Pirate; the Bill Depends on What's Broken," the *New York Times,* Mar. 19, 1972. © 1972 by The New York Times Company. Reprinted by permission.

RUSSELL BAKER, "Strike Four," the *New York Times,* June 22, 1976. © 1976 by The New York Times Company. Reprinted by permission.

JAMES BALDWIN, from "White Man's Guilt," *Ebony,* August 1965.

JACQUES BARZUN, from *Teacher in America* (Boston: Atlantic–Little, Brown, 1945).

EDWARD BELLAMY, from *Looking Backward* (New York: Random House).

ROBERT BENCHLEY, "Family Life in America," (pp. 41–43) by Robert Benchley from *The Benchley Roundup* edited by Nathaniel Benchley. Copyright 1922 by Harper & Row, Publishers, Inc. Reprinted by permission of the publisher.

URIE BRONFENBRENNER, "Why Do the Russians Plant Trees along a Road?" from *The Language of Man,* 4 (Evanston, Ill.: McDougal, Littel & Company, 1971).

JACOB BRONOWSKI, "The Reach of the Imagination," *American Scholar,* Spring 1967. Reprinted by permission of the Academy of Arts and Letters and the permission of the estate of Jacob Bronowski.

CLEANTH BROOKS AND ROBERT PENN WARREN, from *Understanding Poetry,* 3rd ed. Copyright 1938, 1950, © 1960 by Holt, Rinehart and Winston, Reprinted by permission of Holt, Rinehart and Winston.

MARGARET BRYANT, from *Modern English and Its Heritage.* Copyright © 1962 Macmillan Publishing Company. Reprinted by permission of the publisher.

MARGARET BRYANT, from "Our Changing Language," in *Reflections on High School English*: NDEA Institute Lectures, 1965, ed. Gary Tate, University of Tulsa. Reprinted by permission.

TRUMAN CAPOTE, from *In Cold Blood* (New York: Random House, Inc., 1967).

PETER CARLSON, "The Intellectual Taxicab Company," *Newsweek,* June 1975. Copyright © 1975 by Newsweek Inc. All rights reserved. Reprinted by permission.

JOHN CIARDI, from "The Concurrence of Myth," *Saturday Review,* Mar. 9, 1974; from "Tongues," *Saturday Review,* Feb. 27, 1973. Copyright © 1974, 1973. Reprinted by permission of the author and the Saturday Review.

KENNETH B. CLARK, from *The Language of Man,* 5 (Evanston, Ill.: McDougall, Littel & Company, 1971).

WILLIAM H. CLARK, from *Ships and Sailors: The Story of Our Merchant Marine* (Boston: Page, 1938).

RICHARD CONDON, from "A Private Audience—Or Maybe Two?" in *The Vertical Smile* (New York: Dial Press, 1971).

DONNA CORD, "Diary of a Mad Housewife," *Newsweek*, Feb. 18, 1974. Copyright © 1974 by Newsweek, Inc. All rights reserved. Reprinted by permission.

PAUL COREY, "How to Build a Tall A-Frame Alone," excerpted from *Build a Home* by Paul Corey. Copyright © 1946, 1974 by Paul Corey. Reprinted by permission of the Dial Press.

ROBERT E. COULSON, from "Let's Not Get out the Vote," in *Harpers*, November 1975. Reprinted by the permission of Robert E. Coulson.

NORMAN COUSINS, "The Third Most Powerful Man in the World," *Saturday Review*, Apr. 17, 1976. Copyright © 1976. Reprinted by permission of the author and the Saturday Review.

E. E. CUMMINGS, "Buffalo Bill's defunct," Copyright 1923, renewed 1951 by E. E. Cummings. Reprinted from his volume *Complete Poems 1913–1962* by permission of Harcourt Brace Jovanovich.

ROALD DAHL, from "The Visitor," from *Switch Bitch*, by Roald Dahl. Copyright © 1965, 1974 by Roald Dahl. Reprinted by permission of Alfred A. Knopf, Inc. Originally appeared in *Playboy* magazine.

MICHAEL DEMAREST, "The Fine Art of Putting Things off," in *Time*, June 10, 1974. Reprinted by permission from Time, The Weekly Newsmagazine; copyright Time, Inc.

PETER DEVRIES, "Compulsion," from *Without a Stitch in Time, A Selection of the Best Humorous Short Pieces* by Peter DeVries. Copyright © 1953 by Peter DeVries. This story originally appeared in *The New Yorker*. By permission of Little, Brown and Co.

PAUL DICKSON, "Tomorrow's Automated Battlefield," *The Progressive*, August 1974. Reprinted by permission from *The Progressive*, 408 West Gorham Street, Madison, Wisconsin 53703. Copyright © 1947, The Progressive, Inc.

C. A. DOXIADIS, "Two Letters to an American," Reprinted by permission of *Daedalus*, Journal of the American Academy of Arts and Sciences, Boston, Massachusetts. Fall 1972, *How Others See the United States*.

GERALD DURRELL, from "The World in a Wall," from *My Family and Other Animals* by Gerald Durrell. Copyright © 1956 by Gerald M. Durrell. Reprinted by permission of The Viking Press and Curtis Brown Ltd.

LOREN EISELEY, "The Cosmic Orpan," from *Propaedia*, The Encyclopedia Britannica.

HELEN EPSTEIN, "A Sin or a Right," The *New York Times Magazine*, Sept. 8, 1974. © 1974 by The New York Times Company. Reprinted by permission.

JOSEPH EPSTEIN, from "Obsessed with Sport." Reprinted from the July 1976 issue by the permission of Harpers Magazine.

BERGEN EVANS, from *The Language of Man*, 5 (Evanston, Ill.: McDougall, Littel and Co., 1971).

Family Medical Guide, V. C. Branham and S. B. Kutash, eds. A Better Homes and Gardens Book. © 1973 by the Meredith Corporation.

WILLIAM FAULKNER, from *The Reivers* (New York: Random House, 1962).

PATRICK FENTON, "Confessions of a Working Stiff"; *New York*, Mar. 3, 1973. Copyright © 1973 by the NYM Corp. Reprinted with permission of New York Magazine.

ANNE TAYLOR FLEMING, "Up from Slavery—to What?" *Newsweek*, Jan. 21, 1974. Copyright © 1974 by Newsweek, Inc. All rights reserved.

ABRAHAM FLEXNER, "The Usefulness of Useless Knowledge," *Harpers*, October 1939. Reprinted by the permission of Harpers Magazine.

WALKER GIBSON, from *Tough, Sweet and Stuffy* (Bloomington: Indiana University Press, 1966).

FRANÇOISE GILOT AND CARLTON LAKE, from *Life with Picasso* (New York: McGraw-Hill, 1962).

ROBERT GORRELL, "Very Like a Whale," *College Composition and Communication*, October 1965. Copyright © 1965 by the National Council of Teachers of English. Reprinted by permission.

DAN GREENBERG, "Catch Her in the Oatmeal," *Esquire*, February 1958. Reprinted by permission of Esquire Magazine. © 1958 by Esquire Inc.

RALPH GREENSON, from a review of *The Exorcist, Saturday Review*, June 15, 1974. Copyright © 1974. Reprinted by permission of the author and the Saturday Review.

W. W. GREG, from "The Function of Bibliography and Criticism Illustrated in a Study of the Text of King Lear," *Neophilologus*, Vol. XVIII, 1933. Reprinted by permission of the editors.

ARTHUR HAILEY, excerpt from *The Final Diagnosis*. Copyright © 1959 by Arthur Hailey. Reprinted by permission of Doubleday & Company, Inc.

J. B. S. HALDANE, from *Possible Worlds* (New York: Harper & Row, 1928).

STEPHANIE HARRINGTON, "Two Faces of the Same Eve," *New York Times Magazine*, Aug. 11, 1974. © by The New York Times Company. Reprinted by permission.

ERNEST HEMINGWAY, from "Fishing for Trout," from the *Toronto Star*; from *Islands in the Stream* (New York: Charles Scribner's Sons, 1970).

THOR HEYERDAHL, excerpt from *The Ra Expeditions*. English translation © 1971 by George Allen & Unwin Ltd. Translation from the Norwegian © Thor Heyerdahl, 1970. Reprinted by permission of Doubleday & Company, Inc.

STEWART HOLBROOK, from *Iron Brew* (New York: Macmillan, 1939).

LANGSTON HUGHES, "Salvation," from *The Big Sea* (New York: Hill and Wang, 1963).

VERNON E. JORDAN, JR., "The Truth about the Black Middle Class." *Newsweek*, July 8, 1974. Copyright © 1974 by Newsweek, Inc. All rights reserved.

BEL KAUFMAN, from the book *Up the Down Staircase*, © 1964 by Bel Kaufman. Published by Prentice-Hall, Inc., Englewood Cliffs, N.J.

X. J. KENNEDY, "Who Killed King Kong," *Dissent*, Spring 1960. Reprinted by permission of Dissent.

JEAN KERR, from *Please Don't Eat the Daisies*, copyright 1954 by Jean Kerr. Used by permission of Doubleday & Company, Inc.

JOSEPH WOOD KRUTCH, from "Scorpians," *American Scholar*, Vol. 24, No. 1, Winter 1955. Copyright © 1955 by the estate of Joseph Wood Krutch. Reprinted by permission of Marcelle Krutch.

JAMES KUNEN, "The Rebels of '70," the *New York Times Magazine*, Oct. 28, 1973. Copyright © 1973 by James S. Kunen. Reprinted by permission of The Sterling Lord Agency, Inc.

CHARLTON LAIRD, "Learned, Professional and Official Turgidity," from *Language in America*, World Publishing Company. Copyright © 1970 by Charlton Laird. Reprinted with permission.

GEORGE LANG, "How to Make a Caesar Salad," *Bon Appetit*, February 1976. Reprinted by permission of the author.

ROBERT LASSON AND DAVID EYNON, "The Poll's the Thing," the *New York Times*, Oct. 8, 1976. © 1976 by the New York Times Company. Reprinted by permission.

STEPHEN LEACOCK, from *Last Leaves* (New York: Dodd, Mead & Company, 1945). Reprinted by permission.

MAXWELL LEHMAN, "Sanity Note: We Can Still Laugh at Government," *Human Communications Research*, 1974.

Contents

PART TWO

Writer, Reader, Order, *153*

SECTION V

The Audience and Its Needs, 155

SECTION VI

The Writer's Stance: Voice, Point of View, Tone, 177

SECTION VII

Organizing Your Writing: The Paragraph, 207

PART THREE

Prose Strategies: The Writer's Building Blocks, 235

SECTION VIII

Development: Details, Examples, 237

SECTION IX

Classification and Analysis, 274

Thematic Contents

III

Youth

IV

Human Relationships

V

Human Endeavors

VI

Values

XIII

Fantasy and Fable

Preface

For the Student:*

Reading should be fun—because it makes you feel or think or laugh or all three. We have tried to make this book fun, by bringing together different sorts of readings that we liked. And we hope you will like most of them.

Some of the selections are funny. A piece (67), purportedly by one Giles Bullstable, is a spoof describing a pollster's report on the opening night of *Hamlet*. Another (30) tells what happened when a scorpion and a dozen of her babies got dumped on the dining room table. The last section of the book concentrates on some of the different ways humor turns up in writing.

But reading can be fun in other ways; we picked some of the pieces because they told us things we didn't know about but found interesting. Judith Searle (3) tells about what happens to an actress when she works on television commercials. Ted Morgan (4) recounts some of the adventures of a woman cop. There's a description (9) of what may be the oddest restaurant in the world, called *Le Pirate*. X. J. Kennedy (17) talks about the career of King Kong. We put in a number of selections about language, because we have found that most people are interested in how language works.

*A preface for instructors appears in the *Teacher's Manual*.

We picked these pieces mainly because we liked them and hoped you would too, but you can use them in several ways. You can look on the selections as interesting reading, giving you something to think about or disagree with or discuss. You can also let the selections show you some of the ways in which professional writers go about their job. The book is organized to help you see how the selections illustrate different ways of handling writing problems. You can also use the selections as starting points for your own writing, as models or just to get your ideas flowing.

We have tried to give you some help, both in reading the selections and in using the readings to learn more about writing. For one thing, each section has an introduction pointing to some of the writing techniques you will want to notice in the selections. Then, after each selection, there are questions of two sorts. One set of questions suggests ways in which you may want to think about what the selections say — ways to question the writer's ideas, to relate them to your own ideas, or perhaps to compare them with other readings. Another set of questions calls attention to tricks of the trade the author has learned, devices you may want to try.* Some of the selections also have questions intended to help you use the readings to develop your vocabulary. These questions are not quizzes; many of them do not have clearly right or wrong answers. They are intended only to help you read and use your reading.

As another study help, many of the selections have notes in the margins. These are linked to the introductions and to the questions at the end of the selections. We hope that these marginal notes will make both the readings and the questions easier.

We had help in putting the book together, and we are grateful to colleagues who read all or parts of the manuscript and made valuable suggestions: William J. Connelly, Middle Tennessee State University, Maebelle L. Jones, Lansing Community College, and Mike Gillespie, Kansas State University. We also wish to thank Nancy Rutyna for her editorial assistance. Once more we have benefited from the helpfulness and wisdom of William Oliver and Robb Reavill of Prentice-Hall, and once more we are grateful.

Charlton Laird / Robert M. Gorrell / William Lutz / Ronald E. Freeman

*The authors have discussed these devices in more detail in another book, *Modern English Handbook*, and have used the same general basis for organization in both books. The two books may be used together, but need not be.

Writing for a Purpose

Narration: Using Experience

"It was a dark, stormy night, and bandits large and bandits small sat around the campfire. Said a bandit large to a bandit small, 'Tell us a story.' And the bandit small began—"

What the bandit small says is, "It was a dark, stormy night—" and anybody who does not know that this introduction is the whole of the "story" is automatically convicted of never having been a Boy Scout or a Campfire Girl, and of never having gone on a picnic that lasted until the fire began to die down. Likewise, anyone who does not know what constitutes a "story" probably has no younger brothers or sisters, since such small petitioners are notoriously addicted to demanding stories before they go to bed.

Nor is the love of stories limited to the American young. People everywhere have loved them. Scheherazade, we are told, saved her neck by telling the Sultan stories and always leaving one unfinished at beheading time. American Indians in the Western desert, although in danger of freezing to death, have nonetheless convened to tell one another stories, such as how Coyote tricked a maiden and split a mountain in two. A Renaissance Belgian nobleman, ordering his castle hung with tapestries, said he did not care much about the artist or the quality of the weaving, just so the hangings told "good old stories." By "good old stories" he probably meant what happened when Helen ran off with a paramour to Troy, how Dido

3

stabbed herself for Aeneas, and the way some officials shot St.
Sebastian full of arrows.

Such twice-told tales are narratives, but they are not the only
kind. Assume that you come into a room with your coat torn, your
clothes muddy, and around your head a blood-stained bandage made
of somebody's torn-up shirt. Your friends want to know what
happened. You say you were riding double on a motorcycle when the
driver ran into a truck. As the talk develops, you give more details
about what happened to the driver, about what the police did to
investigate the accident, and the like. Your friends wanted to know
what had happened, who did what, and you tried to tell them. As a
result you produced narration.

In rhetorical terms, you had a "purpose." You meant to tell
what happened. Within limits, no doubt you did, but you may have
been in shock and unable to remember some details. And you did
not know everything anyhow; the police would know more about the
skid marks than you would, and the driver of the motorcycle would
know more about what he did to avoid hitting the truck. And you
may have deliberately concealed some details; wanting to protect
your friend, you may not have mentioned that he turned to say
something to you when he should have been watching the road. But
in spite of any such inadequacies, accidental or deliberate, your
account was a narrative, some sort of attempt to tell what happened.

Your report may not have been all narrative, in the sense that it
was a sequence of events and nothing but that. You may have
described the slippery pavement that contributed to the skidding—
which is description. You may have explained why the driver
thought he had to hurry and exceeded the speed limit—which is
exposition. You may even have emphasized the need for clearer and
more visible traffic warnings—which is argument. But with these
variations included or not, your report is still narrative because your
main purpose was to tell your friends what happened.

In giving details about your accident, you have produced the
first of what are sometimes called "The Four Forms of Discourse,"
narration, description, argument, and *exposition.* They are determined
by the purpose of the writer or speaker. Narration may be an attempt
to recover details of a known event, such as the motorcycle accident
above. It may be the account of imagined happenings, such as those
in Heller's novel, *Catch-22,* in which the author insists that these
events did not occur and that these people did not exist, although he
believes he can say something by pretending that all this is a true
account. It may be what might happen but has not as yet, as in a
science fiction yarn. It may even be the report of what probably
could not happen, as in the tale of Rumpelstiltskin. Different as all
these pieces are, they have this in common: the author tried to

recount events, real or imaginary. (Determining the purpose is not the only way to catalog writing, but it is one of them. Others will be considered later.)

The readings in this section are not exclusively storytelling, but they are all more or less narrative. In the reminiscences of Langston Hughes a man remembers what he did as a little boy and what people did to him. The piece by Judith Searle illustrates a different use of narration, to prepare for an explanation of how to succeed in television commercials—most of the advice has been cut from the excerpt. Similarly, the piece by Ted Morgan starts as narration, but uses the narrative to support an argument, trying to prove that women make good police officers. And the report called "Diary for TuTu" uses description to narrate a scientific expedition.

BRIEF ENCOUNTERS

1

Following are narrative bits recording what various sorts of people did or witnessed. **a. Tom Wolfe,** *known for amusing and sensitive interpretive reporting, records a scene in* The Marvelous Mouth; **b. Virginia Woolf,** *distinguished English novelist, comments on the death of another important novelist in an entry in* A Writer's Diary; **c. Françoise Gilot,** *who lived for a time with Pablo Picasso, and her collaborator, Carlton Lake, reminisce about the great Spanish Painter in* Life with Picasso; **d. Mark Twain** *reports on an incident from his youth in a selection from* Life on the Mississippi; **e. James Boswell,** *eighteenth-century man about town and biographer of Samuel Johnson, writes about his youth in an untitled autobiographical sketch;* **f. James Michener,** *whose best sellers include* Hawaii *and* Tales of the South Pacific, *visits a famous bird sanctuary in a scene from* Iberia; **g. Aleksandr Solzhenitsyn,** *Soviet novelist and Nobel Prize winner, reports on the sentencing of fellow prisoners in a scene from* The Gulag Archipelago.

a.   Tom Wolfe

ONE minute Cassius would be out in the middle of the floor re-enacting his "High Noon" encounter with Sonny Liston in a Las Vegas casino. He has a whole act about it, beginning with a pantomime of him shoving open the swinging doors and standing there bowlegged, like a beer delivery man. Then he plays the part of the crowd falling back and whispering, "It's Cassius Clay, Cassius Clay, Cassius Clay, Cassius Clay." Then he plays the part of an effete Las Vegas hipster at the bar with his back turned, suddenly freezing in mid-drink, as the hush falls over the joint, and sliding his eyes around to see the duel. Then he plays the part of Cassius Clay stalking across the floor with his finger pointed at Sonny Liston and saying, "You big ugly bear," "You big ugly bear," about eighteen times, "I ain't gonna fight you on no September thirtieth, I'm gonna fight you right now. Right here. You too ugly to run loose, you big ugly bear. You so ugly, when you cry, the tears run down the back of your head. You so ugly, you have to sneak up on the mirror so it won't run off the wall," and so on, up to the point where Liston says, "Come over here and sit on my knee, little boy, and I'll give you your orange juice," and where Cassius pulls back his right and three guys hold him back and keep him from throwing it at Liston, "And I'm hollering, 'Lemme go,' and I'm telling them out the side of my mouth, 'You better *not* lemme go.' " All this time Frankie Tucker, the singer, is contorted across one of the Americana's neo-Louis XIV chairs, breaking up and exclaiming, "That's my man!"

effete

(For questions on the words printed in the margins, see "Word Study" at the end of the section.)

contorted

b.   Virginia Woolf

Saturday, March 28, 1931

ARNOLD BENNETT died last night; which leaves me sadder than I should have supposed. A lovable genuine man; impeded, somehow a little awkward in life; well meaning; ponderous; kindly; coarse; knowing he was coarse; dimly floundering and feeling for something else; glutted with success; wounded in his feelings; avid; thicklipped; prosaic intolerably; rather dignified; set upon writing yet always taken in; deluded by splendour and success; but naive; an old bore; an egotist; much at the mercy of life for all his competence; a shopkeeper's view of literature; yet with the rudiments, covered over with fat and prosperity and the desire for hideous Empire furniture; of sensibility. Some real understanding power, as well as a gigantic absorbing power. These are the sort of things that I think by fits and starts this morning, as I sit journalising; I remember his determination to write 1,000 words daily; and how he trotted off to do it that night, and feel some sorrow that now he will never sit down and begin methodically covering his regulation number of pages in his workmanlike beautiful but dull hand. Queer how one regrets the dispersal of anybody who seemed—as I say—genuine: who had di-

ponderous

deluded

dispersal

rect contact with life—for he abused me; and I yet rather wished him to go on abusing me; and me abusing him. An element in life—even in mine that was so remote—taken away. This is what one minds.

c.   Françoise Gilot and Carlton Lake

TOWARD the end of the year Pablo had finished his Góngora and we returned to Paris, to stay a few weeks. One day he said, "Matisse has come back from Vence for a few days. We'll go see him." When we reached Matisse's apartment in the Boulevard Montparnasse, we found the door leading from the hall into the apartment partly open. It looked as though Lydia, Matisse's secretary, had gone to the floor above to fetch something and left the door open, perhaps planning to return almost immediately. We walked into the apartment. The first room, a kind of entrance hall, was rather dark. As we walked from there into the salon, out from behind a wall hanging popped Matisse, shouting, "Coo coo!" When he saw it wasn't Lydia, he looked so embarrassed that I felt sorry for him. Not Pablo, though. He looked Matisse up and down with a satisfied smile and said, "Well, I didn't know you played hide-and-seek with Lydia. We're used to hearing Lydia call you *Monsieur* Matisse." Matisse tried to laugh, rather weakly. Pablo didn't let him off that easily.

"The last time we saw you, in the Midi, you were so taken with the fact that Françoise's eyebrows reminded you of circumflex accents, you wanted her to pose for you," he said. "It looks to me as though you were doing all right with Lydia's." It seemed hardly the moment to make an extended visit so in a few minutes we left. Going down in the elevator Pablo said, "It's unbelievable, catching Matisse at a thing like that."

Lydia, according to Pablo, had first come to Matisse in 1932 or 1933. "Matisse didn't need anyone full-time," he said, "but she told him she'd make herself useful by sharpening his pencils. He found that a practical suggestion so he told her she could stay, for a while anyway, on that basis. Finally Madame Matisse found it a little tiresome to have that young girl coming around every day. She gave him his choice: 'Choose between that girl and me.' Matisse thought it over carefully and after two days of sober reflection told Madame Matisse, 'I've decided to keep her. She's a big help to me in preparing my income-tax returns.'

"After a great deal of wailing and gnashing of teeth, Lydia was installed as the official secretary." Pablo shook his head. "There's a Frenchman for you—always practical."

ONCE a day a cheap, gaudy packet arrived upward from St. Louis, and another downward from Keokuk. Before these events, the day was glorious with expectancy; after them, the day was a dead and empty thing. Not only the boys, but the whole village, felt this. After all these years I can picture that old time to myself now, just as it was then: the white town drowsing in the sunshine of a summer's morning; the streets empty, or pretty nearly so; one or two clerks sitting in front of the Water Street stores, with their splint-bottomed chairs tilted back against the walls, chins on breasts, hats slouched over their faces, asleep—with shingle-shavings enough around to show what broke them down; a sow and a litter of pigs loafing along the sidewalk, doing a good business in watermelon rinds and seeds; two or three lonely little freight piles scattered about the "levee"; a pile of "skids" on the slope of the stone-paved wharf, and the fragrant town drunkard asleep in the shadow of them; two or three wood flats at the head of the wharf, but nobody to listen to the peaceful lapping of the wavelets against them; the great Mississippi, the majestic, the magnificent Mississippi, rolling its mile-wide tide along, shining in the sun; the dense forest away on the other side; the "point" above the town, and the "point" below, bounding the river-glimpse and turning it into a sort of sea, and withal a very still and brilliant and lonely one. Presently a film of dark smoke appears above one of those remote "points"; instantly a negro drayman, famous for his quick eye and prodigious voice, lifts up the cry, *prodigious* "S-t-e-a-m-boat a-comin'!" and the scene changes! The town drunkard stirs, the clerks wake up, a furious clatter of drays follows, every house and store pours out a human contribution, and all in a twinkling the dead town is alive and moving. Drays, carts, men, boys, all go hurrying from many quarters to a common center, the wharf. Assembled there, the people fasten their eyes upon the coming boat as upon a wonder they are seeing for the first time. And the boat *is* rather a handsome sight, too. She is long and sharp and trim and pretty; she has two tall, fancy-topped chimneys, with a gilded device of some kind swung between them; a fanciful pilot-house, all glass and "gingerbread," perched on top of the "texas" deck behind them; the paddle-boxes are gorgeous with a picture or with gilded rays above the boat's name; the boiler-deck, the hurricane-deck, and the texas deck are fenced and ornamented with clean white railings; there is a flag gallantly flying from the jack-staff; the furnace doors are open and the fires glaring bravely; the upper decks are black with passengers; the captain stands by the big bell, calm, imposing, the envy of all; great volumes of the blackest smoke are rolling and tum-

bling out of the chimneys—a husbanded grandeur created with a bit
of pitch pine just before arriving at a town; the crew are grouped on
the forecastle; the broad stage is run far out over the port bow, and
an envied deck-hand stands picturesquely on the end of it with a coil
of rope in his hand; the pent steam is screaming through the gauge- *pent*
cocks; the captain lifts his hand, a bell rings, the wheels stop; then
they turn back, churning the water to foam, and the steamer is at
rest. Then such a scramble as there is to get aboard, and to get ashore,
and to take in freight and to discharge freight, all at one and the
same time; and such a yelling and cursing as the mates facilitate it all *facilitate*
with! Ten minutes later the steamer is under way again, with no flag
on the jack-staff and no black smoke issuing from the chimneys. After ten more minutes the town is dead again, and the town drunkard
asleep by the skids once more.

e. James Boswell

IN my twelfth year I caught a very severe cold. I was given a
great many medicines, and my naturally weak stomach became so
upset that I could hardly digest anything. I confess that the fear of
having to go back to what were called my studies made me hope I
could stay ill. The greatest doctors in Scotland were called in. I was
naughty enough to take measures to prevent their medicines from
having any effect on me. I could somehow or other control the operations of my stomach, and I immediately threw up everything they
made me take. I even endured blisters, congratulating myself on not
having to *work*. The Faculty decided that I was suffering from an extraordinary nervous illness, and I confess I laughed heartily to myself
at their consultations. I was weakened in body and mind, and my
natural melancholy increased. I was sent to Moffat, the Spa of Scotland. I was permitted a great deal of amusement. I saw many lively
people. I wished to be lively myself, and insensibly regained my *insensibly*
health, after having imagined that I should certainly be ill all my life.

At thirteen I was sent to the University. There I had more freedom. The place rather pleased me, and during the three years that I
was studying languages, I attained high distinction and my professors said I would be a very great man.

My youthful desires became strong. I was horrified because of
the fear that I would sin and be damned. It came into my troubled
mind that I ought to follow the example of Origen. But that madness
passed. Unluckily a terrible hypochondria seized me at the age of six- *hypochondria*
teen. I studied logic and metaphysics. But I became Methodist. I went

back to Moffat. There I met an old Pythagorean. I attached myself to him. I made an obstinate resolve never to eat any flesh, and I was resolved to suffer everything as a martyr to humanity. I looked upon the whole human race with horror. That passed, I know not how; I think by yielding to received opinions. For even now it does not seem clear to me.

At eighteen I became a Catholic. I struggled against paternal affection, ambition, interest. I overcame them and fled to London with the intention of hiding myself in some gloomy retreat to pass my life in sadness. My Lord _____ made me a deist. I gave myself up to pleasure without limit. I was in a delirium of joy. I wished to enter the Guards. My father took me back to Scotland. I spent two years there studying Civil Law. But my mind, once put in ferment, could never apply itself again to solid learning. I had no inclination whatever for the Civil Law. I learned it very superficially. My principles *superficially* became more and more confused. I ended a complete sceptic. I held all things in contempt, and I had no idea except to get through the passing day agreeably. I had intrigues with married actresses. My fine feelings were absolutely effaced.

I was in love with the daughter of a man of the first distinction in Scotland. She married a gentleman of great wealth. She let me see that she loved me more than she did her husband. She made no difficulty of granting me all. She was a subtle philosopher. She said, "I love my husband as a husband, and you as a lover, each in his own sphere. I perform for him all the duties of a good wife. With you I give myself up to delicious pleasures. We keep our secret. Nature has so made me that I shall never bear children. No one suffers because of our loves. My conscience does not reproach me, and I am sure that God cannot be offended by them." Philosophy of that sort in the mouth of a charming woman seemed very attractive to me. But her father had heaped kindnesses on me. Her husband was one of the most amiable of men. He insisted that I make extended visits at his seat in the country. I was seized with the bitterest remorse. I was unhappy. I was almost in despair, and often wished to confess everything to Mr. _____ , so as to induce him to deprive me of my wretched life. But that would have been madness of the most fatal sort. I opened my heart to Mrs. _____ . Although she was affectionate and generous, she was set in her ideas. She reproached me for my weakness. What could I do? I continued my criminal amour, and the pleasures I tasted formed a counterpoise to my remorse. *counterpoise* Sometimes even in my very transports I imagined that heaven could not but smile on so great a happiness between two mortals.

At twenty-two my father allowed me to go to London. I was glad to escape from Mrs. _____ 's vicinity. I made a resolve never to write to her, and for two years we have had no news of each other excepting merely that we were in health. At London I had an intrigue with a woman hackneyed in the ways of gallantry. For that I could not reproach myself. But I fell into a heartless commerce with girls who belonged to any man who had money.

hackneyed

f.   James A. Michener

"LOOK!" Ybarra cried. "Eagles!" We stopped to watch two imperial eagles chasing a goose who must have had experience with them, for he not only dodged the upper eagle but did it in such a way as to stay well clear of the one waiting below. We cheered the clever goose and with this appropriate introduction I entered one of the rare spots of Europe, or the world either for that matter, the Coto Doñana (Wildlife Preserve of Doña Ana). We turned a corner in the road and saw a lake on which there must have been a thousand ducks. Ybarra said, "They're back! Early, but they're back." When we had passed this check point I saw ahead of me a compact, very old three-story stone building rising mysteriously out of the swampland, a true fifteenth century palace set down here God knows how, a refuge inhabited in times past by kings who sat for Velázquez, by the Duquesa de Alba, who is said to have posed here for Francisco de Goya, and by the man whose spirit seems to haunt the place, King Alfonso XIII, who came here in his impeccable hunting suits and was driven over the swamps and dunes in a 1922 Citroën fitted with tank tracks. This was the palace of Coto Doñana, and in the past fifty years almost every leading naturalist in the world, if his specialty was birds, has caught his breath with excitement as he came upon this unbelievable building in the marshes.

g.   Aleksandr I. Solzhenitsyn

AND we were all cases for the OSO's—the Special Boards attached to the GPU-NKVD. And it turned out that each of us had been imprisoned for nothing much.

No one touched us for three hours. No one opened the doors. We paced up and down the box and, finally, tired out, we sat down on the slab benches. And the little twig kept bobbing and bobbing outside the opening, and the sparrows screamed as if they were possessed.

Suddenly the door crashed open, and one of us was summoned, a quiet bookkeeper, thirty-five years old. He went out. The door was locked. We started running about our box even more agitatedly than before. We were on hot coals.

Once more the crash of the door. They called another one out and readmitted the first. We rushed to him. But he was not the same man! The life had gone out of his face. His wide-open eyes were unseeing. His movements were uncertain as he stumbled across the smooth floor of the box. Was he in a state of shock? Had they swatted him with an ironing board?

"Well? Well?" we asked him, with sinking hearts. (If he had not in fact just gotten up from the electric chair, he must at the very least have been given a death sentence.) And in the voice of one reporting the end of the universe, the bookkeeper managed to blurt out:

"Five . . . years!"

And once more the door crashed. That was how quickly they returned, as if they were only being taken to the toilet to urinate. The second man returned, all aglow. Evidently he was being released.

"Well, well, come on?" We swarmed around him, our hopes rising again. He waved his hand, choking with laughter.

"Fifteen years!"

It was just too absurd to be believed.

Reading and Interpreting

1. Which of these pieces appealed to you most? Which least? Did you dislike any of them? Can you identify what made one of them appeal to you?

2. These excerpts are all narrative in the sense that each represents an attempt to tell what happened. Some of the authors were writing deliberately for publication, some were not. Can you detect which are which? How does this difference in purpose seem to affect the writing?

3. Most events never get recorded, and probably are not much worth recording. All these writers seemed to think they had a good reason to record just what they did. Can you identify the reasons with any confidence?

Writing Techniques

1. Some of these pieces are reminiscence, recalling an event or events long past. Others are the sort of notes that might be part of a journal, something written while the event is still fresh in the writer's mind. Does each method have advantages as a technique for writing? What are the advantages?

2. These pieces cover various stretches of time: some, or at least parts of some, cover only moments; some cover an hour or more; some survey years. Can you notice any effects of this diversity in time?

Word Study

From the context write a brief definition of the words in the margins of the preceding selections (*effete, contorted, ponderous, deluded, dispersal, prodigious, pent, facilitate, insensibly, hypochondria, superficially, counterpoise, hackneyed*). Then look them up in the dictionary and make any necessary revisions in your definitions. Write a note on the origin of *counterpoise* and of *hackneyed.*

Suggestions for Writing

Obviously, a reminiscence can make a good student theme. You have grown up with a family, each member of which was an individual. What was one of them like? You have had experiences which may mean more to you now than they did at the time. You could recall one of them. These possibilities may suggest to you that there is much to be said for a journal—writing down something significant soon after it has happened. Some of the preceding readings may suggest events around you; the campus comes alive at the end of a class period, very much as Mark Twain's home town came alive when a steamboat docked. Your reading may trigger an idea, as might one of your classes, or a committee meeting, or a movie, or a basketball game.

NOT REALLY SAVED
Langston Hughes

2

James Langston Hughes *has been one of the leaders of the black movement in American literature, writing poetry, novels, a play that became a musical, and many reminiscent sketches like that printed below. The following selection is from* The Big Sea (1940).

I was saved from sin when I was going on thirteen. But not really saved. It happened like this. There was a big revival at my Auntie Reed's church. Every night for weeks there had been much preaching, singing, praying and shouting, and some very hardened sinners had been brought to Christ, and the membership of the church had grown by leaps and bounds. Then just before the revival ended, they held a special meeting for children, "to bring the young lambs to the fold." My aunt spoke of it for days ahead. That night I was escorted to the front row and placed on the mourners' bench with the other young sinners, who had not yet been brought to Jesus.

My aunt told me that when you were saved you saw a light, and something happened to you inside! And Jesus came into your life! And God was with you from then on! She said you could see and hear and feel Jesus in your soul. I believed her. I had heard a great many old people say the same thing and it seemed to me they ought to know. So I sat there calmly in the hot crowded church, waiting for Jesus to come to me.

The preacher preached a wonderful rhythmical sermon, all moans and shouts and lonely cries and dire pictures of hell, and then he sang a song about the ninety and nine safe in the fold, but one little lamb was left out in the cold. Then he said: "Won't you come? Won't you come to Jesus? Young lambs, won't you come?" And he held out his arms to all us young sinners there on the mourners' bench. And the little girls cried. And some of them jumped and went to Jesus right away. But most of us just sat there.

A great many old people came and knelt around us and prayed, old women with jet-black faces and braided hair, old men with work-gnarled hands. And the church sang a song about the lower lights are burning, some poor sinners to be saved. And the whole building rocked with prayer and song.

Still I kept waiting to *see* Jesus.

Finally all the young people had gone to the altar and were saved, but one boy and me. He was a rounder's son named Westley. Westley and I were surrounded by sisters and deacons praying. It was very hot in the church, and getting late now. Finally Westley said to me in a whisper: "God damn! I'm tired o' sitting here. Let's get up and be saved." So he got up and was saved.

Then I was left all alone on the mourners' bench. My aunt came and knelt at my knees and cried, while prayers and songs swirled all around me in the little church. The whole congregation prayed for me alone, in a mighty wail of moans and voices. And I kept waiting serenely for Jesus, waiting, waiting—but he didn't come. I wanted to see him, but nothing happened to me. Nothing! I wanted something to happen to me, but nothing happened.

I heard the songs and the minister saying: "Why don't you come? My dear child, why don't you come to Jesus? Jesus is waiting for you. He wants you. Why don't you come? Sister Reed, what is this child's name?"

"Langston," my aunt sobbed.

"Langston, why don't you come? Why don't you come and be saved? Oh, Lamb of God! Why don't you come?"

Now it was really getting late. I began to be ashamed of myself, holding everything up so long. I began to wonder what God thought about Westley, who certainly hadn't seen Jesus either, but who was now sitting proudly on the platform, swinging his knickerbockered legs and grinning down at me, surrounded by deacons and old women on their knees praying. God had not struck Westley dead for taking his name in vain or for lying in the temple. So I decided that maybe to save further trouble, I'd better lie, too, and say that Jesus had come, and get up and be saved.

So I got up.

Suddenly the whole room broke into a sea of shouting, as they saw me rise. Waves of rejoicing swept the place. Women leaped in the air. My aunt threw her arms around me. The minister took me by the hand and led me to the platform.

When things quieted down, in a hushed silence, punctuated by a few ecstatic "Amens," all the new young lambs were blessed in the name of God. Then joyous singing filled the room.

That night, for the last time in my life but one—for I was a big boy twelve years old—I cried. I cried, in bed alone, and couldn't stop. I buried by head under the quilts, but my aunt heard me. She woke up and told my uncle I was crying because the Holy Ghost had come into my life, and because I had seen Jesus. But I was really crying because I couldn't bear to tell her that I had lied, that I had deceived everybody in the church, and I hadn't seen Jesus, and that now I didn't believe there was a Jesus any more, since he didn't come to help me.

Reading and Interpreting

1. What impression of the religious ceremony do you get? How do you interpret the description of the preaching in paragraph 3?

2. How does Westley's attitude differ from that of the narrator?

3. Describe the role of the narrator's aunt in the incident.

4. Does the narrative do more than report an experience? That is, does it use the experience to comment more broadly on religion, on relations between children and adults, or on society generally?

5. What is the long-range importance of the incident to the nar-

rator? Does the reader feel that the narrator has been lacking some-how in not being able to see Jesus? Should the narrator have refused to "get up and be saved"?

Writing Techniques

1. From what point of view is the story told? Is the narrator speaking as an older man looking back or as a twelve-year-old com-menting on the event? Would the story have been as effective from another point of view—in the third person, for instance?

2. How are the events ordered in the account?

3. The narrator frequently uses short sentences. What is their ef-fect? Try combining some of the short sentences with the sentences preceding or following them. What happens when you do this?

4. Check the instances in which the narrator varies from the generally objective account of what happened and reports his feel-ings. What do these comments add to the narrative?

Suggestions for Writing

Recall a childhood incident that seems important as you look back on it. Write an account putting the events in chronological or-der, including any specific details you can now recall and recon-structing necessary details that you can now see would have been re-vealing, although you may not have noticed them at the time. Then on revision try to adjust the narrative in any way that will show the reader, without direct statements, how the incident means some-thing. Possibilities are a religious experience like that of Hughes, an unjust punishment, a quarrel, a disappointment in puppy love, the death of a pet.

MY LIFE IN TV COMMERCIALS   **3**
Judith Searle

Judith Searle *is one of the coming American actresses who, like many of her sisters, served an apprenticeship in TV commercials. The fol-lowing selection was published in* Cosmopolitan.

HE lay there stolidly, waiting for me to come to bed, com-templating the day's frustrations at the office: how his boss didn't understand him, how they weren't using his talents to the fullest. I finished brushing my hair, adjusted the strap on my Pucci night-gown and climbed in beside him, whispering sympathetic words. Colored lights began to flash . . .

"Cut!" came a voice from the darkness beyond. "Not your fault, honey. We had a problem with the camera. Let's do it again."

I moved back to my starting position at the dressing table. The hairdresser rushed to adjust my fall; the makeup man blotted my forehead with tissue. No need to touch up my co-star, lying impassively in the bed. Computers do not perspire . . .

"O.K. Everybody ready? Scene Number 5A, Take 7. Action!"

I repeated the moves I'd already made six times. My square gray bedmate flashed his lights and spun his wheels. I snuggled into the pillows, reached out to pat my computer-husband affectionately on the . . .

◄A transition from what to what?

"Cut! Mike doesn't think those lights flash *sexy* enough. Let's figure out something else."

Well, it took hours to get my co-star to behave in proper bedroom fashion, and we couldn't finish the computer-company commercial until the next day. Typical? In a way. In the seven years I've been acting in television commercials, I've come to expect anything. Every job is totally different from the last: different people, places, products, demands. Different crazy accidents. Making TV commercials is a great profession for someone who loves novelty and has a tolerance for long stretches of frustration, rejection and financial insecurity interspersed with spurts of intensely hard work and the prospect of sudden windfalls. Oh yes—and a liking for carnival atmosphere inside a pressure cooker.

Not all commercials are filmed in studios, of course; many are shot on location, often in exotic places. Working out of New York, I've done jobs in St. Thomas, Puerto Rico, Nassau, Florida, Colorado, North Carolina, Toronto, Baltimore and Washington. Among my favorite location trips was the one on which I played a nun for a soft-drink commercial shot atop a large hill in Poughkeepsie, New York, sixty or so miles north of Manhattan. It was a warm, sunny day, and the hillside took on the look of a giant UN picnic, what with sixteen actors and some fifty extras dressed to represent a veritable General Assembly of nations and lazing about on the grass waiting for their turn to be called. Sometime toward midafternoon, I played my scene, strolling in my nun's habit through the fields with an actor dressed as a construction worker. As we walked, he took thirsty swigs from The Product. The vignette finished uneventfully, and I relaxed again on the grass.

Is this narration or something else?

Then, suddenly, it was panic time. The final shot was to be of all of us in our various costumes coming over the crest of the hill, holding hands, just as the sun disappeared below the horizon. Here, finally, was the reason for busing hundreds of us—cast, crew, ad-agency reps—to this particular site in Poughkeepsie: that final, dramatic long-shot of people of all ages and races joining hands in a unanimity of love for one another and The Product. But wait—the sun was sinking *fast!*

The voice of the director, slightly hysterical, came through a megaphone: "Get those people to the top of that goddamned hill . . . and make it snappy!" But the going was not so easy. The vegetation on the hill was waist-high, nearly over the heads of some of the children—and many of our costumes were cumbersome. I hiked my nun's robe up around my waist and struggled to the top, twisting my ankle on the way. Somehow, we got the shot on the first take. Lucky thing, too, because the sun was gone an instant after that.

Next came the problem of getting back down the hill. Night was falling, and several of the children were crying. A frail, white-haired actress announced tearfully that she didn't think she could make it. Somehow, though—stumbling, swearing, helping each other—we all reached bottom, arriving in the pitch-dark. Most of us felt we'd earned our money that day.

The money you make in commercials can vary, but there are union minimums: $158 per eight-hour session for principal actors (those of us whose faces are seen on-screen) and $120 for extras (who have no lines to speak and whose faces are never seen in the final cut). After taxes and the 10 percent agent's commission are taken out, I generally get a check for less than half my salary. The big money, of course, can come once the spot is on the air. Each time a commercial is shown nationally, the principal actors receive a residual payment. I once made nearly $30,000 on an aspirin pitch over a two-year period, but that sort of long run is unusual these days. Most of us now feel content if a commercial nets us a total of $4,000. And we also have to face the possibility that a spot may never be shown on the air, so there's no guarantee that we'll make more than our daily-session payment.

◄Another break—again, from what to what?

Sometimes, making a commercial can actually *cost* you money. A few years ago I made one for a home permanent in which, for truth-in-advertising reasons, I had to be given a permanent with The Product. And by a nonprofessional (not a hairdresser)—for the same reason. I should have sensed danger when I was asked to sign a statement promising not to hold the advertising agency responsible for any damage. But I was naïve in those days.

At any rate, a week or so after the filming, my hair began falling out. I tried to ignore what was happening. Finally, when my hairbrush started to look like a brier patch, I went in panic to a scalp specialist, who told me I was likely to go bald if I didn't begin a series of treatments immediately. In the end, I spent more on salvaging my hair than I received in residual payments.

As any actress will tell you, there is nothing like an intimate acquaintance with the making of commercials to give you an idea of how the process can go wrong—despite the best efforts of the advertisers involved. One spot I did for a dishwashing liquid will stick forever in my mind. I was given the usual role of the happy wife who loves cooking and housekeeping but detests dirt. She has just discovered a brand-new detergent that demolishes grease, and she demonstrates its effectiveness by dumping a cupful of hamburger drippings into a clear plastic dishpan containing The Product. The script at this point calls for the camera to zoom in on a close-up of the grease dissolving in the suds. After all, that's what had happened in tests at the factory.

How many topic sentences here?

But not in the television studio. I confidently poured in my cup of grease, talking all the while about the extraordinary properties of The Product as the camera zoomed in on a close-up of . . . the grease lying in a cloudy yellow mass at the bottom of the pan. The confident young chemist from the soap company who had designed the commercial was certain I was pouring the grease wrong, or that the water in the pan was too cold or too hot, or that the appropriate amount of The Product had not been used. However, after an afternoon of pouring grease from every conceivable angle, testing the water temperature and concentration of The Product in the dishpan, the chemist seemed to have shrunk four inches.

Then came numerous conferences and phone calls to the client in the Midwest, and it was decided that the villain in the case must be the New York City water. While we were having dinner, several hundred bottles of distilled water were hastily brought in and heated in huge tubs with big immersion coils. The dishpan was filled with the hot mountain-spring water, then The Product was measured and added. For the eighty-seventh time that day, I forced my aching jaws into a smile, uttered a silent prayer and poured the eighty-seventh cup of grease into the pan. Well, it was *better*, but you could still see all that grease.

Finally, the combination of distilled water, a smaller amount of grease and a particular rate and angle of pouring—and maybe the fact that as midnight approached the standards were not so high—produced a take that everybody agreed was the best we were likely to get. Somebody somewhere, however, must have decided it wasn't good enough, because the commercial never appeared on the air. Nor did The Product, to the credit of the advertiser, ever appear on supermarket shelves.

◄A marker of some sort of conclusion?

I am occasionally asked if an actress doesn't have to sleep with certain people to get cast in commercials. The mystique of the advertising world encourages this notion, but I'm here to tell you it is pure myth. Anyone who knows the mechanics of the business also knows that commercials are generally cast by committee. If sleeping with the right people were important, a girl would have to seek out and bed a majority of the men working on an account, most of whom she will never meet anyway; the only ad-agency person she comes face to face with, often, is the female casting director.

Interestingly enough, the one person I've ever felt took unfair advantage of me on a commercial was a fellow actor. We had been filming in a studio in Baltimore for three days, and this particular commercial for a stain- and wear-resistant fiber involved a sword fight between hero and villain in a pseudomedieval setting. As draperies were slashed and bottles of perfume smashed on the carpet, I managed to wander coolly through the perilous action, forcing myself to be unperturbed by the cutlery flashing around my ears, talking about how nice it was not to have to worry about stains and mess when you had curtains and rugs made from The Product.

pseudomedieval

perilous
unperturbed
cutlery

Finally, the fencing scene was finished, and only the closing remained to be shot: my clinch with the hero, an actor who appeared to fancy himself the world's champion French kisser. I still don't know if the tongue down my throat was the actor's idea or the director's, but the last seconds of the commercial show me on Take Number 75 looking like a near-drowning victim, an effect which was apparently just what the director wanted.

This piece has a formal conclusion. Why?

All of which adds up to the commercials field being a scary, demanding, ever-changing and occasionally lucrative place to toil.

Reading and Interpreting

1. The article purports to reveal the "inside" story on television commercials. How much inside information does Searle give you? Cite specific information you learned from the article that you did not know before. Does the article reinforce any ideas about television commercials that you already had?

2. Does the account make you want to act in television commercials? Explain.

3. What seems to be the attitude of the author toward commercials and the lives of those who act in them? Cite specific passages that seem to you to express this attitude.

4. The final paragraph is a summary. Do the incidents that precede it support it as a conclusion?

Writing Techniques

1. Describe how the article uses narration as a device for exposition. For example, what point is the author making with the narrative in the first half dozen paragraphs?

2. The opening incident begins with a story and then comments on its significance. How does the author vary the pattern in the other incidents?

3. Glosses suggest the organization of the piece, which is somewhat unusual for narrative. You may want to contrast this organization with devices used in some of the narratives that follow, those by Ted Morgan and Bill O'Hallaren, for example.

Word Study

Searle uses familiar words, mainly, along with some rarer ones. In the margins you will find the following: *pseudomedieval, perilous, unperturbed,* and *cutlery.* First be sure you know the meaning of each word; then propose a synonym as a possible substitute in the article. How do your words change the effect of the paragraph? Did Searle do well to use the words she chose?

Suggestions for Writing

Try using incidents as Searle does to reveal something about a job or other experience. Almost any experience would do: Sunday School teaching, camp counseling, working in an office, helping at registration, working at a sports event, selling newspapers, being part of a gang or club, washing cars. Create or recall incidents as Searle does to let us see the characters and understand why people act as they do.

WOMEN MAKE GOOD COPS
Ted Morgan

4

"Ted Morgan" *is the pseudonym of Swiss-born Sanche de Grammont. Graduated* summa cum laude *from Yale University, he won a Pulitzer prize for reporting. He has published several books, including* The French *and* The Way Up. *This article is from the* New York Times Magazine.

IT was a muggy summer night in the high-crime Washington, D.C., area known as "the strip." On the corner of 14th and L Streets, a man built like a construction worker stood spread-eagled with his arms stretched out, touching the roof of his car. "Oh, my God," he repeated over and over. Behind him stood a young blond woman half his size, pretty and fresh-faced enough to pose for a shampoo ad. She held a .38 Smith and Wesson pointed at the man's back. With her free hand, she pulled a two-way radio from a pocket of her lime-green pants suit, gave her location and asked for transport.

Moments later, a patrol car pulled up. Lieut. James R. Clark, a sandy-haired veteran of the Washington vice squad, got out and said to the woman: "Don't take your gun out in a normal arrest situation."

"He was trying to pull off," the woman said. "I nearly got run over last week, but I've never had one run out when I showed the gun."

The woman was one of a task force of 24 Washington policewomen who had been sent to patrol the strip in "old clothes" (civilian dress) and break up its dense concentration of prostitutes. When a man solicited a policewoman, she arrested him. When prostitutes harassed the policewomen or interfered with their work, they were arrested for disorderly conduct. In the first two weeks of July, the policewomen had made 238 arrests, including three "man with a gun" arrests.

Is some of this article narration and some not?

The 24 volunteers who nightly infiltrated the capital's busiest red-light district were recruited from the 266 women on the 4,786-strong Washington police force. One hundred and sixty women are on full-time patrol duty, giving Washington the highest percentage of women on patrol of any police department in the country. (As of the first week of April, 172 Washington policewomen were black, 85 were white and 2 were of Spanish descent. Seven were listed as undercover agents without racial or national identity.) New York City, by comparison, has 735 women in its 31,000-member department (about 2½ percent of the total compared to 6 per cent in Washington), with 400 on patrol, and there is a good deal of soul-searching going on over whether they can do the job.

infiltrated

Meanwhile, Audrey A. Williams, a tall, 26-year-old policewoman in black slacks and a yellow T-shirt, had been approached by a man on the corner of 14th and K Streets. Wise by now in the ways of soliciting, Audrey knew that to make an arrest she had to be careful not to say anything that might give grounds for entrapment.

Something different begins here, does it not?

A young, blond man, who looked like a sailor on leave, asked, "What you doin'?"

"I'm workin'," Audrey said.

"How much do you want?"

"What do you mean?"

"I've got $20 I want to spend."

"Spend on what?"

"A good time."

"What do you mean, a good time?"

The man explained what he wanted, and Audrey said, "I am a policewoman, and you are under arrest for soliciting for prostitution."

The man was so dumbfounded he did not resist. Audrey and her partner, Phyllis Knight, put handcuffs on him and called for transport. Lieutenant Clark responded just in time to see the man being carried to the substation in a patrol wagon. "A lot of men resist because their reputation is at stake," Audrey said. "They're from out of town; their family life is placed in jeopardy. I had to chase one two blocks yesterday before I caught him." In the cases that have come to court thus far, first offenders are being given suspended sentences. One man was told to write a 500-word essay on the evils of prostitution.

jeopardy

Another call for transport came over the radio, and Lieutenant Clark drove to a corner where a tall thin man stood in the street in handcuffs next to a car with diplomatic plates. The policewoman who had made the arrest on charges of soliciting, was 5 feet 2 inches, long-lashed and doe-eyed and wore satin slacks and a sequined sweater. Her gun was in her purse. She gave Lieutenant Clark the man's name and he asked headquarters to check it out. A minute later, he got out of the scout car and told the man, "Do you understand what happened to you? You committed a crime." The man shook his head, indicating that he spoke no English. The policewoman said in a low voice that he spoke enough to give her the elements of the offense. "You are free to go because you have diplomatic immunity," Lieutenant Clark told the man. The policewoman unsnapped the cuffs. Lieutenant Clark got back in the cruiser and said, "He's supposed to be from the Republic of Senegal. Never heard of it."

diplomatic

What would you say about the combination of what is seen and what is heard?

In the Seventh District, I went on the 4-to-midnight shift with 23-year-old Steve Odell, blond and energetic, and 27-year-old Stella Jordan, who has large, soft brown eyes and still seemed a bit uneasy in her uniform. Steve and Stella patrolled Anacostia, a tough black neighborhood where the police are viewed as an occupation army rather than a public service. Everywhere they went they were greeted with insults and obscene gestures. "Stella and I agree it's the hate that's hard to put up with," Steve said. "People think you're harassing them; they hate the uniform."

"It sounds dumb," Stella said, "but I thought I could help combat crime and have a part in that. I was tired of people doing wrong things. It's not what I thought it would be though."

Is this conversation worth the space it takes?

"The kids," Steve said, spotting a group of 10- and 12-year-old boys on a corner, "they're our only hope." He waved and called out, "How ya doing?" and one of the boys, no more than 12, replied, "I'm gettin' ready to hurt you someday."

In the scout car, Steve and Stella adopted a tone of good-natured mutual teasing. "We got 160 women on patrol," Steve said, "159½ not counting Stella."

"I thought you were O.K.," Stella said, threatening Steve with her baton.

"Boy, the perfume on some of these women," he said, "I got into the car and almost choked to death."

"Some men are just as bad with their male eau de cologne," Stella replied.

Steve, a bachelor, said, "This night shift sure messes up my personal life."

"Why don't you go out with someone who's got the same hours as you do, like a nurse, or a policewoman?"

"I don't mess with no policewoman," Steve said.

"And I don't mess with no policeman," Stella replied.

Steve did all the driving, explaining that there was something wrong with the transmission. Stella sat quietly beside him, her clipboard on her lap, writing reports. Around 10 P.M., there was a "man with a gun" call, and Steve turned on the siren, and turned corners on two wheels, but it was only a teen-ager with a cap pistol. Four scout cars had responded to the scene (it was a slow night), and a small crowd had gathered. A little girl with black-braided hair came up to Stella and said, "I'm gonna be a policewoman when I grow up."

On the following evening, I rode along in the First District, downtown Washington, on the 4-to-midnight shift with 22-year-old Velma Holmes and Phil Parks, 25. Velma had a nice smile and eyes that squinted. She seemed to enjoy her work. There was an odd contrast between her feet, shod in combat boots, and her hands, with very long, carefully manicured fingernails. The reason for the boots, she said, was that she had been on scooter duty, "and the kick start had my ankle hurting very bad." As for her mandarin-length nails, she showed me the index finger of her right hand and said, "See, my trigger finger is short."

A break in time. Is there any other shift?

Velma and Phil addressed each other rather formally as Holmes and Parks. They shared the driving and the report-writing. Chief Wilson had ruled that scout cars must respond to all complaints, no matter how slight. Patrol officers find themselves acting as judges in the street court of petty disputes. The dispatcher at headquarters called out Parks's and Holmes's scout-car number and told them to go to the Bellevue Cafeteria, near Union Station, where there was a disturbance.

petty

At the cafeteria, a woman said she had been overcharged for her turkey dinner and wanted her $2 back. The manager said she had taken the food on her plate and he could not give her a refund. Velma and Phil, a placid man whose very presence seems to calm people down, took the manager aside and talked to him quietly: "Your job is to please the customers. Why don't you give it back to her? She feels you weren't treating her the way you would treat a white person. Let's make a deal: Give her her $2 back and we'll tell her to stay out of your place." As trivial as this was, I could see that it could have been handled differently. With an overbearing police officer, it could have escalated into a shouting match and several arrests for disorderly conduct.

What do Velma and Phil contribute to the effect of the narrative?

escalated

Velma held the scout-car door open for Phil, and said, "How do you like that for service, Clark? One guy kept holding the door for me when I started," she said. "It made me so self-conscious I told him to stop. Another guy, we had a burglary, he said, 'You wait here, I'm goin' up.' 'No, you ain't,' I said, 'I'd rather go up with you than stay here and have to explain why you're hurt and I'm not.' But I like patrol: It really gives you a chance to get out there and *po-lice*."

The dispatcher sent them to a Salvation Army residence in the shadow of Capitol Hill. A man sat on the stoop holding a bloody T-shirt. He had a bad cut over his right eye and sat there shaking his head.

"He beat me so bad my blood run free," the man said.

"What did you do to him?" Phil asked.

"He said he gonna kill me," the man said.

It developed that the man had gone to a construction site—where he had recently been fired on suspicion of theft—to retrieve some personal belongings, and had been worked over by a watchman.

retrieve

The night manager at the Salvation Army said the man could not stay there again until he had talked to "the major."

"Do you have any money to stay somewhere?" Velma asked.

"He took my money and my cigarettes," the man said. "I'll sleep in the park across the street."

"Don't you have any friends?" Velma asked.

The man shook his head.

"You're in bad shape," Phil said, "you know that? You're going to have to pull yourself together. As far as the guy who beat you is concerned, the best thing to do is swear out a warrant."

◀More talk. What about it as a narrative device?

Velma had been driving and took the wheel again. The battery was dead, a common occurrence since scout cars are used around-the-clock. "We're disabled," Phil called in. "Send us a unit to assist us." Velma moaned. "Now they're going to say I can't drive," she said.

What is the use of such details as these?

On my last night in Washington, I rode along with Ann Scott and Bob Vacin of the Fifth District on the Saturday midnight-to-8 patrol. It seemed to me by now that the women I had observed on various types of patrol performed in a cool, professional manner. Admittedly, I had not seen any shoot-outs or armed robberies. But what I had seen made up the bulk of police work. It was true that the man seemed to act as leader in scout cars, but this seemed to be the result of longer service on the force, rather than a matter of sex roles. In my conversations with men and women officers, both voiced complaints about partners of the opposite sex.

But the man-woman partners I rode with seemed to get along well. In fact, as I heard from several sources, the real danger was that scout-car couples might get along too well. Basically, I felt that the presence of women humanized the police force, and made it a more precise reflection of the population it was intended to serve. Men police officers imbued with the importance of their station could, in certain situations, provoke citizens into committing assaults, while women were more likely to overlook minor offenses and have a cooling effect in domestic quarrels.

However, despite Chief Wilson's assurance that the issue was closed, I felt that, to the men on the force, women on patrol were still on probation. I remembered the remark of Lieut. Joyce Leland, the highest-ranking woman on the Washington force: "Let me tell you, policewomen couldn't do this work if the men didn't help them. They can make or break you." Every patrolman I talked to said that, given the choice, he would rather have a man than a woman partner. The police department still seemed like an exclusive club which tolerates women only in token numbers.

A conclusion a transition, or what?

Ann Scott is 30, a former buyer for a department store. On her, the policewoman's uniform looks good. She joined the department after "my baby brother got strung out on dope," she told me. "The pusher lived in the suburbs, and his kids went to private schools and their playmates were screened. That really got to me. It's corny, you know, but that made me want to help someone else."

corny

Her partner, Bob Vacin, was the only patrolman I talked to who genuinely seemed to feel that women could help improve the quality of police work. "Women bring a new dimension," he said. "It helps some of these guys who have an infatuation with power and who forget that police work is based on service. The girls help break

What about sentence structure? Does Morgan ever use the passive voice?

down that attitude. I don't have any regrets working with a girl. Particularly, a girl like Scottie: She's been around, she knows the score."

That night, as on many other nights, Ann and Bob swept up the crumbs of disorder in their district. Nothing happened that might have tested a woman's bravery or physical prowess. There was an argument over a cab fare. There was a woman in curlers and Bermuda shorts who called the police when her boyfriend tried to kick her door in. There was an M.O. (mental observation, or someone behaving irrationally) in a quiet tree-lined street of frame houses. A woman in a raincoat stood outside one of the houses and said her husband had started throwing furniture. Ann and Bob opened the front door. The house was dark, and they trained the beams of their flashlights into the living room where they found the husband passed out on the floor.

"You better not stay here tonight," Ann told the woman.

After they gave her a ride to the home of a relative, Ann told the dispatcher: "Family affair settled." The dispatcher then sent them to an attempted assault in the same area. A bare-chested man with a shaved head stood on a corner, holding a torn white T-shirt. He said he had been attacked by a woman with a knife.

What does this sort of thing suggest about policewomen?

"Do you know who it is?" Ann asked.

"I don't know her. I know the dude she go with," the man said. "She had some kind of knife. 'I been workin' to get you'—that's what she said. But I don't know her personal like."

"Did she rob you?" Ann asked.

"I still got my money."

"Why did she want to cut you?"

"Her dude got tired of her, and I supposed to be the cause of it."

They drove around the block with the man in the back of the scout car, and he pointed to a large woman with short hair and a puffy face. She was clearly overwrought; and when Ann took her aside, she blurted out, "I had nothing but trouble from him. He pulled out a little penknife, and he supposed to be a man, and I whipped his tail fair-and-square. I'm gonna kill him."

The woman directed a long stream of obscenities at the man, who sat in the scout car pretending not to listen. The woman lunged toward the man, and the two officers blocked her way. Ann, with the help of neighbors, finally quieted the woman down, and she and Bob drove the man about a mile from the scene. "Now you know you're on parole," Bob told him. "For your own good, I wouldn't have anything to do with her."

"She doesn't own the goddamn street," the man said, as he got out.

"Family affair temporarily settled," Ann told the dispatcher.

Reading and Interpreting

1. Morgan uses the examples of specific women officers to illustrate his contention that "women make good cops." Does Morgan state his central idea anyplace in the article, or does he leave it implied?

2. Did you begin reading this article with any preconceived ideas (prejudices) about women police officers on street duty? If so, has reading this article changed those ideas at all? What in the article prompted the change?

3. Does Morgan admit to any prejudices? Does he get personally involved in the article, or does he remain uninvolved, objective? Cite evidence from the article to support your opinion.

Writing Techniques

1. In what sense is this narrative? The title, "Women Make Good Cops," would suggest that Morgan's purpose is argument, to convince his reader of something he probably expects many readers would doubt. On the other hand, much of the text here is telling what happened, what certain people did. That must be narration. If so, how can you describe the part that narration plays in this piece? Does that lead you to any observations about interrelations among the four forms of discourse?

2. Morgan uses at least two kinds of evidence. One begins with the third paragraph. Another takes up later. How would you characterize each, and what is the advantage of each, or the disadvantage?

3. Where does the introduction begin and end? Is it narrative, argument, exposition, or what?

4. Locate statements that shift from narration to make direct comments about the subject. How do these contribute to the development of the overall purpose of the essay?

Word Study

1. From the context write a brief definition of the words in the margins (*infiltrated, jeopardy, diplomatic, corny, petty, escalated, retrieve*). Then look them up in a dictionary and make any necessary revisions in your definitions. What is the origin of *corny?*

2. Morgan is using words to distinguish among the dialects of different persons. The dialects include that of the narrator (the author), that of certain police, and that of various civilians. The narrator speaks of "mandarin-length nails." Steve says, "This night shift sure messes up my personal life." The narrator would not have written that as his own comment. A victim says, "He beat me so bad my blood run free." Identify three other examples that characterize each of these ways of speaking.

Suggestions for Writing

Morgan tries to demonstrate that women make good cops, although many persons, women as well as men, would not have expected this. There was a time when women were not supposed to be good students—they were not admitted to universities, and the old "finishing schools" were pretty pallid affairs. Only recently have women been admitted in any numbers into colleges of law, medicine, dentistry, and some others. Do they make good students in these subjects? How about mathematics, physical sciences, and engineering? And do men make good students in nursing and home economics? Are times changing, and should they change more? Write a paper using any evidence you have on questions such as these, perhaps narrating your own experience as Morgan does.

DIARY FOR TUTU
Bill O'Hallaren

5

Bill O'Hallaren *is a free-lance television writer who has worked on large feature films. One of his recent sequences was filmed in the backwoods of Idaho and Oregon. This article is from the* New York Times Magazine.

SATURDAY, Aug. 25—There is only one customs officer on duty in Winnipeg and he is not amused. Before him, the customs officer in Vancouver took one look at our gear and passed it, presuming that the Winnipeg man would have more time to cope with such craziness. But now the Winnipeg man is perturbed by our two portable swimming pools. "I would think," he announces icily, "that as long as there are only six of you, one pool would be enough." We explain that the pools will hold the whales we plan to capture in Hudson Bay—two whales to a pool. It turns out, however, that our whale-catching permits from the Canadian Government don't carry any weight with customs. We may proceed, the man says, but our scientific equipment for testing and treating whales must stay behind un-

What does the author think he needs to get into the introduction?

til the appropriate ministries can scrutinize it. Bill Flynn, a veteran aquarium curator and leader of our expedition, tells us not to panic. He has been on two previous white whale hunts and nothing went right on those expeditions either.

Besides Flynn, our group includes Roger Stevenson, a marine biologist; John Seeker, a TV cameraman; Dick Gilmore, a TV soundman (all of whom are employes of the Sea World Oceanarium in San Diego); Phil Thornton, a CBS-TV director, and myself, a free-lance television writer. Our main purpose is to capture four yearling white whales and return them safely to San Diego. Secondarily, we hope the capture will make a good television show.

In the preceding year, each of us has been involved in one way or another with Gigi, the only gray whale ever to survive in captivity. A Sea World expedition captured the baby gray off Baja California and it thrived in its Sea World home for a year, growing to 26 feet and a weight of 14 tons, at which point it was released in the ocean. Marine scientists had never had a chance to study a living gray before and troops of them swarmed to Gigi's side during her year in captivity. Her televised story, "Gigi Goes Home," won a series of awards and we are all hopeful that the whites we capture on this expedition will live as happily in Sea World and will provide as good a TV show.

We are a confident and even jaunty crew, certain we will bring off another scientific and dramatic success. In fact, however, we are heading for a few rounds of low comedy (an adventure which will include getting lost at sea with a bunch of drunken Indians), then some exciting encounters with whales and, finally, a horrifying tragedy. *Introduction of a different sort.*

Now officials of Trans Air, a small Canadian airline, review plans for the whale lift. Our party is to fly to Churchill on Hudson Bay this afternoon. We will be met by Indian guides who will take us to the whaling grounds. By next Saturday we should have safely in captivity the four whales authorized by our permit. A Trans Air 737 will arrive in Churchill on Saturday night, pick up our whales in their swimming pools and deliver them to the Sea World Aquarium in San Diego seven hours later.

The white, or beluga, whale is a snub-nosed, saucy eyed animal with marvelous intelligence and a merry disposition. There are only four such whales in captivity in the United States (all in the New York Aquarium). The whites live in Arctic waters and have only rarely been able to endure being transported to aquariums located in temperate zones. Now jet planes shorten the trip and make it more bearable for the whales. In addition, once the whales are safely in the aquarium, marine biologists will only very gradually raise the temperature of the water in which the whales have been kept so as to minimize the shock.

A few hours after our encounter with the customs man in Winnipeg we are flying over Churchill. The old DC-4 has been sputtering over Canada all afternoon at what seems like little more than treetop height. Northern Canada appears to be half forest and half lake and there has been a series of stops at clearings to drop off loggers, hunters and trappers returning from their annual visits to the dazzling urbanity of Winnipeg. A few minutes ago the last of the trees beneath us disappeared and now there is only tundra.

◄ What would you call this?

We gain some altitude and now we approach the wide-mouthed Churchill River, which empties into Hudson Bay at Churchill. The pilot swings low over the river and points down. Those flashing silvers down there in the water are white whales, having a last frolic before heading north. The Arctic fish they live on travel south in summer and north in winter and the whales follow in close pursuit. There must be hundreds of whites in a two- or three-mile stretch of river. Bill Flynn grins and begins to relax. This shouldn't be so hard after all.

Flynn has been worried that the weather may defeat us. Hudson Bay does not thaw until mid-July and it begins to freeze over again in early September. Flynn applied for the whaling permit early in the year, but the Canadian Government stalled for months, and now there are only a few good hunting days left. The Government, sensitive to the wrath of conservationists over the slaughter of fur seals, probably would not have issued the permit at all except for pressure from the Indian community at Churchill. The Indians will help us capture the whales and they will receive $1,500 for each capture.

Is this narration or something else within the story?

The temperature is 75 degrees when we step off the plane. Our heavy coats and boots suddenly seem ridiculous. Churchill's buildings are stark—wooden, unpainted or peeling. The roads are muddy and the mosquitoes are out in force. The natives fan their hands steadily across their faces like windshield wipers.

Our cab driver proudly displays his super heater. It cost $143, and on the coldest winter night it can raise the temperature inside his cab to an even zero, Fahrenheit. The best a standard car heater can do is raise it to 20 below. The driver explains that a man loses efficiency when he sits all night in 20-below temperature; zero, however, is bearable. He adds that the nighttime winter temperatures in Churchill often drop to 40 or 50 below zero and, of course, the effect of the wind may drive the actual temperature even lower. We decide not to gripe about the mosquitoes. . . .

Later that evening we meet the chief in the bar of the Churchill Hotel to hear his plan of operations. The six of us Americans together with seven Indians, he says, will leave at dawn in six motor-powered open boats. We will travel 35 miles across the bay to a fishing and hunting lodge near the mouth of the Caribou River. The Indians will then use the boats to herd the whales into shallow coastal waters. Flynn will pick the animals he wants and the Indians will jump overboard in the shallow water, and wrestle the whales into the boats. These whales are ordinarily hunted with rifle or harpoon, he tells us, and some American and Canadian hunters travel all the way to Churchill to kill the animals in that manner. The Indians used to harpoon or shoot them, too, he says, once regarding whale meat as a staple. Today, however, they don't care for whale meat, now that they have been introduced to beef and pork.

Why should this conversation be reported?

The chief reports that his men have been rehearsing live whale captures and there won't be any problem in getting the four specimens we want. To us, however, it doesn't sound easy. White whales are six feet long at birth and grow to 15 feet and more. The yearlings Bill Flynn hopes to bring back alive will be nine or ten feet long and will weigh at least a ton. A whale of that size can do a tremendous amount of thrashing, especially when it feels threatened.

Flynn asks the chief why we have to venture all the way across the bay when there are plenty of whales in the river only a few hundred feet from where we are sitting. The chief replies that the river does not have the wide, shallow inlets his men require and, besides, everyone will enjoy the trip across the bay. It is difficult to pursue this discussion with the chief because we are sitting in the bar of the Churchill Hotel on a Saturday night in the summer and it is like a Klondike Gold Rush saloon only with 10 times the cast and 50 times the volume of noise. There are bearded construction workers down for a holiday from their posts on the DEW line (the U.S.-Canadian defensive radar system), crewmen from the Russian wheat ships anchored in the bay, mackinawed trappers, Indians, Mounties, town girls, young Canadians who have been backpacking in the wilderness and young Americans who appear to be on the lam from the draft. The country-style music produced by a trio is amplified until the walls tremble. There is not a tie or a dress in the house and the drink is beer, out of the bottle, with Canadian whiskey on the side. A burly man with a red beard explains it's much better to get drunk in the summer, because there's no danger of freezing to death afterwards.

What use have these details?

Sunday, Aug. 26—Dawn. It is a clear warm morning and the bay stretching to the horizon is blue and peaceful. The mosquitoes and gnats are as thick as ever but we are already getting used to them. We are eager to depart, but there seems to be one hitch. No Indians. About 9 o'clock a small boy comes to report that the chief will be along at 11. . . .

Now it is two o'clock in the afternoon. We are told we are leaving immediately. We meet the boats at the Port of Churchill dock a half mile from the Whaler's Motel. Our first sight of this armada is a bit unnerving. The motorboats so confidently mentioned in our briefing turn out to be little more than canoes equipped with outboard motors. The Indians are in a party mood. Their summers are short and every chance for outdoor fun is savored. Besides, the expedition should bring $6,000 into the Indian Council's treasury. A tall, blond Port Authority policeman watches and finally asks Phil Thornton, the television director, what's going on. Thornton explains. The policeman meditates a bit and then asks, "Will the Indians be a help or a hindrance?" He isn't being nasty; it's just that tall, blond whites in Churchill tend to look upon the Indians as bumbling children.

Does this narrative have a social as well as a physical setting?

The supplies being loaded into each boat include several cases of beer and a bottle of Canadian whiskey. The chief hasn't squandered much money on food, but there is some bacon, hot dogs and bread. The chief predicts we will catch our whales in the morning and be back in Churchill tomorrow night.

We depart. The name Hudson Bay conjures up thoughts of adventurers, ice floes and starkness, but nothing prepares a newcomer for the richness of the bay's life. Harbor seals bob just beyond our boats, their faces jovial, round and whiskered. A half dozen varieties of ducks are visible overhead, singly and in formation, and now and then we see a lordly arrow of snow geese. TuTu, the ancient, leathery Eskimo in the bow of my canoe, says there are plenty of fish beneath us and before long we see a fisherman. He is an adult polar bear, with only his head and part of his massive shoulders above water. He is visibly annoyed at us humans who dare to gape at him and he fixes us with a beady gaze until we go away. TuTu explains to us that the bears stay in the water for two or three days at a time, catching an occasional fish but mainly hoping for a white whale or seal. It's no problem for a polar bear to drag a whale or seal through 10 or 15 miles of water to the family on shore.

◄Are we being prepared for something here?

After a couple of hours, all of the Indians in all of the boats are quite drunk. TuTu and Paul, the Cree who is at the helm of my canoe, have downed a fifth of Canadian whiskey since we started and they are now working on the beer. Sometimes Paul steers a straight course and sometimes he wheels in wonderful, dizzying circles, while TuTu applauds. The five other boats on the horizon are doing pinwheels of their own. Suddenly it strikes me that it will soon be dark and I will be in a canoe in the middle of Hudson Bay with a couple of jolly fellows who are feeling no pain. The canoe has no lights or radio, not even a horn, but I need not worry about our going in the wrong direction because the motor has just died. TuTu pulls a rusty single-barreled shotgun from beneath his seat to show we have nothing to fear. Besides, there is still plenty of beer. I observe that there are no life jackets aboard and then reflect that would not be much use anyway because the water temperature is not much above freezing.

At dusk the chief's canoe pulls up and throws us a line. By the time we are hooked up the four other boats heave to and an argument begins among the Indians over where we are and which way we should go. There is no land in sight and having done so many pinwheels in the water has affected our sense of direction. The chief cups a hand to his forehead, surveys the horizon and finally points to his right. We will go that way. TuTu argues vehemently for going to the left, but the majority side with the chief and we go his way. "Lost, lost, lost," TuTu tells me, in a quite matter-of-fact voice. But the chief is right. Just before sunset a smudge of land appears and then we see a stark, lonely building. It is the hunting and fishing lodge. Soon we pull the canoes ashore and unload. The lodge has a butane stove, sink, some cabinets and three cubicles filled with triple-tiered bunks. There is no electricity and it is a three-mile walk to the nearest river which has potable water. Someone will go for water in the morning and meantime there is plenty of beer. . . .

As the fire burns into the night and the beer cans pop, the Indians become animated story tellers. Their yarns often deal with their mortal enemy, the polar bear. The fact is, the Indians would completely dominate this harsh land if it were not for the bears, who steal from them and sometimes maim or kill them. The Canadian Government protects the bears as a priceless natural resource, but the Indians would like to wipe them out. Francis, a rugged middle-aged Cree, tells what seems to be a favorite story. It seems he was hunting in mid-winter and entered an abandoned cabin. A bear, rummaging inside, tore his shoulder out of its socket and slashed his side. Francis killed the bear with a blast from his shotgun and then whipped his dog team into making the 75-mile trip to Churchill in 48 hours, an almost unbelievably rapid journey. The doctors saved his arm. He displays scars and the Indians join in a general cursing of polar bears and Government officials. As we turn in, we hear the honking of tens of thousands of snow geese. They have finished their summer nesting on the tundra and are about to begin their long flight south. There are a million stars and the aurora borealis plays along the horizon. Tomorrow morning, the whales.

Monday, Aug. 27—It is raining and cold and there will be no whale hunting today. It is just as well because our guides are shaky, sullen and withdrawn and sit along the walls, heads nestled in their arms, waiting for their hangovers to pass.

On our return, the chief scolds us. No one should go more than

◄Time blended into the sequence of events.

Notice that this talk prepares you for something coming up.

Why is so much made of these tales?

a hundred yards from the lodge without a gun, he says. Polar bears. We decide the Indians are paranoid about bears.

Tuesday, Aug. 28—Rain. No hunting, no food, no beer. Everyone is sullen. By midafternoon the chief and Francis appear, having shot a brace of geese. The geese are quickly plucked, tossed in a pot and boiled for three quarters of an hour. We are offered shares but we only nibble. The taste for briefly boiled snow geese has to be acquired. It isn't goose season yet but Indians are allowed to kill anything, except polar bears, any time of year.

Wednesday, Aug. 29—The skies are leaden and there's a definite threat of rain, but the chief decides we'll go this morning, come what may. The wind stiffens and the temperature drops into the low forties as we head to sea. By 9 we are in the boats cruising off the shallow inlets the chief had in mind. Now our six canoes begin a sweep toward shore. Every engine is at full throttle. Suddenly, there is a cry and an Indian points from the bow of one canoe. We are herding a pod of whales to shore. Some of the animals dash past the boats and out to sea, but there must be at least 50 between us and the shore. If these animals only knew their own strength, they might smash or capsize one of our boats and make their escape, but they are fleeing in terror. Everyone seems to be screaming, yet the outboards are drowning out all voices. Flynn points to a white sliver just ahead of his canoe and the chief steers alongside like a cowboy guiding his mustang after a rampaging steer. The water is just four to five feet deep and, at a signal, Francis and the chief plunge overboard on the whale's back and begin wrestling the animal. The chief has an arm firmly around the whale's head but Francis' grip on its tail is less sure. The wrestling match goes on savagely for a full minute and then the whale, with one climactic flash of its tail, knocks Francis under the water and breaks free.

What is the impact of this continued use of the present tense?

Paul and TuTu, however, have a better grip on another whale. Other Indians join them and after a brief struggle there are cries of triumph as the exhausted whale is lifted onto the canoe. Our captive, so strong in the water, is nearly helpless in the boat, the great mass of its weight, no longer supported by water, almost crushing its lungs. The whale is a female about nine feet long, and she is quivering with fear. Flynn assigns himself the job of sitting at the whale's side, dousing her with water. Her skin is creamy white and incredibly smooth to the touch. Every inch of skin must be kept wet because if it dries it will blister and the whale will quickly die. The whale has a large, rounded forehead and a wide mouth that seems almost as expressive as a human's. She is a member of the dolphin family and, to a layman, seems quite similar to the dolphins we see in aquariums and aquatic shows. Her breath comes in what seem to

Does description come in here? Explanation?

be agonized gasps but in time she becomes a bit calmer, perhaps in response to the motherly gentle clucking sounds Flynn is making. The discharge from her blow-hole is clear, and free of mucus — an indication of good health. Flynn is elated. But he wants three more.

There are two more wrestling matches, but each animal finally bursts free and two of the Indians are knocked breathless and almost drowned. A hard sleety rain is now falling and all of the Indians who have been in the water are almost numb with cold. The chief orders his party ashore, except for one man left behind to keep pouring water on our captive. Someone scrapes up some brush and pours gasoline on it. The fire is quick, hot and life saving, but also brief, and now the chief must decide whether to make the 5-mile trip back to the lodge, where there is shelter and warmth but no food, or risk the 30-mile trip across the bay back to Churchill. The water is rough and we have no dry clothing, but the chief elects for Churchill.

The crossing is punctuated by a series of engine failures. As one outboard conks out, other canoes circle about helplessly, and then one takes the stricken boat in tow. By now two motors are dead and the four others seem to take turns in giving out death rattles. The rain gets colder and meaner and the bay, which had seemed so vibrant and alive on Sunday, is now an ominous monster waiting to swallow us. At least the whale's breathing is steady and the rain will keep her skin wet even if the human bucket brigade fails her.

Our attention is being focused on the baby whale.

By about 8 o'clock the lights of Churchill slowly emerge and it seems to us like the flowering of civilization. The Whaling Center Motel is grander than the palace of the Sun King. Thornton, with shaking fingers, heats a can of tomato soup and later, wrapped in a blanket, writes an ode to tomato soup. Flynn decides to name the whale TuTu, in honor of the senior Eskimo hunter. It takes eight men to carry TuTu from the canoe to the first of the portable swimming pools. The pool is about 14 feet in diameter and is quickly filled with water pumped from the river. TuTu swims around uneasily in her tiny new home, carefully testing the plastic walls with her nose. Flynn says the biggest problem will be teaching her to eat dead fish. Some captured whales never learn.

Thursday, Aug. 30 — TuTu is the star of Churchill. There has been a shuffle of townspeople, tourists and Indians to her side since dawn. The local radio station broadcast an in-depth report from poolside, including the views of several citizens on what the export of live whales could mean to Churchill's economy. The local stringer for the CBC has filmed a report, and TuTu's debut into show business seems auspicious. An elderly woman asks anxiously if we really believe the whale will recover from its harpoon wounds. When assured TuTu was taken without a scratch, she scolds, "That's just for the press, dearie, but you mustn't lie to me."

There are about 20 spectators, mostly children, watching as Flynn tries unsuccessfully to tempt TuTu with a chunk of fish. Suddenly there are hisses from the audience and they begin to fade back toward the buildings, their eyes fixed on the river. A mother polar bear and her half-grown cub have emerged from the water some 50 yards away and the two are now ambling cautiously toward the whale. The bears pause every few steps and the mother raises her snout high to sniff the wind. Flynn backs carefully toward the lodge. We've been told that polar bears aren't interested in humans as food and only attack when cornered or angered. But running, according to the locals, angers them, and, besides, no human could outrun a polar bear. Someone in the lodge calls the chief and he emerges with his rifle and begins firing against nearby rocks. The combined sound of the shots and richocheting bullets are all the warning the mother bear needs and, after standing her ground only long enough to emit a couple of growls, turns with her cub and returns to the water. She stops at water's edge for a final growl and then she and the cub wade in and swim upriver, two large, bobbing white heads slowly melting into the waves. . . .

Why is this scene developed with detail?

Friday, Aug. 31—There has been growing dissension all week between the younger Indians, led by the chief, and the older men. Now it breaks into the open. Francis, who hasn't made any secret of his doubts about the chief's leadership, tells us he can go out today within a couple of miles of Churchill and catch the three additional whales we want. Besides, the weather is too bad and the time too short for another trip across the bay to the lodge. Flynn, knowing he had little to lose, agrees to let Francis lead an expedition. Two of us stay behind to tend TuTu. The chief, after some hesitation, decides to join the whale hunters.

This diversion might have been omitted in a fictional account.

At about 4 in the afternoon, Francis' party returns, whooping lustily with joy. They have two male whales, one nearly 10 feet long, the other almost 11 feet. It is decided to put these two whales in the pool with TuTu. Flynn is more than happy to be able to ship home three healthy whales, and he notifies the airline and aquarium of his success.

Saturday, Sept. 1—The six of us are sitting in Flynn's room, looking contentedly out the window at the spotlighted pool some 30 yards away. There has been a triumphal dinner earlier in the evening and now all that remains for us to do is to load the whales onto the plane that will arrive tomorrow. Flynn has hired round-the-clock guards to keep a watchful eye on our prizes, but everyone is too excited to sleep, so Flynn has released the guards for a few hours to join a party in progress at the chief's. One or another of us is constantly going out for still another look at the whales. All three animals seem to be healthy and respiring normally.

In light of what is to come, note the economy of this transition.

We all catch sight at almost the same moment of a white shape at the water's edge. It is a massive polar bear moving like a tank up the beach toward the pool. We know exactly what to do, and, fortified with confidence, and beer, we race outside. Flynn has the rifle and begins slamming shots at the rocks closest to the bear. The rest of us shout and bang folding aluminum chairs. At sight of us the bear rears up and suddenly it is as if we are in the presence of the monster from some science fiction movie. The bear is not more than 30 yards away and seems completely contemptuous of our shots, shouts and rattling chairs. It gets down on all fours again, lumbers to the edge of the pool, stands up, and, with one swipe of its paw, rips a top-to-bottom slash. The water gushes through the break and now the bear strides into the empty pool and contemplates the flopping, helpless whales. With a sudden stroke of its paws, the bear slashes the smaller of the two whales across the head and then administers the same killing blow to the larger male. The bear's claws are like huge steel hooks and one fierce swipe with them is enough to crush the skull of a 10- or 11-foot whale. The bear decides it prefers the larger of the two males and sinks a paw into the flesh behind the head and half lifts, half drags, the dying animal through the break in the pool and down the beach. The whale weighs more than a thousand pounds, but the bear drags it as easily as a man might pull a short branch of a tree. TuTu threshes fearfully in the bloody bottom of the pool. Suddenly one of the Indians, whose sleep in the motel office has been broken by the shots, emerges with a rifle and begins firing, but he is shooting to kill. The bear, bellowing angrily as it is struck by several shots, drops the whale at water's edge and lopes off into the night.

Notice how the topical matter and the details develop in this narrative paragraph.

Two whales are dead and TuTu is in a state of shock. The pool is quickly patched and half filled to keep TuTu alive. The reserve pool will be ready in an hour. Four Mounties now have arrived and they are furious about the wounding of the bear. The crippled animal will take cover somewhere near and might kill anyone who stumbles on it. By 1 A.M. it seems as though everyone in Churchill is on hand, and no one is telling who fired at the bear. Flynn, broken-hearted, cancels the chartered flight and plans to stay up all night with TuTu.

Sunday, Sept. 2 — After sweeping the tundra with field glasses, a party of game wardens in a Land Rover spots the wounded bear almost a mile from the Whalers Motel. A skirmish line of Mounties and wardens, 20 in all, with rifles and shotguns, moves slowly forward and, when the animal rises, quickly executes it. The bear is sheer magnificence, over eight feet tall and weighing better than 800 pounds. Its hide will be tanned and auctioned off by the Government. TuTu still lives, but she is an intelligent and emotional animal and it is hard to know how deeply she has been damaged by shock.

Why are TuTu and the bear combined in one paragraph?

Flynn is with her constantly and with each hour his hopes rise that she will survive. It is now too cold and wet for any more whale hunting and Thornton and I are told to return home. There will be no TV show. When we leave, TuTu is circling slowly in her pool and Flynn is trying to tempt her with a chunk of fish. A half dozen Indians watch impassively.

Postscript—Later in the week TuTu was flown by cargo plane to the Sea World aquarium in Ohio because this seemed a shorter and safer flight. TuTu spent four days in the Ohio aquarium and seemed to be thriving. At the end of the week, she was placed on a direct flight to San Diego, with Flynn and his three assistants at her side. TuTu seemed to make the flight in good spirits. At San Diego, she and her pool of icy water were hoisted aboard a truck, but when the truck arrived at Sea World, TuTu was dead.

Reading and Interpreting

1. Who is the TuTu referred to in the title of this selection? How did she get her name?

2. Whales are not normally considered sympathetically. How does O'Hallaren portray TuTu so that you are drawn to her not as a whale but as a sympathetic character? Cite specific passages in the essay that prompt you to sympathize with TuTu.

3. A whale hunt sounds like adventure; but what kind of hunt was this, and what was its purpose? Was the hunt an adventure? Before answering, you may want to define adventure and consider whether there may be quite different kinds of adventure.

Writing Techniques

1. Obviously this is narrative. The purpose is presumably narrative, and most of the time O'Hallaren is telling what happened. But there are other parts, both descriptive and expository. Identify some of these; notice how brief they are, but how they fit into the story. Do your observations tell you anything about how writings with different purposes blend into one another?

2. Ostensibly this is a diary. But it is more than a series of private notes or an outline of daily events. Describe the kind of diary we have here. What advantages are there in writing the story of TuTu in diary form?

3. The last paragraph is not part of the diary. What is the effect of this shift in style and tone?

Suggestions for Writing

Everybody has gone on trips of some sort: moving, taking a hike, going camping or on a picnic, attending summer camp, reporting for a job in a strange place. Usually accounts of such trips are pretty dull, but you probably did not find the account of a whale hunt dull. Why not? Part of the answer will be that going on a hunt like this is more exciting than most weekend picnics. But part of the reason, also, is that O'Hallaren saw, heard, and recorded more than most travelers do. If you can observe as much as O'Hallaren did, you may be able to make even a picnic interesting.

CONFESSIONS OF A WORKING STIFF
Patrick Fenton

6

If this piece can be accepted as the autobiographical account it seems to be, **Patrick Fenton** *tells you who he is and what he does. This selection appeared in* New York *magazine.*

THE Big Ben is hammering out its 5:45 alarm in the half-dark of another Tuesday morning. If I'm lucky, my car down the street will kick over for me. I don't want to think about that now; all I want to do is roll over into the warm covers that hug my wife. I can hear the wind as it whistles up and down the sides of the building. Tuesday is always the worst day—it's the day the drudgery, boredom, and fatigue start all over again. I'm off from work on Sunday and Monday, so Tuesday is my blue Monday.

I make my living humping cargo for Seaboard World Airlines,   *humping* one of the big international airlines at Kennedy Airport. They handle strictly all cargo. I was once told that one of the Rockefellers is the major stockholder for the airline, but I don't really think about that too much. I don't get paid to think. The big thing is to beat that race with the time clock every morning of your life so the airline will be happy. The worst thing a man could ever do is to make suggestions about building a better airline. They pay people $40,000 a year to come up with better ideas. It doesn't matter that these ideas never work, it's just that they get nervous when a guy from South Brooklyn or Ozone Park acts like he actually has a brain.

I throw a Myadec high-potency vitamin into my mouth to ward off one of the ten colds I get every year from humping mailbags out in the cold rain at Kennedy. A huge DC-8 stretch jet waits impatiently for the 8,000 pounds of mail that I will soon feed its empty belly. I wash the Myadec down with some orange juice and grab a brown bag filled with bologna and cheese. Inside the lunch bag there is sometimes a silly note from my wife that says, "I Love You—Guess Who?" It is all that keeps me going to a job that I hate.

I've been going there for seven years now and my job is still the same. It's weary work that makes a man feel used up and worn out. You push and you pull all day long with your back. You tie down pallets loaded with thousands of pounds of freight. You fill igloo- *pallets* shaped containers with hundreds of boxes that all look the same. If you're assigned to work the warehouse, it's really your hard luck. This is the job all the men hate most. You stack box upon box until the pallet resembles the exact shape of the inside of the plane. You get the same monotonous feeling an adult gets when he plays with a child's blocks. When you finish one pallet, you find another and start the whole dull process over again.

The airline pays me $192 a week for this. After they take out the taxes and $5.81 for the pension, I go home with $142. Once a month they take out $10 for term life insurance, and $5.50 for union dues. The week they take out the life insurance is always the worst: I go home with $132. My job will never change. I will fill up the same igloos with the same boxes for the next 34 years of my life, I will hump the same mailbags into the belly of the plane, and push the same 8,000-pound pallets with my back. I will have to do this until I'm 65 years old. Then I'll be free, if I don't die of a heart attack before that, and the airline will let me retire.

In winter the warehouse is cold and damp. There is no heat. The large steel doors that line the warehouse walls stay open most of the day. In the cold months, wind, rain and snow blow across the floor. In the summer the warehouse becomes an oven. Dust and sand from the runways mix with the toxic fumes of fork lifts, leaving a dry, stale taste in your mouth. The high windows above the doors are covered with a thick, black dirt that kills the sun. The men work in shadows with the constant roar of jet engines blowing dangerously in their ears.

Working the warehouse is a tedious job that leaves a man's mind empty. If he's smart he will spend his days wool-gathering. He will think about pretty girls that he once knew, or some other daydream of warm, dry places where you never had a chill. The worst thing he can do is to think about his problems. If he starts to think about how he is going to pay the mortgage on the $30,000 home that he can't afford, it will bring him down. He will wonder why he comes to the cargo airline every morning of his life, and even on Christmas Day. He will start to wonder why he has to listen to the deafening sound of the jets as they rev up their engines. He will wonder why he crawls on his hands and knees, breaking his back a little bit more every day.

To keep his kids in that great place in the country in the summer, that great place far away from Brooklyn and the South Bronx, he must work every hour of overtime that the airline offers him. If he never turns down an hour, if he works some 600 hours over, he can make about $15,000. To do this he must turn against himself, he must pray that the phone rings in the middle of the night, even though it's snowing out and he doesn't feel like working. He must hump cargo late into the night, eat meatball heroes for supper, drink coffee that *heroes* starts to taste like oil, and then hope that his car starts when it's time to go home. If he gets sick — well, he better not think about that.

All over Long Island, Ozone Park, Brooklyn, and as far away as the Bronx, men stir in the early morning hours as a new day begins. Every morning is the same as the last. Some of the men drink beer for breakfast instead of coffee. Way out in Bay Shore a cargoman snaps open a can of Budweiser. It's 6 A.M., and he covers the top of the can with his thumb in order to keep down the loud hiss as the beer escapes. He doesn't want to awaken his children as they dream away the morning in the next room. Soon he will swing his Pinto wagon up onto the crowded Long Island Expressway and start the long ride to the job. As he slips the car out of the driveway he tucks another can of beer between his legs.

All the men have something in common: they hate the work they are doing and they drink a little too much. They come to work only to punch a timecard that has their last name on it. At the end of the week they will pick up a paycheck with their last name on it. They will never receive a bonus for a job well done, or even a party. At Christmastime a card from the president of the airline will arrive at each one of their houses. It will say Merry Christmas and have the president's name printed at the bottom of it. They know that the airline will be there long after they are dead. Nothing stops it. It runs non-stop, without sleep, through Christmas Day, New Year's Eve, Martin Luther King's birthday, even the deaths of Presidents.

It's seven in the morning and the day shift is starting to drift in. Huge tractors are backing up to the big-mouth doors of the warehouse. Cattle trucks bring tons of beef to feed its insatiable appetite for cargo. Smoke-covered trailers with refrigerated units packed deep with green peppers sit with their diesel engines idling. Names like White, Mack, and Kenworth are welded to the front of their radiators, which hiss and moan from the overload. The men talk through the factory-type gates of the parking lot with their heads bowed, oblivious of the shuddering diesels that await them.

Once inside the warehouse they gather in groups of threes and fours like prisoners in an exercise yard. They stand in front of the two time clocks that hang below a window in the manager's office. They smoke and cough in the early morning hour as they await their work assignments. The manager, a nervous-looking man with a stomach that is starting to push out at his belt, walks out with the pink work sheets in his hand.

Eddie, a young Irishman with a mustache, has just bolted in through the door. The manager has his timecard in his hand, holding it so no one else can hit Eddie in. Eddie is four minutes late by the time clock. His name will now go down in the timekeeper's ledger. The manager hands the card to him with a "you'll be up in the office if you don't straighten out" look. Eddie takes the card, hits it in, and slowly takes his place with the rest of the men. He has been out till four in the morning drinking beer in the bars of Ozone Park: the time clock and the manager could blow up, for all he cares. "Jesus," he says to no one in particular, "I hope to Christ they don't put me in the warehouse this morning." *hit*

Over in another group, Kelly, a tall man wearing a navy knit hat, talks to the men. "You know, I almost didn't make it in this morning. I passed this green VW on the Belt Parkway. The girl driving it was singing. Jesus, I thought to myself, it must be great going somewhere at 6:30 in the morning that makes you want to sing." Kelly is smiling as he talks. "I often think, why the hell don't you keep on going, Kelly? Don't get off at the cargo exit, stay on. Go anywhere, even if it's only Brooklyn. Christ, if I was a single man I think I would do just that. Some morning I'd pass this damn place by and drive as far away as Riverhead. I don't know what I'd do when I got there—maybe I'd pick up a pound of beefsteak tomatoes from one of those roadside stands or something."

The men laugh at Kelly but they know he is serious. "I feel the same way sometimes," the man next to him says. "I find myself daydreaming a lot lately; this place drives you to that. I get up in the morning and I just don't want to come to work. I get sick when I hit that parking lot. If it wasn't for the kids and the house I'd quit." The men then talk about how hard it is to get work on "the outside." They mention "outside" as if they were in a prison.

Each morning there is an Army-type roll call from the leads. The leads are foremen who must keep the men moving; if they don't, it could mean their jobs. At one time they had power over the men but as time went by the company took away their little bit of authority. They also lost the deep interest, even enjoyment, for the hard work they once did. As the cargo airline grew, it beat this out of them, leaving only apathy. The ramp area is located in the backyard of the warehouse. This is where the huge jets park to unload their 70,000-pound payloads. A crew of men fall in behind the ramp lead as he *leads* mopes out of the warehouse. His long face shows the hopelessness of another day.

A brutal rain has started to beat down on the oil-covered concrete of the ramp as the 306 screeches in off the runway. Its engines scream as they spit off sheets of rain and oil. Two of the men cover their ears as they run to put up a ladder to the front of the plane. The airline will give them ear covers only if they pay for half of them. A lot of the men never buy them. If they want, the airline will give them two little plugs free. The plugs don't work and hurt the inside of the ears.

The men will spend the rest of the day in the rain. Some of them will set up conveyor belts and trucks to unload the thousands of pounds of cargo that sit in the deep belly of the plane. Then they will feed the awkward bird until it is full and ready to fly again. They will crawl on their hands and knees in its belly, counting and humping hundreds of mailbags. The rest of the men will work up topside on the plane, pushing 8,000-pound pallets with their backs. Like Egyptians building a pyramid, they will pull and push until the pallet finally gives in and moves like a massive stone sliding through sand. They don't complain too much; they know that when the airline comes up with a better system some of them will go.

The old-timers at the airline can't understand why the younger men stay on. They know what the cargo airline can do to a man. It can work him hard but make him lazy at the same time. The work comes in spurts. Sometimes a man will be pushed for three hours of sweat, other times he will just stand around bored. It's not the hard work that breaks a man at the airline, it's the boredom of doing the same job over and over again.

At the end of the day the men start to move in off the ramp. The rain is still beating down at their backs but they move slowly. Their faces are red and raw from the rain-soaked wind that has been snapping at them for eight hours. The harsh wind moves in from the direction of the city. From the ramp you can see the Manhattan skyline, gray- and blue-looking, as it peeks up from the west wall of the warehouse. There is nothing to block the winter weather as it rolls in like a storm across a prairie. They head down to the locker room, heads bowed, like a football team that never wins.

With the workday almost over, the men move between the narrow, gray rows of lockers. Up on the dirty walls that surround the lockers someone has written a couple of four-letter words. There is no wit to the words; they just say the usual. As they strip off their wet gear the men seem to come alive.

"Hey, Arnie! You want to stay four hours? They're asking for overtime down in Export," one of the men yells over the lockers.

Arnie is sitting about four rows over, taking off his heavy winter clothing. He thinks about this for a second and yells back, "What will we be doing?"

"Working the meat trailer." This means that Arnie will be humping huge sides of beef off rows of hooks for four hours. Blood will drip down onto his clothes as he struggles to the front of the trailer. Like most of the men, he needs the extra money, and knows that he should stay. He has Master Charge, Korvettes, Times Square Stores, and Abraham & Straus to pay.

"Nah, I'm not staying tonight. Not if it's working the meat trailer. Don wanted to stop for a few beers at The Owl; maybe I'll stay tomorrow night."

It's four o'clock in the afternoon now—the men have twelve minutes to go before they punch out. The airline has stopped for a few seconds as the men change shifts. Supervisors move frantically across the floor pushing the fresh lot of new men who have just started to come in. They hand out work sheets and yell orders: "Jack, get your men into their rain gear. Put three men in the bellies to finish off the 300 flight. Get someone on the pepper trailers, they've been here all morning." *punch*

pepper trailers

The morning shift stands around the time clock with three minutes to go. Someone says that Kevin Delahunty has just been appointed to the Fire Department. Kevin, a young Irishman from Ozone Park, has been working the cargo airline for six years. Like most of the men, he has hated every minute of it. The men are openly proud of him as they reach out to shake his hand. Kevin has found a job on "the outside." "Ah, you'll be leaving soon," he tells Pat. "I never thought I'd get out of here either, but you'll see, you're going to make it."

The manager moves through the crowd handing out timecards and stops when he comes to Kevin. Someone told him Kevin is leaving. "Is that right, Delahunty? Well I guess we won't expect you in tomorrow, will we? Going to become a fireman, eh? That means you'll be jumping out of windows like a crazy man. Don't act like you did around here," he adds as he walks back to his office.

The time clock hits 4:12 and the men pour out of the warehouse. Kevin will never be back, but the rest of them will return in the morning to grind out another eight hours. Some of them will head straight home to the bills, screaming children, and a wife who tries to understand them. They'll have a Schaefer or two, then they'll settle down to a night of *The Courtship of Eddie's Father, The Rookies, Here's Lucy,* and the late news.

Some of them will start to fill up the cargo bars that surround Kennedy Airport. They will head to places like Gaylor's on Rockaway *cargo bars*

Boulevard or The Dew Drop Inn down near Farmers Boulevard. They will drink deep glasses of whiskey and cold mugs of Budweiser. The Dew Drop has a honky-tonk mood of the Old West to it. The barmaid moves around like a modern-day Katie Elder. Like Brandy, she's a fine girl, but she can out-curse any cargoman. She wears a low-cut blouse that reveals most of her breasts. The jukebox will beat out some Country & Western as she says, "Ah, hell, you played my song." The cargomen will hoot and holler as she substitutes some of her own obscene lyrics.

They will drink late into the night, forgetting time clocks, Master Charge, First National City, Korvettes, mortgages, cars that don't start, and jet engines that hurt their ears. They will forget about damp, cold warehouses, winters that get longer and colder every year, minutes that drift by like hours, supervisors that harass, and the thought of growing old on a job they hate. At midnight they will fall dangerously into their cars and make their way up onto the Southern State Parkway. As they ride into the dark night of Long Island they will forget it all until 5:45 the next morning—when the Big Ben will start the whole grind all over again.

Reading and Interpreting

1. Fenton relates a typical day in his life. Has he done much else? What observations does he make? What conclusions does he draw? How has he universalized the common in his account?

2. In a sense, what Fenton gives us is a detailed diary entry for one day in his life, except that—if we may believe him—most of his days for seven years have been much like this one. Compare and contrast Fenton's sketch with Morgan's account of the life of a policewoman.

3. Why does Fenton keep his job if it is so hard and if he dislikes it so much? Does Fenton provide a specific answer to this question? Does he imply one? Are the answers the same?

Writing Techniques

1. This essay is a narrative, but it is also an example. What does Fenton want to illustrate with his use of example? (You may want to recall this narrative when we study examples in Section VIII.)

2. Examine the first and last paragraphs. How has Fenton tied his account together in his introduction and conclusion? What devices does Fenton use to indicate the chronological structure of his narrative?

3. Usually narrative profits from good characterization. Do the people here become individual, believable, human beings? If so, how does Fenton get this effect? If not, what is lacking?

4. In narrative, two of the devices for variety are change of scene and change of pace. You will recall that in films or television shows the whole screen may be occupied for a time with one person's face; then in the next scene you may be able to see for miles, with the human beings shrinking to dots. Are there such differences in the intimacy of scenes in the Fenton account? What about pace? Do some paragraphs record only minutes or seconds, whereas others survey hours or even more time?

Word Study

1. This is a first-person narrative. What effect does this fact have on the word choice?

2. Most of the words in the selection are common and familiar, but a few are used in unfamiliar ways. Define each of the common words printed in the margins as it is used in the selection (*humping, pallets, heroes, hit, leads, punch, pepper trailers, cargo bars*).

Suggestions for Writing

1. Analyze the selection, identifying various parts, giving each a heading, and leaving space for notes to be added later. The first two headings might be:

a. Introduction: Going to work, Tuesday morning (first paragraph).

b. General description of the job (next two paragraphs).
Then assume you are Fenton. In the spaces you have left for notes, indicate what you would try to do in each part.

2. Fenton's autobiographical sketch suggests a long diary entry or, even more, the kind of paper that might grow from a diary entry. Write the sort of diary jottings that might have been prewriting for one part of a sketch such as this.

3. You might write a paper on "A Day in My Life," using Fenton's account as a kind of model, particularly observing his use of concrete details rather than general comments. Notice, for example, how in the last three paragraphs Fenton names specific TV shows, actual bars, the particular highway the cargomen will take, and so on.

7

THE USE OF FORCE
William Carlos Williams

William Carlos Williams *studied medicine at the University of Pennsylvania and practiced for fifty years in New Jersey. During this time, he published more than a dozen volumes of verse, novels, short stories, plays, essays, criticism, and an autobiography. He won a posthumous Pulitzer Prize for poetry (1963).*

THEY were new patients to me; all I had was the name, Olson. Please come down as soon as you can, my daughter is very sick.

When I arrived I was met by the mother, a big startled looking woman, very clean and apologetic who merely said, Is this the doctor? and let me in. In the back, she added, You must excuse us, doctor, we have her in the kitchen where it is warm. It is very damp here sometimes.

The child was fully dressed and sitting on her father's lap near the kitchen table. He tried to get up, but I motioned for him not to bother, took off my overcoat and started to look things over. I could see that they were all very nervous, eyeing me up and down distrustfully. As often, in such cases, they weren't telling me more than they had to, it was up to me to tell them: that's why they were spending three dollars on me.

The child was fairly eating me up with her cold, steady eyes, and no expression to her face whatever. She did not move and seemed, inwardly, quiet; an unusually attractive little thing, and as strong as a heifer in appearance. But her face was flushed, she was breathing rapidly, and I realized that she had a high fever. She had magnificent blonde hair, in profusion. One of those picture children often reproduced in advertising leaflets and the photogravure sections of the Sunday papers.

She's had a fever for three days, began the father, and we don't know what it comes from. My wife has given her things, you know, like people do, but it don't do no good. And there's been a lot of sickness around. So we tho't you'd better look her over and tell us what is the matter.

As doctors often do I took a trial shot at it as a point of departure. Has she had a sore throat?

Both parents answered me together, No . . . No, she says her throat don't hurt her.

Does your throat hurt you? added the mother to the child. But the little girl's expression didn't change nor did she move her eyes from my face.

Have you looked?

I tried to, said the mother, but I couldn't see.

As it happens we have been having a number of cases of diphtheria in the school to which this child went during that month and we were all, quite apparently, thinking of that, though no one had as yet spoken of the thing.

Well, I said, suppose we take a look at the throat first. I smiled in my best professional manner and asking for the child's first name I said, come on, Mathilda, open your mouth and let's take a look at your throat.

Nothing doing.

Aw, come on, I coaxed, just open your mouth wide and let me take a look. Look, I said opening both hands wide, I haven't anything in my hands. Just open up and let me see.

Such a nice man, put in the mother. Look how kind he is to you. Come on, do what he tells you to. He won't hurt you.

At that I ground my teeth in disgust. If only they wouldn't use the word "hurt" I might be able to get somewhere. But I did not allow myself to be hurried or disturbed but speaking quietly and slowly I approached the child again.

As I moved my chair a little nearer suddenly with one catlike movement both her hands clawed instinctively for my eyes and she almost reached them too. In fact she knocked my glasses flying and they fell, though unbroken, several feet away from me on the kitchen floor.

Both the mother and father almost turned themselves inside out in embarrassment and apology. You bad girl, said the mother, taking her and shaking her by one arm. Look what you've done. The nice man . . .

For heaven's sake, I broke in. Don't call me a nice man to her. I'm here to look at her throat on the chance that she might have diphtheria and possibly die of it. But that's nothing to her. Look here, I said to the child, we're going to look at your throat. You're old enough to understand what I'm saying. Will you open it now by yourself or shall we have to open it for you?

Not a move. Even her expression hadn't changed. Her breaths however were becoming faster and faster. Then the battle began. I had to do it. I had to have a throat culture for her own protection. But first I told the parents that it was entirely up to them. I explained the danger but said that I would not insist on a throat examination so long as they would take the responsibility.

If you don't do what the doctor says you'll have to go to the hospital, the mother admonished her severely.

Oh yeah? I had to smile to myself. After all, I had already fallen in love with the savage brat, the parents were contemptible to me. In the ensuing struggle they grew more and more abject, crushed, exhausted while she surely rose to magnificent heights of insane fury of effort bred of her terror of me.

The father tried his best, and he was a big man but the fact that she was his daughter, his shame at her behavior and his dread of hurting her made him release her just at the critical times when I had almost achieved success, till I wanted to kill him. But his dread also that she might have diphtheria made him tell me to go on, go on though he himself was almost fainting, while the mother moved back and forth behind us raising and lowering her hands in an agony of apprehension.

Put her in front of you on your lap, I ordered, and hold both her wrists.

But as soon as he did the child let out a scream. Don't, you're hurting me. Let go of my hands. Let them go I tell you. Then she shrieked terrifyingly, hysterically. Stop it! Stop it! You're killing me!

Do you think she can stand it, doctor! said the mother.

You get out, said the husband to his wife. Do you want her to die of diphtheria?

Come on now, hold her, I said.

Then I grasped the child's head with my left hand and tried to get the wooden tongue depressor between her teeth. She fought, with clenched teeth, desperately! But now I also had grown furious—at a child. I tried to hold myself down but I couldn't. I know how to expose a throat for inspection. And I did my best. When finally I got the wooden spatula behind the last teeth and just the point of it into the mouth cavity, she opened up for an instant but before I could see anything she came down again and gripping the wooden blade between her molars she reduced it to splinters before I could get it out again.

Aren't you ashamed, the mother yelled at her. Aren't you ashamed to act like that in front of the doctor?

Get me a smooth-handled spoon of some sort, I told the mother. We're going through with this. The child's mouth was already bleeding. Her tongue was cut and she was screaming in wild hysterical shrieks. Perhaps I should have desisted and come back in an hour or more. No doubt it would have been better. But I have seen at least two children lying dead in bed of neglect in such cases, and feeling that I must get a diagnosis now or never I went at it again. But the worst of it was that I too had got beyond reason. I could have torn the child apart in my own fury and enjoyed it. It was a pleasure to attack her. My face was burning with it.

The damned little brat must be protected against her own idiocy, one says to one's self at such times. Others must be protected against her. It is a social necessity. And all these things are true. But a blind fury, a feeling of adult shame, bred of a longing for muscular release are the operatives. One goes on to the end.

In a final unreasoning assault I overpowered the child's neck and jaws. I forced the heavy silver spoon back of her teeth and down her throat till she gagged. And there it was—both tonsils covered with membrane. She had fought valiantly to keep me from knowing her secret. She had been hiding that sore throat for three days at least and lying to her parents in order to escape just such an outcome as this.

Now truly she was furious. She had been on the defensive before but now she attacked. Tried to get off her father's lap and fly at me while tears of defeat blinded her eyes.

Reading and Interpreting

1. Does this seem to you "a short story"? What do you think it is about—the title may suggest what the author thought it was about. Why does not Williams tell us whether or not the girl went to a hospital, whether she died of diphtheria or not?

2. The essence of a piece of fiction is often said to appear as conflict. What is the conflict in this story? Is it resolved?

3. With whom do you sympathize in the story? Why? Does your sympathy shift as the story grows?

4. At times, the doctor becomes angry at other characters. What is the sequence of his anger? Does he ever get angry at himself? Does his attitude toward himself seem to change after the events he recounts and before his recording them?

Writing Techniques

1. Presumably this is fiction, although it may well have been founded on an actual occurrence. How would it have differed if it were the autobiographical account it purports to be, if it were the doctor's entry in his journal after a busy day?

2. What does the author do to make you see and hear this incident? What does he do to gain your sympathy for a character at a particular point in this story?

3. Ostensibly, the central character in the story is Mathilda. Is she? In what sense is the doctor a character in the story as well as the narrator?

Word Study

Contrast the terms used by the parents and by the author when he writes as though he is the doctor. The parents use only short, common words; *ashamed* is perhaps the longest. The doctor mainly uses short, homey words, also, but being an educated man he employs terms the parents do not command. Skim through and record the first ten words you notice that the parents would be unlikely to use. Obviously the doctor can say things the parents could not express, whether for lack of brains, language, education, or whatever. Note specific points that the doctor can pin down exactly because he commands the necessary words.

Suggestions for Writing

Write a brief fictional account of an incident that seems to you to mean something, as Williams apparently thinks his story means something about force and its place in society and about what it does to people. Base your account on some event you took part in, or some occurrence that you observed. You may change any details that will help make your point, as probably Williams changed some of the details about a house call, hoping thereby to make his point.

Description: Observing and Reporting

Have you ever seen a really old film comedy, say one made about 1905? If you have, you were probably amused at the way the people flitted over walls. Usually there was a wild chase, with the runners upsetting applecarts and bumping into funny fat men, and sooner or later, whoever was running away would face a wall about ten or twelve feet high. This would have stopped a less agile runner, but not our hero. He would face a wall and pretend to climb, and up he would go, zip! zip! zip! It would take him perhaps a dozen zips to get over. You would see him there, facing the wall; then suddenly he would be a foot or so off the ground, and then another foot, until he disappeared over the top. And the pursuers would go over the wall the same way, in a series of upward jerks.

Movies were pretty amateurish affairs in those days, and one can imagine how these over-the-wall shots were taken. The photographer took some stills of our hero at the foot of the wall. Then the stagehands heaved him up a bit, with a wire or whatever, and the photographer took some more stills. They kept moving him up the wall, taking stills as they went, until they got him over. Later they ran the stills consecutively and the result was a moving picture, i.e., a series of pictures of our hero having been moved. Of course, a movie is still a series of still pictures, although now the sequence is so rapid and the difference between any still picture and the next still picture is so infinitesimal that the eye cannot detect the breaks and the actors seem to move naturally.

Thus, a story can be told with a series of pictures in film. You can tell the same story with a series of pictures drawn with words, spoken by a narrator or written on paper. Some writers have done this in obvious ways. The poet Edmund Spenser wrote some long allegorical stories partly that way. In one stanza we see the Lady Una and the Red Cross Knight riding across a plain. In the next stanza a dragon comes roaring out of its den. In the following stanza the knight is fighting the dragon, and thus the succeeding pictures-in-words become a narrative.

Looked at in one way, all narratives are series of pictures, or to use terms more suited to writing, are a sequence of descriptions. Usually they are not broken up much, nor are the individual scenes as complete as were the still photographs in the movies of the fugitive being jerked over the wall. Most narratives are more like a modern movie, in which the action of one scene blends into the action of the next. The reader will not be distracted by a series of complete pictures: a novelist does not feel he has to describe everything in a room all over again every time a new character enters. But any novel can be thought of as a series of descriptions, most of them only sketchily suggested by a few details.

Thus description contributes to all narratives. It can also serve in all other kinds of writing. If you are trying to convince somebody that a factory should be prevented from spewing cancer-causing fumes into the air, you are engaged in argument, but you may want to describe what such fumes are doing to a community. If you are trying to show how a machine works—or a legislature, or a dance committee, or the principle of biofeedback, or almost anything—your ultimate purpose may be to explain, but your immediate purpose and your means to that end may be to describe.

In the section on narration, you probably noticed that although narrative can use almost any technique of writing, some devices appeared more than did others. Time was important, as evidenced in the sequence of events; so were cause and effect. Vivid details made a difference. Sentences tended to have actors for subjects, and to rely on active verbs. Characterization helped; we had to know what kinds of people the persons in the narrative were. In a simple nursery tale you might not need to know why Rumpelstiltskin acted the way he did, whether he was badly toilet-trained or suffered a trauma in a ghetto, but in any adult narrative the actors and their characters become important.

In description, also, you can probably observe some ways of

writing that stem from purpose. In description you would expect space to be prominent, as well as spatial relationships. The novelist Joseph Conrad, in an oft-quoted passage, identifies his purpose; he is talking about a novel, but he seems to think of himself as describing. "My task," he says, "is by the power of the written word to make you hear, to make you feel—it is above all to make you *see*." Similarly if you describe a piece of laboratory equipment by which a rat gets a sugar pill for solving a problem, you also will be trying to make us see, and if you describe a symphony you will probably be trying to make us hear. If you want to know how all this can be done, you might notice how others have done it.

Not all the pieces below are made equally of description. The pleasant little piece about "Le Pirate" includes description, but it is much more the report of a visit to a restaurant than it is an undeviating attempt to make us see. And this is in part the importance of description for most college students: it will inevitably enter into reports of all kinds. You will want to ask yourself what description can do for you and how you can best handle it.

BRIEF GLIMPSES

8

Here are brief descriptions, a paragraph or two each, which contribute to some larger plan the author is working on. **a. Herman Melville,** *best known as the author of* Moby Dick *(1851), source of the selection below, was neglected in his own century but is now considered one of America's great novelists:* **b. Vilhelm Moberg,** *contemporary Swedish novelist, writing in* The Emigrants, *describes the crowded living quarters in a sailing vessel, ca. 1850;* **c. Henry David Thoreau** *is known especially for* Walden *(1854), from which the selection below is taken, for his extensive journals, and for his stands as a social rebel;* **d. Charles Darwin** *revolutionized nineteenth-century thought with his discussions of evolution in* The Origin of Species *(1859); the selection is from an earlier work, popularly known as* The Voyage of the Beagle; **e. Katherine Mansfield,** *English novelist and short story writer, was influential in literary movements of the 1920's; the selection is from a short story, "Feuille d'Album,";* **f. Vincent Starrett's** *poem, from* Flame and Dust *(1924), is said to be a sketch of Anthony Comstock, who made himself famous by getting honest books banned in Boston;* **g. Stewart Holbrook** *looks down on a Pennsylvania steel town.; the selection is from his* Iron Brew *(1939).*

CROSSING the deck, let us now have a good long look at the Right Whale's head.

As in general shape the noble Sperm Whale's head may be compared to a Roman war-chariot (especially in front, where it is so broadly rounded); so, at a broad view, the Right Whale's head bears a rather inelegant resemblance to a gigantic galliot-toed shoe. Two hundred years ago an old Dutch voyager likened its shape to that of a shoemaker's last. And in this same last or shoe, that old woman of the nursery tale, with the swarming brood, might very comfortably be lodged, she and all her progeny.

progeny

But as you come nearer to this great head it begins to assume different aspects, according to your point of view. If you stand on its summit and look at these two *f*-shaped spout-holes, you would take the whole head for an enormous bass-viol, and these spiracles, the apertures in its sounding-board. Then, again, if you fix your eye upon this strange, crested, comb-like incrustation of the top of the mass—this green, barnacled thing, which the Greenlanders call the "crown," and the Southern fishers the "bonnet" of the Right Whale; fixing your eyes solely on this, you would take the head for the trunk of some huge oak, with a bird's nest in its crotch. At any rate, when you watch those live crabs that nestle here on this bonnet, such an idea will be almost sure to occur to you; unless, indeed, your fancy has been fixed by the technical term "crown" also bestowed upon it; in which case you will take great interest in thinking how this mighty monster is actually a diademed king of the sea, whose green crown has been put together for him in this marvelous manner. But if this whale be a king, he is a very sulky looking fellow to grace a diadem. Look at that hanging lower lip! what a huge sulk and pout is there! a sulk and pout, by carpenter's measurement, about twenty feet long and five feet deep; a sulk and pout that will yield you some 500 gallons of oil and more.

apertures

diadem

IN the hold enormous pieces of canvas had been hung to separate the space into three compartments: one for married couples and children, one for unmarried men, and one for unmarried women. The family bunks were toward the stern, partitioned off by bulkheads of rough boards nailed together. The small cells looked like cattle pens or horses' stalls. Beds were made on the deck of the hold with mattresses and loose straw. Unmarried passengers slept in bunks, strung longships between the stanchions. There were one-man and two-man bunks, "upper and lower berths."

stanchions

Dust rose from unaired mattresses, blankets, and skins as the emigrants spread their bedding and made up their bunks in the hold of the *Charlotta*—berths for seventy-eight people. Each passenger kept his belongings at the foot of his bunk. The overhead was low, and the air thick and choking. The three small compartments with canvas bulkheads seemed even smaller than they were, with this cargo of knapsacks, food baskets, bedding, and bundles. Here and there stood crude little tables or food boards, where people could sit and eat. These also were crowded with baskets and tubs, which must be put somewhere. At last there was hardly a spot left for the people to step on.

Only through the main hatch did light filter into the hold. After dark a few weak, smoking, kerosene lanterns were lit and hung along the sides of the ship.

c.   Henry David Thoreau

FOR sounds in winter nights, and often in winter days, I heard the forlorn but melodious note of a hooting owl indefinitely far; such a sound as the frozen earth would yield if struck with a suitable plectrum, the very *lingua vernacula* of Walden Wood, and quite familiar to me at last, though I never saw the bird while it was making it. I seldom opened my door in a winter evening without hearing it. *Hoo hoo hoo, hoorer hoo,* sounded sonorously, and the first three syllables accented somewhat like *how der do;* or sometimes *hoo hoo* only. One night in the beginning of the winter, before the pond froze over, about nine o'clock, I was startled by the loud honking of a goose, and, stepping to the door, heard the sound of their wings like a tempest in the woods as they flew low over my house. They passed over the pond toward Fair Haven, seemingly deterred from settling by my light, their commodore honking all the while with a regular beat. Suddenly an unmistakable cat owl from very near me, with the most harsh and tremendous voice I ever heard from any inhabitant of the woods, responded at regular intervals to the goose, as if determined to expose and disgrace this intruder from Hudson's Bay by exhib-

plectrum

iting a greater compass and volume of voice in a native, and *boo-hoo*
him out of Concord horizon. What do you mean by alarming the
citadel at this time of night consecrated to me? Do you think I am
ever caught napping at such an hour, and that I have not got lungs
and a larynx as well as yourself? *Boo-hoo, boo-hoo, boo-hoo!* It was one
of the most thrilling discords I ever heard. And yet, if you had a dis-
criminating ear, there were in it the elements of a concord such as   concord
these plains never saw nor heard.

d.   Charles Darwin

WHILE going one day on shore near Wollaston Island, we
pulled alongside a canoe with six Fuegians. These were the most abject and miserable creatures I anywhere beheld. On the east coast the
natives, as we have seen, have guanaco cloaks, and on the west, they
possess seal-skins. Amongst these central tribes the men generally
have an otter-skin, or some small scrap about as large as a pocket-
handkerchief, which is barely sufficient to cover their backs as low
down as their loins. It is laced across the breast by strings, and according as the wind blows, it is shifted from side to side. But these
Fuegians in the canoe were quite naked, and even one full-grown
woman was absolutely so. It was raining heavily, and the fresh water, together with the spray, trickled down her body. In another har-
bour not far distant, a woman, who was suckling a recently born
child, came one day alongside the vessel, and remained there out of
mere curiosity, whilst the sleet fell and thawed on her naked bosom,
and on the skin of her naked baby! These poor wretches were
stunted in their growth, their hideous faces bedaubed with white
paint, their skins filthy and greasy, their hair entangled, their voices
discordant, and their gestures violent. Viewing such men, one can
hardly make oneself believe that they are fellow-creatures, and inhabitants of the same world. It is a common subject of conjecture   *conjecture*
what pleasure in life some of the lower animals can enjoy: how much
more reasonably the same question may be asked with respect to
these barbarians! At night, five or six human beings, naked and
scarcely protected from the wind and rain of this tempestuous climate, sleep on the wet ground coiled up like animals. Whenever it is
low water, winter or summer, night or day, they must rise to pick
shell-fish from the rocks; and the women either dive to collect sea-
eggs, or sit patiently in their canoes, and with a baited hair-line
without any hook, jerk out little fish. If a seal is killed, or the floating

carcass of a putrid whale discovered, it is a feast; and such miserable food is assisted by a few tasteless berries and fungi.

e.   Katherine Mansfield

HE really was an impossible person. Too shy altogether. With absolutely nothing to say for himself. And such a weight. Once he was in your studio he never knew when to go, but would sit on and on until you nearly screamed, and burned to throw something enormous after him when he did finally blush his way out—something like the tortoise stove. The strange thing was that at first sight he looked most interesting. Everybody agreed about that. You would drift into the café one evening and there you would see, sitting in a corner, with a glass of coffee in front of him, a thin, dark boy, wearing a blue jersey with a little grey flannel jacket buttoned over it. And somehow that blue jersey and the grey jacket with the sleeves that were too short gave him the air of a boy that has made up his mind to run away to sea. Who has run away, in fact, and will get up in a moment and sling a knotted handkerchief containing his night-shirt and his mother's picture on the end of a stick, and walk out into the night and be drowned. . . . Stumble over the wharf edge on his way to the ship, even. . . . He had black close-cropped hair, grey eyes with long lashes, white cheeks and a mouth pouting as though he were determined not to cry. . . . How could one resist him? Oh, one's heart was wrung at sight. And, as if that were not enough, there was his trick of blushing. . . . Whenever the waiter came near him he turned crimson—he might have been just out of prison and the waiter in the know. . . .

f.   Vincent Starrett

Kinsella was obscenely bald,
   And militantly pure.
Impedimenta, people called
   His mental furniture.
But no opprobrium could taint
   That splendid rectitude—
He would have looked no more than quaint
   Deploying in the nude.

IT was dusk, and we stood looking down into a valley that often knew the night but never day. Smoke poured from a few of the scores of stacks below us, and when the wind rose a bit a mild warm shower of cinders fell where we stood. They were light cinders, falling silently like so much tarnished snow.

One was conscious of more smoke than could be seen coming from the stacks. I actually felt that smoke was everywhere in the valley, and on the hills, too—an all-prevailing smoke, not black, not white, simply a haze that clouded everything from a fly to a building and left nothing in true perspective.

There it was below us, Aliquippa in western Pennsylvania, at work under a smoky moon.

Aliquippa is a mighty enough steel town in a region that knows steel and little else. I looked down at it through the enveloping haze and knew that the place held secrets that neither the sun nor the moon ever discovered. Even its vast noises seemed muted, here on the hill. Only a dull rumbling, rising and falling on the breeze, remained of the accumulated sound of ten thousand men working and sweating in a madhouse that thundered until it shook the walls around them.

But the eye told better of doings in the valley. Now the haze was streaked with bursts of flame, with billows of smoke, and again with small volcanoes of orange and yellow sparks. I thought of Aliquippa as an old man sitting there in the gloom of the valley, sullenly smoking his pipe in the evening: a moody old man, given to expressing visibly his fits of silent temper. When he thought of something long past that made him seethe, he puffed furiously, and the sparks came.

Suddenly, as if the smoke and sparks and streaks of fire had been but a mere kindling of it, the whole valley blazed with a lurid *lurid* glow—not lightning, not heavy artillery, nor yet a flame thrower, but all three together. One saw the stacks plainly now, stark black silhouettes against a background of red and yellow. . . . The old man and his pipe had gone wholly mad.

That, said my friend, is a Bessemer in blow.

We went down into the murky lowland and into the steel plant, a place that took in more acres within its high fence than do most farms. Cinders were thicker here, and heavier. The noise was such as to discourage talk. Men spoke with their fingers, their hands, their arms.

On and on we walked, past the glittering coke ovens that winked with eight hundred eyes, past the furnaces muttering over their nightly fare of Mesabi ore, and on to the hulking Bessemer shed. Its outside was lost in gloom. Inside was a scene to stop the late Dante Alighieri dead in his tracks.

Here were three tall Bessemer converters in a row. How a Bessemer looks to a veteran steelworker's eye, I don't know. To a layman it looks like the egg of a roc, that fabulous bird which was said to have borne off the biggest elephant in its flight. A roc's egg with one end cut off and gaping. It is a container of brick and riveted steel, twice as tall as the tallest man and supporting near its middle on axles. It is set high up on a groundwork of brick. Into this caldron goes molten ore, fifty thousand pounds at a time. Through the iron is blown cold air—oxygen forced through the hot metal with the power of a giant's breath. Out of the egg, in good time, comes steel. It is little short of pure magic.

fabulous

One of the converters was in blow as we entered the shed. Tilted almost but not quite straight up, the mouth of it belched flame like a cannon built for the gods. It was a terrifying sight, and hypnotic. I didn't want to look elsewhere, to turn my eyes from that leaping flame which towered thirty, perhaps forty, feet above the converter.

The roar was literally deafening; and little wonder, for here was a cyclone attacking a furnace in a brief but titanic struggle, a meeting in battle of carbon and oxygen, cleverly arranged by the sweating gnomes whose red faces appeared white in the Bessemer's glow. Both carbon and oxygen would lose, each consuming the other, and men would be the winners by twenty-five tons of bright new steel.

literally

The roaring continued. The red fire changed to violet, indescribably beautiful, then to orange, to yellow, and finally to white, when it soon faded. "Drop," the boys call it. I saw the great vessel rock uneasily on its rack, moved with unseen levers by an unseen workman. A locomotive pushed a car close under. On the car was a big ladle. The hellish brew was done.

Slowly the converter tilted over, and from its maw came a flow of seething liquid metal—Bessemer steel. A Niagara of fire spilled out, pouring into the waiting ladle, and sixty feet away the heat was too much for comfort. A cascade of sparks rolled out and over, a sort of spray for this cataract, and it seemed everything in the shed danced with light.

Steel was being born in a light so blinding that one must wear dark glasses to look on it long. It was a dreadful birth. The pygmy men who ran about on the floor seemed entirely too puny to cope with such a thing. One preferred subconsciously to trust in the tall shadows on the walls, for the weird towering shapes looked more in character for this business.

In perhaps five minutes the ladle was filled with the running fire. The bell on the locomotive rang. The ladle was pulled away, out into the darkness of the yard, and a sudden deep gloom settled down in the Bessemer shed. The devil's pouring was over.

It is the most gorgeous, the most startling show that any industry can muster, a spectacle to make old Vulcan's heart beat faster, enough to awe a mortal. No camera has ever caught a Bessmer's full grim majesty, and no poet has yet sung its splendor.

Reading and Interpreting

1. Description provides an opportunity to bring in concrete detail. Do the amount and the sharpness of this detail have much to do with your reaction to the writing?

2. Most of the subjects here described you have never seen and will never have a chance to see. A Bessemer furnace is now as out of date as the head of a right whale lying on a whaler's deck. Anthony Comstocks and shy boys like the Mansfield youth are not so common as they used to be. The Tierra del Fuegians do not now live as Darwin saw them. Perhaps you disliked all these pieces. If you did, you might remind yourself that people who have seen a particular football game are more likely to read an account of it than are those who did not. What does such evidence signify about you and the kind of descriptions that would interest you? In this, do you seem to be like almost everybody else or different?

3. Which of these pieces was easiest to read? Which hardest to read? Why? Can you draw any conclusions from your answers about your own reading and writing?

Writing Techniques

1. Assume that Melville's piece about the right whale is a good example of classical description, a passage that is purely description and little else. Read it carefully, noticing the progression. From it can you work out the basic pattern for extended description? How does it start? How does it develop? How does it end?

2. One piece differs from all the others in one basic descriptive device. Which one is it? What effect does this restricted use of one approach have on the writing and its effect?

3. Contrast the pieces by Moberg and Mansfield. The tone is different, of course; tone is discussed in Section VI. The pieces differ also in descriptive pattern; Moberg gives you a scene, Mansfield a single individual. What differences in technique do these two kinds of descriptions seem to need?

4. A similar contrast can be drawn between the journal entry of

Darwin and the poem by Starrett. These pieces are alike, however, in that in each the author tries to draw some kind of moral, some comment on man and society. Does description seem to be well suited to such purposes? How do these use examples to make their point?

5. The Holbrook excerpt can be thought of as typical of a rather long description. What problems in technique does it raise that do not appear so prominently in most of the shorter pieces?

Word Study

1. From the context write a brief definition of the words in the margins (*progeny, apertures, diadem, stanchions, plectrum, concord, conjecture, lurid, fabulous, literally*). Then look them up in the dictionary and make any necessary revisions in your definitions.

2. Metaphorical writing is especially useful in description, as selection **a,** by Melville, demonstrates. Point out at least three uses of metaphor in the second and third paragraphs of the selection.

3. Selection **f,** Starrett's poem, depends heavily on the meanings of the words, the associations they suggest as well as their denotations. Look up especially *impedimenta, opprobrium, rectitude,* and *deploying*. How do the relationships of the usual connotations of *militantly, impedimenta,* and *deploying* affect the meaning of the poem?

Suggestions for Writing

1. Recall your conclusions about the Melville piece in question 1 of Writing Techniques above. Then try to write a classic description of a place, person, or object you know.

2. Select a scene you know well and write a brief description of it, using only details you can see. Then, recalling the Thoreau piece, write a description of the same scene, insofar as you can, using only what can be heard. (Even if the place is completely noiseless, that is worth describing.) Attempt the same description using only smell. Then try to put the three together into one balanced picture. Notice whether the description improves as you use more than one sense.

LE PIRATE
Richard Atcheson

9

Richard Atcheson, *who writes also under the name Charles Tressilian, has had a diversity of editorial and reportorial experience with* Playboy, Holiday, Show, Chicago Daily News, *and other periodicals.*

He is a frequent contributor to Saturday Review, Cosmopolitan, Vista, *etc., and has published several books, including* What the Hell Are We Trying to Prove, Martha? *and* The Bearded Lady. *This article appeared in the* New York Times.

THERE is a crazy restaurant in the south of France where you are expected to eat well and copiously, to drink to excess, to listen to music and perhaps to spin to it — and also to break up the joint before you leave. The name of the place is Le Pirate. It sits on an otherwise empty stretch of rocky beach at Cap Martin and commands an unobstructed view across a bay to the lights of Menton. Relatively few people can avail themselves of the prospect, however, because Le Pirate, in addition to being wild, is wildly expensive.

The night I was there I was a guest in a party of 10 and so I never did discover what our bill was. Cost was never mentioned during the evening, and no prices are displayed, but I learned later that the *addition* at Le Pirate depends to a great extent on how much you break. Two American millionaires who departed one night without settling up must have done considerable damage because next morning they sent a messenger around with a leather pouch containing 2,000 gold pieces said to be worth about $1,000 altogether. For ordinary citizens, I am told, the equivalent of $50 a person would be on the lower end of the scale.

Frenchmen who know Le Pirate say it is very "American," a reference perhaps to the fact that what is of paramount importance is not the food but the total experience. The secret of the restaurant's success, put simply, is excess — loud, raw, tasteless, outrageous waste and profligacy. And for that one must pay plenty.

My introduction to the place came when a French friend of mine called me up in Monte Carlo. "Tonight," he said, "we make a big party at Le Pirate. Americans like it very much. Frank Sinatra likes it very much. We shall break up the place. You come and you will see."

We drove along the coast to a rocky beach and parked in front of a high barricade with a gate in it. Some roughneck was leaning against the gate, picking his teeth with a knife. He could have been just another Côte d'Azur hippie, for he was stripped to the waist, had a scarf tied around his head and wore one gold earring, but in fact he was Le Pirate's only road sign, a sort of Elsa Maxwell version of a proper pirate.

My companions and I passed through the barricade and found ourselves in an open-air court with a few tables and chairs scattered around, and big rocky outcrops with open fires blazing away furiously in them. There were torches set on poles to provide flickering illumination as the twilight deepened.

Is there a theme sentence? What kind of introduction?

Narrative with brief bits of description.

Several bare-chested "pirates" were rushing around with trays of drinks, and popping flat round loaves of bread into and out of the fires. There was much yelling, swaggering, wrestling and showing off of high spirits. I took a martini from a nearby pirate and tried to get into this thing.

The people I was with were standing around making witty conversation, but I noticed that their eyes were rolling like crazy trying to take everything in, and when Le Pirate himself showed up—a tall, sallow, Satanic-looking guy with jangling gold coin necklaces and a toothy smile—our party gazed at him with undisguised amazement. His name is really Robert Viale, and he is as much entertainer as restaurateur; when he's doing his number (which is apparently all the time) he is given to grand and sweeping gestures, grandiloquent overstatement ("Eeeuuu are all my darrling fraahnds") and a sort of balletic direction of his staff. While he talks to you, hands out his business card and caresses the gold coins around his neck, he is simultaneously twitching, ogling and going "pssst" at his youthful employes, who are alert to his merest shrug, leaping six feet through the air to light the cigarettes of women who've only just started to fumble with their packs, bounding back to produce chairs for portly gentlemen who've only just begun to glance around for one. Le Pirate and his crew do nothing without flourish; you begin to realize that you are not just at a restaurant for dinner but are an integral part of a carefully choreographed event.

Description of a person.

The drinks keep coming (this is *not* French) and the sunset is, perhaps therefore all the more remarkable. The yelping youths and Le Pirate himself begin to jolly and cajole you toward the door of the restaurant proper, then down a set of stairs into a low-ceilinged, wood-paneled room where colored-glass balls hang in fishnets from the pillars, the tables are covered with red-and-white checkered cloths and candles sputter everywhere. On one wall is a signed photograph of Frank Sinatra; lesser celebrities flank him.

Description of a place.

As you sit down, more drinks are produced; then pirates rush forward with bowls and crocks and soon a steaming pile of *moules marinière* is before you, and other pirates are pouring white wine. Though you attempt to converse with your neighbors, there is such an urgency about these young men serving you and such an intrusive concern on the part of Le Pirate, who is swaggering from table to table, that it's hard to maintain a line of thought. Particularly when the mussels taste so good, and when Le Pirate suddenly claps his hands imperiously and shrieks for gypsies. Immediately the room is full of beautiful girls in bare-midriff dresses with polka-dot flounces, all going "yi-yi-yi" and "yip-yip-yip" and whirling and clapping their hands and stomping furiously on the floor right by your chair. Guitars are whanging, people are dancing and screaming,

What would you call this?

and you are so busy looking that you can hardly find your mouth with your fork.

The pace never slackens. On comes the soup, on comes the steak and the lobster (all very non-French this, but fine eats), and you scarcely notice because of the high jinks, not to mention the wine—bottle after bottle. And it's amazing how witty you've become after so much wine; whenever you can make yourself heard above the din your flushed companions positively roar with laughter at everything they think you're saying.

◄A good topic sentence? Transition?

Le Pirate is keeping up a steady monologue in French; it's all about his life, about love and joy and unutterable sadness, and sometimes he's speaking and at other times singing. Soon the two become interchangeable, and at a certain point, he embarks on this long, melancholy song about how he's growing older and how his beloved son (there stands the lout, tall and blond and blushing a bit, accompanying his father on the guitar) wants to go his own way, to leave him (sob). But the song concludes that this is Right, this is Good, this is Joy. So out come the gypsies, screaming and stamping even louder; it's dessert time, champagne time, and while you're breaking a meringue with your spoon, the bubbly is surging forth from 10 bottles at a time, and Le Pirate is sampling each and the ones he doesn't like, he hurls full force into the fire.

So the corks are popping, the bottles are smashing, and you're still dining in a frenzy of drunken excitement when suddenly you find serpentine streamers by your plate and then the air is full of uncoiling colored paper and everybody is pelting everybody else. Now the music is augmented by horns and trumpets. There is screaming in the background and you turn to see that a braying donkey, garlanded with flowers, has been introduced into your midst; he is plodding up to your table and lowering his great gray muzzle into your plate; he is eating up your meringue and grazing your chin with his soft ears. At this point a lot of people are starting to fling their champagne glasses at the fireplace, so of course you do, too.

Sight and sound plus narrative details.

There is no shortage of champagne glasses—there are always more champagne glasses—and you keep drinking and throwing and find you have stepped directly Through The Looking Glass. Because the plates now start to go SMASH! CRASH! Shards of glass and crockery are flying around the room. People seize the vases, flowers and all: ZOOM BOOM! The salts and the peppers, the tablecloths, the silverware are all in the air. Madness! Your companions are lifting up the table itself; tables rise on shoulders all over the room. There's a big parade of tables and drunks and gypsies and horn players out of the room, into the courtyard. The big fires in the stone outcrops are still burning, and the tables are flung into the flames, with everybody cheering and hollering and applauding. And as the heat rushes forward to your cheeks in the night air, as the warmth flares around you, people look at one another with wild eyes and wicked, heedless grins, and there is laughter from some deep-down, dangerous, untapped place.

And is the evening over now, in the light of these hungry flames? Hardly, because the son of Le Pirate happens to have a discotheque just across the road, and we can all skip and dance over there by the light of the moon, the moon, and rush in and dance off our energies in a final paroxysm of sweat, laughter, drinks and fragmented conversation.

How is the conclusion handled?

The trouble for members of the bourgeoisie like me is that it's hard for us to take stuff like this in our stride. The rich don't have any problems with things like breaking up a joint; that's one of the ways in which they are different from us. They break something, they buy something else. The bourgeoisie survive Le Pirate, though, but their hearts may go boom-boom the whole night afterward.

Only the other Sunday there was a mention, in a story I read about Americans who like to live on the Riviera, of some "affluent American" who particularly prizes his Côte d'Azur villa because Le Pirate, his favorite restaurant, is only 20 minutes away. Never in a million years could I describe Le Pirate as my favorite—and I guess that marks one obvious difference between the rich (him) and the bourgeois (me). For all that I wouldn't have missed it for anything.

Reading and Interpreting

1. Many people assume that descriptions are dull. Is this piece dull? If not, how does it differ from descriptions that you have found dull or have heard others condemn as dull?

2. Atcheson says that Frenchmen considered Le Pirate very "American." He makes a guess at why they thought it American. Would you make the same guess, or a different one? Does the characterization do Americans and America injustice? If the Frenchmen are right, what would this identification reveal about the nature of the United States and its people?

3. State the main idea of the piece in one sentence. Your answer will need to take account of the first and the last paragraphs, but it will also need to consider if the author is trying mainly to amuse you or to make an important comment or revelation. Is Atcheson trying to (1) recount an experience, (2) describe an unusual place, (3) make a deeply philosophic observation about human nature, or (4) do something else—or all four in varying degrees?

Writing Techniques

1. What gives this piece its appeal? Is it the material itself? Atcheson as a professional newsman recognizes that one of the ingredients of news is the bizarre. Is the key to be sought in Atcheson's way of writing? It is familiar, even colloquial, some would say slangy. Would you? Or does Atcheson's charm grow from something else?

2. The forms of discourse are mixed here. Go through the article, marking those sections that are mainly narrative, those mainly descriptive, those in which narrative and description are almost indistinguishably blended, those that are something else. What would you conclude about the role of description in this piece?

3. How is the piece put together? What details are given in the introductory paragraph? Which of these appear later in developed form? What does this arrangement of details do for the article? Does Atcheson use any other means of giving order to his writing?

4. Atcheson is aware that the restaurant is as "phony," to use a term he doubtless would have employed, as a vaudeville show or a comedy skit on television. How does he reveal this fact without saying so bluntly?

Word Study

Examine the paragraph that describes Le Pirate himself, beginning, "The people I was with." This paragraph is description, but many terms in it imply action: *caresses the gold coins; twitching, ogling, and going psssst; leaping six feet through the air.* Record some more. Some rather rare words are used to good effect, for example, *balletic* and *choreographed.* Be sure you know what they mean, and then find four more words that tell a great deal because of the way Atcheson has used them. Atcheson once tries to suggest Le Pirate's manner of speaking. What is the effect of this?

Suggestions for Writing

You probably have not smashed champagne glasses in an establishment so exotic as *Le Pirate,* but you have been to places that had their own character—a pizza parlor patronized by students, for example. Describe such a place, making use of Atcheson's techniques insofar as they will work, making us see the place, hear it, and maybe even smell it, in part by showing what people do there and are expected to do. That is, try making your theme a report, one that is descriptive in purpose but uses narrative in the sense that the account becomes in part a detailing of your experience.

GOODBYE, ASHEVILLE
Perry Deane Young

10

Like a number of practitioners in what we might call the American School of Factual Writing, **Perry Deane Young** *started by reporting for local newspapers, in his case, in North Carolina. He graduated into the big time with the UPI and the* New York Journal, *and eventually into free-lance writing, doing articles for magazines. He also wrote,* Two of the Missing: A Reminiscence of Some Friends in the War. *The following piece is from* Harper's.

MY return to the small city of Asheville, North Carolina, where I was born and lived until I was eighteen years old, was a shattering experience. I can only compare it to what a German refugee might feel going back in 1974 to a town he left in the 1930s. It looked as if my hometown had been destroyed in some terrible miscalculation of the war and subsequently rebuilt in the same gaudy new glass, concrete, and steel molds found in practically every other town and city in America. Every landmark of my childhood that had survived was in a new setting so foreign to me that all earlier meaning was lost. That place so vital to my memories no longer exists.

And mine was a magical place. Others may talk of their hometowns as narrow, inhibiting places, but Asheville was my first connection to a better life than I was born to—a life of music and literature, of interesting people, exotic places.

The town is situated on a rolling plateau, at the confluence of the French Broad and the Swannanoa Rivers, in between the high Blue Ridge Mountains to the east and the Great Smoky Mountains to the west. The steep, dark mountains, with their coves and gorges, offered an omnipresent backdrop of mystery; frequent mists lent romance to everyday scenes; and at dusk and dawn there was no telling where the mountains began and ended or how many creatures might be wandering in the densely wooded wilderness preserves. ◄Important breaks mark the beginning and the end of this paragraph.

For most of its first hundred years, Asheville was an isolated village of a few hundred people living in low wooden houses clustered around the Buncombe County Courthouse. (Our Congressman gave the language the word *buncombe*—bunkum—after a colleague asked him why he had talked so long when he had nothing to say. "I was speaking to Buncombe," he replied.) The courthouse was the first reason for the village, but the reason for Asheville's growth from a population of less than 3,000 in the 1870s to a small city of more than 50,000 in the 1920s was the setting itself.

After the Civil War, several German physicians had called Asheville's climate the best for the cure of tuberculosis, so when the Swannanoa Tunnel opened the town to rail traffic in 1879, thousands of patients, lured by brochures, came to live in sumptuous English manor houses and French chateaux built by the doctors. By the late 1800s Asheville began to attract the healthy and rich. Among them was young George Vanderbilt, who had boasted that he would one day build the most magnificent estate in America. He could have bought any land he wanted, but after taking in the view from the old Battery Park Hotel in Asheville, he promptly bought more than his eyes could see—more than 120,000 acres, beyond and including Mount Pisgah, the highest mountain visible from town.

Does Young use active or passive sentence structures?

Vanderbilt's Biltmore (inspired by the Château de Blois) was designed by the fashionable architect Richard Morris Hunt; its grounds were laid out by Frederick Law Olmstead. Still the largest private house in America, Biltmore is now open to the public—turn right at the McDonald's by the railroad tracks, pay your $4.50, and drive on in. Another rich man built a replica of Gunston Hall, another built a medieval fortress (complete with battered towers), and still others built half-timbered Tudor mansions and severe German castles.

Meanwhile, other, more economy-minded visitors built spacious mountain lodges with big bay windows and wide porches where guests could sit and rock and gaze at the mountains. In my childhood, several of the main streets in Asheville were still lined with these lovely old houses in colorful, landscape gardens.

By the 1920s, Asheville was a real boomtown. The tunnel under Beaucatcher Mountain was built then, and a city hall and a new courthouse—enormous, ugly buildings—were erected for a projected metropolis of 250,000.

The time shifts. Does anything else shift with it?

When the crash came, Asheville, was one of the hardest-hit towns in the country. My father and hundreds of others were left with boxes full of worthless deeds. The mayor, unable to face the indebtedness of the city, killed himself. The population now is still less than 60,000 despite the expansion of the city limits. Until about 1959, when I left Asheville, there was virtually no major construction. The old and historic buildings had been preserved more because of the owners' timidity about investing in change than out of appreciation of the past.

Black Thursday, 1929, has additional significance to anyone born in Asheville. Six days before the day the stock market crashed,

Charles Scribner's Sons published Thomas Wolfe's first novel, *Look Homeward, Angel.*

The picturesque Altamont of Wolfe's book was Asheville, his hometown. He left a portrait of Asheville almost photographic in detail which, over the years, soulful Wolfe buffs have used to trace the author's footsteps through the town's streets. Wolfe's characterizations resulted in rave reviews in the local newspaper, but also in lawsuits and family bitterness. His response was to stay away, writing voluminous letters to his mother about how he missed Asheville, and voluminous novels, such as *You Can't Go Home Again,* about the town and his life in exile.

Scott and Zelda Fitzgerald started visiting Asheville at about the same time. When Fitzgerald found that the local library had never stocked Wolfe's books, he bought them himself and put them on the shelves. Fitzgerald loved the town, and mentions it in most of his novels. Zelda put her trust in a doctor in Asheville who felt that faith in Jesus Christ, exercise, and long hikes cured mental illness. The hospital where she stayed was close to our house; when I was eight, Zelda died in a fire there.

My family lived in a big old drafty house on a hilltop at the north edge of town. We raised acres of broccoli, eggplant, cauliflower, spinach, beans, mustard greens, turnips, peppers, and corn. My old man eventually bought a truck, but he never used a tractor or any other mechanized equipment on the farm; there are photographs of me riding on one of his mule-drawn wagons. I was his thirteenth child, and he would laugh and call me "quits" when he took me along to deliver vegetables or play checkers and get his hair cut at a place on Lexington Avenue, an open market street as enchanting as the rue Mouffetard in Paris.

◄Is this a theme sentence? If so, of what?

Suppers in our house included numerous kinsmen, field hands, and a wonderful assortment of hermits who would stop by our place on their way to sell the bundles of ginseng root and balsam extract they had collected in the mountains. My mother willingly fixed any sort of game my father and his hunting friends brought in—squirrels, rabbits, quail, pheasant, deer, bear, coon, possum; once we even had mud turtles.

Young uses concrete detail.

My mother had finished one year of college, but she still fervently believed in the near-animistic mysteries told and retold by the mountain people. An old conjurewoman read her life in a cup of herb tea when she was fifteen, and even today she refuses to divulge the part relating to me, because all the rest has come to pass.

Hollywood presents *The Last Picture Show* and *American Graffiti* as stories of an American childhood. They seem shallow and drab compared to the wonder and excitement I knew as a boy in Asheville. The one movie that might have been made about an Asheville childhood could not be filmed there. I have heard that the would-be producers felt the town simply did not look like the one in *Look Homeward, Angel.*

I knew many things had changed: our farm was condemned in the mid-1950s because the city kept dumping raw sewage in the irrigation water; a school bus garage and parking lot now covered the area where our house and greenhouses had been; the Appalachian Development Highway plowed over the cliff and pasture; the same road took the lovely hill of dogwood trees around the cottage where O. Henry once lived; an older expressway downtown had lopped off most of the Lexington Avenue market and taken the house where Wolfe was born; a housing development was creeping across the bluff where Sidney Lanier had camped out.

But, there were still the mountains. Or, so I thought.

Why does he make a paragraph of ten words?

It was when I heard that the city council had voted to cut Beaucatcher Mountain in two in order to widen the narrow tunnel underneath that I decided I had to go home again. The protagonist of *Look Homeward, Angel,* like every other Asheville boy, takes his girlfriend on a picnic on Beaucatcher. It was the eastern wall of the town, a gentle backdrop that changed with the seasons.

About ten years ago, with the careless planning that has always characterized Asheville, two four-lane roads had been built right up to either end of the tunnel. It was inevitable that someday something would have to be done about the bottleneck that had been created. And so, since widening the tunnel would be too expensive, the issue was decided solely on the question of economy. When I questioned people about the open cut, everybody said they would rather see the mountain instead of a hole. But, they said, "What can you do? Just try driving that road during rush hour."

The man actually charged with the job of tearing down the mountain was Frank Hutchison, regional engineer for the North Carolina Department of Transportation. "After a few years, I don't think people will even notice," he said. "The side of that mountain is going to be plastered with houses anyway." (Indeed, several of the hills I remembered as green already resemble those around Los Angeles.) Speaking of a similar situation when a local television station built a tower on top of Mount Pisgah, he recalled, "There was a lot of hullabaloo raised then about 'the beauty of the mountains,' but now you don't ever hear anything about it."

Critics talk about symbols. Is the mountain a symbol?

With a last glimpse toward the mountain, I looked back on the town itself. Four banks had erected enormous new buildings, completely changing the character of the town's main squares. (When I commented on the precious little amount of green space left in the town, one city official said, "Look at downtown Charlotte. There's no green space there at all.")

The merchants' escape from downtown—whole blocks of stores have been abandoned—to suburban shopping centers happened in Asheville a decade later than in most small towns. But, it followed a similar pattern. Haphazard planning had not provided for an increase in parking places. Property owners were unwilling to compromise, so no places were made available for parking garages until after the land could be sold for nothing else.

I visited the old Battery Park Hotel, which I remembered as bustling and elegant, famous for its many notable guests and their parties. A new owner had tried to renovate the hotel, but financial difficulties had forced him to abandon the project. The wide terraces were now littered with debris; many windows were broken, their shades flapping out; a rusted padlock held two sagging screen doors closed across the front entrance.

Why should not the piece stop here?

The major source of what I call destruction, and what Asheville officials call progress, is Urban Renewal funds, which were poured into the city in the mid-1960s. The Civic Urban Renewal Project has demolished more than 150 structures in a seventy-six-acre "renewal area." Some very usable structures were destroyed, to be replaced mostly by the gaudiest of "modern" buildings—some of flimsy glass and steel, others of heavy bunker style.

If this is description, what does it describe?

The Urban Renewal people were not satisfied with their demolition of the old David Millard Junior High School—a sturdy, adequate structure; they also leveled the hill under it. So far, the lot has had no takers; every way you look there are more like it, some "cleared for development" fifteen years ago.

Will King of the Asheville Housing Authority told me everybody was "very pleased" with this demolition area. "It's a beginning point to salvage the downtown area."

"In other words, you had to destroy it in order to save it?"

"Yes," he said.

Not by coincidence, the Asheville Chamber of Commerce has discovered the city's major problem, which is directly related to the destruction of these familiar landmarks. Two years in succession, the Chamber officials agreed that the major problem of Asheville had to do with the "quality of life." And so they voted to stage a "Quality '76" campaign for the national Bicentennial celebration.

Neither of the retired businessmen named as codirectors could tell me—or a group of volunteer firemen assembled to publicize the program—what they meant by the quality of life. Although they did recognize that it was a spiritual thing having to do with the appearance of the town, they were only concerned with planting grass and shrubs around factories and giving new coats of paint to old buildings. Listening to these men, I felt that they would never understand that the quality of life had to do with those huge sections of town

Is this what the article is about?

that had been leveled for development. What had been destroyed could never be put back.

There is no way now that anyone can ever experience what I knew so casually—strolling down pleasant, treelined streets where Thomas Wolfe, F. Scott Fitzgerald, O. Henry, and Sidney Lanier once walked. On the square in Asheville, there was once a pawnshop, and a cleaners where you could get hats blocked; there was an open-air fruit store and a pharmacy that stayed open late and delivered anywhere in town. All these were pushed aside for one enormous burnt-umber glass-and-steel bank building, and for a second bank that, when completed, will match the first. There is no way I can take any-one to the square and say: "This is my hometown." It's just not the same place.

Reading and Interpreting

1. What is this piece about? Is it a description of Young's home town? The account of how a home community became a thriving town-becoming-a-city? What are the implications of the title? As the text tells you, Thomas Wolfe wrote a novel subsequent to his experiences in Asheville that he entitled *You Can't Go Home Again.* In what ways might this serve as a title for Young's piece? Would the impact of the account be any different if the title were "The Case Against Progress?"

2. Thinking over this piece you must be aware that it is made of several rather distinct parts. Which did the most for you? Why? Could any one of them have been left out?

3. A topic sentence of sorts is as follows: "And mine was a magical place." What does Young do to make Asheville magical, if it was? Would this serve as a topic sentence for all of this piece, or only part of it? If only part, which part?

Writing Techniques

1. Is the bulk of the piece narrative? (You might check to find out.) Some parts are almost pure description, for example, the third paragraph. Are there any others? Would it be fair to say that, contrary to much writing where the description contributes to the narration, the narrative here serves a descriptive purpose? Even so, is the entire purpose either narrative or descriptive? Is it argument, persuasion against progress that ruins homes? Or would you say it is exposition, for example, an explaining of what the author means by the first paragraph?

2. There are several different sorts of narrative here. Does each contribute to what you might call a description in the sense that it is part of a report of what the town was like and what it has become? Try to characterize these different sorts of narrative and their impact.

3. What are some of the effects of Young's decision to write in the first person?

4. Young does more than describe the town physically; he describes an atmosphere, an attitude. Point out at least three passages that do more than describe the town physically.

Suggestions for Writing

1. You probably have strong feeling for the town or the neighborhood you grew up in, or even the school you attended. If you have had the experience of going back to such a place, you most likely found it changed. Can you write a "You Can't Go Home Again" piece, reporting your experience?

2. Any one of several parts of Young's account may suggest a similar one for you. Notice the passage beginning, "My family lived. . . ." You might write a similar sketch of how your family lived. Or note the passage beginning, "But there were still the mountains." You could write a sketch having the idea, "But there was (were) still. . . ."

3. Attacking progress used to be almost as bad as attacking motherhood or the flag. But now at least one state has announced its policy, "Come to visit us, but don't stay." Would such a principle make good sense for your community? Try describing a place you know and its probable future if growth and progress continue.

TOMORROW'S AUTOMATED BATTLEFIELD
Paul Dickson

11

A Washington-based free-lance writer, **Paul Dickson** *has long been a close student of armaments and their influence on man's future. He contributes to periodicals—this article comes from* The Progressive—*and for five years was Washington editor of* Electronics. *An introduction, relating the concept of the automated battlefield to the McNamara Line in Vietnam, is here omitted.*

OF all the applications of the electronic battlefield employed, none was more sophisticated, dramatic, or lethal than an operation called Project IGLOO WHITE which was set up to cut traffic on the Ho Chi Minh Trail in Laos. It ran at full tilt from 1969 until the end of 1972 at a cost of about a billion dollars a year. It worked this way: Periodically, sensors were strewn over the landscape from high-speed aircraft, with the most common combination a mix of ADSIDs (Air-Delivered Seismic Intrusion Detectors) and ACOUBUOYs (Acoustic Buoys). The ADSID is a seismic sensor contained in a long spear *seismic* which is flung from an airplane to embed in the ground so that only its antenna—disguised to look like a tropical plant—remains above ground. The ACOUBUOY is a radio-microphone which floats down on a small parachute to snag in the branches of trees, to transmit noises. In all, tens of thousands of ADSIDs and ACOUBUOYs were dropped, along with other sensors including such bizarre items as a sensor produced by Honeywell which was made to look like animal droppings, and another called XM-3 chemical detector or "people sniffer" which was developed to detect the ammonia in human body odors. The "sniffer" device, however, was easily foiled when those on the ground learned it could be thrown out of whack by hanging buckets of urine in the trees.

In Project IGLOO WHITE, these sensors were used to detect activity which, once detected, was picked up by patrolling aircraft. In turn the aircraft relayed the information to a large land-based computer center in Thailand. "Skilled target analysts" monitored the in- *monitored* formation and decided whether or not the movement detected was worth attacking. If an attack was decided upon, planes were sent in to strike in truly electronic fashion; not only did the computer provide the course and coordinates for flight, but the plane's ordnance was released automatically. While most of the IGLOO WHITE missions were conducted by F-4 Phantom jets, some employed other aircraft. One special craft that was used was the Night Hawk, a helicopter gunship outfitted with special devices enabling it to see in the dark.

The actual ordnance used during IGLOO WHITE was as varied as the sensors. Some were such big items as PAVE-PAT II, a 2,500-pound bomb filled with propane under pressure and capable of clearing hundreds of acres of jungle; some were smaller anti-personnel weapons like WAPPUM and DRAGONTOOTH, which are dropped from the air in huge numbers and arm themselves as they spin to the ground. These weapons are so distinctly anti-personnel in nature that Air Force Major Raymond D. Anderson, in the process of testifying to DRAGONTOOTH's effectiveness, said, "If a person steps on it, it could blow his foot off. If a truck rolls over it, it won't [even] blow the tire." Another of the horrifying anti-personnel weapons used with IGLOO WHITE and other electronic battlefield operations in Southeast Asia was the SUU-41, an airborne dispenser which was used to cover an area with hundreds of small GRAVEL mines. A single piece of GRAVEL looks like a small tea bag, but is quite effec-

tive at killing or maiming despite its innocent appearance. The list of
such weaponry is long and diverse enough to include such items as
"spider mines," which throw off long wire tentacles that explode   *tentacles*
when touched, and a small anti-personnel weapon that floats through
the air like a leaf.

The military regarded IGLOO WHITE as a success. In 1971, the
Air Force claimed that it had been able to find and destroy eighty per
cent of the traffic coming down the Ho Chi Minh Trail. The claim at
the end of that year was that 12,000 trucks and large numbers of
troops had been destroyed without putting an American soldier on
the ground.

The American departure from Vietnam did not end the mili-
tary's interest in the electronic battlefield. Rather, that interest has intensified. As IGLOO WHITE and other operations demonstrated, the
concept had proven itself. One of the military's major postwar goals
is to develop and expand the notion. In the matter of sensors alone,
there are many postwar efforts.

As the various services work to develop their own new generation of sensor packages, there are developments in other military
areas. In May 1972, the United States held a major display of the electronic battlefield at a base in West Germany for the benefit of the
other fourteen members of the North Atlantic Treaty Organization.
That display, code-named MYSTIC MISSION, was clearly intended to
induce the rest of NATO to adopt the system. Testifying in support
of the fiscal 1974 military R&D budget, Stephen J. Lukasik, Director
of the Advanced Research Projects Agency, said that the other nations were still making up their minds but that the United States was
going ahead with a program to adapt old components and create new   *components*
ones for the European environment. Whether or not the rest of
NATO adopts the program, the United States is now preparing a European model of the electronic battlefield ready for quick transport to
that area.

Sensor development is just a small slice of the vast electronic
battlefield effort. Among the other ongoing elements that now make
the electronic battlefield a far-ranging concept of offense as well as
defense, and no longer a sort of electronic Maginot Line, are these:

RPVs (Remotely Piloted Vehicles). The Army, Navy, and Air Force
are all working on various pilotless, remotely controlled aircraft. They
range from reusable surveillance fighters and bombers which could   *surveillance*
be built for a few million dollars each (much less than piloted aircraft) to models which would be expended as a ram against enemy
aircraft, or as a guided bomb, and estimated to cost less than $100,000
each to produce.

Laser weapons. All three armed services are spending heavily to develop new laser arms—expected to cost more than $300 million a year for the next five years. First given broad and successful application in the "smart" bombs which are able to home in on a target illuminated by a laser beam, lasers are now being developed for applications such as antiaircraft, antimissile, air-to-air combat, and target location. In May 1973, *Aviation Week and Space Technology* reported an evolving Army program in which small RPVs would be outfitted with small television cameras and a laser designator. "Scenes viewed by the camera would be relayed in real time over a data link to ground observers who could acquire targets from a television monitor, then illuminate them with [RPVs] laser for remotely launched laser-guided missiles."

IBCS (Integrated Battlefield Control System). A major Army program aimed at reducing manpower and increasing combat efficiency by applying automation to battle functions ranging from logistics to psychological tactics. Major elements of the IBCS now under development include the TACFIRE system in which hand-held digital devices (tied into a master computer) are used at the front line to direct firepower, and CS3 (for Combat Service Support System), a mobile computer that tends to the details of logistics and inventory supply in combat areas. This automated effort was described at one point by Army Brigadier General Wilson R. Reed as one ". . . which will electronically tie the sensors to the reaction means—the 'beep' to the 'boom' as it were—and leave the soldiers free to do what they do best—think, coordinate, control. The potential seems limitless."

logistics

digital

The list could go on, but the point is that there are many efforts to link the "beep" to the "boom" which extend all the way down to the development of new techniques and hardware to prevent hostile jamming and other interference with the electronic links between the varied beeps and booms.

Incredibly, this massive proliferation of electronic military developments goes on without attracting the attention of civilian America. Congress has expressed little interest and much of that has been adulatory. . . .

[The article continues with an account of the manner in which this revolution in the military has been accomplished with little civilian awareness, either in or out of the government.]

Reading and Interpretation

1. Dickson is attempting in this essay to describe a future reality. Thus his description must be an extension of present materials, in this case printed research sources. How well has Dickson used his sources to describe what the battlefield of tomorrow will look like?

2. Does Dickson draw a composite picture of what the future battlefield will look like? Or does he give only the pieces and allow you to draw a composite picture for yourself? Is this an effective technique?

3. Dickson implies that the electronic battlefield raises some moral questions? What are they?

4. What gives this piece its appeal? That it is about war? Is it the mystery and wonder of secret weapons? Is it because the future is our future, and we shall have to live and die in it, whether we like it or not? Is it because young people usually bear the brunt of the fighting?

Writing Techniques

1. This is mainly a report, based on documents. What is its purpose? If it is description, how does it differ from the sort we called classic description in Melville's picturing of a whale's head? How does it differ from some other description, like that of Asheville, for example? What kinds of details does it rely on?

2. We have seen above that description readily blends into narration. Would it be true that descriptive reports, like the account of the machines of an automated battlefield, readily blend into exposition and narration?

3. In part this piece is organized by chronology. This device suggests a narrative. The piece is certainly not narrative in the sense that the hunting of TuTu is, but in what sense does narrative enter into the organization?

Word Study

1. The selection contains a number of relatively common words used in special senses in the technical discussions. From the context write brief definitions of the words in the margins (*seismic, monitored, tentacles, components, surveillance, logistics, digital*). Then look them up in a dictionary and make any necessary revisions in your definitions. Describe the origin of *tentacle, logistics,* and *digital.*

2. This essay is filled with what are called *acronyms,* terms like *ABM* for *Anti-Ballistic Missile.* What good are such terms? Is there anything bad about them? How should their use be restricted? Why should this essay make more use of acronyms than previous pieces in this book? *Jeep* and *radar* were once acronyms. Can you think of any other terms that started as acronyms but are now common words? Do you know any acronyms so new that you cannot find them in our dictionary? What does all this suggest about the role of acronyms in modern American English?

Suggestions for Writing

If you are taking other courses, you must be encountering new tools and new methods. Describe some of these. If you are taking geology you may have learned that geologists now have a new way of getting energy from hot rocks far below the surface. If you are studying psychology you may have learned that some individuals are able to hear and taste in color; if so, you might describe the means of testing these abilities. If you have encountered no such exotic devices, you can describe a beginner's tools for a particular endeavor, or the concepts that a beginner must have.

PORTRAIT OF A MUGGER
James Willwerth

12

James Willwerth *is a New York journalist. In an introduction not here reprinted, he says that in the previous year he had been assigned to write part of a survey of "crime in America." His report attracted the attention of a publisher's editor, who suggested he write a book about a criminal who finds himself in a "skirmish with society." Intrigued, Willwerth set about trying to find the right kind of informant, and one who would talk. This article was published in* Harper's.

I searched a long time for the right connection and finally a meeting was arranged with a man I call "Jones"—he would be Vergil to my Dante. I never knew exactly why he agreed to this intrusion; perhaps vanity, the flattery of someone's pervasive interest in him; perhaps loneliness, for I was a sympathetic listener, and he was clearly a troubled man. Perhaps it was simply that our relationship developed into a habit; for although we kept some distance between ourselves by using the pseudonyms "Jones" and "Sam," we soon became friends. It was impossible not to be drawn to Jones, if only for his need to cling to some measure of respectability. During his worst days as a heroin addict, he proudly refused to mug women or elderly people. Neither does he terrorize his victims. He had debts, relatives, a doting mother, an argumentative father, a drinking problem, children on the way, and a dog in need of housebreaking. He had been a

The description starts.

street fighter, heroin addict, burglar, confidence man, prison inmate, and possibly—though I don't fully believe him—a murderer.

His world is small, a whirlpool of lower-New York street corners, tense friendships, family problems, small-change business deals, people without last names—and sudden violence. It is an insular world where "uptown" means a girlfriend's apartment north of Houston Street and "the Bronx" is your brother's apartment on 287th Street. When it suited him, Jones stayed at his parents' home, a tiny shelter in "the projects," and when it didn't he stayed with one of his women.

Each of our meetings had an unpredictable life of its own, ending when I filled a notebook or simply became too exhausted or frightened to continue. Many of them took place in a cramped, smelly flat on Clinton Street where Carol, one of two women pregnant by him, lived for a while. It was a depressing scene, rubbed raw by the whimpering of Carol's three-year-old boy by another man and the sputtering of a broken-down television set. Sitting with his feet on a coffee table and wondering what it would be like to have anything he wanted, Jones described his fantasy of wealth.

"Wow, I'd like to be richer than the Rockefellers! I'd have a Cadillac and a chauffeur. I would go the whole route, and get a Rolls-Royce, too. I would have a diamond ring for each day of the week. I would change clothes three times a day, and I'd have a whole lotta homes.

"I'd have a beach house, and I'd have a boat. I'd do the same thing the rich people do—fuck it, man! The world isn't ready for the change of making everyone equal, or treating everybody like a *man,* so, fuck it, I would live as well as I could. There are people so rich in this world that they have somebody do their *worrying* for them. I would live like that.

"I would have the best drugs, man. Smoke you could hardly stand, it would get you off so good. And coke—wow, Jack, I would have nothing but the finest crystal. I would be big and everybody would be looking to see what I was gonna do next. I'd have a penthouse for Moms, and so many clothes that I would have to get an extra penthouse just to store them."

"What about a private airplane?"

"Oh, yeah, man. One of those, too."

In reality, when Jones works regularly, he says he makes more than $100 a day. Perhaps several thousand dollars a month, perhaps $20,000 a year. It is tax free. Let's assume he is bragging—that he makes only half that amount; he is still making 10,000 tax-free dollars a year. This doesn't make him a Rockefeller but he is doing better than most of New York City's office workers, deliverymen, cops, and firemen.

Is this description by conversation?

Yet he is constantly broke. He takes money from his women, borrows from his parents, and hits me up practically every time we get together (and always pays me back). He dresses well and uses expensive drugs—but they can't possibly account for all the money he spends. Yet beyond the drugs and clothes, he lives like a welfare recipient. *Why?*

A short topic sentence. Does it work?

One day we decided to play a rather serious game: we would pretend to be muggers.

Narration plays a part here.

"I don't know all the rules and answers, but the ones I know I'm sure of," Jones is saying as we begin my guided tour of victimland. "Rule number one is that everything's okay as long as you don't get caught." He is pointing out areas of interest along the way—you and your wallet, for example.

I see a jowly, middle-aged man with wavy hair carrying a grocery bag toward a car. We are about fifty yards from him.

Jones sees the man but does not turn. His eyes seem to be aimed at the pavement.

"Yeah, he'd be good. He's got his hands full. You let him get in the car, and you get in with him before he can close the door. You are right on top of him, and you show him the knife. He'll slide over and go along with it."

"After that?"

"If you think he's gonna chase you, you can put him in the trunk."

We turn toward a cluster of buildings. I see a man in a black suburban coat. He is taller and younger.

"Not him," Jones says, again without looking directly at him. "He looks hard. You could take him off in a hallway, but he would give you trouble in the street."

On to bigger things. We walk through one of the project parks. I have a *sense* of us. As a kid I tried to look tough walking with friends—chest out, dour expression. Watch out. I might *do* something. Any moment now. I have this sense today.

An elderly woman sees us. She abruptly changes direction; my paranoia index jumps.

"Did she do that because of us?"

"It doesn't matter. You either hit her or you don't."

We walk to Second Avenue, moving among crowds of shoppers—sad faces, tired arms filled with packages, coats, purses, flat hip-pocket wallets in the sunny afternoon . . . so much *money* in this speckled fool's gold afternoon.

Point of view becomes important.

We are inside a bank. A dozen people stand in line before the paying/receiving window. Jones takes a withdrawal slip at a back counter and begins writing on it. I look around nervously, scanning people in the line, wondering if the bank guard sees anything funny about us. Again, Jones seems to be watching no one. He writes "$48" on the slip.

"What do you see?" I whisper.

"That dude in the striped pants."

I see a short, nervous man in his mid-fifties who waits while the cashier helps the person ahead of him in line.

Middle-class money.

He gives the teller some small slips and a check; the teller gives him a big bill, a few smaller ones, and several pieces of paper.

"He's making a drop," Jones says without looking up from the bank slip. "You saw the receipts. If I wanted to do a thing, I would follow him to his store. Then I'd watch for a few days to see the times he goes to the bank. I'd get him on a Monday. Then you get the money he made on Friday night, Saturday, and Monday. Maybe Sunday, too, depending on the type of store."

The man counts his money. He glances over his shoulder—at us?—and starts toward the door.

The mugger sees things the journalist cannot.

Now I see a tall man in suede boots and a raincoat in the line; he holds a paycheck and seems to be irritated at the delay.

"Him?"

"Uh-*uh*—he don't look right. Today's Friday. There's a precinct house a couple of blocks away—cops get paid today."

I look again—I can't tell a thing. The man is tall and his face is hard.

"Let's go out," Jones says, "I'll show you something else."

We stand before a bakery display window, pretending to look at strawberry cake. Jones nods toward the first man, who is half a block away, walking north.

"You can watch him in the reflection and let him get a little ahead; then you follow him."

"How do you watch him so closely in the bank?"

"You learn how to look like you are doing something else. There's a line on the withdrawal paper, you know? You can keep writing on it and look around without being conspicuous."

Jones moves his hand slightly as if he were writing and swivels his head. As I watch him, my eyes fall naturally to his hand.

"You look around. Then you put your head down and think about what you've seen. Then you look up, but your hand is still writing, so it looks like you are doing business. You have to blend in, be another face. The better you look, the less they think about you. You want to look like a workingman—like, my gold ring is a good thing to play on, it looks like I have money, so nobody thinks I am a mugger."

Jones may be a crook, but he is interested in words.

He chuckles at the wordplay he is about to make.

"Or that they will be a *muggee*. You get careful like this, because you are doing wrong, and you know people are out to get you for it."

He looks across the street.

"There's a precinct house on that block. The check-cashing place near it is a good place to pull rips. Nobody thinks a dude would have the heart to do it so close to a cop station; so nobody watches it very closely."

We walk into a grimy side street between First and Second Avenues and stop across from a storefront. The red-and-blue sign— Checks Cashed/Money Orders Filled—is ringed with light bulbs, and the windows are covered with wire and protective devices. Half a block away, the precinct house has patrol cars clustered in front. Brawny plainclothes detectives pass by every few minutes.

A shifting point of view.

Jones looks at my watch and sees that it is two-fifteen.

"It's a little early now. Pretty soon, this place will be doin' business." We lean against a store window and wait.

Jones nudges me. "That dude's got cash. Watch him."

Across the street, I see a tall man with snow-white hair. He walks confidently, head erect, wearing a black cashmere coat; in profile he bears a striking resemblance to the late Chief Justice Earl Warren, the same bright eyes, broad nose, and prominent cheekbones. I mention this to Jones, who laughs, only vaguely familiar with the Warren court.

Jones's street sense is astounding. The man hasn't moved directly toward the store, only stepped off the curb. He could be headed anywhere on the block.

Jones says he will cash a check.

He passes a storefront, then stops, steps backward, and disappears into the doorway.

"He is being careful. That means he's got cash."

"A good victim?"

"Yeah."

Three minutes later, the man emerges and continues walking down the block.

"From the way he walks, I think he lives on this block."

"Why?"

"The way he moves. He looks like he knows where he's going. He's afraid to move too fast, but he looks like he knows where he wants to get to."

More close observation, coupled with an economy of words.

As Jones finishes the sentence, the tall old man turns on one foot and walks into a brownstone apartment building.

"When would you move?"

"I'd wait until he gets through the door. The building is old, so the second door won't lock fast. If you time it right, the lock won't stop you."

Jones drags on the cigarette he is holding.

"I'd be in there now. I'd let him start climbing the stairs. Then I'd take him."

And the old man, who looks like a statesman but lives on a bad block, would lose something. His Social Security check? A stock dividend? His life? I have this crazy vision of Earl Warren scurrying along this grimy block, flowing robes trailing in the gutter, clutching his lawbooks and stealing glances behind him. He is followed by a mob of street people. They will follow him into the doorway now and beat him, stepping all over his robes, searching his books for dollar bills between the pages, screaming and kicking at him when he tries to talk. What are you to *me*, they are yelling—another rich bastard who thinks he knows about poor people!

Two detectives drive by. They look at us carefully.

"Let's move," Jones says.

We walk farther down the block, past the cavernous precinct building. Its flag juts out like an arm in a plaster cast.

"These cops think they're slick," Jones is saying in low tones. "There used to be a guy dealing a lot of dope in this building here"—he points to a tenement next to the precinct house—"and they think I don't know there are three of them behind me now."

Suddenly I am aware of three men in step with us. They seem to be walking aimlessly. One mentions a card game, another says something about an "easy mark." But they don't look like cops. Is Jones paranoid?

> The criminal studies dialects—a sort of "applied linguistics."

" 'Mark' is an old word," Jones is saying. "Cops give themselves away by their language. Nobody in the streets uses that word anymore. They probably wondered what we were doing hanging around."

We turn at the next block and walk toward a group of projects several blocks away. The tour is over.

That was one of the lighter times; Jones's mood was good; on the street he can run away from himself, get involved with his craft. But I remember a gray, drizzling day when the sky was falling upon the city streets, and the corner where we'd meet was nearly flooded. Jones is hunched over in the drizzle, sucking sullenly on a wet cigarette. We turn and walk south. He wants cocaine before we do anything else. He wants it so badly he does not mind walking through the rain.

> Description of a more conventional sort.

"I've got to get out of Carol's apartment. It's goin' too fast with her. She's makin' too many demands. I just can't deal with it. This is on my mind all the time. It's getting hard to live."

"Maybe it's the rain."

He brightens. "Yeah." But the smile folds. "No, I went to bed feeling like this. *Everything* is fucked up. I'm gettin' high too much— but I have to. I can be an expressionless dummy. I don't show happiness or disappointment."

He turns and looks at me savagely.

"And I *know* where that leads. When I am buying coke rather than clothes, when I put a quarter down on coke first, then dig it, something is happening. I'm not goin' back to dope, but this is how it could happen."

A bus pulls up, splashing water at us. We go inside. Jones talks in a low, angry whine.

What kind of description is this?

"I don't know ... if ... I should ... talk ... about this ... maybe it's too deep." He plays with his hands in his lap.

"But ... when that baby is born ... I hope it is ... *dead.*"

The air is still. The bus rumbles noisily through the traffic. There is nothing to say.

"I don't want her to have it—she wants it to keep me." The chunky hands start to move.

"Wow ... I don't even know if it's *mine.* Carol is hot-blooded, and she was seeing some other dudes when we started up. I don't ... *want* that baby."

He falls back into the seat, relieved at having said it.

Nearly midnight now, a hot summer night filled with poor people. We sit in the parked car near the project, finishing a bottle.

"There's one thing I haven't told you," Jones says, cupping his hands around a cigarette. "I don't know if it should be in the story."

I hold the bottle in my lap and wait.

"I've done some hits—you know, a contract. It was right after I got out of prison, and I needed some bread."

I believed all along—and I still want to believe—that Jones hurts his victims only as a last resort. Murder!

Silence; a stillness in the air smothering sound.

"Tell me about it."

Jones shifts in the seat. He starts slowly. "It was ... up in the Bronx. I was known to some people up there ... I had the rep that I could come down heavy if there was a fight. So one night I'm high on smoke, and I walk into this bar. I see a dude named Cuba. He is from the island, you dig it, and he is into numbers and he does some things in drugs.

Jones's narrative used to describe him.

"We started rapping, and after a while he was telling me he had some business to do. I asked how much it paid. He said four thousand, and I said, wow, I'll do that thing! He said okay. He would give me half before I did it and the other half afterward. I was high on smoke, you know? I didn't really know whether I would do it, but the money looked good. I figured maybe I would beat him for it.

"Anyway, I said I'd do this thing. But I really figured I would beat him for the two thousand. He gives me the money and takes me down to this place to get a weapon. They had everything there except tanks! He gave me a .38 and told me to throw it away if I used it, or bring it back if I didn't."

Jones is loosening up now.

"I had this gun and I was still gonna beat him, but then I remembered something my uncle said. He said you don't take money from the Family unless you do the job. Or you don't get to spend it."

I nod.

"So I went to this street where these two dudes lived. They were black dudes and they had done wrong, I guess. I laid for them one at a time. I caught the first one in a hallway, and I cut his throat. It was very fast."

I am numb. Here is the man Hobbes talked about; he can remove all civilized restraints when he wishes; all the spiritual and legal codes intended to keep people from tearing each other to pieces mean nothing to him.

This interrupts a story. Why does the author use it?

He stops. He doesn't like talking about this, and I am not taking notes.

"What about the other dude?"

He is finishing the wine and offers me a last chance at it before he takes the final swill.

"I laid for the second one the same way. I caught him from behind in a hallway and did the job with a hammer. I left fast. I don't even remember seeing him hit the ground."

"What did you do with the gun?"

"I took it back. I didn't use it because I figured I could do the jobs better with my hands. It's safer to do things quietly."

Jones throws his head back, finishing the bottle with a long pull.

"The man was impressed, real impressed that I didn't use it. He asked if I wanted to do other jobs. I said no. I didn't want to be a hit man. I didn't feel there was any future in it."

He throws the bottle out the window.

"Besides, I had enough money to keep me going for a while."

Silence. I can't think of a thing to say. . . .

Jones was still living with Carol when we last talked. Carol had now given birth to the baby whose arrival he so feared, and between her semimonthly welfare checks and his job they seemed to be doing pretty well.

Time provides a transition.

It was Christmas Eve, and he took me to his parents' place; a tinfoil Christmas tree laden with blinking blue lights and candy canes stood in one corner of the living room. Moms served pot roast, and we all crowded around the tiny kitchen table to get at the rolls Pops was pulling out of a small toaster-oven. As far as I could tell, Jones was supporting himself legitimately. He'd tried dealing marijuana for a while, but that didn't work out. He hadn't mugged anyone for a long time, he said—and probably wouldn't as long as he was employed.

Something starts here. Is it a conclusion? If so, of what?

He had little else to say. His life seemed to have stabilized, although Pops (who is black but who had always angrily preferred Jo-Anne, who is white, over Carol) kept saying he wanted his son out of "that nigger's house." Everyone asked about the book. I said I was still working on it; and I warned them that it would not hide anything. They nodded and accepted this.

Once that night, I felt I saw Jones's family for the first time. I hadn't realized how deeply they loved each other, despite all that had happened. Pops told me that he and Jones had fought bitterly the previous night, and both men had cried afterward. They talked again and again of their love for each other. Jones nodded as his father talked and Moms smoked cigarettes. And Jerry, Jones's brother, stood behind the table and agreed with all that was said.

For several days after that, I carried a picture in my head of this besieged family. It is impossible, indeed foolish, to conclude that Jones is merely a product of his environment. It says too little about him, or the nature of our common interest. Jones is a failed human being—a sociopath—one of the millions among us. He is trying to die. The schools, therapists, and prisons in his life have not changed that. In a middle-class family he might have caused trouble in less frightening ways: drag racing, pills, vandalism. But he grew up in a ghetto. He found his friends on street corners; he became a junkie, then a mugger. In a more prosperous community, he might have chosen a corporate president or politician as his predator-hero.

In theory, then, it would be easy to rid our cities of people like Jones. First we could abolish ghettos. As long as they exist, we will endure what they spawn: police technology cannot change that. Secondly, we could develop ways to deal more positively with troubled human beings. For now, therapy is available to the wealthy; the poor go to prison. And lastly, we could stop heaping cultural approval on predators ... successful gangsters, ruthless businessmen, violent Hollywood stereotypes.

Is this conclusion by contrast?

In reality such solutions are remote. So I think mostly of Jones standing on the corner that night with Christmas lights behind him as we said goodbye, and I am reduced to wondering how good and evil exist so easily within the same person. I've stopped looking for simple answers. I only know that each of us must continue to look at the other without turning away.

Reading and Interpreting

1. This is a close portrait of a man, but it is a portrait that tells you more than the man's physical appearance. In fact, you know little about the physical appearance of Jones. What, then, is this essay describing?

2. Why does Willwerth find Jones fascinating?

3. What kind of person is Jones? He is not bad at all. What is the evidence? Could you make a case for his being a practical, prudent, sensible fellow? He is intelligent—or at least he has a certain sort of intelligence. Clearly, he had trained himself to see and interpret. Is there intelligence he does not have? Is he at the mercy of his emotions? Whom and what does he seem to hate most? There must be some weakness in him. What is it?

4. What is your reaction to Jones? Before you get too outraged at this criminal, what do you think of Willwerth? Are there any moral implications in Willwerth knowing that Jones is a criminal and doing nothing about it? Does Willwerth express any concern about the morality of his own actions?

5. According to Willwerth, what makes a criminal? Where is his conclusion stated in the essay? Many of Jones's attitudes and actions are contradictory. At times the man is a paradox. How is this consistent with the conclusion Willwerth arrives at about Jones, the criminal, and crime?

Writing Techniques

1. Much of the description of Jones in this essay comes through dialogue. Examine the dialogue carefully and point to those passages which particularly contribute to the description of Jones.

2. Jones is a creature of the street; it is his natural habitat, his jungle. As Willwerth discovers, Jones feels most comfortable on the street, on the move. Examine the essay and note where Jones is described in terms of his relation with his physical surroundings.

Word Study

Several of the glosses call your attention to the way Jones uses words. Many of these are highly expressive, but you would probably not use them in a theme, except in quotations. Why not? Because you consider them slang? Or you assume that others would call them slang? Some of the terms Jones uses might be called *argot*, the usage of a particular group of people. If terms like *rap, mark,* and *take* are slang as Jones uses them—they are at least what is sometimes called *unconventional English*—what can you conclude about the use and limitations of such terms?

Suggestions for Writing

You probably do not hobnob with criminals, but you must know some people who are disapproved by society. Or you must now see, if you did not see it then, that many of your playmates were misjudged. Mediocre, dull, or even vicious boys or girls may be popular, admired for what you will now feel were quite unadmirable qualities. On the other hand, boys and girls who grow up to be superb human beings may be tormented and ostracized as children. Try to picture somebody who you believe is, or was, misunderstood. You may want to take some tips from Willwerth in making us see this person.

Argument:
Making Your Point

"You're a liar."

"So are you!"

This is argument, no question about it. But it is not good argument. Probably neither of the small boys who are here being quoted convinced the other, nor was he likely to convince anybody else. Why is this bad argument, and what would good argument contain that this exchange does not?

Most argument is, and always has been, more crucial than schoolyard squabbles. A murder trial is an argument between the state and the accused; a foreign policy is the result of argument among various experts espousing conflicting proposals; even a scientific discussion of what Mars is made of will include argument.

In ancient Greece, the term *rhetoric,* which now refers to all talk about writing or speaking, was mainly limited to discussions of argument. Rhetoric concerned the doings of a *rhetor,* a public speaker, who argued the case of a client in court, addressed a public forum, or—as a sort of sport or an artistic display—delivered a set speech. Ancient writers like Aristotle codified the means of formalized oral persuasion.

We tend to use the word *rhetoric* in a less limited way. We apply it to the good use of language in any form; we can consider the rhetoric of a public address as the Greeks did, or we can study the rhetoric of written language, even the rhetoric of fiction. And if the signals that a programmer exchanges with a computer ever become so nearly adequate that we can call them a language, we shall be able to discuss the Rhetoric of Resselrig—or whatever this elaborated computer talk might be called. At present we could even define argument by its opposite, saying it is communication of the kind a computer does not use. A computer never argues with a programmer; it does what it is told or it does not do it.

The computer has no intellect, but all creatures relying on complex, well-stocked brains find they must argue. Such argument must have a rhetoric or rhetorics that differ from narration and description, for the purposes are different. Argument—or if you prefer the term, *persuasion*—is concerned with beliefs, with getting somebody else to agree with you, with getting a listening or reading audience to accept one claim rather than another, with trying to move somebody to do something. But is argument limited to only one sort of thing?

In the readings below, obviously Thomas Jefferson, penning the Declaration of Independence, is involved in argument. He was trying to get others to believe that the English colonies in America had legal and moral right to declare themselves independent. But Jefferson knew that many good men and women would say that the king's subjects had no right to break their oaths of allegiance to the British crown; and he knew that many devout people believed that God himself had chosen the king, and so to deny the king was to be disobedient to God's will. But is Jefferson's argument in reality the same sort of composition as X. J. Kennedy's speculations about King Kong? And is either the same sort of thing as Jonathan Swift's ironic attack on absentee landlords suppressing Irish people? You may want to ask yourself such questions.

You will want to ask, also, what makes good argument and what keeps argumentative writing from being good. You are likely to find that kinds of development discussed later in the book are relevant here. Definition enters abnormally into argument, and certainly analysis and classification will. You may have to raise questions about evidence: how much is needed, what sort is needed, when is it needed? You will need to observe the roles of induction and deduction. And you will want to notice how narration and description can be turned to the purpose of an author who is engaged in argument.

13

Following are bits of argument or attempted persuasion. **a. Bergen Evans,** *author of many books and articles, is Professor of English at Northwestern University;* **b. Kenneth B. Clark** *is Professor of Psychology in the City University of New York;* **c. J. R. Oppenheimer** *was a key figure in developing atomic fission; the paragraph is from "Atomic Weapons."* **d. Bertrand Russell** *was one of the distinguished philosophers and mathematicians of our time; the selection below is from his* An Outline of Philosophy; *among Lord Russell's honors was the Nobel Prize for Literature, 1950;* **e. Oscar Wilde** *shocked the late nineteenth century with his witty plays;* **f. Abraham Flexner,** *who was long one of the directors of research in America, wrote this in an article for* Harper's Magazine; *g.* **Robert E. Coulson's** *piece was printed in* Harper's; *h. the* **Shakespeare** *excerpt is the beginning of Mark Antony's funeral address for Caesar in* Julius Caesar, III, 2; *i.* **Ralph R. Greenson,** *M.D., speaks as a psychoanalyst; his review was printed in* Saturday Review, June 15, 1974.

a.   Bergen Evans

I am much more concerned with sadism than with sex in the entertainment media. The movies have always settled all human problems with a quick right to the jaw—and perhaps this has led many of our young people to assume that the answer to any problem is to smash things up.

b.   Kenneth B. Clark

IT would be extremely difficult for young people, on the basis of what they see now in movies, to have any clear picture of what the important things are in this country and world, what the things are in which human beings must believe. Our media apparently are suggesting to them that nothing is important, that everything is absurd and ridiculous and utterly trivial. And this is intolerable.

c. J. R. Oppenheimer

ONE of our colleagues, a man most deeply committed to the welfare and growth of science, advised me not long ago not to give too much weight in any public words to the terrors of atomic weapons as they are and as they can be. He knows as well as any of us how much more terrible they can be made. "It might cause a reaction," he said, "hostile to science. It might turn people away from science." He is not such an old man, and I think it will make little difference to him, or to any of us, what is said now about atomic weapons if before we die we live to see a war in which they are used. I think that it will not help to avert such a war if we try to rub the edges off this new terror that we have helped bring to the world. I think that it is for us among all men, for us as scientists perhaps in greater measure because it is our tradition to recognize and to accept the strange and the new, I think it is for us to accept as fact this new terror, and to accept with it the necessity for those transformations in the world which will make it possible to integrate these developments into human life. I think we cannot in the long term protect science against this threat to its spirit and this reproach to its issue unless we recognize the threat and the reproach and help our fellow men in every way suitable to remove their cause. Their cause is war.

d. Bertrand Russell

IMAGINATION is not, as the word might suggest, essentially connected with images. No doubt images are often, even usually, present when we imagine, but they need not be. A man can improvise on the piano without first having images of the music he is going to make; a poet might write down a poem without first making it up in his head. In talking, words suggest other words, and a man with sufficient verbal associations may be successfully carried along by them for a considerable time. The art of talking without thinking is particularly necessary to public speakers, who must go on when once they are on their feet, and gradually acquire the habit of behaving in private as they do before an audience. Yet the statements they make must be admitted to be often imaginative. The essence of imagination, therefore, does not lie in images.

e. Oscar Wilde

THE real Don Juan is not the vulgar person who goes about making love to all the women he meets, and what the novelists call "seducing" them. The real Don Juan is the man who says to women "Go away! I don't want you. You interfere with my life. I can do without you." Swift was the real Don Juan. Two women died for him!

f. Abraham Flexner

I suggested that he might ask the physicists of the University of Rochester precisely what Hertz and Maxwell had done; but one thing I said he could be sure of, namely, that they had done their work without thought of use and that throughout the whole history of science most of the really great discoveries which had ultimately proved to be beneficial to mankind had been made by men and women who were driven not by the desire to be useful but merely the desire to satisfy their curiosity.

"Curiosity?" asked Mr. Eastman.

"Yes," I replied, "curiosity, which may or may not eventuate in something useful, is probably the outstanding characteristic of modern thinking. It is not new. It goes back to Galileo, Bacon, and to Sir Isaac Newton, and it must be absolutely unhampered. Institutions of learning should be devoted to the cultivation of curiosity and the less they are deflected by considerations of immediacy of application, the more likely they are to contribute not only to human welfare but to the equally important satisfaction of intellectual interest which may indeed be said to have become the ruling passion of intellectual life in modern times."

g. Robert E. Coulson

NONVOTERS are often more intelligent, more fair-minded, and just as loyal as voters. The right not to vote is as basic as the right to. If voting is made a duty, it ceases to be a privilege.

Let's look at the voting behavior of Mr. and Mrs. Whipcord and Mrs. Whipcord's brother Harold, on the day of the local school-board election. Mrs. Whipcord says, "I have studied the candidates and have made up my mind. I will vote for Jones." Mr. Whipcord says, "I know nothing about the candidates or the issues. I will stay home, and allow the election to be decided by the votes of those who have made a study and formed an opinion." Harold says, "I don't know anything about the candidates or the problems, but by golly, I'm going to vote. It's my duty. I'll pick the fellows with the shortest names."

If there is a bad citizen among these three, which one is it? Whose procedure is least likely to bring good government to the school district?

h.   William Shakespeare

Mark Antony: Friends, Romans, countrymen, lend me your
    ears;
I come to bury Cæsar, not to praise him.
The evil that men do lives after them;
The good is oft interred with their bones;
So let it be with Cæsar. The noble Brutus
Hath told you Cæsar was ambitious:
If it were so, it was a grievous fault,
And grievously hath Cæsar answer'd it.
Here, under leave of Brutus and the rest—
For Brutus is an honourable man;
So are they all, all honourable men—
Come I to speak in Cæsar's funeral.
He was my friend, faithful and just to me:
But Brutus says he was ambitious;
And Brutus is an honourable man.
He hath brought many captives home to Rome,
Whose ransoms did the general coffers fill:
Did this in Cæsar seem ambitious?
When that the poor have cried, Cæsar hath wept:
Ambition should be made of sterner stuff:
Yet Brutus says he was ambitious;
And Brutus is an honourable man.
You all did see that on the Lupercal
I thrice presented him a kingly crown,

Which he did thrice refuse: was this ambition?
Yet Brutus says he was ambitious;
And, sure, he is an honourable man.
I speak not to disprove what Brutus spoke,
But here I am to speak what I do know.
You all did love him once, not without cause:
What cause withholds you then, to mourn for
   him?
O judgement! thou art fled to brutish beasts,
And men have lost their reason. Bear with
   me;
My heart is in the coffin there with Cæsar,
And I must pause till it come back to me.

i. Ralph R. Greenson

THE EXORCIST is a menace, the most shocking major movie I have ever seen. Never before have I witnessed such a flagrant combination of perverse sex, brutal violence, and abused religion. In addition, the film degrades the medical profession and psychiatry. At the showing I went to, the unruly audience giggled, talked, and yelled throughout. As well they might: Although the picture is not X-rated, it is so pornographic that it makes *Last Tango in Paris* seem like a Strauss waltz.

Reading and Interpreting

1. Most of the selections, which are only parts of longer arguments, differ considerably in their methods. Which of them seem to you most convincing? Which least? Explain your reasons for your ranking.

2. Which selections are mainly assertions of an opinion? Which support a contention with factual evidence, with details, or with reasons?

Writing Techniques

1. Oscar Wilde's paragraph could be called an epigram. What would seem to be the qualities of a good epigram? Try to write one.

2. How much evidence does Greenson present to support his attitude toward the film he is discussing? Compare his method with that of Flexner, another physician.

3. Read Antony's speech from *Caesar* out loud, as if you were playing the part. How would you handle the repetition of phrases like "honourable men" and "he was ambitious"? How does Antony use factual evidence of the behavior of Caesar? Does it demonstrate that Caesar has been ambitious? To what extent is Antony's argument emotional? In what ways does the speech suggest that Antony is conscious of his audience (see Section V)?

4. Is the second line of Antony's speech an adequate topic sentence for the whole? Explain.

5. What are the examples that Bertrand Russell uses to support his opening sentence? Are they valid as evidence for his thesis?

6. How do the examples used by Robert Coulson differ from those of Russell? How does Coulson expect you to answer the final question of the paragraph?

Suggestions for Writing

Write a short paragraph in two versions. In one begin with a topic sentence in which you anticipate that your argument will be read by sympathetic readers; in the other, begin with a topic sentence assuming that your readers may resent your position. You may wish to use the topic of one of the selections, either agreeing or disagreeing with the author's views.

THE DECLARATION OF INDEPENDENCE
Thomas Jefferson

14

Thomas Jefferson, *third president of the United States, has been called "the most versatile of the founding fathers." A tremendously productive man, his draft of the Declaration, which when revised established July 4, 1776, as the birthdate of a nation, was the product of little more than an inspired week or so of feverish writing. Following are some words you may want to be sure you understand before trying to read the Declaration, consulting your dictionary and learning to use the word in a sentence:* acquiesce, candid, convulsions, depository, dissolutions, endowed, harass, impel, inestimable, invested, magnanimity, providence, rectitude, sufferance, tenure, unalienable, usurpations.

In CONGRESS, July 4, 1776.

The Unanimous Declaration of the Thirteen
United States of America.

WHEN in the Course of human events, it becomes necessary for one people to dissolve the political bands which have connected them with another, and to assume among the powers of the earth, the separate and equal station to which the Laws of Nature and of Nature's God entitle them, a decent respect to the opinions of mankind requires that they should declare the causes which impel them to the separation.

Introduction.

We hold these truths to be self-evident, that all men are created equal, that they are endowed by their Creator with certain unalienable Rights, that among these are Life, Liberty and the pursuit of Happiness.

Basic belief becomes a theme sentence.

That to secure these rights, Governments are instituted among Men, deriving their just powers from the consent of the governed.

That whenever any Form of Government becomes destructive of these ends, it is the Right of the People to alter or to abolish it, and to institute new Government, laying its foundation on such principles and organizing its powers in such form, as to them shall seem most likely to effect their Safety and Happiness. Prudence, indeed, will dictate that Governments long established should not be changed for light and transient causes; and accordingly all experience hath shewn, that mankind are more disposed to suffer, while evils are sufferable, than to right themselves by abolishing the forms to which they are accustomed. But when a long train of abuses and usurpations, pursuing invariably the same Object evinces a design to reduce them under absolute Despotism, it is their right, it is their duty, to throw off such Government, and to provide new Guards for their future security.

Such has been the patient sufferance of these Colonies; and such is now the necessity which constrains them to alter their former Systems of Government. The history of the present King of Great Britain is a history of repeated injuries and usurpations, all having in direct object the establishment of an absolute Tyranny over these States. To prove this, let Facts be submitted to a candid world.

A new topic.

He has refused his Assent to Laws, the most wholesome and necessary for the public good.

Details and examples.

He has forbidden his Governors to pass Laws of immediate and pressing importance, unless suspended in their operation till his Assent should be obtained; and when so suspended, he has utterly neglected to attend to them.

He has refused to pass other Laws for the accommodation of large districts of people, unless those people would relinquish the right of Representation in the Legislature, a right inestimable to them and formidable to tyrants only.

He has called together legislative bodies at places unusual, uncomfortable, and distant from the depository of their public Records, for the sole purpose of fatiguing them into compliance with his measures.

He has dissolved Representative Houses repeatedly, for opposing with manly firmness his invasions on the rights of people.

He has refused for a long time, after such dissolutions, to cause others to be elected; whereby the Legislative powers, incapable of Annihilation, have returned to the People at large for their exercise; the State remaining in the mean time exposed to all the dangers of invasion from without, and convulsions within.

He has endeavoured to prevent the population of these States; for that purpose obstructing the Laws for Naturalization of Foreigners; refusing to pass others to encourage their migrations hither, and raising the conditions of new Appropriations of Lands.

Coherence by reference.

He has obstructed the Administration of Justice, by refusing his Assent to Laws for establishing Judiciary powers.

He has made Judges dependent on his Will alone, for the tenure of their offices, and the amount and payment of their salaries.

He has erected a multitude of New Offices, and sent hither swarms of Officers to harass our people, and eat out their substance.

He has kept among us, in times of peace, Standing Armies without the Consent of our legislatures.

He has affected to render the Military independent of and superior to the Civil power.

He has combined with others to subject us to a jurisdiction foreign to our constitution, and unacknowledged by our laws; giving his Assent to their Acts of pretended Legislation:

For Quartering large bodies of armed troops among us:

For protecting them, by a mock Trial, from punishment for any Murders which they should commit on the Inhabitants of these States:

Why this shift in sentence structure?

For cutting off our Trade with all parts of the world:

For imposing Taxes on us without our Consent:

For depriving us in many cases, of the benefits of Trial by Jury:

For transporting us beyond Seas to be tried for pretended offenses:

For abolishing the free System of English Laws in a neighbouring Province, establishing therein an Arbitrary government, and enlarging its Boundaries so as to render it at once an example and fit instrument for introducing the same absolute rule into these Colonies:

For taking away our Charters, abolishing our most valuable

Laws, and altering fundamentally the Forms of our Governments:

For suspending our own Legislatures, and declaring themselves invested with power to legislate for us in all cases whatsoever.

He has abdicated Government here, by declaring us out of his Protection and waging War against us:

He has plundered our seas, ravaged our Coasts, burnt our towns, and destroyed the lives of our people.

He is at this time transporting large Armies of foreign Mercenaries to compleat the works of death, desolation and tyranny, already begun with circumstances of Cruelty & perfidy scarcely paralleled in the most barbarous ages, and totally unworthy the Head of a civilized nation.

He has constrained our fellow Citizens taken Captive on the high Seas to bear Arms against their Country, to become the executioners of their friends and Brethren, or to fall themselves by their Hands.

He has excited domestic insurrections amongst us, and has endeavoured to bring on the inhabitants of our frontiers, the merciless Indian Savages, whose known rule of warfare, is an undistinguished destruction of all ages, sexes and conditions. In every stage of these Oppressions We have Petitioned for Redress in the most humble terms: Our repeated Petitions have been answered only by repeated injury. A Prince, whose character is thus marked by every act which may define a Tyrant, is unfit to be the ruler of a free people. Nor have We been wanting in attentions to our British brethren. We have warned them from time to time of attempts by their legislature to extend an unwarrantable jurisdiction over us. We have reminded them of the circumstances of our emigration and settlement here. We have appealed to their native justice and magnanimity, and we have conjured them by the ties of our common kindred to disavow these usurpations, which, would inevitably interrupt our connections and correspondence. They too have been deaf to the voice of justice and of consanguinity. We must, therefore, acquiesce in the necessity, which denounces our Separation, and hold them, as we hold the rest of mankind, Enemies in War, in Peace Friends.

Climax of both time and intensity.

WE, THEREFORE, the Representatives of the UNITED STATES OF AMERICA, in General Congress Assembled, appealing to the Supreme Judge of the world for the rectitude of our intentions, do, in the Name and by Authority of the good People of these Colonies, solemnly publish and declare, That these United Colonies are, and of Right ought to be FREE AND INDEPENDENT STATES; that they are Absolved from all Allegiance to the British Crown, and that all political connection between them and the State of Great Britain, is and ought to be totally dissolved; and that as Free and Independent States, they have full Power to levy War, conclude Peace, contract Alliances, es-

Conclusion of Declaration.

tablish Commerce, and to do all other Acts and Things which Independent States may of right do.

And for the support of this Declaration, with a firm reliance on the protection of divine Providence, we mutually pledge to each other our Lives, our Fortunes and our sacred Honor.

Reading and Interpreting

1. In 1776 all major Continental European countries were governed by absolute rulers, and ideas like republicanism and democracy were thought to be as dangerous as communism has been considered in the twentieth century. (Be sure you know the meaning of *republican* and *democratic*.) Would the doctrines in the second, third, and fourth paragraphs of the Declaration have been widely accepted?

2. In popular American belief, the Declaration is one of the major documents on which modern democracy is founded. What evidence of a belief in democracy do you find in the Declaration?

3. Much of the document is a list of charges against George III. Is this attack appropriate? Some members of Jefferson's committee objected to the first draft of this section and eliminated parts, including a passage accusing George III of fostering slavery, which Jefferson called "an execrable commerce." What does this deletion suggest about the attitudes behind the document?

Writing Techniques

1. Analyze this argument for its parts. One way is to recognize four subdivisions: (1) introduction and topical statement, (2) evidence, (3) conclusion, and (4) declaration. If you use this breakdown, where do the various parts begin and end?

2. Jefferson refers to "Facts . . . submitted to a candid world." What are some of the facts Jefferson lists? How much of his argument is composed of facts?

Word Study

You probably noticed that Jefferson uses the spellings *unalienable, compleat,* and *behaviour,* which were once standard—the last still is, in England. How does he seem to be using capitalization? It is not the system you have been taught. Does it make sense? Are there changes in the apparent meaning of terms in two hundred years? For *bands* in the first sentence we might use *bonds*. Can you find other words that seem to have a meaning not now common?

Suggestions for Writing

Do you have any strong beliefs? That you and other students should be freed of parental control? That you should be freed from control by the faculty? By the administration? That no woman has or is likely to get equal opportunities with men? That women, blacks, and other so-called "minority groups" are now so favored that a white male has little chance of getting a good job? That no black male can expect to get justice in this country? That all drunk drivers should be locked up, say for two years? That nobody has the right to dictate the driving habits of anyone else? That the owning of handguns should be strictly controlled? That control of the citizens' right to bear arms is un-American and dangerous? If so, try to write some kind of "declaration." You may or may not want to pattern your essay on Jefferson's. However, you will want to present some concrete, specific evidence.

THE INTELLECTUAL TAXICAB COMPANY
Peter Carlson

15

As will be apparent from the context, when **Peter Carlson** *wrote this for* Newsweek *in 1975 he was an undergraduate at Boston University.*

MY friend Danny hung his Boston University diploma below the hack license in his cab.

After seventeen years of education in the finest schools in America, Danny, at 22, couldn't fix his stopped sink, repair a burnt connection in his fuse box, replace a pane of glass in his kitchen or locate the carburetor in his car.

Danny is an educated man. He is a master of writing research papers, taking tests, talking and filling out forms. He can rattle off his social-security number as easily as he can his name because it was also his student identification number. He can analyze Freud from a Marxian viewpoint and he can analyze Marx from a Freudian viewpoint.

In short, Danny is an unskilled worker and he has a sociology degree to prove it. He is of very little use to American industry.

This is nothing new. Colleges have been turning out unskilled workers for decades. Until five years ago, most of these unskilled workers took their degrees in sociology, philosophy, political science or history and marched right into the American middle class. Some filled executive positions in business and government but many, if not most, went into education, which is the only thing they knew anything about. Once there, they taught another generation the skills necessary to take tests and write papers.

But that cycle broke down. Teachers are overabundant these days, college applications are down, plumbers are making $12 an hour and liberal-arts graduates are faced with a choice—graduate school or the taxicab.

Danny chose the taxicab because driving was about the only marketable skill he possessed. Danny refers to his job as "Real World 101." He has been shot at, punched, sideswiped and propositioned. But he has also acquired some practical skills—he can get his tickets fixed; he knows how to cheat the company out of a few extra dollars a week; he found his carburetor and can fix it.

Soon, I will be in the same position. I'll graduate from Boston University with a B.S. in journalism. Whatever skills that degree symbolizes are not currently in demand. I suppose I could go to the graduate school but, Christ, I've been doing the same thing for seventeen years and I'm getting a little tired of it. Besides, there are a lot of grad-school graduates who are driving cabs, too.

And that brings me to the Intellectual Taxicab Company.

Danny and I were discussing the hack business recently and we came up with the idea. It is the simple answer to a simple question: why should all that college education go to waste reading road signs when masses of people are looking for knowledge and riding in cabs?

What America needs is a system to bring together all the knowledgeable cabbies and the undereducated rest of the country. The system we propose is the Intellectual Taxicab Company.

The Intellectual Taxicab Company would consist of a dispatcher and a fleet of cabs driven by recent college graduates. When you need a ride, you call the company and say something like: I'd like to go from Wall Street over to East 83rd and I'd like to discuss the world monetary situation."

"All right, sir, we'll have an NYU economics graduate over in five minutes."

Or: "Hello, I'm in Central Square and I'd like to go to Brookline and discuss whether or not there is a God."

"You're in luck, madame, we have a Harvard philosophy graduate who minored in Comparative Religions right in the neighborhood."

The educational possibilities of this plan are staggering. English and Drama graduates could take the after-theater run, explaining the literary ramifications of the shows. Political Science graduates could hack around Capitol Hill or City Hall. Regular bus runs could be set up to conduct seminars on popular topics.

The Intellectual Taxicab Company would bring adult education to the streets. It would also give all those alienated college graduates a feeling that they didn't waste four years and all that tuition money. And it would elevate the snotty cabdriver to an art form: cabbies would quote Voltaire while they rant about how bad the mayor is.

Surely there must be some foundation money or unimpounded Federal funds available to begin such a noble experiment in education. If there is, Danny and I are ready to start immediately. In fact, Danny is licking his lips in anticipation. "Just think how much my tips will go up," he said.

Reading and Interpreting

1. What is the main purpose of this essay? What is it criticizing? Is it trying to persuade an audience that there should be a change?

2. What is the attitude of the essay toward education? What is its view toward contemporary society?

Writing Techniques

1. What main devisions can you point out in the organization of the essay?

2. Like the Declaration of Independence, this essay makes use of fact to support its point of view. How does its use differ from that in the Declaration?

3. Most of Carlson's paragraphs are short, only two or three sentences. Can you make any rhetorical justification for relying so consistently on brief paragraphs?

Suggestions for Writing

Try writing an essay on the relations between education and society as you see them today, either marshaling arguments seriously or imitating Carlson's method of proposing an absurd alternative to usual assumptions.

16

HISTORY IS BUNK
Peter Steinfels

Peter Steinfels *is a professor of history who has published articles in various scholarly journals, as well as* Commonweal, *from which the following article is taken.*

THERE have recently been complaints that young people are not sufficiently interested in history, that they feel the study of the past to be "irrelevant" and to have no connection with the problems we face today.

Of course these young people are absolutely right. Let me give you an example. I have wasted (as it turns out) a small but significant portion of my life studying the history of modern Germany. One of the most general conclusions of such study, reached by almost anyone who undertakes it for more than 15 minutes, is that a nation can achieve the pinnacle of material, intellectual and artistic civilization and yet, because of deep flaws in its political culture, perpetrate unthinkable evils. Obviously that is the kind of lesson that has no relevance to us. You can see how my time has been wasted.

But let me illustrate the matter in more detail. Students of German history are forced by their pedantic professors to pay attention to something known as the Prussian "Constitutional Crisis." This episode began in 1862 when the Prussian Chamber of Deputies, dissatisfied with King William I's proposed strengthening of the military and believing that the constitution meant what it said about the budget's having to be approved by the Chamber, refused to vote the funds the king's ministers requested. In turn, the feudal upper house, at the government's behest, threw out the Chamber's budget; and so there was no budget at all.

In a constitutional regime, one would think that the government would then have resubmitted a compromise to the Chamber or simply have abided by the Chamber's will. But constitutional theorists are never at a loss for cleverness. Those in Prussia pointed out that, yes, the constitution did seem to insist on the Chamber's approval for the budget, but, on the other hand, the constitution also gave the government the right to collect the current taxes and duties until ordered otherwise. Therefore, a "gap" existed in the constitution; and necessity being the mother of invention for constitutional theorists as for everyone else, it was decided that in the unresolved situation created by the gap, the necessity of maintaining the state implied the government could pretty much do what it pleased.

Such a conclusion was obviously not to everyone's taste, and in the midst of the resulting tumult, the king called a brash, 47-year-old nobleman, politician and diplomat to head the government. This was Otto von Bismarck. (In the midst of this kind of useless study, it is nice to have a familiar personality on which to hang your hat.) Mr. Bismarck was not well received. He immediately defied the Chamber, proclaiming that power—blood and iron—would resolve the great questions of the day. The moderates and liberals replied that the legal and moral order was not violated with impunity. The historian Heinrich von Treitschke termed Bismarck's defiance a shallow and ridiculous vulgarity. But government without a budget continued.

Meanwhile, Bismarck dissolved the Chamber and called new elections. In the intervening period, when there was no Chamber to counter his moves, he attacked the press, obtaining a royal order allowing the suppression of critical newspapers. He further maligned his opponents as unpatriotic and even as traitors. When the elected deputies wished to question Bismarck about a semisecret agreement that allowed Russian troops to cross into Prussia to exterminate fugitive Polish rebels, Bismarck refused even to explain his policy publicly.

By now, you must be convinced that none of these ridiculous goings-on has the slightest relevance to our own politics; but it is too late—you have to hear the story out, so you will know exactly what we inflict upon our poor students.

None of these maneuvers—censorship, public disparagement of the character and loyalty of his opponents and even intimidation through the courts—had obtained for Bismarck the pliable legislative majority that he desired. The constitutional crisis remained unresolved.

But Bismarck was to find the solution in international politics. He adroitly manipulated a series of international crises in a pyrotechnic display of diplomatics; waged two swift and successful wars, against Denmark and Austria; and successfully united all of northern Germany under the Prussian crown. He was the hero of the hour.

That part of the tale, I admit, possesses a certain melodrama, but now we descend to the truly dry-as-dust details. In the wake of his victory, Bismarck submitted to the Chamber an indemnity bill, legalizing his government's three years of illegal rule. Who could resist the successful Bismarck? Certainly not the German liberals. Had he not demonstrated that ruthlessness and toughness are crowned with success, whereas moral principles count for naught? Had he not stolen the cause of German unity from the liberals' own agenda, and even admitted the liberal principle of universal suffrage into the new constitution for the North German Confederation?

The liberals did more than vote Bismarck his indemnity. They fell over themselves to recant the naïve and impractical ideals of their former liberalism. They learned a new "realism" at Bismarck's school. "It does not become the German," wrote Treitschke, "to repeat the commonplaces of the apostles of peace . . . or to shut his eyes to the cruel truth that we live in an age of war."

The tale, as you can see, not only is boring and useless, it is rather sad. The backbone of German liberalism, never much to boast about, was now broken for good. Bismarck was no Nazi; he accomplished his ends with a minimum of bloodshed, in a diplomatic performance that has been justly admired ever since. But the heritage he left Germany was one of submission to the strong and decisive leader, faith in power, cynicism about political principles and contempt for public and parliamentary accountability. Brutality and force were rendered respectable, adorned with a certain mystique. The opposition always cringed in fear of being branded disloyal. The results eventually were tragic for Germany, and for the rest of the world.

But the young people are right; none of this has anything to do with us.

Reading and Interpreting

1. What does Steinfels believe about the value of history? How is the reader expected to take the sentence in the middle of the essay that the reader must be "convinced that none of these ridiculous goings-on has the slightest relevance to our own politics"; or how is he to interpret the final sentence of the essay?

2. Can you cite specific incidents of modern politics that parallel those described by Steinfels?

Writing Techniques

1. Describe how Steinfels uses narrative as a way of developing an argument. What does the essay suggest about the distinctions among narration, description, argument, and exposition as discrete categories of writing?

2. What is the proposition Steinfels states and then asserts at the end that he has proved? Is this proposition to be taken as ironic? You may wish to keep this essay in mind for further consideration after discussions of point of view in Section VI.

3. The essay develops as a series of incidents, with a comment on the significance of each. Indicate the divisions of the essay produced by this technique.

Word Study

Notice the kinds of words Steinfels uses. Are they longer or shorter than those in most of the earlier selections? Are they more general or more specific. Does the character of the words seem to reflect the way Steinfels writes, or might it also have something to do with the subject, with argument as against narration or description? In this connection you may want to compare the choice of words in the story about Bismarck toward the end of the essay with the first two paragraphs.

As you may recognize, many of the words Steinfels uses come from Latin or Greek. Such words make much use of prefixes and suffixes. Look up in your dictionary the following words from the first two paragraphs and make a list of the prefixes and suffixes they utilize. Be sure you know what each of them means. Notice how the meaning of the prefix enters into the use of the word in English. (You will find that the same affix may be spelled in more than one way; in the list below, *in-* and *ir-* are the same prefix, as are *com-* and *con-*.)

recently	complaints	interested	sufficiently
irrelevant	connection	absolutely	significant
general	conclusions	undertake	intellectual
civilization	unthinkable	political	obviously

Suggestions for Writing

Try using Steinfels' method for writing an essay about some discipline that has been questioned—for example, creative writing, philosophy, art, chemistry, foreign languages, space travel, home economics. Or adapt it to a comment on a statement like one of the "self-evident truths" of the Declaration of Independence.

WHO KILLED KING KONG?   17
X. J. Kennedy

X. J. Kennedy, *of Tufts University, is best known as a poet and an editor of poetry, but he has also written biography and criticism, including* Mark Twain's Frontiers *(1963). This discussion appeared in* Dissent.

THE ordeal and spectacular death of King Kong, the giant ape, undoubtedly have been witnessed by more Americans than have ever seen a performance of *Hamlet, Iphigenia at Aulis,* or even *Tobacco Road.* Since RKO-Radio Pictures first released *King Kong,* a quarter-century has gone by; yet year after year, from prints that grow more rain-beaten, from sound tracks that grow more tinny, ticket-buyers by thousands still pursue Kong's luckless fight against the forces of technology, tabloid journalism, and the DAR. They see him chloroformed to sleep, see him whisked from his jungle isle to New York and placed on show, see him burst his chains to roam the city (lugging a frightened blonde), at last to plunge from the spire of the Empire State Building, machine-gunned by model airplanes.

Though Kong may die, one begins to think this legend unkillable. No clearer proof of his hold upon the popular imagination may be seen than what emerged one catastrophic week in March 1955, when New York WOR-TV programmed *Kong* for seven evenings in a row (a total of sixteen showings). Many a rival network vice-president must have scowled when surveys showed that *Kong*—the 1933 B-picture—had lured away fat segments of the viewing populace from such powerful *fat segments* competitors as Ed Sullivan, Groucho Marx and Bishop Sheen.

But even television has failed to run *King Kong* into oblivion. Coffee-in-the-lobby cinemas still show the old hunk of hokum, with the apology that in its use of composite shots and animated models the film remains technically interesting. And no other monster in movie history has won so devoted a popular audience. None of the plodding mummies, the stultified draculas, the white-coated Lugosis with their shiny pinball-machine laboratories, none of the invisible stranglers, berserk robots, or menaces from Mars has ever enjoyed so many resurrections.

Why does the American public refuse to let King Kong rest in peace? It is true, I'll admit, that *Kong* outdid every monster movie be- *monster* fore or since in sheer carnage. Producers Cooper and Schoedsack *movie* crammed into it dinosaurs, headhunters, riots, aerial battles, bullets, bombs, bloodletting. Heroine Fay Wray, whose function is mainly to scream, shuts her mouth for hardly one uninterrupted minute from first reel to last. It is also true that *Kong* is larded with good healthy *reel* sadism, for those whose joy it is to see the frantic girl dangled from cliffs and harried by pterodactyls. But it seems to me that the abiding appeal of the giant ape rests on other foundations.

Kong has, first of all, the attraction of being manlike. His simian nature gives him one huge advantage over giant ants and walking vegetables in that an audience may conceivably identify with him. Kong's appeal has the quality that established the Tarzan series as American myth—for what man doesn't secretly image himself a huge hairy *myth* howler against whom no other monster has a chance? If Tarzan recalls the ape in us, then Kong may well appeal to that great-granddaddy primordial brute from whose tribe we have all deteriorated.

Intentionally or not, the producers of *King Kong* encourage this identification by etching the character of Kong with keen sympathy.   *etching*
For the ape is a figure in a tradition familiar to moviegoers: the tradition of the pitiable monster. We think of Lon Chaney in the role of Quasimodo, of Karloff in the original *Frankenstein*. As we watch the Frankenstein monster's fumbling and disastrous attempts to befriend a flower-picking child, our sympathies are enlisted with the monster in his impenetrable loneliness. And so with Kong. As he roars in his chains, while barkers sell tickets to boobs who gape at him, we perhaps feel something more deep than pathos. We begin to sense something of the problem that engaged Eugene O'Neill in *The Hairy Ape:* the dilemma of a displaced animal spirit forced to live in a   *spirit*
jungle built by machines.

King Kong, it is true, had special relevance in 1933. Landscapes of the depression are glimpsed early in the film when an impresario, seeking some desperate pretty girl to play the lead in a jungle movie, visits souplines and a Woman's Home Mission. In Fay Wray — who's been caught snitching an apple from a fruitstand — his search is ended. When he gives her a big feed and a movie contract, the girl is magic-carpeted out of the world of the National Recovery Act. And when, in the film's climax, Kong smashes that very Third Avenue landscape in which Fay had wandered hungry, audiences of 1933 may well have felt a personal satisfaction.

What is curious is that audiences of 1960 remain hooked. For in the heart of urban man, one suspects, lurks the impulse to fling a bomb. Though machines speed him to the scene of his daily grind, though IBM comptometers ("freeing the human mind from drudgery") enable him to drudge more efficiently once he arrives, there comes a moment when he wishes to turn upon his machines and kick hell out of them. He wants to hurl his combination radio-alarm-clock out the bedroom window and listen to its smash. What subway commuter wouldn't love — just for once — to see the downtown express smack head-on into the uptown local? Such a wish is gratified in that memorable scene in *Kong* that opens with a wide-angle shot: interior of a railway car on the Third Avenue El. Straphangers are nodding, the literate refold their newspapers. Unknown to them, Kong has torn away a section of trestle toward which the train now speeds. The motorman spies Kong up ahead, jams on the brakes. Passengers hurtle together like so many peas in a pail. In a window of the car appear Kong's bloodshot eyes. Women shriek. Kong picks up the railway car as if it were a rat, flips it to the street and ties knots in it, or something. To any commuter the scene must appear one of the most satisfactory pieces of celluloid ever exposed.   *celluloid*
Yet however violent his acts, Kong remains a gentleman. Re-

markable is his sense of chivalry. Whenever a fresh boa constrictor threatens Fay, Kong first sees that the lady is safely parked, then manfully thrashes her attacker. (And she, the ingrate, runs away every time his back is turned.) Atop the Empire State Building, ignoring his pursuers, Kong places Fay on a ledge as tenderly as if she were a dozen eggs. He fondles her, then turns to face the Army Air Force. And Kong is perhaps the most disinterested lover since Cyrano: his attentions to the lady are utterly without hope of reward. After all, between a five-foot blonde and a fifty-foot ape, love can hardly be more than an intellectual flirtation. In his simian way King Kong is the hopelessly yearning lover of Petrarchan convention. His forced exit from his jungle, in chains, results directly from his single-minded pursuit of Fay. He smashes a Broadway theater when the notion enters his dull brain that the flashbulbs of photographers somehow endanger the lady. His perilous shinnying up a skyscraper to pluck Fay from her boudoir is an act of the kindliest of hearts. He's impossible to discourage even though the love of his life can't lay eyes on him without shrieking murder.

The tragedy of King Kong then, is to be the beast who at the end of the fable fails to turn into the handsome prince. This is the conviction that the scriptwriters would leave with us in the film's closing line. As Kong's corpse lies blocking traffic in the street, the entrepreneur who brought Kong to New York turns to the assembled reporters and proclaims: "That's your story, boys—it was Beauty killed the Beast!" But greater forces than those of the screaming Lady have combined to lay Kong low, if you ask me. Kong lives for a time as one of those persecuted near-animal souls bewildered in the middle of an industrial order, whose simple desires are thwarted at every turn. He climbs the Empire State Building because in all New York it's the closest thing he can find to the clifftop of his jungle isle. He dies, a pitiful dolt, and the army brass and publicity-men cackle *cackle* over him. His death is the only possible outcome to as neat a tragic dilemma as you can ask for. The machine-guns do him in, while the manicured human hero (a nice clean Dartmouth boy) carries away Kong's sweetheart to the altar. O, the misery of it all. There's far more truth about upper-middle-class American life in *King Kong* than in the last seven dozen novels of John P. Marquand.

A Negro friend from Atlanta tells me that in movie houses in colored neighborhoods throughout the South, *Kong* does a constant business. They show the thing in Atlanta at least every year, presumably to the same audiences. Perhaps this popularity may simply be due to the fact that Kong is one of the most watchable movies ever constructed, but I wonder whether Negro audiences may not find some archetypical appeal in this serio-comic tale of a huge black powerful free spirit whom all the hardworking white policemen are out to kill.

Every day in the week on a screen somewhere in the world, King Kong relives his agony. Again and again he expires on the Empire State Building, as audiences of the devout assist his sacrifice. We watch him die, and by extension kill the ape within our bones, but these little deaths of ours occur in prosaic surroundings. We do not die on a tower, New York before our feet, nor do we give our lives to smash a few flying machines. It is not for us to bring to a momentary standstill the civilization in which we move. King Kong does this for us. And so we kill him again and again, in much-spliced celluloid, while the ape in us expires from day to day, obscure, in desperation.

Reading and Interpreting

1. In the general introduction to this section it was suggested that the subject of this article about a fictional gorilla—if he is a gorilla—may be as serious as Jefferson's subject, which involves such concepts as liberty and justice. Can you find any justification for such a thesis?

2. At this writing, broadcasters try feverishly, making a new set of attempts each year, to find some pattern of programming that moralists and critics will approve and viewers will watch. Thus far they have been notably unsuccessful. What can one infer from this? Is modern television as revealing as Kennedy believes *King Kong* was?

Writing Techniques

1. In what sense is this piece argument? Surely not in the same way as the Declaration of Independence, which follows formal patterns. You might describe it as a pleasant blend of exposition, narration, and description that near the end is turned toward an argumentative purpose. Could you provide details for such a characterization?

2. How would you describe the tone of this piece? And could you account for it? Superficially the piece is chatty; does this seeming nonchalance obscure a carefully worked out organization, or is the piece as loose as at first it appears?

3. Kennedy finishes his opening sentence by referring to three specific plays rather than making a general comment such as "... a performance of more highly regarded popular dramas." Find five other instances in which Kennedy uses specifics to make a general point.

Word Study

Most common words have more than one use. They may have dozens. Usually, we guess from the context which use is intended in any instance, although a reader with a weak vocabulary may misunderstand a sentence or a whole paragraph through choosing the wrong use. According to a joke, a computer translated the passage, "The spirit is willing, but the flesh is weak," as "The Scotch is all right, but the steak is rotten." If that actually happened, the machine had chosen the wrong use for a number of words. Below are words and phrases that have more than one use. You probably chose the right one, and hence understood the sentence; now, using your dictionary, find other uses for the word, which would have given the sentence a different meaning or changed the whole into nonsense: *fat segments, monster movie, reel, myth, etching, spirit, celluloid, cackle.*

Suggestion for Writing

Write an essay in which you try to account for the popularity of something—a specific film, a soap opera, a detective novel, a television program, a kind of advertising, a sport like professional basketball or football.

A MODEST PROPOSAL
Jonathan Swift

18

As an established figure in English literature, **Jonathan Swift** (1667–1745) may need little introduction, but few men of whom we know so much have remained so enigmatic. Early in his life he was an intellectual maverick, enamored of a charming woman, but he died a bachelor, Dean of St. Patrick's Cathedral in Dublin. A Modest Proposal is only one of his satires, which include some of the bitterest in the language.

A MODEST PROPOSAL For Preventing the Children of Poor People From Being a Burthen to Their Parents or Country, and for Making Them Beneficial to the Public.

It is a melancholy object to those who walk through this great town, or travel in the country, when they see the streets, the roads, and cabin-doors crowded with beggars of the female sex, followed by three, four, or six children, *all in rags,* and importuning every passenger for an alms. These mothers, instead of being able to work for their honest livelihood, are forced to employ all their time in strolling, to beg sustenance for their helpless infants, who, as they grow up, either turn thieves for want of work, or leave their dear Native Country to fight for the Pretender in Spain, or sell themselves to the Barbadoes.

I think it is agreed by all parties that this prodigious number of children, in the arms, or on the backs, or at the heels of their mothers, and frequently of their fathers, is in the present deplorable state of the kingdom a very great additional grievance; and therefore whoever could find out a fair, cheap, and easy method of making these children sound useful members of the common-wealth would deserve so well of the public as to have his statue set up for a preserver of the nation.

Introduction describes a problem.

But my intention is very far from being confined to provide only for the children to professed beggars; it is of a much greater extent, and shall take in the whole number of infants at a certain age who are born of parents in effect as little able to support them as those who demand our charity in the streets.

As to my own part, having turned my thoughts, for many years, upon this important subject, and maturely weighed the several schemes of other projectors, I have always found them grossly mistaken in their computation. It is true a child, just dropped from its dam, may be supported by her milk for a solar year with little other nourishment, at most not above the value of two shillings, which the mother may certainly get, or the value in scraps, by her lawful occupation of begging, and it is exactly at one year old that I propose to provide for them, in such a manner as, instead of being a charge upon their parents, or the parish, or wanting food and raiment for the rest of their lives, they shall, on the contrary, contribute to the feeding and partly to the clothing of many thousands.

Advantages of proposal cited without revealing what it is.

There is likewise another great advantage in my scheme, that it will prevent those voluntary abortions, and that horrid practice of women murdering their bastard children, alas, too frequent among us, sacrificing the poor innocent babes, I doubt, more to avoid the expense than the shame, which would move tears and pity in the most savage and inhuman breast.

The number of souls in this kingdom being usually reckoned one million and a half, of these I calculate there may be about two hundred thousand couple whose wives are breeders, from which number I subtract thirty thousand couple who are able to maintain their own children, although I apprehend there cannot be so many under the present distresses of the kingdom, but this being granted, there will remain an hundred and seventy thousand breeders. I again subtract fifty thousand for those women who miscarry, or whose children die by accident or disease within a year. There only remain an hundred and twenty thousand children of poor parents annually born: The question therefore is, how this number shall be reared, and provided for, which, as I have already said, under the present situation of affairs, is utterly impossible by all the methods hitherto proposed, for we can neither employ them in handicraft, or agriculture; we neither build houses (I mean in the country), nor cultivate land: they can very seldom pick up a livelihood by stealing till they arrive at six years old, except where they are of towardly parts, although I confess they learn the rudiments much earlier, during which time they can however be properly looked upon only as *probationers*, as I have been informed by a principal gentleman in the County of Cavan, who protested to me that he never knew above one or two instances under the age of six, even in a part of the kingdom so renowned for the quickest proficiency in that art.

If this is a fair sample, has word choice changed in 250 years?

I am assured by our merchants that a boy or girl, before twelve years old, is no saleable commodity, and even when they come to this age, they will not yield above three pounds, or three pounds and half-a-crown at most on the Exchange, which cannot turn to account either to the parents or the kingdom, the charge of nutriment and rags having been at least four times that value.

I shall now therefore humbly propose my own thoughts, which I hope will not be liable to the least objection.

I have been assured by a very knowing American of my acquaintance in London, that a young healthy child well nursed is at a year old a most delicious, nourishing, and wholesome food, whether stewed, roasted, baked, or boiled, and I make no doubt that it will equally serve in a fricasse, or a ragout.

I do therefore humbly offer it to public consideration, that of the hundred and twenty thousand children already computed, twenty thousand may be reserved for breed, whereof only one fourth part to be males, which is more than we allow to sheep, black-cattle, or swine; and my reason is that these children are seldom the fruits of marriage, a circumstance not much regarded by our savage, therefore one male will be sufficient to serve four females. That the remaining hundred thousand may at a year old be offered in sale to the persons of quality, and fortune, through the kingdom, always advising the mother to let them suck plentifully in the last month, so as to render them plump, and fat for a good table. A child will make two dishes at an entertainment for friends, and when the family dines alone, the fore or hind quarters will make a reasonable dish, and seasoned with a little pepper or salt will be very good boiled on the fourth day, especially in winter.

The proposal.

I have reckoned upon a medium, that a child just born will

weigh 12 pounds, and in a solar year if tolerably nursed increaseth to 28 pounds.

Details worked out seriously.

I grant this food will be somewhat dear, and therefore very proper for landlords, who, as they have already devoured most of the parents, seem to have the best title to the children.

Infant's flesh will be in season throughout the year, but more plentiful in March, and a little before and after, for we are told by a grave author, an eminent French physician, that fish being a prolific diet, there are more children born in Roman Catholic countries about nine months after Lent than at any other season; therefore reckoning a year after Lent, the markets will be more glutted than usual, because the number of Popish infants is at least three to one in this kingdom, and therefore it will have one other collateral advantage by lessening the number of Papists among us.

I have already computed the charge of nursing a beggar's child (in which list I reckon all cottagers, labourers, and four-fifths of the farmers) to be about two shillings *per annum,* rags included, and I believe no gentleman would repine to give ten shillings for the carcass of a good fat child, which, as I have said, will make four dishes of excellent nutritive meat, when he hath only some particular friend or his own family to dine with him. Thus the Squire will learn to be a good landlord, and grow popular among his tenants, the mother will have eight shillings net profit, and be fit for work till she produces another child.

Those who are more thrifty (as I must confess the times require) may flay the carcass; the skin of which, artificially dressed, will make admirable gloves for ladies, and summer boots for fine gentlemen.

What is the meaning of *shambles* here?

As to our City of Dublin, shambles may be appointed for this purpose, in the most convenient parts of it, and butchers we may be assured will not be wanting, although I rather recommend buying the children alive, and dressing them hot from the knife, as we do roasting pigs.

A very worthy person, a true lover of this country, and whose virtues I highly esteem, was lately pleased, in discoursing on this matter, to offer a refinement upon my scheme. He said that many gentlemen of this kingdom, having of late destroyed their deer, he conceived that the want of venison might be well supplied by the bodies of young lads and maidens, not exceeding fourteen years of age, nor under twelve, so great a number of both sexes in every country being now ready to starve, for want of work and service: and these to be disposed of by their parents if alive, or otherwise by their nearest relations. But with due deference to so excellent a friend, and so deserving a patriot, I cannot be altogether in his sentiments; for as to the males, my American acquaintance assured me from frequent experience that their flesh was generally tough and lean, like that of

A variation rejected as impractical.

our schoolboys, by continual exercise, and their taste disagreeable, and to fatten them would not answer the charge. Then as to the females, it would, I think with humble submission, be a loss to the public, because they soon would become breeders themselves: And besides, it is not improbable that some scrupulous people might be apt to censure such a practice (although indeed very unjustly) as a little bordering upon cruelty, which, I confess, hath always been with me the strongest objection against any project, however so well intended.

But in order to justify my friend, he confessed that this expedient was put into his head by the famous Psalmanazer, a native of the island Formosa, who came from thence to London, above twenty years ago, and in conversation told my friend that in his country when any young person happened to be put to death, the executioner sold the carcass to persons of quality, as a prime dainty, and that, in his time, the body of a plump girl of fifteen, who was crucified for an attempt to poison the emperor, was sold to his Imperial Majesty's Prime Minister of State, and other great Mandarins of the Court, in joints from the gibbet, at four hundred crowns. Neither indeed can I deny that if the same use were made of several plump young girls in this town, who, without one single groat to their fortunes, cannot stir abroad without a chair, and appear at the playhouse, and assemblies in foreign fineries, which they never will pay for, the kingdom would not be the worse.

Some persons of a desponding spirit are in great concern about that vast number of poor people, who are aged, diseased, or maimed, and I have been desired to employ my thoughts what course may be taken to ease the nation of so grievious an encumbrance. But I am not in the least pain upon that matter, because it is very well known that they are every day dying, and rotting, by cold, and famine, and filth, and vermin, as fast as can be reasonably expected. And as to the younger labourers they are now in almost as hopeful a condition. They cannot get work, and consequently pine away for want of nourishment, to a degree, that if at any time they are accidentally hired to common labour, they have not strength to perform it; and thus the country and themselves are happily delivered from the evils to come.

Does a different sort of satire enter here?

I have too long digressed, and therefore shall return to my subject. I think the advantages by the proposal which I have made are obvious and many, as well as of the highest importance.

For first, as I have already observed, it would greatly lessen the number of Papists, with whom we are yearly over-run, being the principal breeders of the nation, as well as our most dangerous enemies, and who stay at home on purpose with a design to deliver the kingdom to the Pretender, hoping to take their advantage by the absence of so many good Protestants, who have chosen rather to leave

Advantages of proposal formally summarized.

their country than stay at home, and pay tithes against their conscience to an Episcopal curate.

Secondly, the poorer tenants will have something valuable of
their own, which by law be made liable to distress, and help to pay
their landlord's rent, their corn and cattle being already seized and
money a thing unknown.

Thirdly, Whereas the maintenance of an hundred thousand children, from two years old, and upwards, cannot be computed at less
than ten shillings a piece *per annum,* the nation's stock will be
thereby increased fifty thousand pounds *per annum,* besides the
profit of a new dish, introduced to the tables of all gentlemen of fortune in the kingdom, who have any refinement in taste, and the
money will circulate among ourselves, the goods being entirely of our
own growth and manufacture.

Fourthly, The constant breeders, besides the gain of eight shillings sterling *per annum,* by the sale of their children, will be rid of
the charge of maintaining them after the first year.

Fifthly, This food would likewise bring great custom to taverns,
where the vintners will certainly be so prudent as to procure the best
receipts for dressing it up to perfection, and consequently have their
houses frequented by all the fine gentlemen, who justly value themselves upon their knowledge in good eating; and a skillful cook, who
understands how to oblige his guests, will contrive to make it as expensive as they please.

Sixthly, This would be a great inducement to marriage, which
all wise nations have either encouraged by rewards, or enforced by
laws and penalties. It would increase the care and tenderness of
mothers toward their children, when they were sure of a settlement
for life, to the poor babes, provided in some sort by the public to
their annual profit instead of expense. We should see an honest emu-
lation among the married women, which of them could bring the fat-
test child to the market, men would become as fond of their wives,
during the time of their pregnancy, as they are now of their mares in
foal, their cows in calf, or sows when they are ready to farrow, nor
offer to beat or kick them (as it is too frequent a practice) for fear of a
miscarriage.

Many other advantages might be enumerated: For instance, the
addition of some thousand carcasses in our exportation of barrelled
beef; the propagation of swine's flesh, and improvement in the art of
making good bacon, so much wanted among us by the great destruction of pigs, too frequent at our tables, which are no way comparable
in taste or magnificence to a well-grown, fat yearling child, which
roasted whole will make a considerable figure at a Lord Mayor's
feast, or any other public entertainment. But this and many others I
omit, being studious of brevity.

What does *made liable to distress* mean?

What is the impact of terms like "fat yearling child"?

Supposing that one thousand families in this city would be constant customers for infants' flesh, besides others who might have it at merry-meetings, particularly weddings and christenings, I compute that Dublin would take off annually about twenty thousand carcasses, and the rest of the kingdom (where probably they will be sold somewhat cheaper) the remaining eighty thousand.

I can think of no one objection that will possibly be raised against this proposal, unless it should be urged that the number of people will be thereby much lessened in the kingdom. This I freely own, and it was indeed one principal design in offering it to the world. I desire the reader will observe, that I calculate my remedy for this one individual *Kingdom of Ireland, and for no other that ever was, is, or I think, ever can be upon earth.* Therefore let no man talk to me of other expedients: *Of taxing our absentees at five shillings a pound: Of using neither clothes, nor household furniture, except what is of our own growth and manufacture: Of utterly rejecting the materials and instruments that promote foreign luxury: Of curing the expensiveness of pride, vanity, idleness, and gaming in our women: Of introducing a vein of parsimony, prudence, and temperance: Of learning to love our Country, wherein we differ even from* **Laplanders**, *and the inhabitants of* **Topinamboo**: *Of quitting our animosities and factions, nor act any longer like the Jews, who were murdering one another at the very moment their city was taken: Of being a little cautious not to sell our country and consciences for nothing: Of teaching landlords to have at least one degree of mercy toward their tenants. Lastly, of putting a spirit of honesty, industry, and skill into our shopkeepers, who, if a resolution could now be taken to buy only our native goods, would immediately unite to cheat and exact upon us in the price, the measure, and the goodness, nor could ever yet be brought to make one fair proposal of just dealing, though often and earnestly invited to it.*

Therefore I repeat, let no man talk to me of these and the like expedients, till he hath at least some glimpse of hope that there will ever be some hearty and sincere attempt to put them in practice.

But as to myself, having been wearied out for many years with offering vain, idle, visionary thoughts, and at length utterly despairing of success, I fortunately fell upon this proposal, which as it is wholly new, so it hath something solid and real, of no expense and little trouble, full in our own power, and whereby we can incur no danger in *disobliging* England. For this kind of commodity will not bear exportation, the flesh being too tender a consistence to admit a long continuance in salt, *although perhaps I could name a country which would be glad to eat up our whole nation without it.*

After all I am not so violently bent upon my own opinion as to reject any offer, proposed by wise men, which shall be found equally innocent, cheap, easy, and effectual. But before something of that

In Swift's day these details were timely. Why?

What country?

kind shall be advanced in contradiction to my scheme, and offering a better, I desire the author, or authors, will be pleased maturely to consider two points. First, as things now stand, how they will be able to find food and raiment for an hundred thousand useless mouths and backs. And secondly, there being a round million of creatures in human figure, throughout this kingdom, whose whole subsistence put into a common stock would leave them in debt two millions of pounds sterling; adding those, who are beggars by profession, to the bulk of farmers, cottagers, and labourers with their wives and children, who are beggars in effect. I desire those politicians, who dislike my overture, and may perhaps be so bold to attempt an answer, that they will first ask the parents of these mortals whether they would not at this day think it a great happiness to have been sold for food at a year old, in the manner I prescribe, and thereby have avoided such a perpetual scene of misfortunes as they have since gone through, by the oppression of landlords, the impossibility of paying rent without money or trade, the want of common sustenance, with neither house nor clothes to cover them from the inclemencies of the weather, and the most inevitable prospect of entailing the like, or greater miseries upon their breed for ever.

An eighteenth-century opinion poll. Does Swift trust it?

I profess in the sincerity of my heart that I have not the least personal interest in endeavoring to promote this necessary work, having no other motive than the *public good of my country, by advancing our trade, providing for infants, relieving the poor, and giving some pleasure to the rich.* I have no children by which I can propose to get a single penny; the youngest being nine years old, and my wife past childbearing.

Why this final paragraph?

Reading and Interpreting

1. What is the serious purpose of Swift's argument? What is the significance for this purpose of the list of "other expedients" in the fifth paragraph from the end?

2. When do you first realize in reading the essay that it is ironic? What is the effect in the early paragraphs of phrases like "dropped from its dam" and "no saleable commodity" in referring to children or "breeders" to refer to women?

Writing Techniques

1. Analyze the organization of the essay; can you discover a planned order for the material? Is there also an order in the development of the emotional impact of the essay?

2. The piece is obviously satire; does it also get some of its effects by parody—that is, by imitating and ridiculing another kind of writing?

3. In what ways are Carlson and Steinfels, in readings number 15 and 16, using techniques like those of Swift?

Word Study

One of the glosses suggested that the use of words had changed in the last 250 years. You probably noticed in that paragraph that Swift uses the singular *couple* where you would use *couples*. You probably would not say that a child who was a deft thief was *of towardly parts*, not even in satire. Nor would you be likely to use the combinations *quickest proficiency* and *situation of affairs*. Using your dictionary, be sure you know what these terms mean as Swift employs them. Now notice four other words or phrases in the essay that you are not sure of, and identify the meaning Swift intends.

Suggestions for Writing

You may be lucky enough never to have seen any of the kind of misery and indifference that infuriated Swift, but you probably know about situations in our own society that you feel need reform: life in some inner-city ghettos, the circumstances of some migrant workers, or conditions in some undeveloped parts of the world. Or you may have opinions about some other situations that need changing: integrity in some governmental unit, pollution of waterways or wilderness areas in America, or a college curriculum. Write an essay advocating some reform. You may wish to do it straight, seriously and directly presenting arguments for change. Or you may have an idea for writing it satirically, using techniques like those of Carlson or Swift. You might even want to try it both ways, comparing the results.

Exposition: Helping People Understand

The world is a question mark. And the universe is a still bigger question mark. One definition of being human might be: man is that creature who knows enough and has brains enough to see that nobody has ever explained the world or himself.

Life is full of questions. Children pester their parents with them: Why do I have to go to bed? Why are so many cats black and none of them green? Who made water wet? Nor are questions limited to small children. The most competent physician is likely to tell you that the more he learns about disease, the less he is able to explain it. The most learned scientist is likely to tell you that the more he discovers, the more he raises questions he cannot answer.

But man can be defined also as the kind of creature who attempts to find and to phrase answers. The result is what is called *exposition,* the serious attempt to explain. It is one of the most common kinds of writing, and the more complex modern society becomes, the more we must use it and rely on it.

It is the stuff you are reading right now. All textbooks are by nature exposition. Reports use exposition, although they may use description and other types of writing as well. Much of what students say when they compose answers is exposition. Even a biography or an autobiography—ostensibly narrative—may be at

least partly exposition in purpose and development. In his
Autobiography Jean Jacques Rousseau told about his life, so he said,
because he wanted to explain what kind of person he was. Even little
masterpieces like the Sermon on the Mount and the Gettysburg
Address could be called expositions, insofar as they are not lyric
poetry.

If you want the course you are taking to be practical, you may
care to study how writers get the effects they want with exposition.
Most of the people who make up the college curricula believe that
students need skill in exposition. You need it to understand your
courses, and to do the writing associated with courses. And you will
need it after you have been graduated: professional people, business
executives, social and political leaders deal all the time with
expository composition, written and oral. The course you are taking
now, however much it may make of narration and description, even
of argument, may be aimed in the end at showing you how to handle
exposition.

This may be another way of saying that exposition makes
extensive use of the other three forms. Even though your purpose is
to explain, you may find that you can explain best by telling what
happened. We have already seen that narration is more or less built
of sequential description. And description can appear directly in
exposition. Once we see something clearly, see how it works, can
picture its parts and its uses, explanation may become obvious. You
may have had the experience of arguing with yourself, being devil's
advocate for first one side and then the other, hoping that a good
argument would lead to the best explanation.

Expositions complete the first of the three main parts of this
book. You may find that the selections in this section serve well to
tie this part of the book together and, to continue the figure, to wrap
it up. Consider how much, and in what ways, each of the four forms
of discourse—narration, description, argument, and exposition—
enters into the others, every form of writing taking part in every
other form. In all likelihood you can find examples of such
interreliances in this set of readings and your recollections of earlier
sets.

In viewing these interactions you are likely to be looking at the
forms of discourse as ways of writing, as well as the results from
purposes in writing. This is a world in which ends get all mixed up
with means, in which purposes engender devices, and devices
prompt purposes. Such fluidity is not least apparent in anything so
subtle and varied as the use of language and the creations of the
mind. But if an awareness of such interactions helps you to write
better and read more perceptively, well and good.

The following are brief expositions, or selections from longer essays.
a. Ambrose Bierce, *a minor maverick, who became for a time one of the most powerful of American editors, included this definition in* The Devil's Dictionary; **b. François Marie Arouet,** *called Voltaire, best known for the satirical novel* Candide, *wrote on kissing in the* Philosophical Dictionary *(1764);* **c.** *The* Report on Attorney General's Conference on Drug Abuse in Schools *appeared October 25 and 26, 1966;* **d. James Thurber** *was one of America's great humorists, especially identified with* The New Yorker, *where this example from* Fables for Our Time *first appeared;* **e. Urie Bronfenbrenner,** *psychologist, published his question in* The Language of Man *(1971);* **f. James Baldwin** *is one of the most distinguished writers on problems of blacks; this excerpt appeared in* Ebony; **g. Joseph Wood Krutch** *spent a vigorous lifetime as a New York critic, then retired to the southwestern desert and wrote as a desert naturalist, with descriptions like this from* The American Scholar; **h. William Faulkner** *is considered by many critics as America's finest novelist; the selection is from* The Reivers *(1962).*

a. Ambrose Bierce

LOVE, *n.* A temporary insanity curable by marriage or by removal of the patient from the influences under which he incurred the disorder. This disease, like *caries* and many other ailments, is prevalent only among civilized races living under artificial conditions; barbarous nations breathing pure air and eating simple food enjoy immunity from its ravages. It is sometimes fatal, but more frequently to the physician than to the patient.

b. Voltaire

KISSING—There was among the ancients I know not what of symbolic and sacred attached to the kiss, since one kissed the statues of the gods and their beards, when the sculptors had shown them with a beard. Initiates kissed each other at the mysteries of Ceres, as a sign of concord.

The early Christians, men and women, kissed each other on the mouth at their *agapæ*. This word signified "love-feast." They gave each other the holy kiss, the kiss of peace, the kiss of brother and sister, ἄγιον φίλημα. This custom lasted for more than four centuries, and was abolished at last on account of its consequences. It was these kisses of peace, these *agapæ* of love, these names of "brother" and "sister," that long drew to the little-know Christians, those imputations of debauchery with which the priests of Jupiter and the priestesses of Vesta charged them. You see in Petronius, and in other profane authors, that the libertines called themselves "brother" and "sister." It was thought that among the Christians the same names signified the same infamies. They were innocent accomplices in spreading these accusations over the Roman empire. ... In one of Shakespeare's tragedies called "Othello," this Othello, who is a black, gives two kisses to his wife before strangling her. That seems abominable to honourable people; but Shakespeare's partisans say it is beautifully natural.

c. Report on Attorney General's Conference on Drug Abuse in Schools and Colleges

ADMISSIONS for LSD-caused psychic problems were one every other month in 1964 and within the past year have increased to 15 to 20 per month. Ten million people are currently taking amphetamines and 20 million people are taking barbiturates. All of the LSD currently used is black market. There is no legal manufacture of the drug. Of the people using LSD, 40% were on other drugs in addition to LSD, and 30% on morphine. Some of these exist in a "chuckwagon" drug world where they are sampling a "smorgasbord" of drugs alternately.

d. James Thurber

The Sheep in Wolf's Clothing

NOT very long ago there were two sheep who put on wolf's clothing and went among the wolves as spies, to see what was going on. They arrived on a fete day, when all the wolves were singing in the taverns or dancing in the street. The first sheep said to his companion, "Wolves are just like us, for they gambol and frisk. Every day is fete day in Wolfland." He made some notes on a piece of paper (which a spy should never do) and he headed them "My Twenty-Four Hours in Wolfland," for he had decided not to be a spy any longer but to write a book on Wolfland and also some articles for the *Sheep's Home Companion.* The other sheep guessed what he was planning to do, so he slipped away and began to write a book called "My Ten Hours in Wolfland." The first sheep suspected what was up when he found his friend had gone, so he wired a book to his publisher called "My Five Hours in Wolfland," and it was announced for publication first. The other sheep immediately sold his manuscript to a newspaper syndicate for serialization.

Both sheep gave the same message to their fellows: wolves were just like sheep, for they gambolled and frisked, and every day was fete day in Wolfland. The citizens of Sheepland were convinced by all this, so they drew in their sentinels and they let down their barriers. When the wolves descended on them one night, howling and slavering, the sheep were as easy to kill as flies on a windowpane.

Moral: Dont' get it right, just get it written.

e.   Urie Bronfenbrenner

A few weeks ago I was showing some photographs I had taken in Russia to a class of fifth and sixth graders in an American school. Most of the children came from middle class faculty and professional families. Among my pictures were a number of shots of roads lined with young trees.

A child's hand went up:
"Why do they have trees along the road?"

A bit puzzled, I turned the question back to the class:
"Why do you suppose they have trees?"

Another child's hand rose for eager answer:
"So that people won't be able to see what's going on beyond the road."

A girl had a different idea,
"It's to make work for the prisoners."

I asked why some of *our* roads have trees planted along the side.

"For shade," the children said.
"To keep the dust down."

Where did the children get the idea that the Russians have different reasons than we have for planting trees?

f. James Baldwin

I have often wondered, and it is not a pleasant wonder, just what white Americans talk about with one another. I wonder this because they do not, after all, seem to find very much to say to *me,* and I concluded long ago that they found the color of my skin inhibitory. This color seems to operate as a most disagreeable mirror, and a great deal of one's energy is expended in reassuring white Americans that they do not see what *they* see. This is utterly futile, of course, since *they do* see what *they* see. And what they see is an appallingly oppressive and bloody history, known all over the world. What they see is a disastrous, continuing, present, condition which menaces them, and for which they bear an inescapable responsibility. But since, in the main, they appear to lack the energy to change this condition, they would rather not be reminded of it. Does this mean that, in their conversations with one another, they merely make reassuring sounds? It scarcely seems possible, and yet, on the other hand, it seems all too likely.

g. Joseph Wood Krutch

AS one observer has put it, if you see two [scorpions] together then they are either making love or one of them is being eaten. . . .

So far as I know no detailed account of the mating habits of the Arizona species has ever been published, but in a creature which varies so little they are probably the same as those described in Henri Fabre's classic account of the kind which live in Provence and also, more recently, of a Philippine species. Male and female stand face to face with their tails raised and their stings touching. The male takes his partner by the claw and then backs away, leading her with him. This holding of hands in a sort of dance may last for more than an hour, after which the couple disappears under a stone or into some other recess, the male walking backward as he conducts his partner. This sounds almost romantic and it probably does involve a sort of courtship. But the holding of hands is also probably necessary because creatures which are deaf and almost blind can't afford to lose one another once happy accident has brought them together. And though human lovers have been known on occasion to call one another "good enough to eat," we are likely to be shocked when the female scorpion takes this extravagant metaphor literally, as she frequently does.

h. William Faulkner

[*The old man who is the narrator in the novel interrupts a story about an accomplished mule for an expository discourse on intelligence, especially of mules and other animals.*]

A mule which will gallop for a half-mile in the single direction elected by its rider even one time becomes a neighborhood legend; one that will do it consistently time after time is an incredible phenomenon. Because, unlike a horse, a mule is far too intelligent to break its heart for glory running around the rim of a mile-long saucer. In fact, I rate mules second only to rats in intelligence, the mule followed in order by cats, dogs, and horses last—assuming of course that you accept my definition of intelligence: which is the ability to cope with environment: which means to accept environment yet still retain at least something of personal liberty.

The rat of course I rate first. He lives in your house without helping you to buy it or build it or repair it or keep the taxes paid; he eats what you eat without helping you raise it or buy it or even haul it into the house; you cannot get rid of him; were he not a cannibal, he would long since have inherited the earth. The cat is third, with some of the same qualities but a weaker, punier creature; he neither toils nor spins, he is a parasite on you but he does not love you; he would die, cease to exist, vanish from the earth (I mean, in his so-called domestic form) but so far he has not had to. (There is the fable, Chinese I think, literary I am sure: of a period on earth when the dominant creatures were cats: who after ages of trying to cope with the anguishes of mortality—famine, plague, war, injustice, folly, greed—in a word, civilised government—convened a congress of the wisest cat philosophers to see if anything could be done: who after long deliberation agreed that the dilemma, the problems themselves were insoluble and the only practical solution was to give it up, relinquish, abdicate, by selecting from among the lesser creatures a species, race optimistic enough to believe that the mortal predicament could be solved and ignorant enough never to learn better. Which is why the cat lives with you, is completely dependent on you for food and shelter but lifts no paw for you and loves you not; in a word, why your cat looks at you the way it does.)

The dog I rate fourth. He is courageous, faithful, monogamous in his devotion; he is your parasite too: his failure (as compared to the cat) is that he will work for you—I mean, willingly, gladly, ape any trick, no matter how silly, just to please you, for a pat on the head; as sound and first-rate a parasite as any, his failure is that he is a sycophant, believing that he has to show gratitude also; he will debase and violate his own dignity for your amusement; he fawns in return for a kick, he will give his life for you in battle and grieve himself to starvation over your bones. The horse I rate last. A creature capable of but one idea at a time, his strongest quality is timidity and fear. He can be tricked and cajoled by a child into breaking his limbs or his heart too in running too far too fast or jumping things too wide or hard or high; he will eat himself to death if not guarded like a baby; if he had only one gram of the intelligence of the most backward rat, he would be the rider.

The mule I rate second. But second only because you can make him work for you. But that too only within his own rigid self-set regulations. He will not permit himself to eat too much. He will draw a wagon or a plow, but he will not run a race. He will not try to jump anything he does not indubitably know beforehand he can jump; he will not enter any place unless he knows of his own knowledge what is on the other side; he will work for you patiently for ten years for the chance to kick you once. In a word, free of the obligations of ancestry and the responsibilities of posterity, he has conquered not only life but death too and hence is immortal; were he to vanish from the earth today, the same chanceful biological combination which produced him yesterday would produce him a thousand years hence, unaltered, unchanged incorrigible still within the limitations which he himself had proved and tested; still free, still coping.

Reading and Interpreting

1. Consider Bronfenbrenner's question about why Russians plant trees along the road. The professor writes as though he is puzzled as to the proper answer. Do you think he is? Or is he sure of the answer, but trying to get you to make the same answer yourself? Is there more than one possible answer?

2. Baldwin, a black, is deeply resentful of the treatment of his race in many parts of the world, including the United States. But you would probably not call him a militant; at least he is not recommending burning the White House or dynamiting the Statue of Liberty. He is, of course, a very intelligent, highly educated man. How would

you characterize his attitude? Does this attitude have any effect on the impact made by his paragraph?

3. Thurber offers a statement that he calls a moral. Do you think he means it? If not, what could he mean?

Writing Techniques

1. The introduction to this section suggests that a great variety of devices in writing can be used for exposition. Here are possible characterizations of one quality of each of the brief expositions, not in the order above. See if you can match them to the passages: (1) implied definition based on historical details; (2) logical conclusion from examples; (3) statistical details; (4) description of a typical example; (5) collected evidence leading to a question; (6) satirical moral drawn from fictitious narrative; (7) pretended definition, leading to satirical statement; (8) comparison and contrast.

2. Readers and listeners always want to know on what basis an author speaks, especially in exposition. But truth is hard to come by, and is usually not quite certain. Clearly, Krutch, among others, is weighing his evidence and trying to let his reader know how much this evidence can be trusted. What does he do to keep his reader quietly informed?

3. On what definition does the character from Faulkner's novel depend for his discussion of intelligence among animals? Could the discussion be classified as argument? Are the reasons for the ranking valid evidence? In what ways does the style of the passage seem like that of a person speaking rather than writing?

Suggestions for Writing

1. Try writing a "fable for our time." Before you do so, you will want to study Thurber's fable. If it is both good reading and good sense, what makes it so? Is the moral ironic? That is, does Thurber perhaps mean the opposite of what he says?

2. Consider the selection from Faulkner. Some psychologists say that the pig is the most intelligent barnyard animal, and anybody who has tried to keep a pig from going through a hole in a fence may be willing to agree, even by Faulkner's definition of intelligence. And some say that chickens are the most stupid, even stupider than geese. You might try to evaluate a bird or an animal. But if you do not know much about barnyards, try human beings. They are not as varied as animals, but some are brighter than others, and presumably

the more intelligent gravitate toward certain professions and occupations. Can you make some comments? You may need a definition of intelligence different from Faulkner's.

YOU COULD HAVE KNOCKED ME DOWN WITH A FENDER **20**
Goodman Ace

Goodman Ace *is one of the entertainment media's contributions to modern literature. He writes an occasional column, including this one, for the* Saturday Review *called "Top of My Head."*

LEO ROSTEN in his column in the January 12, 1974, issue of this magazine had this to say:

> A word about malapropisms. That word came into English *not* with Sheridan's character Mrs. Malaprop, in *The Rivals* (1775), . . . but a century earlier. *Malaprop* was coined by Dryden, and it happens to be erroneous, incorrect, and cockeyed. . . . The phrase *mal à propos* does not designate a comical misuse of words; it means not appropriate, not in season, not relevant. It does not mean what we use it for—*lapsus comicus,* as my . . . colleague in the Chaos Club, Felix Kaufmann, neatly dubbed it. . . .

Well, that shook me up. It also gave me pause. Also, it sent me to my dictionary. I would have gotten into this wrangle earlier, but I've been in bed with a bad case of lifting a heavy dictionary.

Besides, having been in the malaprop-writing business for the fifteen years when my wife, Jane, and I were the major stars of a minor radio program, "Easy Aces," I wanted to assemble my facts before disagreeing. I never cross my unabridges until I'm sure I'm on safe ground.

That mixed metaphor is widely and erroneously described as a malaprop. It isn't. In my book, the one I don't lift anymore, a malaprop is defined as "the use of a word sounding somewhat like the one intended, but ludicrously wrong in the context."

I could rest my case here. But I feel compelled to carry on, because here all these years I've been thinking I was malapropping, when according to Mr. Rosten's friend Mr. Kaufmann, I've been *lapsus comicusing.* (I like to use a newly found word in all its grammatical forms.)

There are those who refer to a malaprop as a pun. Not true. There is a fine distinction, which you will recognize in the definition

my English teacher gave us: "A pun is a word that is played upun."
There is no such word as *upun*. Repeating, I submit that a true malaprop must be an actual word with a meaning of its own even though
the meaning is out of context.

Amos 'n' Andy were often said to have used malaprops. False.
When Andy said, "I'se regusted," he was not using a malaprop.
There is no such word as *regusted* (and lately there is no such word
as *I'se*). As a pure example, I offer Jane's saying on radio that she
took a drive way downtown on the East Side: "I saw all those old
testament houses."

Or any of the following:

"You get up at the crank of dawn and don't talk to me, just sitting there being unspeakable."

"You can't tell a book by its lover."

"Marge and I are insufferable friends."

"Do you want me to strangle a couple of eggs for you?"

"I ate in a restaurant today, and the food was abdominal."

"Absinthe makes the heart grow fonder."

"Familiarity breeds attempt."

"Be it ever so hovel, there's no place like home."

"We had a baffle of wits."

"Home wasn't built in a day."

"Just explain it to me in words of one cylinder."

"Sure, I believe people should learn to live together. We're all
cremated equal."

"He's as old as Macushla."

"I think he's very sweet. That's my candied opinion."

"I didn't tell them who I was. I used a facetious name."

"At school I took a course in domestic silence."

"That's a wonderful picture of Abraham Lincoln, except that he
looks so thin and emancipated."

These are pure malaprops. If they were not, Mr. Rosten's colleague, Mr. Kaufmann, could have saved us this one-sided debate by
advising Mr. Sheridan, who wrote *The Rivals,* not to name his leading character Mrs. Malaprop but to call her Mrs. Lapsus Comicus.

Lapsus comicus is an apt description for "verbal boners" that do
not contain similar-sounding words. As an example, Mr. Rosten
quoted a statement made by Samuel Goldwyn: "A verbal contract is
not worth the paper it's written on." Or, as Jane used to say, "Love
makes the world go round together," adding a word to complement
the warmth of her statement.

These are two classic examples of *comicus lapsing,* when the
tongue trips lightly and hurriedly ahead of the speech figure formed
in a busy and cluttered mind, grasping at straws to make a point.

However, malapropisms or *lapsus comicusisms* notwithstanding, we used to call them Janeaceisms. A word that came into the language in 1930.

Reading and Interpreting

1. What is Goodman Ace explaining? How serious is his exposition? Would punsters you know accept his distinction between malapropism, *lapsus comicus,* and pun? For what purpose does he make the distinction?

Writing Techniques

1. In perhaps the most common pattern for exposition, the writer presents a proposition or question and then supports or illustrates it with examples. How much of Ace's piece uses this method?

2. How extensively is the piece developed by definition? Identify the definitions and comment on their validity.

3. Ace ends his essay with a sentence fragment. Would it have been better to attach it to the preceding sentence or to make it a complete sentence?

Suggestions for Writing

Ace says that Rosten's column sent him to his dictionary. The dictionary can provide ideas and materials for interesting writing. Try writing a paper about some aspect of language that interests you, using the dictionary for examples when it can be useful. There are innumerable possibilities—the history of a simple word like *hit* or *dig* or *tap* or a discussion of its various uses, dialect differences, common usage slips, palindromes, rhymes, spelling problems.

THE CONCURRENCE OF MYTH, OR LISTENING TO WORDS ALL THE WAY BACK
John Ciardi

21

John Ciardi *is best known as a lyric poet (more than a dozen volumes to date) and as poetry editor of the* Saturday Review, *for which he*

*also writes columns, including the one below. He has long been at work
on a verse translation of Dante's* Divine Comedy.

DAYS and their divisions are calculated from the earth's spin,
years from its orbit, and months from the moon (Anglo-Saxon *mona,*
moon; *monath,* month, from the same Germanic root). Our week,
however, is an erratic concept. The "week" of primitive societies varied from three to eight days and seems to have been related, not to
heavenly motions, but to market and trading days. In the language of
the Congo today, the same word serves for both "week" and "market."

The Egyptians probably started with a variable market week
and later named their days for the seven planets they knew about
(sun and moon included), starting with Saturn as the remotest and
then, in order of succession, Jupiter, Mars, the Sun, Mercury, Venus,
and the Moon. The Greeks did not calculate weeks. Nor did the Romans, until the reign of Theodosius at the end of the fourth century
A.D. When they did adopt the concept, they followed the basic Egyptian system, though naming their days in a different order: *dies solis,
dies lunae, dies Martis, dies Mercurii, dies Jovis, dies Veneris, dies Saturni.*

The early Teutons calculated a five-day week. When they
adopted the seven-day week from the Romans, they simply translated
dies solis as *sunnan dagaz* (Anglo-Saxon *sunnan daeg*), Sunday; and
dies lunae as *monnan dagaz* (Anglo-Saxon *monan daeg*), Monday. The
names of their original five days derive from lost myth, from the
Mesopotamian heartland in which earliest civilized man evolved
the Indo-European language that has provided the base for most of
the languages of the Middle East, Europe, and the Indian subcontinent. Simultaneously, early man was evolving the myths that un-
derlie most of our religions. The names of the five original Norse
weekdays, especially as compared with the names given the corresponding days on the Latin calendar, are full of clues to that lost
myth and its divergent evolutions. Of the five, Thursday (Thor's day
north and Jove's day south) and Saturday (named north and south for
Saturn) correspond exactly, testifying to some common cultural base.
The remaining three days suggest a more complicated story.

Tuesday is the Nordic day of Tiu and the Latin day of Mars.
Since both can be glossed as gods of war, the correspondence seems
neat enough, but only on the surface. The name Tiu derives from the
Indo-European root *diew-,* the base of Greek *theos,* Latin *deus,* Italian
dio, French *dieu,* and English *deity.* Try the variations of Tiu as *Tchiu,
Djieu,* join them to the root *p'te(r)-,* father, and Sanskrit *Dyaus pitar,*
Greek *Zeus pater,* and Latin *Jupiter* (earlier *Dies-piter*) all become ob-
viously related as variants of one name. The name Tiu once meant

"God," and not "a god" but "God the father of gods," the original Jahveh. *The Nordic people demoted their supreme deity to the status of war god.* But was it a demotion, or did they move him to the central place in their warlike culture? The question is for paleoethnologists and may be unanswerable. The point is that the roots of the language have remembered to ask it.

Wednesday is the Nordic day of Wodan, Wotan, Woden, Odin, and the Roman day of Mercury. But Wodan was the father god who replaced Tiu at the summit of Valhalla. What one-to-one connection can he have with Mercury, an important god, to be sure, but only a messenger boy by comparison with the Supreme Deity? There are no clues in the name Mercury: Its origins are lost in the silence of the Etruscans, and the Greek equivalent, Hermes, is untraceable. The one clue is that among the attributes of Mercury is emotional as well as physical volatility, a quality we still respond to when we speak of a "mercurial temperament." The name Wodan derives from the Indo-European root *wet-*, Germanic variant *wod-*, signifying "madness, devine madness, inspired frenzy." (Compare the obsolete English adjective *wood*—pronounced wod—meaning "mad.") The connection is a thin one, but myth leaves traces, not paved highways, and the trace cannot fail to suggest that in the complex evolution of the god-myths, Mercury and Wodan are related through some common ancestor.

Friday is Frigga's day in Norse and the day of Venus in Latin—another strange pairing. Frigga being the supreme mother of gods and Venus only the sub-goddess of love and beauty, a patronage assigned by Norse myth to the minor goddess Freya, or Freyja. But here the clues locked in the word roots are all but conclusive. The name Freyja is more than coincidentally similar to the name Frigga and must suggest that Freyja is a later and separate manifestation of attributes once associated with Frigga (the maturity of the god-mother and the assignment of her earlier role to a daughter). The theory itself is guesswork, but the confirming clue is at the root of the language: The Indo-European root of the name Frigga is *pri-*, to love.

In the beginning was the Word. And words, when we reach for all that is locked in them, still echo our beginning.

Reading and Interpreting

1. Ciardi's column, and that by Goodman Ace (number 20) have the same subject—words—but they differ in purpose. Describe this difference. Can you state any central thesis for Ciardi's column?

2. Why is Ciardi's column more or less interesting than Ace's?

3. How does Ciardi organize his essay?

Writing Techniques

1. Notice the last sentence in Ace's and Ciardi's columns. Does the difference throw any light on question 1, above?

2. How does Ciardi organize the fourth paragraph in order to present technical information clearly?

Word Study

Ciardi is a poet. Would you know it in his choice of words when he writes prose? Do you find his using supposedly "poetic" words such as *e'en* and *poesy*? Figures of speech characterize some verse. Do you find him making much use of figurative language? He uses some history. Where? And he uses etymology (be sure you know the meaning of this word). He is using the results of etymological study when he talks about the Indo-Europeans and when he relates Friday to the Goddess of Love, Venus. Would you say he is using etymology, also, when he discusses Tuesday? If Ciardi does not use "poetic" words, does he seem to have considerable knowledge of words, and a love for them?

Suggestions for Writing

Ace said that Rosten's column sent him to the dictionary. To what kind of books has Ciardi gone for his information? Try combining the kinds of books that Ciardi and Ace used into source material for a paper.

THE FINE ART OF PUTTING THINGS OFF
Michael Demarest

22

Michael Demarest *is an associate editor of* Time *magazine. The following article appeared in* Newsweek.

"NEVER put off till tomorrow," exhorted Lord Chesterfield in 1749, "what you can do today." That the elegant earl never got around to marrying his son's mother and had a bad habit of keeping worthies like Dr. Johnson cooling their heels for hours in an anteroom attests to the fact that even the most well-intentioned men have been postponers ever. Quintus Fabius Maximus, one of the great Roman generals, was dubbed *"Cunctator"* (Delayer) for putting off battle until the last possible *vinum* break. Moses pleaded a speech defect to rationalize his reluctance to deliver Jehovah's edicts to Pharaoh. Hamlet, of course, raised procrastination to an art form.

Examples provide an introduction.

The world is probably about evenly divided between delayers and do-it-nowers. There are those who prepare their income taxes in February, prepay mortgages and serve precisely planned dinners at an ungodly 6:30 P.M. The other half dine happily on leftovers at 9 or 10, misplace bills and file for an extension of the income tax deadline. They seldom pay credit-card bills until the apocalyptic voice of Diners threatens doom from Denver. They postpone, as Faustian encounters, visits to barbershop, dentist or doctor.

apocalyptic

Yet for all the trouble procrastination may incur, delay can often inspire and revive a creative soul. Jean Kerr, author of many successful novels and plays, says that she reads every soup-can and jam-jar label in her kitchen before settling down to her typewriter. Many a writer focuses on almost anything but his task — for example, on the Coast and Geodetic Survey of Maine's Frenchman Bay and Bar Harbor, stimulating his imagination with names like Googins Ledge, Blunts Pond, Hio Hill and Burnt Porcupine, Long Porcupine, Sheep Porcupine and Bald Porcupine islands.

focuses

From *Cunctator's* day until this century, the art of postponement had been virtually a monopoly of the military ("Hurry up and wait"), diplomacy and the law. In former times, a British proconsul faced with a native uprising could comfortably ruminate about the situation with Singapore Sling in hand. Blessedly, he had no nattering Telex to order in machine guns and fresh troops. A U.S. general as late as World War II could agree with his enemy counterpart to take a sporting day off, loot the villagers' chickens and wine and go back to battle a day later. Lawyers are among the world's most addicted postponers. According to Frank Nathan, a nonpostponing Beverly Hills insurance salesman, "The number of attorneys who die without a will is amazing."

ruminate

Even where there is no will, there is a way. There is a difference, of course, between chronic procrastination and purposeful postponement, particularly in the higher echelons of business. Corporate dynamics encourage the caution that breeds delay, says Richard Manderbach, Bank of America group vice president. He notes that speedy action can be embarrassing or extremely costly. The data explosion fortifies those seeking excuses for inaction — another report to be

A new thesis.

fortifies

read, another authority to be consulted. "There is always," says Manderbach, "a delicate edge between having enough information and too much."

His point is well taken. Bureaucratization, which flourished amid the growing burdens of government and the greater complexity of society, was designed to smother policymakers in blankets of legalism, compromise and reappraisal—and thereby prevent hasty decisions from being made. The centralization of government that led to Watergate has spread to economic institutions and beyond, making procrastination a worldwide way of life. Many languages are studded with phrases that refer to putting things off—from the Spanish *mañana* to the Arabic *bukra fil mishmish* (literally "tomorrow in apricots," more loosely "leave it for the soft spring weather when the apricots are blooming").

Notice the topic sentences. Are most of them long or short?

Academe also takes high honors in procrastination. Bernard Sklar, a University of Southern California sociologist who churns out three to five pages of writing a day, admits that "many of my friends go through agonies when they face a blank page. There are all sorts of rationalizations: the pressure of teaching, responsibilities at home, checking out the latest book, looking up another footnote."

Psychologists maintain that the most assiduous procrastinators are women, though many psychologists are (at $50-plus an hour) pretty good delayers themselves. Dr. Ralph Greenson, a U.C.L.A. professor of clinical psychiatry (and Marilyn Monroe's onetime shrink), takes a fairly gentle view of procrastination. "To many people," he says, "doing something, confronting, is the moment of truth. All frightened people will then avoid the moment of truth entirely, or evade or postpone it until the last possible moment." To Georgia State Psychologist Joen Fagan, however, procrastination may be a kind of subliminal way or sorting the important from the trivial. "When I drag my feet, there's usually some reason," says Fagan. "I feel it, but I don't yet know the real reason."

subliminal

In fact, there is a long and honorable history of procrastination to suggest that many ideas and decisions may well improve if postponed. It is something of a truism that to put off making a decision is itself a decision. The parliamentary process is essentially a system of delay and deliberation. So, for that matter, is the creation of a great painting, or an entrée, or a book, or a building like Blenheim Palace, which took the Duke of Marlborough's architects and laborers 15 years to construct. In the process, the design can mellow and marinate. Indeed, hurry can be the assassin of elegance. As T. H. White, author of *Sword in the Stone*, once wrote, time "is not meant to be devoured in an hour or a day, but to be consumed delicately and grad-

Conclusion echoes introduction.

marinate

ually and without haste." In other words, *pace* Lord Chesterfield, what you don't necessarily have to do today, by all means put off until tomorrow.

Reading and Interpreting

1. How does this piece differ from the Ace and Ciardi columns? What would you say is the best thing about this essay?

2. Could this piece be classified as argument?

3. What is Demarest's thesis? Is it stated or implied? How convincingly is it asserted?

Writing Techniques

1. How does the main purpose of Demarest's piece differ from that of Ciardi? How serious is Demarest? Is the tone of the essay consistent, or does it shift?

2. Discuss Demarest's use of examples.

3. Demarest's sentences show notable variety in length. Can you tell why he uses long sentences, and why short ones?

Word Study

1. Demarest likes figurative language and figures of speech. The following are used more or less figuratively: *apocalyptic, focuses, ruminate, fortifies, subliminal, marinate,* also note the sequence beginning *to smother,* paragraph 6. Be sure you know about each word to enjoy the fun; looking up the word and its etymology is likely to help.

2. Demarest also uses such devices as alliteration ("mellow and marinate"). Locate other examples of sound figures and comment on their effect.

3. What is a "Faustian encounter," paragraph 2? Is Demarest exaggerating with the phrase?

Suggestions for Writing

Demarest tries to demolish a hoary but commonly accepted belief. Try writing a paper questioning a different belief or common attitude. Proverbs are likely subjects: A stitch in time saves nine; a rolling stone gathers no moss; A penny saved is a penny earned; and so on. Or try something like the statement that the exception proves the rule.

THE TRUTH ABOUT THE BLACK MIDDLE CLASS
Vernon E. Jordan, Jr.

23

Vernon E. Jordan, Jr., *in addition to being an official of the National Urban League and a former official of the NAACP, writes a syndicated column that appears in newspapers throughout the United States. This selection appeared in* Newsweek.

RECENT reports of the existence of a vast black middle class remind me of daring explorers emerging from the hidden depths of a strange, newly discovered world bearing tales of an exotic new phenomenon. The media seem to have discovered, finally, black families that are intact, black men who are working, black housewives tending backyard gardens and black youngsters who aren't sniffing coke or mugging old ladies.

And out of this "discovery" a new black stereotype is beginning to emerge. Immaculately dressed, cocktail in hand, the new black stereotype comes off as a sleek, sophisticated professional light-years away from the ghetto experience. As I turn the pages of glossy photos of these idealized, fortunate few, I get the feeling that this new black image is all too comforting to Americans weary of the struggle against poverty and racism.

But this stereotype is no more real than was the old image of the angry, fire-breathing militant. And it may be just as damaging to black people, for whom equal opportunity is still a theory and for whom a national effort to bring about a more equitable distribution of the fruits of an affluent society is still a necessity. After all, who can argue the need for welfare reform, for guaranteed jobs, for integrated schools and better housing, when the supposed beneficiaries are looking out at us from the pages of national magazines, smiling at the camera between sips from their martinis?

> Is there a thesis statement here?

The "new" black middle class has been seen recently in prime time on a CBS News documentary; it has adorned the cover of *The New York Times* Magazine, and it has been the subject of a *Time* cover story. But its much ballyhooed emergence is more representative of wishful thinking than of reality. And important as it is for the dedication and hard work of countless black families finally to receive recognition, the image being pushed so hard may be counter-productive in the long run.

The fact is that the black middle class of 1974, like that of earlier years, is a minority within the black community. In 1974, as in 1964, 1954 and in the decades stretching into the distant past, the social and economic reality of the majority of black people has been poverty and marginal status in the wings of our society.

The black middle class traditionally included a handful of professionals and a far larger number of working people who, had they been white, would be solidly "working class." The inclusion of Pullman porters, post-office clerks and other typical members of the old black middle class was due less to their incomes—which were well below those of whites—than to their relative immunity from the hazards of marginal employment that dogged most blacks. They were "middle class" relative to other black people, not to the society at large.

A distinction between middle classes.

Despite all the publicity, despite all the photos of yacht-club cocktail parties, that is where the so-called black middle class stands today. The CBS broadcast included a handyman and a postal worker. Had they been white they would be considered working class, but since they were black and defied media-fostered stereotypes, they were given the middle-class label.

Well, is it true that the black community is edging into the middle class? Let's look at income, the handiest guide and certainly the most generally agreed-upon measurement. What income level amounts to middle-class status? Median family income is often used, since that places a family at the exact midpoint in our society. In 1972 the median family income of whites amounted to $11,549, but black median family income was a mere $6,864.

Facts to support a thesis.

That won't work. Let's use another guide. The Bureau of Labor Statistics says it takes an urban family of four $12,600 to maintain a "intermediate" living standard. Using that measure, the average black family not only is *not* middle class, but it earns far less than the "lower, non-poverty" level of $8,200. Four out of five black families earn less than the "intermediate" standard.

What about collar color? Occupational status is often considered a guide to middle-class status, and this is an area in which blacks have made tremendous gains, breaking into occupations unheard of for non-whites only a decade ago. When you look at the official occupation charts, there is a double space to separate higher-status from lower-status jobs such as laborer, operative and service worker. That gap is more than a typographical device. It is an indicator of racial separation as well, for the majority of working whites hold jobs above that line, while the majority of blacks are still confined to the low-pay, low-status jobs below it. At the top of the job pinnacle, in

Notice the short topic sentences.

the elite categories of the professions and business, the disparity is most glaring, with one out of four whites in such middle-class jobs in contrast to every tenth black worker.

Yes, there are black doctors, dentists and lawyers, but let no one be fooled into thinking they are typical—these professions include only 2 per cent blacks. Yes, there are black families that are stable, who work, often at more than one job, and who own cars and homes. And yes, they are representative of the masses of black people who work the longest hours at the hardest jobs for the least pay in order to put some meat on the table and clothes on their backs. This should be emphasized in every way possible in order to remind this forgetting nation that there is a dimension of black reality that has never been given its due.

A qualification. What effect does it have?

But this should not blind us to the realization that even with such superhuman efforts, the vast majority of blacks are still far from middle-class status. Let us not forget that the gains won are tenuous ones, easily shaken from our grasp by an energy crisis, a recession, rampant inflation or nonenforcement of hard-won civil-rights laws.

How much is conclusion? How does it grow from the introduction?

And never let us fall victim to the illusion that the limited gains so bitterly wrenched from an unwilling nation have materially changed the conditions of life for the overwhelming majority of black people—conditions still typified by discrimination, economic insecurity and general living conditions inferior to those enjoyed by the majority of our white fellow citizens.

Reading and Interpreting

1. Summarize in a sentence the main point of this essay. Is this point adequately supported with evidence?

2. What is the basis for the appeal of this piece? Would it have more interest for some audiences than for others?

3. Does the essay deal with a broader problem than the one identified in the title?

Writing Techniques

1. How much of this essay is argument and how much exposition? Should it have been classified as argument?

2. Do you find any shift in the tone of the last three paragraphs? Explain.

3. The essay could be roughly divided into four sections. Try making such a division and giving each section a heading.

Suggestions for Writing

This essay might be called a "modern problem" essay, providing evidence to clarify an attitude toward the problem. Try writing a paper in which you deal with a problem by examining the validity of comments about it. For example, many writers are saying these days that students can neither write nor read as well as did their predecessors. You might examine the accuracy of such comments.

THE COSMIC ORPHAN
Loren Eiseley

24

Loren Eiseley, *trained in biology and long a professor at the University of Pennsylvania, has brought his scientific background and his command of literate prose to the consideration of what used to be thought of as philosophic problems, such as: What is man, and what is his business on earth? This selection is from* Propaedia.

WHEN I was a young lad of that indefinite but important age when one begins to ask, Who am I? Why am I here? What is the nature of my kind? What is growing up? What is the world? How long shall I live in it? Where shall I go? I found myself walking with a small companion over a high railroad trestle that spanned a stream, a country bridge, and a road. One could look fearfully down, between the ties, at the shallows and ripples in the shining water some 50 feet below. One was also doing a forbidden thing, against which our parents constantly warned. One must not be caught on the black bridge by a train. Something terrible might happen, a thing called death.

An incident, narration as an introduction.

From the abutment of the bridge we gazed down upon the water and saw among the pebbles the shape of an animal we knew only from picture books—a turtle, a very large, dark mahogany-coloured turtle. We scrambled down the embankment to observe him more closely. From the little bridge a few feet above the stream, I saw that the turtle, whose beautiful markings shone in the afternoon sun, was not alive and that his flippers waved aimlessly in the rushing water. The reason for his death was plain. Not too long before we had come upon the trestle, someone engaged in idle practice with a repeating rifle had stitched a row of bullet holes across the turtle's carapace and sauntered on.

My father had once explained to me that it took a long time to make a big turtle, years really, in the sunlight and the water and the mud. I turned the ancient creature over and fingered the etched shell

with its forlorn flippers flopping grotesquely. The question rose up
unbidden. Why did the man have to kill something living that could What can you
never be replaced? I laid the turtle down in the water and gave it a observe about
little shove. It entered the current and began to drift away. "Let's go sentence
home," I said to my companion. From that moment I think I began to structure?
grow up.

"Papa," I said in the evening by the oil lamp in our kitchen.
"Tell me how men got here." Papa paused. Like many fathers of that
time, he was worn from long hours, he was not highly educated, but
he had a beautiful resonant voice and he had been born on a frontier
homestead. He knew the ritual way the Plains Indians opened a
story.

"Son," he said, taking the pattern of another people for our
own, "once there was a poor orphan." He said it in such a way that I
sat down at his feet. Once there was a poor orphan with no one to The story of the
teach him either his way, or his manners. Sometimes animals helped orphan.
him, sometimes supernatural beings. But above all, one thing was
evident. Unlike other occupants of Earth he had to be helped. He did
not know his place, he had to find it. Sometimes he was arrogant and
had to learn humility, sometimes he was a coward and had to be
taught bravery. Sometimes he did not understand his Mother Earth
and suffered for it. The old ones who starved and sought visions on
hilltops had known these things. They were all gone now and the
magic had departed with them. The orphan was alone; he had to
learn by himself; it was a hard school.

My father tousled my head; he gently touched my heart. "You
will learn in time there is much pain here," he said. "Men will give
it to you, time will give it to you, and you must learn to bear it all,
not bear it alone, but be better for the wisdom that may come to you
if you watch and listen and learn. Do not forget the turtle, nor the
ways of men. They are all orphans and they go astray; they do wrong
things. Try to see better."

"Yes, papa," I said, and that was how I believe I came to study
men, not the men of written history but the ancestors beyond, be- The meaning of
yond all writing, beyond time as we know it, beyond human form as the story.
it is known today. Papa was right when he told me men were orphans, eternal seekers. They had little in the way of instinct to in-
struct them, they had come a strange far road in the universe, passed
more than one black, threatening bridge. There were even more to
pass and each one became more dangerous as our knowledge grew.
Because man was truly an orphan and confined to no single way of
life, he was, in essence, a prison breaker. But in ignorance his very
knowledge sometimes led from one terrible prison to another. Was
the final problem, then, to escape himself, or, if not that, to reconcile
his devastating intellect with his heart? All of the knowledge set

down in great books directly or indirectly affects this problem. It is the problem of every man, for even the indifferent man is making, unknown to himself, his own callous judgment.

Long ago, however, in one of the Dead Sea Scrolls hidden in the Judaean Desert, an unknown scribe had written: "None there be, can rehearse the whole tale." That phrase, too, contains the warning that man is an orphan of uncertain beginnings and an indefinite ending. All that the archaeological and anthropological sciences can do is to place a somewhat flawed crystal before man and say: This is the way you came, these are your present dangers; somewhere, seen dimly beyond, lies your destiny. God help you, you are a cosmic orphan, a symbol-shifting magician, mostly immature and inattentive to your own dangers. Read, think, study, but do not expect this to save you without humility of heart. This the old ones knew long ago in the great deserts under the stars. This they sought to learn and pass on. It is the only hope of men.

Is this, too, introduction, marking the thesis idea?

What have we observed that might be buried as the Dead Sea Scrolls were buried for 2,000 years, and be broken out of a jar for human benefit, brief words that might be encompassed on a copper scroll or a ragged sheet of vellum? Only these thoughts, I think, we might reasonably set down as true, now and hereafter. For a long time, for many, many centuries, Western man believed in what we might call the existent world of nature; form as form was seen as constant in both animal and human guise. He believed in the instantaneous creation of his world by the Deity; he believed its duration to be very short, a stage upon which the short drama of a human fall from divine estate and a redemption was in progress.

What use is being made of time as a device for organizing?

Worldly time was a small parenthesis in eternity. Man lived with that belief, his cosmos small and man-centered. Then, beginning about 350 years ago, thoughts unventured upon since the time of the Greek philosophers began to enter the human consciousness. They may be summed up in Francis Bacon's dictum: "This is the foundation of all. We are not to imagine or suppose, but to *discover*, what nature does or may be made to do."

When in following years scientific experiment and observation became current, a vast change began to pass over Western thought. Man's conception of himself and his world began to alter beyond recall. " 'Tis all in pieces, all coherence gone," exclaimed the poet John Donne, Bacon's contemporary. The existing world was crumbling at the edges. It was cracking apart like an ill-nailed raft in a torrent—a torrent of incredible time. It was, in effect, a new nature comprising a past embedded in the present and a future yet to be.

Bacon and a crumbling world.

First, Bacon discerned a *mundus alter*, another separate world that could be drawn out of nature by human intervention—the world that surrounds and troubles us today. Then, by degrees, time depths of tremendous magnitude began, in the late 18th century, to replace the Christian calendar. Space, from a surrounding candelabrum of stars, began to widen to infinity. The Earth was recognized as a mere speck drifting in the wake of a minor star, itself rotating around an immense galaxy composed of innumerable suns. Beyond and beyond, into billions of light years, other galaxies glowed through clouds of wandering gas and interstellar dust. Finally, and perhaps the most shocking blow of all, the natural world of the moment proved to be an illusion, a phantom of man's short lifetime. Organic novelty lay revealed in the strata of the Earth. Man had not always been here. He had been preceded, in the 4,000,000,000 years of the planet's history, by floating mollusks, strange fern forests, huge dinosaurs, flying lizards, giant mammals whose bones lay under the dropped boulders of vanished continental ice sheets.

The Orphan cried out in protest, as the cold of naked space entered his bones, "Who am I?" And once more science answered, "You are a changeling." "You are linked by a genetic chain to all the vertebrates. The thing that is you bears the still aching wounds of evolution in body and in brain. Your hands are made-over fins, your lungs come from a creature gasping in a swamp, your femur has been twisted upright. Your foot is a reworked climbing pad. You are a rag doll resewn from the skins of extinct animals. Long ago, 2,000,000 years, perhaps, you were smaller, your brain was not so large. We are not confident that you could speak. Seventy million years before that you were an even smaller climbing creature known as a tupaiid. You were the size of a rat. You ate insects. Now you fly to the Moon."

Does Eiseley's thesis keep growing as he goes?

"This is a fairy tale," protested the Orphan. "I am here, I will look in the mirror."

"Of course it is a fairy tale," said the scientists, "but so is the world and so is life. That is what makes it true. Life is indefinite departure. That is why we are all orphans. That is why you must find your own way. Life is not stable. Everything alive is slipping through cracks and crevices in time, changing as it goes. Other creatures, however, have instincts that provide for them, holes in which to hide. They cannot ask questions. A fox is a fox, a wolf is a wolf, even if this, too, is illusion. You have learned to ask questions. That is why you are an orphan. *You are the only creature in the universe who knows what it has been.* Now you must go on asking questions while all the time you are changing. You will ask what you are to become. The world will no longer satisfy you. You must find your way, your own true self."

Does his sentence structure change as he moves into more exposition?

"But how can I?" wept the Orphan, hiding his head. "This is magic. I do not know what I am. I have been too many things."

"You have indeed," said all the scientists together. "Your body and your nerves have been dragged about and twisted in the long effort of your ancestors to stay alive, but now, small orphan that you are, you must know a secret, a secret magic that nature has given to you. No other creature on the planet possesses it. You use language. You are a symbol-shifter. All this is hidden in your brain and transmitted from one generation to another. You are a time-binder, in your head the symbols that mean things in the world outside can fly about untrammelled. You can combine them differently into a new world of thought or you can also hold them tenaciously throughout a lifetime and pass them on to others."

Thus out of words, a puff of air, really, is made all that is uniquely human, all that is new from one human generation to another. But remember what was said of the wounds of evolution. The brain, parts of it at least, is very old, the parts laid down in sequence like geological strata. Buried deep beneath the brain with which we reason are ancient defense centres quick to anger, quick to aggression, quick to violence, over which the neocortex, the new brain, strives to exert control. Thus there are times when the Orphan is a divided being striving against himself. Evil men know this. Sometimes they can play upon it for their own political advantage. Men crowded together, subjected to the same stimuli, are quick to respond to emotion that in the quiet of their own homes they might analyze more cautiously.

Scientists have found that the very symbols which crowd our brains may possess their own dangers. It is convenient for the thinker to classify an idea with a word. This can sometimes lead to a process called hypostatization or reification. Take the word "Man," for example. There are times when it is useful to categorize the creature briefly, his history, his embracing characteristics. From this, if we are not careful of our meanings, it becomes easy to speak of all men as though they were one person. In reality men have been seeking this unreal man for thousands of years. They have found him bathed in blood, they have found him in the hermit's cell, he has been glimpsed among innumerable messiahs, or in meditation under the sacred bô tree; he has been found in the physician's study or lit by the satanic fires of the first atomic explosion.

In reality he has never been found at all. The reason is very simple: men have been seeking Man capitalized, an imaginary creature constructed out of disparate parts in the laboratory of the human imagination. Some men may thus perceive him and see him as either totally beneficent or wholly evil. They would be wrong. They are wrong so long as they have vitalized this creation and call it Man. There is no Man; there are only men: good, evil, inconceivable mixtures marred by their genetic makeup, scarred or improved by their societal surroundings. So long as they live they are *men*, multitu-

Two rare
words. Is some
definition
provided?

How is this
paragraph tied
together?

dinous and unspent potential for action. Men are great objects of study, but the moment we say "Man" we are in danger of wandering into a swamp of abstraction.

Surveying our fossil history perhaps we are not even justified as yet in calling ourselves true men. The word carries subtle implications that extend beyond us into the time stream. If a remote half-human ancestor, barely able to speak, had had a word for his kind, as very likely he did, and just supposing it had been "man," would we approve the usage, the shape-freezing quality of it, now? I think not. Perhaps no true orphan would wish to call himself anything but a traveller. Man in a cosmic timeless sense may not be here.

The point is particularly apparent in the light of a recent and portentous discovery. In 1953 James D. Watson and Francis H. C. Crick discovered the structure of the chemical alphabet out of which all that lives is constituted. It was a strange spiral ladder within the cell, far more organized and complicated than 19th-century biologists had imagined; the tiny building blocks constantly reshuffled in every mating had both an amazing stability and paradoxically, over long time periods, a power to alter the living structure of a species beyond recall. The thing called man had once been a tree shrew on a forest branch; now it manipulates abstract symbols in its brain from which skyscrapers rise, bridges span the horizon, disease is conquered, the Moon is visited.

Why is the discovery portentous?

Molecular biologists have begun to consider whether the marvellous living alphabet which lies at the root of evolution *can* be manipulated for human benefit. Varieties of domesticated plants and animals have been improved. Now at last man has begun to eye his own possible road into the future. By delicate excisions and intrusions could the mysterious alphabet we carry in our bodies be made to hasten our advancement into the future? Already our urban concentrations, with all their aberrations and faults, are future-oriented. Why not ourselves? Is it in our power to perpetuate great minds *ad infinitum*? But who is to judge? Who is to select this future man? There is the problem. Which of us poor orphans by the roadside, even those peering learnedly through the electron microscope, can be confident of the way into the future? Could the fish unaided by nature have found the road to the reptile, the reptile to the mammal, the mammal to man? And how was man endowed with speech? *Could* men choose their way? Suddenly before us towers the blackest, most formidable bridge of our experience. Across what chasm does it run?

The style shifts to asking questions. Is it a good device here?

Biologists tell us that in the fullness of time over ninety percent of the world's past species have perished. The mammalian ones in particular are not noted for longevity. If the scalpel, the excising laser ray in the laboratory, were placed in the hands of some one man,

some one poor orphan, what would he do? If assured, would he reproduce himself alone? If cruel, would he by indirection succeed in
abolishing the living world? If doubtful of the road, would he reproduce the doubt? "Nothing is more shameful than assertion without
knowledge," a great Roman, Cicero, once pronounced as though he
had foreseen this final bridge of human pride—the pride of a god
without foresight.

After the disasters of the second World War when the dream of
perpetual progress died from men's minds, an orphan of this violent
century wrote a poem about the great extinctions revealed in the
rocks of the planet. It concludes as follows:

> I am not sure I love
>   the cruelties found in our blood
>   from some lost evil tree in our beginnings.
> May the powers forgive and seal us deep
>   when we lie down,
> May harmless dormice creep and red leaves fall
>   —over the prisons where we wreaked our will—
> Dachau, Auschwitz, those places everywhere.
> If I could pray, I would pray long for this.

How does the conclusion echo the beginning?

One may conclude that the poet was a man of doubt. He did not regret man; he was confident that leaves, rabbits, and songbirds would
continue life, as, long ago, a tree shrew had happily forgotten the ruling reptiles. The poet was an orphan in shabby circumstances pausing by the roadside to pray, for he did pray despite his denial; God
forgive us all. He was a man in doubt upon the way. He was the
eternal orphan of my father's story. Let us then, as similar orphans
who have come this long way through time, be willing to assume the
risks of the uncompleted journey. We must know, as that forlorn
band of men in Judaea knew when they buried the jar, the man's
road is to be sought beyond himself. *No man there is who can tell the
whole tale.* After the small passage of 2,000 years who would deny
this truth?

How has the word orphan *grown in the essay?*

Reading and Interpreting

1. What is Eiseley's central idea here? Try getting it all into one
sentence.

2. With this essay in mind, if you could interview Eiseley what
questions would you think most worth asking him?

3. You may have been surprised to find Eiseley, a biologist, at-
taching so much importance to language. What is the importance of
language to his central idea?

4. You probably know the meaning of the word *orphan*. Be sure you also know the meaning of *cosmos*. Then try to explain why Eiseley gave his essay the name he did.

Writing Techniques

1. For a time as you read, this piece may have seemed like autobiography, that is, like narrative. When did it shift to exposition?

2. Eiseley uses several sorts of evidence. Which kinds, and do they appear particularly in certain parts of the essay? Why?

3. What are the main parts of this essay? How has so varied a piece of writing been held together?

4. Some of the glosses suggest points at which Eiseley's thesis seems to grow as his essay advances. Another one of these transitional points will be found at the beginning of the tenth paragraph, "Worldly time was a small parenthesis in eternity." Can you find at least one more such point?

Word Study

1. Considering his subject, Eiseley uses few rare words, but you may find him using many that are strange enough to you so that they expand when you know them better. Read again the paragraph, fourth from the last, beginning, "The point is. . . ." Now look up the following words and try to learn enough about each so that you can be comfortable with them: *portentous, chemical alphabet, constituted, paradoxically, manipulates, symbols.* Read the paragraph again. It should now mean more to you.

2. Can you make any observations about Eiseley's choice of words? Does he use any figurative language? Does he use common words along with uncommon ones? Does he use concrete, specific words? Does he use suggestive words, what are sometimes referred to as connotative, that is, words that stimulate feeling as well as have meaning?

Suggestions for Writing

Eiseley's essay is more complex than most of those you have encountered in earlier chapters, and it raises a number of questions which might be explored in separate papers. Consider writing a paper on some topic suggested by this essay—for example, Man as a Symbol-Maker; Words that Make Realities of Abstractions; Biological Improvement of Man; Man as a Changeling.

Writer, Reader, Order

The Audience
and Its Needs

When you try to say something, or when somebody else expresses
something that you need to grasp, there are always at least two
principals: the author (the writer or speaker) and the audience (the
reader or listener). In each of these roles you have powers and
openings you lack when you are cast in the other. And in each you
have obligations. Composition, in other words, assumes a compact
between writer and reader. This group of selections should suggest
how an audience shares in that compact, how the reader helps
determine the way a writer goes about a job.

There may be writing that has no audience. Some poets have
said they write only to produce a poem; once it is finished they
never look at it again or care whether anybody else does. But such
indifference must be rare. Even when you take notes or write in a
diary, you have an audience, yourself if no one else. And most of us
will not go to the trouble of putting words on paper without trusting
that someone sometime may look at them.

For most writing the purpose is communication — of the
emotion behind a poem, the logic of an opinion on politics, even the
information in a telephone directory. To communicate well you need
a notion of whom you are talking to. Most good writing is directed,
more or less consciously, to some kind of audience. And the form

and character of the writing vary to fit the needs, desires, and abilities of the interested readers.

Audiences can be roughly classified as limited, specialized, or general. A letter home is obviously directed to a small group, and you know without thinking much about it what will interest that audience and communicate to it. A business letter also has a limited audience, but this audience is likely to make different demands than your family. Many applicants have failed to get jobs because they inadequately assessed their audience, the prospective employer. Larger groups may also constitute limited audiences—readers of children's books, of women's magazines, or of a student newspaper. Specialized audiences are limited in a different way, to a group having some kind of special knowledge or technical interest. Writing for scholars or scientists or morticians assumes familiarity with a vocabulary and with information that a general audience would not have. Most writing, however, is directed to a general audience, composed of individuals and of many limited audiences. In a sense, even a general audience is limited—for written composition, limited at least to those who can read—and it has expectations that are sometimes hard to anticipate and to meet. Communication with a general audience requires use of a current and widely accepted style, clear organization, and thoughtful development of ideas.

In your reading, you can note how the audience influences the writer. The prospective reader affects the choice of subject; you would not discuss devices for harnessing solar energy with a five-year-old, even though you are a design engineer. Thus the audience helps choose the content; it also alters development.

Abortion may interest both a group of juvenile delinquents and a class of paramedical technicians, but you would use different evidence for each group. Various audiences respond to various types of sentences and choices of words, and the devices you would use to hold the attention of the juvenile delinquents and the paramedics would be quite different.

Some of the selections in this chapter illustrate how the same author may vary his prose to address different audiences. Rudyard Kipling has one approach in *The Jungle Book,* addressed to children, another to begin a short story written for a general adult audience. Compare Margaret Bryant writing in a college textbook with Margaret Bryant addressing an audience of college teachers. Or compare Leo Rosten in a popular magazine column with Leo Rosten in an amusing but serious dictionary of the Yiddish language. Here the audiences will differ only slightly; the same person who reads Rosten's columns may pick up his dictionary, but this reader will have one set of expectations reading a Rosten essay and a somewhat different set consulting the Rosten dictionary. The human animal remains the same, but rhetorically the reader becomes part of separate if overlapping audiences. The selection from *Alice in Wonderland* offers another sort of problem. Carroll was presumably directing his story to a little girl, but does the selection seem to be a children's story?

BRIEF INSIGHTS INTO AUDIENCES   **25**

The following selections provide clues for a sort of sleuthing job, since they can be compared for the audiences they presume. They concern the same subject, ships, but they differ in content and style, partly because they are directed toward different audiences: **a. Frederick Marryat** *was a British sea captain of sailing vessels, who retired to writing novels based on his experiences; this scene is from* Mr. Midshipman Easy *(1836);* **b.** *this entry is from* The Rainbow Dictionary *(1947);* **c.** *the next item is from* Webster's New World Thesaurus *(1971),* **d.** *this description comes from* **Joseph Conrad,** Nigger of the Narcissus, *(1897); Conrad captained ships plying the Pacific and Indian Oceans before he retired to become one of England's most creative novelists;* **e.** *this statement appears in* **Robert Edwards Annin,** Ocean Shipping: Elements of Practical Steamship Operation *(1920);* **f. William H. Clark** *sketches the exotic China Trade in* Ships and Sailors: The Story of Our Merchant Marine *(1938);* **g. Basil Lubbock,** *repeats a personal narrative of the opium ship* Antelope, *reprinted in* The China Clippers *(1914);* **h. Charles D. G. White** *expounds the handling of sail boats in* Handbook of Sailing, *(1947).*

a.   Frederick Marryat

"MAN the braces. We shall be taken aback directly, depend upon it."

The braces were hardly stretched along before this was the case. The wind flew round to the south-west with a loud roar, and it was fortunate that they were prepared — the yards were braced round, and the master asked the captain what course they were to steer.

"We must give it up," observed Captain Wilson, holding on by the belaying pin. "Shape our course for Cape Sicie, Mr. Jones."

And the *Aurora* flew before the gale, under her foresail and top-sails close reefed. The weather was now so thick that nothing could be observed twenty yards from the vessel; the thunder pealed, and the lightning darted in every direction over the dark expanse. The watch was called as soon as the sails were trimmed, and all who could went below, wet, uncomfortable, and disappointed.

"What an old Jonah you are, Martin," said Gascoigne.

"Yes, I am," replied he; "but we have the worst to come yet, in my opinion. I recollect, not two hundred miles from where we are now, we had just such a gale in the *Favourite,* and we as nearly went down, when—"

At this moment a tremendous noise was heard above, a shock was felt throughout the whole ship, which trembled fore and aft as if it was about to fall into pieces; loud shrieks were followed by plaintive cries, the lower deck was filled with smoke, and the frigate was down on her beam ends. Without exchanging a word, the whole of the occupants of the berth flew out, and were up the hatchway, not knowing what to think, but convinced that some dreadful accident had taken place.

On their gaining the deck it was at once explained; the foremast of the frigate had been struck by lightning, had been riven into several pieces, and had fallen over the larboard bow, carrying with it the main topmast and jib-boom. The jagged stump of the foremast was in flames, and burnt brightly, notwithstanding the rain fell in torrents. The ship, as soon as the foremast and main topmast had gone overboard, broached-to furiously, throwing the men over the wheel and dashing them senseless against the carronades; the forecastle, the forepart of the main deck, and even the lower deck, were spread with men, either killed or serious[ly] wounded, or insensible from the electric shock. The frigate was on her beam ends, and the sea broke furiously over her; all was dark as pitch, except the light from the blazing stump of the foremast, appearing like a torch held up by the wild demons of the storm, or when occasionally the gleaming lightning cast a momentary glare, threatening every moment to repeat its attack upon the vessel, while the deafening thunder burst almost on their devoted heads. All was dismay and confusion. . . .

b.   *The Rainbow Dictionary*

SHIP   A **ship** sails on the water

A **very big boat** sails on the water. The **ships** sail on the ocean to all parts of the world.

> The anchor heaves, the ship swings free,
> The sails swell full. To sea! To sea!

ship, *n.* Types of ships include the following—dahabeah, junk, galleon, sampan, xebec, lugger, steamer, steamship, ocean greyhound, liner, freighter, landing barge, packet, ferry, clipper, square-rigged vessel, dhow, sailing ship transport, tanker, fishing smack, lightship, pilot boat, cutter-yacht, pindjajap, lorcha, galiot, casco, patamar caique, bilander, baghla, state barge, battleship, cruiser, destroyer, corvette, aircraft carrier, whaling vessel, bark, barkentine, brigantine, schooner, windjammer, yacht, dragger, cutter, ketch, yawl, bugeye, sloop, brig, tug, trawler, three-master, four-master, billyboy, hoy, felucca, caravel; see also **boat.**

d. Joseph Conrad

A big, foaming sea came out of the mist; it made for the ship, roaring wildly, and in its rush it looked as mischievous and discomposing as a madman with an axe. One or two, shouting, scrambled up the rigging; most, with a convulsive catch of the breath, held on where they stood. Singleton dug his knees under the wheel-box, and carefully eased the helm to the headlong pitch of the ship, but without taking his eyes off the coming wave. It towered close-to and high, like a wall of green glass topped with snow. The ship rose to it as though she had soared on wings, and for a moment rested poised upon the foaming crest as if she had been a great sea-bird. Before we could draw breath a heavy gust struck her, another roller took her unfairly under the weather bow, she gave a toppling lurch, and filled her decks. Captain Allistoun leaped up, and fell; Archie rolled over him, screaming:—"She will rise!" She gave another lurch to leeward; the lower deadeyes dipped heavily; the men's feet flew from under them, and they hung kicking above the slanting poop. They could see the ship putting her side in the water, and shouted all together:—"She's going!" Forward the forecastle doors flew open, and the watch below were seen leaping out one after another, throwing their arms up; and, falling on hands and knees, scrambled aft on all fours along the high side of the deck, sloping more than the roof of a house. From leeward the seas rose, pursuing them; they looked wretched in a hopeless struggle, like vermin fleeing before a flood; they fought up the weather ladder of the poop one after another, half naked and staring wildly; and as soon as they got up they shot to leeward in clusters, with closed eyes, till they brought up heavily with their ribs against the iron stanchions of the rail; then, groaning, they rolled in a confused mass.

FIFTH, such ships approximate the economical speed limit for vessels of that type. In a general trader, loaded sea speed is one of the most important factors to be considered. But, while it is always present in the mind of the time charterer, it is potent with him only to the limit of commercial profit. He will not pay a fancy charter hire merely to save a few hours on a long voyage. The expense of bunkers must be considered. Briefly, there is a point where the extra expense for fuel neutralizes the advantage of the extra speed secured. This varies with the ship and the trade, and beyond it no owner should attempt to go.

f. William H. Clark

THE first ship to dare the tremendous voyage direct was the *Empress of China* of New York. In February, 1784, she left Manhattan and on August 23, 1784, six months later, she was at Macao. On board was Major Samuel Shaw of Boston, charged as supercargo with the business of trading the ship's cargo with the Chinese for silk and tea. The difficulties this Boston young man faced were tremendous. Chinese dignitaries, in their stiff silk robes, welcomed him hospitably, it is true, but between them was the double barrier of language and customs. British merchants had regularly organized channels of trade; Shaw had neither experience or any one to help him. But, unaided, he went to work and traded so successfully that, when the *Empress* arrived home after an absence of 15 months, he showed such a huge profit that the China trade was established firmly by this single voyage.

g. Basil Lubbock

COCKING our pistols, and laying the boarding pikes down at our sides ready for instant use, we waited for them. Directly twenty or thirty leaped upon the low bowsprit, some rushing to the nettings with knives to cut an entrance. We took deliberate aim and fired, about a dozen falling back into the boats as the result of our first and only shot. Dropping the firearms we now took to the pikes and rushed to the bow. Here the battle was for some minutes pretty fierce, and a rent having been made in the boarding net the China-men rushed to it like tigers, but as fast as they came in they were piked and driven back.

Meantime one of the boats had silently dropped alongside, and ere we were aware of it, her crew were boarding us in the rear. But here the doctor (the cook) was prepared for them, and the first that showed their heads above the rail received half a bucket full of scald-ing water in their faces, which sent them back to their boat howling with pain.

"That's it, doctor, give it to them," shouted the old man, who seemed to be quite in his element, and he rushed down off the poop, whither he had gone for a moment to survey the contest, and taking a bucketful of the boiling water forward threw it in among the Chinamen, who were still obstinately contesting the possession of the bow. With a howl of mixed pain and surprise they retreated, and we succeeded in fairly driving them back into the boats.

h.   Charles G. White

IN the early stages of the development of the airplane it was the common belief that the lifting force created by driving a sloping wing against the air furnished all of the lifting power. The study of planes after an accident and the experiment conducted in wind tun-nels led to this most important discovery: that the partial vacuum created *above* the wing gave even more lifting effect than did the un-derside which was driven against the wind (Fig. 35). These experi-ments and the successful results obtained by following the new prin-ciple demonstrated that the same conditions are present in a sail. A

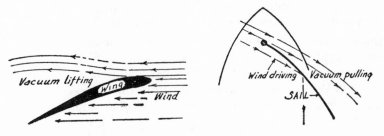

Fig. 35. Airplane wing and the sail

sail does not present a flat surface when under pressure from the wind, but it has a curved surface. This curve is more pronounced near the mast and becomes less as it approaches the leech. This curved surface is almost a duplicate of the shape of the airplane wing. In fact a well-designed and properly setting sail can be considered as an airplane wing in a vertical position. It is now known that the pull of the partial vacuum produced on the leeward side of the sail is even more effective.

Reading and Interpreting

1. Anyone who has seen a plane crash, or even an automobile accident, knows that high-speed transportation can be dangerous. Discuss the kinds of risks in earlier travel suggested in some of these readings.

2. You may have found the last reading the most interesting. What makes a sailing ship move? What keeps an airplane up in the air?

Writing Techniques

1. Readings **b** and **c** are both from word books, both directed at specialized audiences, but they are directed toward different audiences. How is each adapted to its particular audience?

2. Marryat and Conrad are both writing fiction, and thus to a degree both for a general audience. Still, the audiences would differ somewhat. By close reading of the two passages try to describe this difference. (One might add that both authors were former sea captains, that both were describing ship life in the nineteenth century, although Marryat knew mainly sailing vessels and Conrad wrote mainly about engine-powered ships.)

3. White's account is presumably factual. Is it reasonable to suppose that its author may not have thought much about audience?

4. Annin's comment is from a textbook for a course calculated to help students become executives for steamship companies. What does the author do to satisfy the needs of this specialized audience? The selections by Clark and White are also more expository than anything else; how would their audiences differ from one another and from Annin's audience?

5. Some of these pieces use dialogue, some do not. What seem to be the uses of dialogue?

Suggestions for Writing

You may not have thrown boiling water on pirates trying to hijack your cargo of opium or lain unconscious on a deck when a bolt of lightening struck your foremast, but you have had interesting experiences. Recount one of them in two versions directed toward two quite different audiences. Following are obvious possibilities: a younger brother or sister, a close friend, a police officer, a teacher or a school administrator concerned with discipline, a reporter, your mother or father, another person involved in the incident who did not know something you know.

A STORYTELLER AND HIS AUDIENCES
Rudyard Kipling

26

As a British civil servant assigned abroad, **Rudyard Kipling** *learned to know and love the Indian people when they were not as yet appreciated in Europe and America. He used this background for poems, stories, and nonfiction, becoming one of the best-loved writers of his day. Following are the beginnings of two stories.*

a. From "Rikki-tikki-tavi," in *The Jungle Book,* . . . (1894)

THIS is the story of the great war that Rikki-tikki-tavi fought single-handed, through the bathrooms of the big bungalow in Segowlee cantonment. Darzee the Tailorbird helped him, and Chuchundra the Muskrat, who never comes out into the middle of the floor, but always creeps round by the wall, gave him advice, but Rikki-tikki did the real fighting.

He was a mongoose, rather like a little cat in his fur and his tail, but quite like a weasel in his head and his habits. His eyes and the end of his restless nose were pink. He could scratch himself anywhere he pleased with any leg, front or back, that he chose to use. He could fluff up his tail till it looked like a bottle brush, and his war cry as he scuttled through the long grass was: *Rikk-tikk-tikki-tikki-tchk!*

One day, a high summer flood washed him out of the burrow where he lived with his father and mother, and carried him, kicking and clucking, down a roadside ditch. He found a little wisp of grass floating there, and clung to it till he lost his senses. When he revived, he was lying in the hot sun on the middle of a garden path, very draggled indeed, and a small boy was saying, "Here's a dead mongoose. Let's have a funeral."

"No," said his mother, "let's take him in and dry him. Perhaps he isn't really dead."

They took him into the house, and a big man picked him up between his finger and thumb and said he was not dead but half choked. So they wrapped him in cotton wool, and warmed him over a little fire, and he opened his eyes and sneezed.

"Now," said the big man (he was an Englishman who had just moved into the bungalow), "don't frighten him, and we'll see what he'll do."

It is the hardest thing in the world to frighten a mongoose, because he is eaten up from nose to tail with curiosity. The motto of all the mongoose family is "Run and find out," and Rikki-tikki was a true mongoose. He looked at the cotton wool, decided that it was not good to eat, ran all round the table, sat up and put his fur in order, scratched himself, and jumped on the small boy's shoulder.

"Don't be frightened, Teddy," said his father. "That's his way of making friends."

"Ouch! He's tickling under my chin," said Teddy.

Rikki-tikki looked down between the boy's collar and neck, snuffed at his ear, and climbed down to the floor, where he sat rubbing his nose.

"Good gracious," said Teddy's mother, "and that's a wild creature! I suppose he's so tame because we've been kind to him."

"All mongooses are like that," said her husband. "If Teddy doesn't pick him up by the tail, or try to put him in a cage, he'll run in and out of the house all day long. Let's give him something to eat."

They gave him a little piece of raw meat. Rikki-tikki liked it immensely, and when it was finished he went out into the veranda and sat in the sunshine and fluffed up his fur to make it dry to the roots. Then he felt better.

"There are more things to find out about in this house," he said to himself, "than all my family could find out in all their lives. I shall certainly stay and find out."

b.   From *The Man Who Would Be King* (1889)

"Brother to a Prince and fellow to a beggar if he be found worthy."

THE law, as quoted, lays down a fair conduct of life, and one not easy to follow. I have been fellow to a beggar again and again under circumstances which prevented either of us finding out whether the other was worthy. I have still to be brother to a Prince, though I once came near to kinship with what might have been a veritable King and was promised the reversion of a Kingdom—army, law-courts, revenue and policy all complete. But, to-day, I greatly fear that my King is dead, and if I want a crown I must go and hunt it for myself.

The beginning of everything was in a railway train upon the road to Mhow from Ajmir. There had been a Deficit in the Budget, which necessitated traveling, not Second-class, which is only half as dear as First-class, but by Intermediate, which is very awful indeed. There are no cushions in the Intermediate class, and the population are either Intermediate, which is Eurasian, or native, which for a long night journey is nasty, or Loafer, which is amusing though intoxicated. Intermediates do not patronize refreshment-rooms. They carry their food in bundles and pots, and buy sweets from the native sweetmeat-sellers, and drink the roadside water. That is why in the hot weather Intermediates are taken out of the carriages dead, and in all weathers are most properly looked down upon.

My particular Intermediate happened to be empty till I reached Nasirabad, when a huge gentleman in shirt-sleeves entered, and, following the custom of Intermediates, passed the time of day. He was a wanderer and a vagabond like myself, but with an educated taste for whiskey. He told tales of things he had seen and done, of out-of-the-way corners of the Empire into which he had penetrated, and of adventures in which he risked his life for a few days' food. ''If India was filled with men like you and me, not knowing more than the crows where they'd get their next day's rations, it isn't seventy millions of revenue the land would be paying—it's seven hundred millions,'' said he; and as I looked at his mouth and chin I was disposed to agree with him. We talked politics—the politics of Loaferdom that sees things from the underside where the lath and plaster is not smoothed off—and we talked postal arrangements because my friend wanted to send a telegram back from the next station to Ajmir, which is the turning-off place from the Bombay to the Mhow line as you travel westward. My friend had no money beyond eight annas which he wanted for dinner, and I had no money at all, owing to the hitch in the Budget before mentioned. Further, I was going into a wilderness where, though I should resume touch with the Treasury, there were no telegraph offices. I was, therefore, unable to help him in any way.

''We might threaten a Station-master, and make him send a wire on tick,'' said my friend, ''but that'd mean inquiries for you and for me, and I've got my hands full these days. Did you say you are traveling back along this line within any days?''

''Within ten,'' I said.

"Can't you make it eight?" said he. "Mine is rather urgent business."

"I can send your telegram within ten days if that will serve you," I said.

"I couldn't trust the wire to fetch him now I think of it. It's this way. He leaves Delhi on the 23rd for Bombay. That means he'll be running through Ajmir about the night of the 23rd."

"But I am going into the Indian Desert," I explained.

"Well *and* good," said he. "You'll be changing at Marwar Junction to get into Jodhpore territory—you must do that—and he'll be coming through Marwar Junction in the early morning of the 24th by the Bombay Mail. Can you be at Marwar Junction on that time? 'Twon't be inconveniencing you because I know that there's precious few pickings to be got out of these Central India States—even though you pretend to be correspondent of the *Backwoodsman*."

"Have you ever tried that trick?" I asked.

"Again and again, but the Residents find you out, and then you get escorted to the Border before you've got time to get your knife into them. But about my friend here. . . ."

Writing Techniques

The two stories are written by the same author at nearly the same time and are set in roughly the same place. You will surmise at once, however, that they are directed toward different audiences. Identify subject, characters, writing style, choice of words, and the like that lead you to guess this.

Suggestions for Writing

Writing for an audience of children is not as easy as it might seem, but give it a try. One possibility is a story about an animal, with hints from Kipling's mongoose.

ON LANGUAGE   **27**
Margaret Bryant

Margaret Bryant, *long professor of English at Brooklyn College, is one of the more humane writers on present-day American English, producing standard reference works like* Current American Usage *(1962), textbooks like* Modern English and Its Heritage *(2nd ed., 1962), and many professional and scholarly books and articles.*

WORDS are the fundamental stuff out of which language, as we understand the term, is made, and in preceding chapters we have studied words in regard to their sounds. In this section it will be our purpose to deal with the origin and meaning of words, the most fascinating and most popular subject in the whole field of linguistics. Trace back almost any of the common English words and you will get a rich and rewarding glimpse of the history, the customs, and even the beliefs of earlier ages.

Take, for instance, *board*, which at the outset meant nothing more than *a piece of timber*, as it still does. Since theatrical stages were made of wood, the phrase *on the boards* became current for *on the stage*, and a further definition as an *extensive surface of wood* is exemplified by chessboard, from which develops the idea of any flat, thin surface, not necessarily of wood, as in *cardboard* and *pasteboard*, where no timber is present at all. Also, derived directly from the first meaning, *board* conveys the idea of a table for food, as in *bed and board* and *the groaning board*. The word likewise becomes attached to the group of persons who customarily hold meetings around a table, such as *Board of Health* and *Board of Aldermen*.

Or consider the word *lozenge*, which nowadays usually has the humble, prosaic meaning of *cough drop* or *small piece of hard candy*. The word comes from Old French *losange*, also spelled *losenge* and *lozenge*, and denoting, first, *flattery* and then *praise*. The Modern French *losange* still has the meaning *praise, commendation*, or *eulogy*. *Lozenge* broadened in its meaning, however, to denote first the eulogies that appeared as epitaphs on funeral monuments and still later the monuments themselves. But monumental inscriptions usually appeared in diamond-shaped figures; so by a further extension of meaning *lozenge* became the equivalent of such a figure, and thus was used as an architectural term, since many buildings were decorated with *lozenges*. Moreover, other things also took on or already had this diamond-shaped form, especially small confections of sugar, usually medicated. By a final extension of meaning, *lozenge* has come to refer to a cough drop or bit of hard candy, whether or not in the diamond shape.

b. From *Our Changing Language*

IN considering vulgar English, the English of yesterday as well as the English of today must be taken into account for the reason that the term "vulgar English" is identical in meaning with the words "linguistic change." It is easy to perceive that this conclusion is inevitable. For let us take any given change in speech, say one from x to y. The use of y must have a beginning; and from that beginning up to the very moment of its general acceptance, to use y in place of x must constitute a deviation from accepted or conventional practice— that very deviation which we have just defined as vulgarity in speech.

This identification of the changing with the vulgar in language should not be considered a radical notion. For what is it that the self-constituted guardians of the purity of our speech are really truly opposing? Is it not all change? What is it which they call vulgar? Is it not any single locution representing a possible change?

Take as a representative of the purist type Jonathan Swift, who back in the early eighteenth century was denouncing *mob* for *mobile vulgus*. What were his reasons? Not that *mob* was shorter, neater, more expressive—in a word, better English? No, he condemned *mob* as vulgar, i.e., as a linguistic change.

No purist of today would eschew *mob,* and why not? Because despite Jonathan Swift, *mob* has become an educated vulgarism, and hence no vulgarism at all. This gate-crasher, once in the party, is accepted by all, and Swift's strictures are politely ignored.

In other words, once linguistic change has become consummated it becomes not only normal but potentially admirable. Once we all succumb, it's great to be vulgar!

Reading and Interpreting

1. Do the two examples of word development in reading **a** illustrate any general point made in the introduction to this section? If so, are they successful as illustrations?

2. Do you know any other words than the example given in **b** that were formerly considered vulgar but are now respectable? For example, *boss* in the sense "a political boss" used to be considered vulgar, but few people now hesitate to use it. Make a list of ten words that some people consider vulgar but others use frequently.

Writing Techniques

Selection **a** comes from a textbook intended for an elementary college course in language; Professor Bryant may be thinking of someone very much like you as her audience. Selection **b** comes from a public address; Bryant was told to expect that her audience would include local teachers, some interested parents and townspeople, and some students who had come voluntarily. Read the two passages carefully, and isolate in each some things that Bryant has done to adapt her treatment to the somewhat different audiences.

Suggestions for Writing

1. Professor Bryant might have used any of dozens of words for her two illustrative paragraphs in the first selection. Take two other words, and then with the help of an etymological dictionary or a good dictionary having word origins, try writing two paragraphs like those in the selection.

2. Select a word or phrase that some people now avoid as being vulgar: *suspicion* as a verb, *Negro, guts,* and the like. Using reference works, as Bryant does, or interviews with various sorts of people, try to find out something of what has happened to the term and how it is now viewed.

MATZO AND AN EMBARRASSING MOMENT
Leo Rosten

28

Leo Rosten *has been known as one of the most amusing and literate observers of the American scene ever since* The Education of H*Y*M*A*N K*A*P*L*A*N *(1937), published under the pen name Leonard Q. Ross. Before he turned exclusively to writing, he taught political science.*

a.   From *The Joys of Yiddish: A Relaxed Lexicon* (1968)

matzo
matzoh

Pronounced MOTT-*seh* (not MOTT-*so*) to rhyme with "lotsa." Hebrew: The plural in Hebrew is *matzoth,* pronounced MOTT-*sez,* in Yiddish.

Unleavened bread (it comes in thin, flat, ridgy oblongs, and is semiperforated to facilitate neat breaking).

DURING Passover, no bread, no yeast or leavened products are eaten. *Matzos* commemorate the kind of unleavened bread the Jews, fleeing from Egypt in the thirteenth century B.C., ate because they could not pause in their perilous flight long enough to wait for the dough to rise. Exodus 12 : 15: "Seven days shall ye eat unleavened bread. . . ."

Today, *matzos* are enjoyed all year round, and are served in many restaurants.

The following story has nothing to do with *matzos* but may give you an irreverent slant on Exodus. It is Hollywood's version of the flight from Egypt:

Moses, racing his harassed people across the desert, came to the Red Sea and, snapping his fingers, called: "Manny!"

Up, breathless, ran Manny, publicity man. "Yes, sir?"

"The boats!"

"What?"

"The *boats*," said Moses. "Where are the boats — to get us across the Red Sea?!"

"Oh, my God! Moses, what with all the news items and human-interest stories — I forgot!"

"You *what?* "

"I forgot!"

"You forgot the *boats?!*" cried Moses. "You idiot! You moron! The Egyptians will be here any minute! What do you expect me to do — talk to God, ask Him to part the waters, let all of us Jews across and drown the pursuing Egyptians? Is *that* what you think——"

"Boss," said Manny, "you do that and I'll get you two pages in the Old Testament!"

b.   *"My Most Embarrassing Moment"*

TWO ambitious women whom I do not remotely know have begged me to contribute to a volume they are compiling entitled "My Most Embarrassing Moment." The anthology will contain the most colorful discomfitures of famous actors, authors, athletes, and (for all I know) glassblowers who inhaled and midgets who grew.

I don't know why people solicit the work of professional writers for free, but the letter I received was so charming that I may send the anthologists "my most embarrassing moment" — after it has been published (and paid for) in these glowing pages.

The place was Hollywood. The time: 1939. I was working on a solemn sociological study of the movie colony. One day, to my surprise, I received a telegram from the Masquers' Club, inviting me to be their guest at a banquet in honor of W. C. Fields.

I was delighted. I was transported. I revered Fields as the funniest misanthrope our land ever produced. So I appeared at the Masquers' Club. No sooner had I entered a jam-packed lobby than I heard my name blaring, over and over, from loudspeakers and an agitated voice pleading that I report to the desk *at once* for an urgent message. My heart sank. Had one of my loved ones fallen into the La Brea tar pits in search of a neglected dinosaur? Had my best researcher been crushed in a stampede outside the Brown Derby?

I plowed through the mob to the desk, where I was told by a tight-lipped factotum that I was "damn late" for one who would be seated *on the dais!* Swiftly, the majordomo led me backstage, where I beheld Fields (already red-nosed from fiery waters), surrounded by such celebrants as Groucho Marx, Bob Hope, Jack Benny, Edgar Bergen, Milton Berle. . . .

"Line up!" called the praetorian guard. He recited name after hallowed name. Mine, unhallowed, was last. "Proceed to the dais!"

As we marched across the stage, the audience rose to its feet, applauding—until I appeared. They must have thought me Sam Goldwyn's nephew from Kankakee.

The dinner was excellent, the cigars sublime, and William Collier, Sr., rose to conduct the festivities. A famous wit, he orated a barrage of dazzling, scathing, yet affectionate "ribs" about our guest of honor. To each barbed line Fields responded with an evil grin, a leering grunt, and a sip of alcoholic disdain. Collier completed his backhanded eulogy, then proclaimed, "Our first speaker to honor Bill Fields is;—he consulted his prep sheet and winced—"Dr. Leo Boston—no—*Rosten*."

It would be wrong to say that I could not believe my ears; the full measure of my horror lay in the fact that I did. I sat paralyzed. It took the elbow either of Red Skelton or of George Burns, jabbing into my ribs, to propel me to my feet.

The "applause" which had greeted Collier's garbled recitation of my name would not have awakened a mouse. My erectness compounded my shame, for the auditorium broke into frowns of confusion and murmurs seeking enlightenment. But there I stood—numb, dumb, unknown—looking into a star-filled sea of faces staring glumly at me. I prayed for a trapdoor to open beneath me or for lightning to strike me dead. Neither happened. Instead I heard a hoarse *sotto voce* "Say *some*thin'!" The voice dripped with unmistakable disgust.

I gulped—then heard someone who was hiding in my throat utter these words: "The only thing I can say about W. C. Fields, whom I have admired since the day he advanced upon Baby LeRoy with an ice pick, is this: any man who hates dogs and babies can't be all bad."

The appearance of Mae West in a G-string would not have produced a more explosive cachinnation. The laughter was so uproarious, the ovation so deafening, the table-slapping and shoulder-punching were so vigorous, that I cleverly collapsed onto my chair.

I scarcely remember the rest of that historic night. The jokes and gags and needlings of Fields (who by now resembled a benign Caligula) put all previous celebrity "roasts" to shame.

But the next morning, all the local papers led off their stories about the banquet with my ad-lib. The AP and UPI and INS flung my remark around the world. CBS and the BBC featured the quip on radio. Overnight, I was an international wit.

Alas. God put bitters in the wine of my enflatterment; for ever since then, "Any man who hates dogs and babies can't be all bad" has been credited to—W. C. Fields. Hardly a week passes in which I do not run across some reference to "Fields' immortal crack."

Let any who question my veracity simply check the newspapers of February 17 (the morning after the banquet), 1939. Or let them consult *Time* or *Newsweek*. All correctly attribute the aphorism to its young and catatonic creator.

Embarrassing moments? Man!

Reading and Interpreting

1. Check another dictionary on the word *matzo.* Do you find any differences from Rosten's account?

2. Is the incident Rosten reports in *b* actually an "embarrassing moment"?

Writing Techniques

1. Try to distinguish between the two audiences for whom Rosten is writing. Any distinction will need to be sharp. As a matter of fact, most of the readers who regularly follow Rosten's column, *Diversions,* in *The Saturday Review* are likely also to know *The Joys of Yiddish.* But the two selections differ somewhat, and close reading should suggest distinctions that may be based on different anticipated audiences.

2. Rosten in the second selection uses more than half his skit in providing an account in detail of what preceded the central incident. What is the value of this long account of preliminary events?

Suggestions for Writing

"My Most Embarassing Moment" is a kind of standard writing assignment, for college classes as well as the "ambitious women" who solicited Rosten. But as Rosten demonstrates, an account of this sort can be interesting. Try writing one, noting particularly that Rosten's account develops constantly with specific details.

SOME KNIGHTS IN NEED OF AN AUDIENCE   **29**
Lewis Carroll

Lewis Carroll *(whose actual name was Charles Lutwidge Dodgson), taught at Oxford University, where he was known as a boring lecturer. He wrote monographs on mathematics, almost entirely forgotten, and books of fantasy and nonsense like* The Hunting of the Snark, *mostly forgotten, but he is known the world over for two little books he wrote to amuse Alice Liddell, the daughter of faculty friends. The books were* Alice in Wonderland *and* Alice Through the Looking Glass, *from which the following selection is taken.*

AT this moment her [Alice's] thoughts were interrupted by a loud shouting of "Ahoy! Ahoy! Check!" and a Knight, dressed in crimson armour, came galloping down upon her, brandishing a great club. Just as he reached her, the horse stopped suddenly: "You're my prisoner!" the Knight cried, as he tumbled off his horse.

Startled as she was, Alice was more frightened for him than for herself at the moment, and watched him with some anxiety as he mounted again. As soon as he was comfortably in the saddle, he began once more "You're my——" but here another voice broke in "Ahoy! Ahoy! Check!" and Alice looked round in some surprise for the new enemy.

Why the word check?

This time it was a White Knight. He drew up at Alice's side, and tumbled off his horse just as the Red Knight had done: then he got on again, and the two Knights sat and looked at each other for some time without speaking. Alice looked from one to the other in some bewilderment.

"She's *my* prisoner, you know!" the Red Knight said at last.

"Yes, but then *I* came and rescued her!" the White Knight replied.

"Well, we must fight for her, then," said the Red Knight, as he took up his helmet (which hung from the saddle, and was something the shape of a horse's head) and put it on.

"You will observe the Rules of Battle, of course?" the White Knight remarked, putting on his helmet too.

"I always do," said the Red Knight, and they began banging away at each other with such fury that Alice got behind a tree to be out of the way of the blows.

The battle begins.

"I wonder, now, what the Rules of Battle are," she said to herself, as she watched the fight, timidly peeping out from her hiding-place. "One Rule seems to be, that if one Knight hits the other, he knocks him off his horse; and, if he misses, he tumbles off himself— and another Rule seems to be that they hold their clubs with their arms, as if they were Punch and Judy—What a noise they make when they tumble! Just like a whole set of fire-irons falling into the fender! And how quiet the horses are! They let them get on and off them just as if they were tables!"

Another Rule of Battle, that Alice had not noticed, seemed to be that they always fell on their heads; and the battle ended with their both falling off in this way, side by side. When they got up again, they shook hands, and then the Red Knight mounted and galloped off.

"It was a glorious victory, wasn't it?" said the White Knight, as he came up panting.

"I don't know," Alice said doubtfully. "I don't want to be anybody's prisoner. I want to be a Queen."

"So you will, when you've crossed the next brook," said the White Knight. "I'll see you safe to the end of the wood—and then I must go back, you know. That's the end of my move."

The end of the move.

"Thank you very much," said Alice. "May I help you off with your helmet!" It was evidently more than he could manage by himself: however she managed to shake him out of it at last.

"Now one can breathe more easily," said the Knight, putting back his shaggy hair with both hands, and turning his gentle face and large mild eyes to Alice. She thought she had never seen such a strange-looking soldier in all her life.

He was dressed in tin armour, which seemed to fit him very badly, and he had a queer-shaped little deal box fastened across his shoulders, upside-down, and with the lid hanging open. Alice looked at it with great curiosity.

"I see you're admiring my little box," the Knight said in a friendly tone. "It's my own invention—to keep clothes and sandwiches in. You see I carry it upside-down, so that the rain can't get in."

"But the things can get *out*," Alice gently remarked. "Do you know the lid's open?"

"I didn't know it," the Knight said, a shade of vexation passing over his face. "Then all the things must have fallen out! And the box is no use without them." He unfastened it as he spoke, and was just going to throw it into the bushes, when a sudden thought seemed to strike him, and he hung it carefully on a tree. "Can you guess why I did that?" he said to Alice.

Alice shook her head.

"In hopes some bees may make a nest in it—then I should get the honey."

"But you've got a bee-hive—or something like one—fastened to the saddle," said Alice.

"Yes, it's a very good bee-hive," the Knight said in a dis-contented tone, "one of the best kind. But not a single bee has come near it yet. And the other thing is a mouse-trap. I suppose the mice keep the bees out—or the bees keep the mice out, I don't know which."

There must be satire here. What does it suggest about the audience?

"I was wondering what the mouse-trap was for," said Alice. "It isn't very likely there would be any mice on the horse's back."

"Not very likely, perhaps," said the Knight; "but, if they *do* come, I don't choose to have them running all about."

"You see," he went on after a pause, "it's as well to be provided for *everything*. That's the reason the horse has all those anklets round his feet."

"But what are they for?" Alice asked in a tone of great curiosity.

"To guard against the bites of sharks," the Knight said. "They're my own invention."

Reading and Interpreting

1. Why does the White Knight say, "That's the end of my move"? What else in the selection suggests the same intention of the author?

2. Obviously this piece is satirical. What does Carroll seem to be making fun of? How much in the piece is simply nonsense included only for amusement?

3. Carroll's Alice stories are still among the most widely read books in the language. From this selection can you suggest why?

Writing Techniques

1. The selection is from *Through the Looking Glass,* one of the books Carroll wrote for an Oxford professor's daughter. Mention spe-cific items of information the selection assumes that the reader will have. Would a modern child be likely to have all the information necessary to understand the selection?

2. The selection is primarily narrative. Does it make direct comments to express any attitude or purpose beyond telling the story? How does it reveal its satiric purpose to the reader?

Word Study

1. How do you account for the spelling of *armour* in the first sentence?

2. What is the meaning of *deal*, used to describe the box the White Knight discusses toward the end of the selection?

Suggestions for Writing

Attempts at direct imitation of Carroll are not likely to be successful, but you might try writing a short narrative for a child, dealing with characters animated from a game or with other imaginary characters.

The Writer's Stance: Voice, Point of View, Tone

When you write, you take what may be called a *stance*. Literally, a stance is "the way a person or animal stands," as in a golfer's stance. In rhetoric the word is used figuratively, to describe the way a writer stands in relation to a subject.

In part, a writer's stance expresses a personality. You write as you do partly because you are the kind of person you are and have had your own experiences. Your sex and your age and your family background alter the attitudes you will take toward your subject. If your father deserted you and you are now working your way through college, you may see class attendance differently than do friends who are given all the money they can use. But your stance also depends on your purposes for any piece of writing, on the subject, and on the audience you anticipate. It appears also in the voice, point of view, and tone you adopt.

In a sense, whenever you write you are a kind of actor, playing a role. You assume a *voice*. Writing a story, you may pretend to be one of the characters and write in the first person, reporting events as your character saw them. You may write as if a child were telling the story, or you may use the voice of a person looking back on events and reminiscing. You may pretend to be an outside observer, who knows even what is going on in your characters' minds. Even

177

when you are not writing fiction you adopt a voice, usually playing some part of yourself, but writing differently for different occasions. In one of the selections following, for instance, Donna Cord writes as an angry housewife—which she probably is—but for other occasions she might write in a different voice. Jean Kerr pretends to be a cowed and bewildered housewife, exasperated with problems of rearing children. At other times she writes as a witty sophisticate, unlikely to be abashed by any youngster, however devious.

Also, when you write, you adopt a *point of view,* a physical position in space and time. Suppose you want to describe a stabbing and you decide to write in the voice of an eyewitness. You could establish a position looking down from a fifteenth-floor window. From that point of view you would be limited; you could not tell much about such details as the kind of shoes the stabber wore or even the weapon he used. But you would have an advantage of being able to describe the entire scene, the arrival of the police, the people moving about, perhaps where the stabber ran. If you wrote as though you were standing beside the victim, you would be able to use intimate details, but you would not have so wide a view. You would also need to take a position in time—looking back at the incident, for instance, or perhaps writing as if it is occurring as you talk. Gerald Durrell in "Knee Deep in Scorpions" is looking back at an incident he remembers; Donna Cord assumes that what she describes exists in the present, while she is writing.

Stance implies also a *tone* or manner, like a tone of voice in speaking—harsh, soft, sarcastic, bitter, straightforward. The three essays on women's rights are written with different voices and in different tones. Donna Cord justifies her title by seeming to be "mad"; the writing is vigorous, direct, angry-sounding. Shana Alexander, as a trained journalist writing a report, is more judicious, more objective in tone. Would you call Anne Taylor Fleming "a swinging feminist"? Or jaunty but too dedicated to be flip? Many other sorts of tone are possible. A writer on women's rights might take a lofty, authoritarian, self-righteous approach, reminding readers that Jehovah is said to have told Eve to obey Adam. Another might be sarcastic, restrained or sentimental, boastful or reticent, flippant or serious. Swift's "A Modest Proposal," which appeared earlier as an example of argument, is ironic and satiric. Section XIII, "Serious Fun," has samples of other tones.

The selections that follow provide an approach to writing. They offer insights into the natures of individual authors and they illustrate various sorts of stances authors may adopt. You can chart the differences by describing for each selection the voice the speaker uses, by identifying the physical point of view, and by observing the tone of the writing.

KNEE DEEP IN SCORPIONS

Gerald Durrell

30

Gerald Durrell, *one of the great collectors of all times, developed his love of all living things while his family was spending five years on the Greek island of Corfu. The excerpt is from* My Family and Other Animals *(1961), which describes their life there. The "Larry" of the account is the novelist Lawrence Durrell, at the time of this piece a scrambling young literateur.*

THEN one day I found a fat female scorpion in the wall, wearing what at first glance appeared to be a pale fawn fur coat. Closer inspection proved that this strange garment was made up of a mass of tiny babies clinging to the mother's back. I was enraptured by this family, and I made up my mind to smuggle them into the house and up to my bedroom so that I might keep them and watch them grow up. With infinite care I manoeuvred the mother and family into a match-box, and then hurried to the villa. It was rather unfortunate that just as I entered the door lunch should be served; however, I placed the match-box carefully on the mantelpiece in the drawing room, so that the scorpions should get plenty of air, and made my way to the dining room and joined the family for the meal. Dawdling over my food, feeding Roger surreptitiously under the table, and listening to the family arguing, I completely forgot about my exciting new captures. At last Larry, having finished, fetched the cigarettes from the drawing room, and lying back in his chair he put one in his mouth and picked up the match-box he had brought. Oblivious of my impending doom I watched him interestedly as, still talking glibly, he opened the match-box.

Now I maintain to this day that the female scorpion meant no harm. She was agitated and a trifle annoyed at being shut up in a match-box for so long, and so she seized the first opportunity to escape. She hoisted herself out of the box with great rapidity, her babies clinging on desperately, and scuttled onto the back of Larry's hand. There, not quite certain what to do next, she paused, her sting curved up at the ready. Larry, feeling the movement of her claws, glanced down to see what it was, and from that moment things got increasingly confused.

He uttered a roar of fright that made Lugaretzia [the maid] drop a plate and brought Roger out from beneath the table, barking wildly. With a flick of his hand he sent the unfortunate scorpion flying down the table, and she landed midway between Margo and Leslie [the two other children], scattering babies like confetti as she thumped onto the cloth. Thoroughly enraged at this treatment, the creature sped towards Leslie, her sting quivering with emotion. Leslie leaped to his feet, overturning his chair, and flicked out desperately with his napkin, sending the scorpion rolling across the cloth towards Margo, who promptly let out a scream that any railway engine would have been proud to produce. Mother, completely bewildered by this sudden and rapid change from peace to chaos, put on her glasses and peered down the table to see what was causing the pandemonium, and at that moment Margo, in a vain attempt to stop the scorpion's advance, hurled a glass of water at it. The shower missed the animal completely, but successfully drenched Mother, who, not being able to stand cold water, promptly lost her breath and sat gasping at the end of the table, unable even to protest. The scorpion had now gone to ground under Leslie's plate, while her babies swarmed wildly all over the table. Roger, mystified by the panic, but determined to do his share, ran round and round the room, barking hysterically.

"It's that bloody boy again . . ." bellowed Larry.

"Look out! Look out! They're coming!" screamed Margo.

"All we need is a book," roared Leslie; "don't panic, hit 'em with a book."

"What on earth's the *matter* with you all?" Mother kept imploring, mopping her glasses.

"It's that bloody boy . . . he'll kill the lot of us. . . . Look at the table . . . knee-deep in scorpions. . . ."

"Quick . . . quick . . . do something. . . . Look out, look out!"

"Stop screeching and get a book, for God's sake. . . . You're worse than the dog. . . . Shut *up*, Roger. . . ."

"By the grace of God I wasn't bitten. . . ."

"Look out . . . there's another one. . . . Quick . . . quick. . . ."

"Oh, shut up and get me a book or something. . . . "

"But *how* did the scorpions get on the table, dear?"

"That bloody boy. . . . Every match-box in the house is a death-trap. . . ."

"Look out, it's coming towards me. . . . Quick, quick, do something. . . ."

"Hit it with your knife . . . *your knife*. . . . Go on, hit it. . . ."

Since no one had bothered to explain things to him, Roger was under the mistaken impression that the family were being attacked, and that it was his duty to defend them. As Lugaretzia was the only stranger in the room, he came to the logical conclusion that she must be the responsible party, so he bit her in the ankle. This did not help matters very much.

By the time a certain amount of order had been restored, all the baby scorpions had hidden themselves under various plates and bits of cutlery. Eventually, after impassioned pleas on my part, backed up by Mother, Leslie's suggestion that the whole lot be slaughtered was quashed. While the family, still simmering with rage and fright, retired to the drawing-room, I spent half an hour rounding up the babies, picking them up in a teaspoon, and returning them to their mother's back. Then I carried them outside on a saucer and, with the utmost reluctance, released them on the garden wall.

Reading and Interpreting

1. What gives the account of the incident its interest? How much does it reveal about the character of the narrator? How much of the interest depends on the use of specific details?

2. The characters other than the narrator are presented only briefly. Try to distinguish the attitudes of each of the characters toward scorpions and toward the episode.

Writing Techniques

1. Describe the voice the writer adopts for the story. At the time he was writing, the author was a mature scientist. Does he make his narrator a child recounting the incident, or is the narrator an adult remembering? What are the advantages of the voice the author adopts?

2. Try to describe the tone of the piece, the attitude the author takes toward the incident and the reader. Is the author making fun of the boy, is he tolerantly amused, is he critical of the boy's carelessness, or is he completely noncommital?

3. What limits does the author's choice of a point of view impose? How does he use his stance to reveal attitudes and thoughts of the actors, especially of those other than the narrator?

Suggestions for Writing

Try telling this incident from the point of view of one of the other characters. The selection reveals only a little about them, but you might think of them in the following ways as they are presented in the complete book from which the selection is taken. Lugaretzia is a somewhat scatterbrained, garrulous peasant woman. The mother loves her children and is tolerant of them, in her quite capable way, but her way includes taking a bit of the British Empire with her wherever she goes, and being somewhat baffled that, as a Victorian lady, she must assume the headship of an upper-class household. Lawrence is trying hard to become the novelist he eventually did become, and is much aware of himself as an artist and an intellectual. Leslie, the brother next in line, a decent, downright sort of fellow, loves guns and hunting. Margo—who has since become an author in her own right—was very much a teenage girl, concerned with being pretty and attractive.

ATTITUDES ON UNPREPARED STUDENTS
Bel Kaufman

31

Bel Kaufman *is a grade school teacher who became a national figure through one best seller,* Up the Down Staircase *(1964), the source of these excerpts. The book is a chronological sequence, composed of her diary and other documents, notably papers from her pupils.*

CIRCULAR # 61

PLEASE KEEP ALL CIRCULARS ON FILE, IN THEIR ORDER

TOPIC: HOMEWORK ADDENDUM

WE HAVE HAD AN EPIDEMIC OF UNPREPARED STUDENTS. A STUDENT UNPREPARED WITH HOMEWORK MUST SUBMIT TO HIS TEACHER, IN WRITING, HIS REASON OR REASONS FOR NEGLECTING TO DO IT. PLEASE KEEP THESE HOMEWORK EXCUSES ON FILE IN THE RIGHT-HAND DRAWER OF YOUR DESK.

James J. McHabe
Adm. Asst.

From the right-hand drawer, Room 304:

I know homework is essential to our well being, and I did it but I got into a fight with some kid on the way to school and he threw it in the gutter.

My dog chewed it up.

I didn't know we were supposed to do it.

I fell asleep on the subway because I stayed up all night doing my homework, so when it stopped at my station I ran through the door not to be late & left it on the seat on the subway.

The cat chewed it up and there was no time to do it over.

The page was missing from my book.

Even though I brought in a legal note for absence he sent me back. That's why I'm unprepared.

I had to take care of my three siblings because my mother is in the hospital.

Why I Didn't Do It. When you tell us to bring a book report I do not like it because I have to go to the library and get a book to read it. It will take me about two month or more to read it and I have to owe money to them and it adds up. It isn't fair to the pocket, Ha-ha! In those hours when I have to read the book I can watch TV or play around or shoot a couple.

As I was taking down the assignment my ballpoint stopped.

I had to study French so didn't have time to study English.

I did it but left it home by mistake.

If a teacher wants to know something why doesn't she look it up herself instead of making we students do it? We benefit ourselves more by listening to her, after all, she's the teacher.

The baby spilled milk on it.

My brother took "my" homework instead of "his."

I have to work after school and they kept me til midnight.

I lost my book & just found it.

There's no room in my house now my uncle moved in and I have to sleep in the hall and couldn't use the kitchen table.

Some one stole it.

I was sick and had to go to bed.

What homework?

My dog pead on it.

Reading and Interpreting

1. Do you accept the examples from McHabe and from the students as real rather than fictional? What makes them convincing? Which of the student reports sound like obvious fibs?

2. Does the selection imply any kind of judgment or comment on the value of either the order from McHabe or the responses of the student?

Writing Techniques

McHabe and the students write from markedly different points of view, but there are also differences in the approaches taken by different students. Distinguish among the stances taken by different students as they approach a practical writing problem—for instance, the tone of the student who wrote sanctimoniously about his "siblings," the next one who decided on a defiant approach, and the final one who wrote that the dog "pead on it."

PLEASE DON'T EAT THE DAISIES
Jean Kerr

32

Jean Kerr *is the author of very funny comedies* (Mary, Mary; Goldilocks; King of Hearts, among others). *Her husband is Walter Kerr, drama critic for* The New York Times. *Her* Please Don't Eat the Daisies, *which includes the following chapter, is a collection of sketches about their family life.*

WE are being very careful with our children. They'll never have to pay a psychiatrist twenty-five dollars an hour to find out why we rejected them. We'll tell them why we rejected them. Because they're impossible, that's why.

It seems to me, looking back on it, that everything was all right when there were two of them and two of us. We felt loved, protected, secure. But now that there are four of them and two of us, things have changed. We're in the minority, we're not as vigorous as we used to be, and it's clear that we cannot compete with these younger men.

You take Christopher—and you *may;* he's a slightly used eight-year-old. The source of our difficulty with him lies in the fact that he is interested in the precise value of words whereas we are only interested in having him pick his clothes up off the floor. I say, "Christopher, you take a bath and put all your things in the wash," and he says, "Okay, but it will break the Bendix." Now at this point the shrewd rejoinder would be, "That's all right, let it break the Bendix." But years of experience have washed over me in vain and I, perennial *perennial* patsy, inquire, "*Why* will it break the Bendix?" So he explains, "Well, if I put *all* my things in the wash, I'll have to put my shoes in and they will certainly break the machinery."

"Very, well," I say, all sweetness and control, "put everything but the shoes in the wash." He picks up my agreeable tone at once, announcing cheerily, "Then you *do* want me to put my belt in the wash." I don't know what I say at this point, but my husband says, "Honey, you mustn't scream at him that way."

Another version of this battle of semantics would be:

"Don't kick the table leg with your foot."

"I'm not kicking, I'm tapping."

"Well, don't tap with your foot."

"It's not my foot, it's a fork."

"Well don't tap with the fork."

"It's not a *good* fork" . . . et cetera, et cetera.

Christopher is an unusual child in other respects. I watch him from the kitchen window. With a garden rake in one hand he scampers up a tree, out across a long branch, and down over the stone wall—as graceful and as deft as a squirrel. On the other hand, he is *deft* unable to get from the living room into the front hall without bumping into at least two pieces of furniture. (I've seen him hit as many as five, but that's championship stuff and he can't do it every time.)

He has another trick which defies analysis, and also the laws of gravity. He can walk out into the middle of a perfectly empty kitchen and trip on the linoleum. I *guess* it's the linoleum. There isn't anything else there.

My friends who have children are always reporting the quaint and agreeable utterances of their little ones. For example, the mother of one five-year-old philosopher told me that when she appeared at breakfast in a new six-dollar pink wrap-around, her little boy chirped, in a tone giddy with wonder, "Oh, look, our Miss Mommy must be going to a wedding!" Now I don't think any one of my children would say a thing like that. (What do I mean I don't *think;* there are some things about which you can be positive.) Of course, in a six-dollar wrap-around I wouldn't look as if I were going to a wedding. I'd look as if I were going to paint the garage. But that's not the point. The point is: where is that babbling, idiotic loyalty that other mothers get?

A while back I spoke of a time when there were two of them

and two of us. In my affinity for round numbers I'm falsifying the *affinity*
whole picture. Actually, there never were two of them. There was one
of them, and all of a sudden there were three of them.

The twins are four now, and for several years we have had gal- *galvanized*
vanized iron fencing lashed onto the outside of their bedroom windows. This gives the front of the house a rather institutional look and
contributes to unnecessary rumors about my mental health, but it
does keep them off the roof, which is what we had in mind.

For twins they are very dissimilar. Colin is tall and active and
Johnny is short and middle-aged. Johnny doesn't kick off his shoes,
he doesn't swallow beer caps or tear pages out of the telephone book.
I don't think he ever draws pictures with my best lipstick. In fact, he
has none of the charming, lighthearted "boy" qualities that precipi-
tate so many scenes of violence in the home. On the other hand, he
has a feeling for order and a passion for system that would be trying
in a head nurse. If his pajamas are hung on the third hook in the
closet instead of on the second hook, it causes him real pain. If one
slat in a Venetian blind is tipped in the wrong direction he can't
have a moment's peace until somebody fixes it. Indeed, if one of the
beans on his plate is slightly longer than the others he can scarcely
bear to eat it. It's hard for him to live with the rest of us. And vice
versa.

Colin is completely different. He has a lightness of touch and a
dexterity that will certainly put him on top of the heap if he ever *dexterity*
takes up safe-cracking. Equipped with only a spoon and an old
emery board, he can take a door off its hinges in seven minutes and
remove all of the towel racks from the bathroom in five.

Gilbert is only seventeen months old, and it's too early to tell
about him. (As a matter of fact, we can tell, all right, but we're just
not ready to face it.) Once upon a time we might have been taken in
by smiles and gurgles and round blue eyes, but no more. We know
he is just biding his time. Today he can't do much more than eat his
shoelaces and suck off an occasional button. Tomorrow, the world.

My real problem with children is that I haven't any imagination.
I'm always warning them against the commonplace defections while
they are planning the bizarre and unusual. Christopher gets up *bizarre*
ahead of the rest of us on Sunday mornings and he has long since
been given a list of clear directives: "Don't wake the baby," "Don't
go outside in your pajamas," "Don't eat cookies before breakfast."
But I never told him, "Don't make flour paste and glue together all
the pages of the magazine section of the Sunday *Times*." Now I tell
him, of course.

And then last week I had a dinner party and told the twins and
Christopher not to go in the living room, not to use the guest towels
in the bathroom, and not to leave the bicycles on the front steps.
However, I neglected to tell them not to eat the daisies on the

dining-room table. This was a serious omission, as I discovered when I came upon my centerpiece—a charming three-point arrangement of green stems.

The thing is, I'm going to a psychiatrist and find out why I have this feeling of persecution . . . this sense of being continually surrounded. . . .

Reading and Interpreting

1. Compare this piece with the selection from *Up the Down Staircase.* Are there any similarities in the pictures presented of the children?

2. What impression do you get of the attitude of the narrator toward her children? What kind of household is she describing— happy, chaotic, normal, tense, or some combination? Do you feel that she really wants "that babbling, idiotic loyalty that other mothers get"?

3. How do you interpret comments like: "they're impossible" in the first paragraph referring to the children; "I haven't any imagination," referring to herself; or the parenthetical "we can tell, all right"?

Writing Techniques

1. The introduction to Part Two points out that a writer's stance in any composition grows from his genuine feelings about a subject and from the voice he adopts. Describe the character of the narrator in this piece? Do you assume that the narrator has the same attitude as the author? Describe the stance of each.

2. The piece is deliberately humorous, and partly ironic in tone. How does the writer convey the impression that she does not really consider her children monsters and herself a downtrodden housewife? What is the effect of her use of exaggeration? She pretends to analyze both herself and her children, and seems not to understand either. What is the effect of her pretended miscalculations?

3. Why is this writing funny? One critic suggested, because the reader so frequently encounters the unexpected. Could you find evidence for such a statement?

Word Study

From the context write a brief definition of the words in the margins (*perennial, deft, affinity, galvanized, dexterity, bizarre*). Then look them up in a dictionary and make any necessary revisions in your definitions. Note especially the etymology of *galvanized, dexterity*, and *bizarre*.

Suggestions for Writing

Write a sketch about children you have known or observed, illustrating as fully as you can with examples of their behavior.

DIARY OF A MAD HOUSEWIFE
Donna Cord

33

Donna Cord *tells us something about herself; the "My Turn" column to which she refers is a weekly editorial in* Newsweek, *each week by a different author, usually distinguished journalists or public figures.*

YOU, my fellow Americans, will probably never read this. Not because my thoughts are not interesting, or important, or valid, or a darn sight better than a lot of the gibberish I have read in the My Turn column. But because I am nobody . . . that is, I am not what the enlightened editors at *Newsweek* would call a distinguished guest writer. But then, how many of those are there around anyway? No, I am just a poor, ordinary schnook—married, mother, citizen. The BankAmericard bill around our house is in four figures and the Sears bill is not far behind. A traveling vacation is in the unforeseeable future, as is a new car (our '68 Chevelle is creaky, but it runs), a new coat, roast beef and air conditioning. How many "My Turn" columnists can match *those* qualifications? *(margin: The writer establishes a stance.)*

The one thing that I have an abundance of at this point in time is anger. Anger and disgust. Not with my country. The United States is blessed (in theory at least) with all the institutions to make it work For The People. I am angry with you, and you, and me. All of us. We have become a nation of sheep—and we are being screwed at every turn. *(margin: She announces her audience.)*

We, the people, are letting go unchallenged atrocities that should warm the hearts of totalitarian leaders everywhere. The governor of California pays no taxes. The President pays laughably little (and by the way—*my* memoirs and personal papers are just sitting here, waiting for someone to appraise them . . .); your rich landlord probably paid less than you. Capital gains, write-offs, loopholes. Everyone acknowledges that only the middle-average-poor get the tax *(margin: Richard Nixon was then president, Gerald Ford vice-president.)*

shaft. So why do we let it happen? Where is a full-fledged taxpayers' revolt? I am tired of being hopelessly debt-ridden while the rich and the super-rich and the politicians go skiing (did you notice our new Vice-President happily giving interviews on the snowy slopes of Colorado?).

My husband belongs to no union; he gets no (ha ha) "cost of living" raises. So each year that he earns the same, our financial condition goes straight downhill. We need gas as much as anyone, but if *we* had dared to block an interstate highway with our rusty car, we would have been arrested in two minutes flat. Why is it that big, profitable airlines have the ear of the government, and plain people do not? Why, if indeed there is a shortage of gasoline, were the huge oil companies allowed to raise their prices to compensate for the reduced supply? All that that accomplished was to keep their profits (amounts so enormous they boggle the mind) at the same level. Well, the oil companies are part of the reason for the energy crisis, so why *should* their profits stay the same (or worse, increase)? What is the tragedy if big business would bear part of the burden of our current troubles?

Argument by asking questions— does it work?

But oh, no, folks. You and I are the ones who pay—60 cents a gallon and no end in sight. Can you believe that the signs of this energy crunch were not apparent to our government three months ago, or six months ago, or two years ago? What the hell have our leaders been doing? Wallowing in Watergate? But, lo and behold, all of a sudden the government announces that there is an energy crisis and a shortage of practically everything, and we meekly accept. Why aren't we outraged? We are taken for fools and suckers—and we must be.

Do the questions fit the stance of a mad housewife?

We are fools because we have uncomplainingly let the big-money interests take over our country. If you're not a conglomerate, you're nobody. I laugh and cry and rage all at the same time when some overeducated economist rattles on about supply and demand and trade deficits and baloney; then he slinks away, back to his well-furnished home and well-padded paycheck, while we nod our heads and eat macaroni again.

We, the people, used to have high moral standards—sometimes downright Victorian and repressive, but high nevertheless. So why are we allowing our beloved country to limp along with a President who is at best morally questionable, surrounding himself with yes men and crooks and perjurers and enriching himself at our expense? My house needs remodeling—will you send me tax money to pay for it?

Congress, a body of elected officials completely surrounded by a vacuum, is supposed to reflect the will of the people. And it is reflecting all right—reflecting our *lack* of will to change what is wrong. What are we afraid of? Have we met the enemy and it is us? Where is our public pressure—our collective will—to either get off the Presi-

Notice her lively phrasing.

dent's back (if his is still truly the leadership we want) or get him out of office?

We have gone along for years accepting the rich getting richer, toys that can maim, built-in obsolescence, unsafe cars, medical costs that threaten bankruptcy, air that chokes us and special-interest lobbies in Washington. Don't we care? Are we indeed such sheep that we must wait for a Ralph Nader to come along and get our cars made safer for us? We are the ones who are getting smashed up in our Tinkertoy two-doors at the rate of 50,000 a year while Pentagon personnel spend their time in chauffeured (and, I might add, sturdy) limousines. Where is the "citizens' lobby" to look out for *your* interests?

There is insanity all about us. Our government sells wheat to Russia, which in turn supports and encourages the Arab countries, which in turn shut off our oil. We pay farmers for *not* growing food, and millions go hungry. The dairy industry is a government pet, and I try powdered milk (ugh!) because real milk sells for $1.50 a gallon. If we elect an almost "ordinary" person—that is, not a millionaire—to high office (like Agnew), he winds up with his hand out for money; and if we elect millionaires, how can they know or care about the ordinary needs of ordinary people?

I have no answers—only a strong faith in the power of the people. I only know that you can't be walked on if you stand up. I know I care about my country and the quality of my life. And so do my neighbors. And the people all across America. Where are our voices? There is a scene from "The Magnificent Seven" in which the outlaw says of the poor villagers whose town he has just plundered, "If God didn't want them shorn, He would not have made them sheep." Have we become a nation of sheep?

> The tone shifts. Does the change strengthen or weaken the earlier stance?

Reading and Interpreting

1. Is the piece a personal complaint, or is it a serious criticism of our society? Is it significant that the piece was written by a woman?

2. Are the details she cites accurate? Have any of the "atrocities" she lists been reformed since she wrote?

Writing Techniques

1. The writer directly describes the stance she is adopting as "angry." How does her choice of words reflect that anger?

2. What does the writer gain by adopting the character of an outraged citizen who is personally affected by what she criticizes?

Does she lose anything? Is there any danger that readers will not react entirely favorably because they will suspect her of special pleading, will feel that the case is exaggerated?

3. Try to characterize Cord's tone. It is as tense as though she
were in a shouting match, but that is not all. Does her persistence
bother you? If so, is it possibly true that a striking tone should not
be maintained too consistently? Or is this tautness appropriate, at
least in a short piece?

Suggestions for Writing

Cord's piece is impressive especially because of the wealth of
details she has amassed and classified to make her point. Try a criticism of some institution or activity you find improper—current educational policies, for example, or the defeat by lobbyists of gun-control
laws, or student government, graduation requirements, or fraternity
or sorority regulations—marshalling details to support a point of
view. Or you might try a refutation of Cord's article.

UP FROM SLAVERY—TO WHAT?
Anne Taylor Fleming

34

Anne Taylor Fleming, *a free-lance writer who lives and works in
Los Angeles, publishes in* Newsweek *magazine and other publications. This
article appeared in* Newsweek.

FOR a long time now I've been going to parties and hearing
that creative people in America are—like gasoline, raisins, and happily married couples—becoming scarcer and scarcer. To which I always reply, "Just wait until we 'new' women find our voices. Then
you'll see the real stuff again."

The first
sentence
establishes (1) a
thesis, (2) a
stance.

Apparently, my boast was hasty and naive. We may have come
a long way, baby, but if our first creative efforts—the books, magazines, the films, the canvases, the TV shows, the plays and the
poems—are any indication, it isn't nearly far enough. The sad truth
is that the words women are writing, the magazines they're editing,
the shows they're producing sound almost exactly like what their
husbands, lovers, or masters, if you will, have been turning out for
years.

In fact, women are going men one better: they're running faster,
swinging harder, playing rougher. The writing they are doing in *Ms.*

magazine is so hard-edged, so tough, that it makes any of the magazines for men look softheaded and mushy by comparison. Bella Abzug and Shirley Chisholm, the new kind of female politician, practice their art with a sharpness, a brittleness that their male colleagues and opponents can only envy. Barbara Walters has a stiffer upper lip than Frank McGee, one of her co-hosts on the "Today" show.

This female toughness may be excused as an entrance fee, a survival device that women feel they have to use. But what it really is, it seems to me, is a capitulation and a copout. It's as if we were all sticking our thumbs under our overall straps and saying, "See. See how sharp and quick our little minds are. We can think like men after all. We can even outplay you at your own game." But finding a new and better game, a game where might ain't necessarily right? That never even crossed our minds.

A word of caution. I am a women's liberationist, a feminist. Like any other halfway sane woman in this country, I have to be. I want it, and I want it all, and I want it now. And I concede that this wanting of mine has been made a lot easier by the efforts of some hard-thinking and hard-talking women who have gone before.

What I want is equal rights—professional, emotional and sexual. What I don't want is that good old American brand of equality that insists that we're all equal not only in rights but in body and soul as well. What I don't want is to give up my specialness, my female ethnicity. The trouble is, there seems to be only one game in town. And like the blacks who had to take the kinks out of their hair and the jive out of their language—their recent attempts to put both back in being symbolic, not substantial victories—to get into the game, there will be enormous pressure on me to lay aside my frills of body and mind at the entrance gate. I don't want to think, eat, sleep, talk, laugh, act or write like a man. I don't want to wear a handsome suit, carry a briefcase and anticipate clogged arteries at age 40. I don't even want to wear blue jeans all the time. I don't want to make, in short, all the same mistakes men have been making for years. I don't want to hate homosexuals, co-workers or beautiful women just because they threaten me.

Norman Mailer said at least one correct thing in his book, "The Prisoner of Sex." That is, he stood in awe before the mystery of the female body. Bravo. I have often stood in awe of my own. No woman who has felt her breasts change shape ever so slowly, who has felt the perverse pleasure of a menstrual cramp or labor pain, who has felt herself come alive sexually would deny the wild and strange power of her body, somewhere far beyond the reach of Masters and Johnson, David Reuben, etc. Mailer missed something, though, something that even women ignore or try to hide about themselves: the mystery of the female mind. A woman's head is every bit as fluent

A summary of the thesis.

More keys to stance.

Analyze the development of this paragraph.

A notable periodic sentence.

and highly charged as a man's, and just because it has not been toughened and bruised out there in the "real world" it still has some freshness, some originality, some softness—in other words, some mystery.

We women have been allowed to be scared, fragile, coy, even a little crazy. We've been allowed, in fact encouraged, by men to be daydreamers. Consequently, the way we look at sex is different. Sexologists tell us that while a man will have a graphically physical thought about a woman, a woman's desire is usually embroidered with more diffuse erotic fantasies. "Deep Throat" and its offspring certainly show how sadly limited is the male erotic imagination. Apparently, the readers of the new skin magazines for women are, in the name of liberation, allowing their more sophisticated imaginations to also be limited, to be appeased by the same heavy-handed junk that men have bought for years. Bare hairy chests and flexed behinds just don't get to me. I doubt that they really get to other women either.

Characterize the stance as it develops.

What I worry about as I enter the real world is how much of my fantasizing, my craziness, my intuition I'll have to leave at home in order to be successful out there. I strongly believe that it is our much-mocked feminine intuition that will make us better doctors, lawyers and Indian chiefs. With that intuition, we can operate out of an instinctive wisdom, not out of the pragmatic reflex that propels our men to Watergate and other such sinkholes.

I worry that I've already been seduced, that I'll also do anything to earn an extra buck or an extra pat on the head. I worry that I'll push and pull whatever small talents I have to suit the market. I worry that I'll round off my corners so I can slip into the game unnoticed, that I'll play for "their" stakes—a jazzy job, a jazzy husband and jazzy kids—and abide by their rules. I worry that I'll aspire to be a Sally Quinn or a Gloria Steinem rather than a Frances FitzGerald or a Lillian Hellman because the rewards are more visible. I worry that I'll learn to be clever, to take all the short cuts, to steal all the bases. All of which makes me worry that I'll never hit a home run, or that I may never even try. And if you don't try to hit home runs, why play ball?

A figure of speech as a conclusion.

Reading and Interpreting

1. Summarize Fleming's complaint about current activities of women.

2. What positive solution does she suggest? How valid is her faith in women's intuition?

Writing Techniques

1. What is similar in the stances Fleming and Cord adopt for their essays? How do the two pieces differ in tone? Does Fleming also use exaggeration in making her case?

2. Notice the sixth paragraph, beginning "What I want . . . . " Is it an effective paragraph? Analyze its construction.

3. The last two paragraphs include an unusual device for continuity. Notice the topic sentences: "What I worry about . . . . " "I worry that . . . . " Does it work?

Word Study

Examine the sixth paragraph, beginning "What I want is equal rights." You probably recognize all the words in this paragraph, but some are used as you may not customarily rely upon them. Try to define as exactly as you can, using dictionaries to help you, each of the following words as they are used here, especially in view of the author's stance as she has described it: *specialness, ethnicity, game, jive, threaten.*

WILL POWER CHANGE WOMEN?
Shana Alexander

35

Shana Alexander, *a Washington journalist, was a staff member of* Newsweek *when she wrote the following editorial. She has publicized and participated in feminist movements.*

WOULD a world governed equally by women and men be a better place than the one we have now? Until this week I had always been certain it would, and had damned the Founding Fathers as our original male chauvinists. Nowhere has American "democracy" been more fraudulent than in its consistent 200-year exclusion of women from the political process. For the first 150 years or so woman was disenfranchised. When she got to vote, she failed to use it in her own behalf. She had by then—as feminists say—been "niggerized."

A question as introduction. Has she made her stance firm yet?

"Women in America are much more brainwashed and content with their roles as second-class citizens than blacks ever were," wrote Congresswoman Shirley Chisholm a couple of years back.

She would not say so today. Two years ago, 1,070 women ran

for major state and national office, according to figures compiled by
the National Women's Political Caucus. This year, more than three
times as many women already are off and running. The number of
women legislators has gone up 28 per cent in the past year. But with
no women in the U.S. Senate, and only sixteen in the House, there is
still a long way to go.

To kick off 1974 as "The Year of Women" and declare open season on male candidates, the Caucus recently staged a feminist political rally. Its theme: Will women change power, or will power change
women? A good question. On hand to answer it were three of the
Caucus's Founding Mothers: Congresswoman Bella Abzug, former
White House press secretary Liz Carpenter and writer-editor Gloria
Steinem.

Another question. Which is the thesis?

For me the rally was also a re-entry crisis. Before joining *Newsweek* I was a Founding Mother myself. An honest Cabinet officer gets
rid of his stock portfolio before assuming office; a blackjack dealer
ties a green apron over his pockets. I too wanted to play fair, to write
as a woman but not as a feminist party-liner.

But in truth my own liberation from women's lib had by then
become a matter of personal urgency. After a year in Caucus office, I
was feeling dangerously stir-crazy and figured I was due time off for
good behavior.

In our original Caucus high command were Congresswomen
Chisholm and Abzug, as well as Ms. Steinem and Betty Friedan, plus
the requisite token student and token black—and me. I thought of
myself as House Neutral, someone with no ax to grind beyond the
simple notion that more women should hold office. Women were no
better than men, but we had different priorities from men, and these
special women's concerns were being ignored in the legislatures and
in the Congress. Feeding and caring for young children, rights of
working women, single women and domestic workers, sexual discrimination of 100 subtle varieties, and various legal rights of women
and children had gone essentially unchanged not just for two years
but 50. They will remain unchanged until women legislators and politicians force the change.

But the savage infighting among the feminist leadership wore
me down. I had no heart for the hurly-burly of politics; no stomach
for it and no talent; I was glad to leave. The reason women are such
crude, brutal and destructive combatants, I later decided—the reason
women fighters lack pace, grace, rhythm and mercy—is certainly not
because we are "subject to raging hormonal impulses," as some men
claim. Nor is women's rage entirely blamable on self-hatred long repressed, as psychiatrists of both sexes like to assert.

Narrative paragraphs as development.

I think that hair-trigger female fury, the surge to leap for the
jugular at the merest drop of a glove, the readiness to "drop the

bomb on Luxembourg," results from lack of a female tradition of chivalry. Women have not been trained to fight fair. It will take some time before women learn to act like gentlemen.

Still no clear statement of stance, but some details.

But my re-entry trauma was more than worth it. Most speakers at the Caucus rally had important new things to say, and in two years the decibel level had dropped appreciably. The noises issuing from the podium were no longer the sound of the strident majority. No longer "ladylike," not yet "gentlemanly," the speakers sounded merely human. A grand sound these days.

Said Ms. Abzug, "We are not interested in ripping off a piece of power for women in a society that has no soul. We want to change the society completely. The odds are that we will change power, but power won't change us." I hope it changes us somewhat. The women's movement is still at times too much an uncomfortable parody of *machismo*.

Liz Carpenter is always the practical politician. "Will power change Chuck Colson's grandmother?" she wonders. "Will she just lie there and take it? I hope she's up on her feet, and running for city council, for state legislature. . . ." Thanks to people like Ms. Carpenter there is a Women's Political Caucus today in every state but one. The women who are running for office today are not extraordinary women. They really are housewives and grandmothers.

More details suggesting stance.

Gloria Steinem says that a separate woman's culture does exist. Women are different from men, she says, because we do not have "to prove our masculinity." While this is true enough, we do have to define our femininity, and that we have not yet done. When Ms. Steinem tells us that women constitute our only reservoir of a substantially changed set of values, I applaud. But when feminists reject certain old values, I mourn. Why won't *Ms.* publish articles on how to bake and sew? Men, at least, might read them.

Mary Anne Krupsak, a state senator now running for lieutenant governor of New York, was the most exciting speaker of all, because she was not just talking about changing power, she was out doing it. When she said, "You bet power will change women, because power gives you confidence! Confidence to speak out to women, and not to *waver* in your beliefs," you could feel the confidence level in the entire room lift, as if the audience had begun to levitate. In a sense, we had.

Senator Krupsak is a Roman Catholic, and her stand in favor of a woman's right to choose abortion or not was personally agonizing. The national president of the Right-to-Life movement lives in her district. Rosaries for her soul were said on the steps of the state capitol. Her pious, devoted parents, two pharmacists, received letters suggesting that Mary Anne herself should have been aborted.

What does Krupsak's stand exemplify?

But Senator Krupsak's own political experience, and her own

strong empathy for powerless people, had taught her that one must strive to find decent policies for society as a whole. "I had to tell myself: for some people, like me, the fetus is alive. But for some other people, it isn't! What about them? If *they* are denied abortion, they lose *everything*. You cannot inflict your own position on others in a pluralistic society."

Mary Anne Krupsak is what I meant when I wrote some years back that women are more idealistic than men, and crazily brave. How we need that now!

What can you say about this as a conclusion?

Reading and Interpreting

1. Does Alexander answer either of the questions she poses — the one at the beginning of the essay or the one in the title? Does the final paragraph provide an answer? Is Alexander's position as clear as that of Fleming or Cord?

2. According to Alexander, how did the women's movement change during the two years preceding the Caucus rally she describes?

3. How do you react to Alexander's comment about halfway through the editorial that "It will take some time before women learn to act like gentlemen"? Should women learn to act like gentlemen?

Writing Techniques

1. How does Alexander's writing stance differ from that of Fleming and Cord? How does this stance affect the tone of the piece?

2. Alexander's piece is constructed as a journalistic report on the 1974 Caucus rally. How does the writer use this report as a vehicle for presenting her opinions? She makes considerable use of quotations, presenting opinions of Caucus leaders. Does this device make her writing sound more objective than that of Fleming or Cord? Does it make her piece more convincing?

3. Is Alexander's stance dictated in any way by her status as a professional writer for a news magazine? Is she adopting a stance more deliberately or less so than Fleming or Cord?

Word Study

Examine paragraphs 3 to 5, beginning, "She would not say so today." Record the most notable figures of speech in these paragraphs; one of the first is "off and running," suggesting a race, especially perhaps a horse race. Even the final word, *party-liner* involves a figure. What is the effect of this figurative use of language for an article like this one?

Suggestions for Writing

Making any use you wish of ideas in the three articles by women — with due credit, of course — write a discussion of some aspect of the role of women in society. You might focus on something like the role of women students in college, jobs for women, questions of rearing children, or the Equal Rights Amendment. You might wish to develop or oppose an idea in one of the essays, or you may wish to "update" one of the essays, reviewing what has happened since the selection was written.

THE REBELS OF '70
James Simon Kunen

36

James Simon Kunen, *ten years before he wrote this piece, had been one of the pampered young students who tormented the police, burned campus buildings, and shut down universities. James Simon Kunen first came to prominence with the publication of his book* The Strawberry Statement, *an account of the student rebellion at Columbia University in May, 1968. He is now a free-lance writer who publishes in the* Atlantic Monthly, Esquire, *and the* New York Times Magazine, *from which the following article is taken.*

I'M on my way to California. After 18 months as a conscientious objector, working with juvenile delinquents in the Massachusetts Department of Youth Services, I'm going to "drift around" the country. "You realize, of course, this all comes from the movies," said my friend Phil of the idea. He's right. I'm trying to be a drifter, but by virtue of trying I cannot succeed. I'm a middle-class drifter — a bogus drifter — far too purposeful ever really to cut loose.

In this case my purpose is to gather material for an essay on what my friends are doing these days, to see if it's true that, after shutting down campuses five years ago, they're entering establishment careers — what we used to call "selling out." . . .

Just before I left on the trip a friend asked me how my new Joe

An introduction.

A stance established.

Reporter Tape Recorder was working. I said it seemed to pick up voices very clearly from close up, but I wasn't sure it could pick up a speech at a rally.

"Jim," she said gently, touching my wrist, "they don't have rallies anymore."

"Scab grapes! Scab store! Please don't shop here anymore!"

My prep-school friend Dick Casey and I were picketing, for the United Farmworkers, San Francisco groceries which carried nonunion grapes. It felt good to be good again, out in the streets, shouting for justice, but it also felt a little awkward. Our half-dozen co-picketers seemed strangely young, and the words of their chants sounded almost foreign. Occasionally, Casey and I would quietly slip in a "Ho Ho Ho Chi Minh . . . " or "Hey Hey L. B. J. . . . " — our language.

Case 1: The desultory picketer.

In the old days Casey used to battle police around the University of Buffalo. The students would march through the streets chanting, and then the police would shoot tear gas at them and charge them with clubs, and the students would run away, then reassemble and start marching again, until the police would charge them again.

One day in the spring of '70 Casey had been doing this for several hours, until it was time to go home for supper. There, it struck him. "I was just fighting the police, and now I'm eating supper. If I was really serious, why did I go home for supper, and why did the police let me?" He decided he wasn't really "fighting" police, who, after all, had guns. Whatever he did was at their indulgence. So he stopped. As did many others.

Since then, having graduated with a degree in English and a prize for writing, Casey's been a liquor-store clerk, a cabdriver, a house painter, a shingler of roofs and a cook. The last job avowedly was his idea of a meaningful career. "People gotta eat," he used to say, and he still talks fondly of opening a restaurant called "Working Class Heroes." But he moves around a lot — as does everybody; a six-month-old address book is a keepsake — and is often out of work.

Follow the passage of time as revealed in sequences at the beginning of paragraphs.

In San Francisco he was getting incremental haircuts and going down every day to the "deployment office," as he calls it, looking for a menial job. He and executive positions are not attracted to one another. "What am I supposed to say, 'O.K., I'll *be* vice-president of Coca-Cola'?" More and more he'd like to be something: perhaps a film maker. His latest home effort was a two-minute animated Hamlet.

I told him that our mutual friend John Short had decided to leave his small-town newspaper job and go to law school.

"Dropping out, huh," Casey observed.

"Growers get rich! Farmworkers starve!"

I had been surprised when Short called me last May to break

the news that he was going to law school. Why, I wanted to know. He sounded apologetic: "Getting licensed to drive your car, that's the whole structure of life," he explained. "Besides, I want to be powerful. I've found that whatever you do, you're going to take crap, and I'd rather take crap from people below me than from people above me."

John Short, Andover '66, Harvard '70, springs from an upper-class background. His family is wealthy and well-connected, and among his forebears was one desperate soul who risked everything on the Mayflower. Short used to be known at Andover for being "in a fog," but he had the moral acuity to help barricade a Dow recruiter in an office at Harvard way back in 1967.

Upon graduation he duly set about not making his fortune and not climbing to power, quietly working on a small-town newspaper, *The Provincetown* (Mass.) *Advocate*. He remembers that he "scoffed at the idea" of taking law-school entrance exams as a senior, and was "shocked" at the number of his friends who paused to do so before embarking on their pastoral pursuits. "They were hedging," he says, "and that's what we were against."

I followed Short during his first day of law school this September. Registration at Northeastern University's Gryzmish Law Center was held in a lecture room full of legless black plastic seats attached to long white linoleum-topped tables. The air was conditioned, the windows blinded, the walls cinder-blocked—a law-and-order building. Members of the entering class of '76 looked as though they were there to be booked. Short, an organic if very slightly paunchy 25-year-old in sneakers and permanently unpressed white dungarees, was typical of those shuffling from table to table getting things stamped, except that half of them were women.

"Hello, John!" called a Harvard classmate, Bart Gordon, from a few places back in line.

"Oh God," Short groaned. "I didn't know *you* were going to be here. It kind of cheapens the whole experience."

Gordon was fresh from a commune in Vermont, where he'd lived "till I couldn't handle it anymore—living in a house for four with nine people, seeing people at breakfast every morning that I maybe could have gotten along with if I saw them every three weeks."

I asked Gordon if it were money that had brought him down to school. "No, I don't need money. My wife and the baby and I could live on $3,000 a year, with some help from our parents. But I want a skill. All my jobs in Vermont were unskilled labor. I was an unskilled carpenter, and unskilled farmer, and unskilled teacher. I want a skill—it's the ideal of meaningful labor." He added that it may be "a fantasy" that the law will be "meaningful labor."

Another hint on stance.

Case 2: Short goes back to law school.

Case 3: Gordon from a commune.

When Gordon asked Short his excuse for being there, Short said he wanted to be a D.A., to go after "the real criminals." "The real criminals are sitting in offices, like some people's fathers."

"You're going to be going after people's fathers?" I asked.

"I don't know," Short answered. "What do I know about being a D.A.?"

What does one know about anything after 16 years of school? One knows how to go to school. Short and his classmates completed their computer cards with dispatch, consumed coffee, doughnuts, speeches. The registrar informed them that 2,500 had applied to be in their class of 125.

"Few people here would admit this," Short whispered, "but it feels good in spite of yourself to hear that you're still 'prime material.' "

Afterwards, the freshmen recessed to a nearby room for sherry. Nothing could be more established than sherry. It prompted me to ask John—who, as a Democratic party official helped deliver Provincetown to McGovern—if his commitment to social change was void.

"I'm not committed in the same way I was in college," Short said. "It's such a youthful thing. I thought things then were—not so much *worse,* but—more *disgusting.* Now I just think things *exist.*"

A few of Short's classmates brought a bottle of Taylor Cream over and sat down. The revelation that I was writing an article only confirmed their sense that they—going to law school at 25—represented a trend, a trend that might be called Bourgeois Chic.

Short figures he'll be in a position to do more good as a lawyer than as a demonstrator or anything that he was before. "In college the standard thing to believe was that our parents and even people a few years older than ourselves were incomprehensibly shackled by their occupations. Today I'd say the most important thing in my life is my work."

"And how much would you look to get paid for it?"

"It's hard to say. I've said to friends that my goal is to have a Pontiac with a telephone in it, and that bespeaks a certain amount of income. Pontiacs are basically for *arrivés,* self-made men. That's probably what I want more than the Pontiac—to be known as someone who's really earned his money, because that obviously hasn't been true up to now, being a rich kid, a prepster."

"With a career and a Pontiac you can't help but get married, can you?" I asked.

Short sipped his nth sherry. "Fortunately, I retain a power not to look into the future. The civilizing process of going to law school does make the idea more palatable. The thing is, I just don't know any marriages that are successful among people within shouting dis-

Does Kunen's stance change subtly as he talks with old friends?

Summary: Sherry and a Pontiac.

Each of these former friends also has a stance.

tance of our age. Everyone fails. It's just horrible. The time to go into it would seem to be after you've settled on what you're going to be doing for the rest of your life."

Or it's settled on you. . . .

The goal of middle-class life—from the air inside a Cadillac to the curriculum of a prep school—is insulation and control. Even our "own" youth culture came to us packaged. We had a communal experience, of a sort—though it was not experienced communally—an atomized communal experience. Millions of times in thousands of dorm rooms, the class of '70 heard revolution on the stereo. But however savage the rhythm or radical the words, anything we heard we heard because The Corporation had decided we'd hear it—though its motive be that most innocent of all: making money.

The author's summary.

The youth culture was so pervasive because it filled a vacuum. Affluence had given us, luxury of luxuries, four years with nothing to do: college. Unheard of numbers of "kids" were in college; we were unbelieveably well set up, regaled with music "systems," diverted by studies, and yet feeling a vague malaise, beginning to suspect that we were not in touch with reality and did not know very much about it, that we ourselves were not *relevant*.

The most important activity among this crowd was drug-taking, the principal purpose of which was, as always, escape. But in this case the students were trying to escape a reality they suspected was unreal, and to probe the depths and heights for a more basic or transcendent Reality, which would inform their actions and allow them to begin to live, at last, after having been suspended in a perpetual state of "preparation."

Browsing through the cosmos we found that there were worlds other than the one our parents perceived, a discovery which eroded our received beliefs and certainties; and one side effect of the drugs was to put us all outside the law.

What comes from browsing through other worlds? A major transition?

Meanwhile, our parents' world came up with its war, misrepresented as this and that but obviously—to anyone with the time to look into it, and we, protected by deferments, had time—a cynical imperialist operation. That we were lied to about the war intensified our scrutiny of how much of our given reality was illusion. It set us looking for other lies, which weren't hard to find. Universities not being very portable, many had remained behind after the core cities had turned black and poor. A Columbia student, for instance, didn't have to look very far to see the effects of racism in the land of equal opportunity.

Columbia University sits on a hill overlooking Harlem.

We had concluded, correctly, that we were living in a rotten, corrupt, morally bankrupt, brutally exploitative system, failing to apprehend only that this meant the world was clicking along as usual.

We were outraged. To us the war was a moral offense, not a

question of politics, and we reacted to it in moral, rather than political terms. We didn't try to mobilize interest groups, or manipulate one power concentration against another, or do any of those things that politicians know about. And, of course, we didn't have "a program." Insofar as our rhetoric was political, that was a response to the needs of the conceptual framework of older people.

A recollected stance seen from the present.

When people used to demand of us, "But what's your program?" we'd dutifully come up with something that could pass for one, talking about taxes and things. We should have said, "Why should we have a program? We're the Scourge of the Earth, we're the Wrath of God, and you're asking us about programs?"

I never knew anyone who, at 19, was seriously interested in running the country. We were trying to *stop* something. We felt ourselves to be a purifying force, the force of life. Somehow by the strength of our youth the nation would be wrenched from the grip of death, cleansed, made new.

"The Movement," we were aptly named. Not the party or the revolution. The Movement—an undirected upheaval of the earth, an inarticulate force of nature. We weren't trying to convince the nation of anything. We were just trying to wake it up. Our "tactic" was an appeal to the nation's conscience, the existence of which we posited, apparently in error. . . .

"The Movement" stopped moving.

Not working toward a career, let alone not working at all, was also a rejection of the System within which success and exploitation, work and war, were of a piece in our minds. ("Work! Study! Get ahead! Kill!" we used to chant at Columbia.) It seemed the country was full of people who subsumed themselves in their work roles, deriving their identities from their functions, abdicating human will and responsibility, leaving the country to be run not by people but by a System, capable of anything.

Of course it was the System that enabled us to reject the System. It gave us time. There was no need—or opportunity—for everyone to be producing all the time. You can bet there aren't a lot of sensitive young intellectuals trying to find themselves in The People's Republic: "You can find yourself right out there in the rice paddies with everybody else, buddy."

How has this attitude been anticipated earlier?

We were terrified of working as hard as did our fathers, charter subscribers to the Protestant Ethic: Pay now, fly later. Olson up at Clark University, told me, "When I look at how incredibly difficult it is for me to do very little, then I can't even imagine what it must be like for people to do a lot." He likes to think about the easy fortune he could make marketing draft-evader bracelets, each engraved with the name of an exile, to be worn until amnesty. . . .

It's been three years now that we've been on the outs. The world of the small job, the personal project, inevitably begins to seem

So now, three years later—.

constricting. Our middle-class *instinct* (subliminal, unshakable) to "make something of yourself," abetted by our social commitment— also rather hard to shake—drives us back toward the larger arena. We can't leave the running of the world entirely in the hands of the exec types, can we?

And as we find idealistic gratification hard to come by, materialistic gratification becomes more attractive. I, for instance, used to think I could stop the war; then I thought I'd get realistic and instead save delinquents from lives of crime; finding that beyond my power, I resolved to show them a good time. My success in pursuit of even that modest goal was equivocal. After several months as a supervisor and associate of juvenile delinquents it came to me that I'd feel somehow more *confident* if I had a big car. On May Day of '72, I bought The Dream.

As Dave Warren says, "Whatever else you say about those bourgeois comforts, they sure are comfortable."

I agree with a friend who said, "You don't want to be in the position of not knowing where your next car is coming from." And money can be habit-forming. After the hook, the line and sinker are easy.

Summing up the last three years, John Short said, "People led whatever kind of life they had to in order to convince themselves that they were exercising free will." That done, having gained control of their lives, having insulated themselves from outside pressures, more and more holdouts are becoming late-signers.

The question is: will we, despite the hallucinations and barricades in our backgrounds, become indistinguishable from our parents?

Are the young radicals becoming like their fathers, whom they did not trust?

We still take drugs, but mostly just grass, and that without any imputation of mystic import. In this period of Post-Mumbo-Jumbo Materialism the popularity of psychedelics has fallen along with that of transcendence.

Our attitude toward authority is still shaped by the clashes in college. To quote Olson, "Whenever I see a cop on my block I feel like I better flush all by books down the toilet."

Our political views would still look appropriate on leaflets. I spoke with 11 classmates across the country, and most would agree with Casey that "the United States is the world's leading reactionary force." Though everyone enjoys Watergate, no one buys it as the redemption of the System. It's so American—instead of purging a corrupt government we do a TV show on it. And we can't help recalling that there was no uproar when "radicals" were bugged. No one I know has the slightest doubt that the C.I.A. was behind the coup in Chile, but no one has any plans for doing anything about it either, since there are no bumper-stickers out and no organization to send five dollars to. The activists among us are those who volunteered a few hours for McGovern.

In our rowdy days we were told we couldn't change the world. I think we can't help but change the world, one way or another.

"I think we can't help but change the world."

I was just talking to a friend of mine, who said, "I'm much happier now that I'm not 'a radical.' I stopped feeling guilty over just being alive in America."

And I said, "My father always held to that belief that young people would eventually abandon their idealistic visions and come around to appreciating the verities—like the overwhelming importance of money."

"Your father sounds like a very wise man," she said.

Reading and Interpreting

1. Much of Kunen's article could just as well have been included in Section II as a descriptive report. His method of describing is somewhat different from those used by the writers in Section II. Does it have any advantages? What are its limitations?

2. The essay can be divided into a brief introduction and three parts. Identify these. Are all of them necessary? In part of the introduction not here reprinted Kunen asks himself, "Have I become one of the people I used to be against?" This introduction leads to the third main part of Kunen's article. With such an introduction and conclusion, could the first and second main portions of the article be dropped? What would be lost, if anything, by such cutting?

Writing Techniques

1. Here we have a different handling of point of view, the difference springing from an unusual use of time. Kunen is writing about himself and his friends at various times, which seem to be about as follows: ten or more years ago, five years ago, three years ago, and now. During this decade or so his point of view—as a person, not necessarily as a writer—has changed so much that he now has to ask himself if he has become the kind of person he would formerly have worked against, perhaps even hated. Looking back from his time of writing, how does he manage to reflect the various points of view he has entertained?

2. Kunen's essay, particularly in the light of question 1 above, raises a still better question: Is a point of view entirely stable? Is it ever completely one thing? Or is it a range of attitudes that shift somewhat during the writing? If the latter, what revisions must you make of your earlier conclusions about a stance?

Suggestions for Writing

1. Kunen seems to think he knows what students are like today. Does he? When he was a student he had little desire to be like the adults he knew, and he apparently thought they did not understand him and his friends and their values. Is he right about students today, or is he as wrong as he thought his parents were?

2. Kunen and his fellow students were not very popular with many of the adults of the day. Some students bombed and burned buildings, beseiged deans in their offices, and fomented riots. People were shocked by such conduct and baffled by it. Do you find that adults resent you and your fellow students? Or, if not, do they seem much concerned if a student who has been trained for a special job cannot get such a job and has to take something just to live?

3. Kunen says, "I think we can't help but change the world." If you could change the world, how would you change it? Do you have any plans for changing even a small part of the world?

4. You might try to write on any of the suggestions above by using Kunen's technique of interviewing your fellow students and trying to reach some conclusion after reporting your interviews.

Organizing Your Writing: The Paragraph

The writer's obligations in the writer-reader contract are considerable. As a writer, you take a stance appropriate to the audience and the subject, but above all you have to try to be understood. This is not so easy as it may seem. It requires careful word choice and clear sentences, and especially it requires ordering your material, showing your audience where your prose is going and how it gets there. You need to organize your writing, and you should help your reader see this organization.

Writing is highly varied, and there is no statement that could apply to all writing. Nevertheless you can profit by examining some of the ways writers have found to put their ideas together and give an audience an orderly view of a subject. A good place to begin is the paragraph. Technically, paragraphing is only a kind of punctuation device, a way of breaking prose into segments. Structurally, it is a basic tool for organization, a way of putting ideas into groups so that the reader will not have to swallow too much in one gulp but will have enough to satisfy his appetite.

Many paragraphs follow patterns that are variations of an ideal common model, so that once you have studied this basic type, paragraphs are easier to construct than you might expect. Furthermore, paragraphs reveal more than themselves. A paragraph can be thought of as a sort of scale model of any longer piece of writing. Once you understand organization in the paragraph, you have a good start toward organizing any composition.

To see how this operates, look at the first paragraph of this introduction. It begins with a general statement, recalling the notion of a writer-reader contract from previous introductions and calling attention to the writer's obligations in this contract. It can be considered as both a *theme sentence* and a *topic sentence.* That is, it introduces both the whole introduction and this particular paragraph. It has the ingredients of most passable topic sentences, transition and direction. In recalling the writer-reader contract it provides a transition from what has preceded. It also introduces the new topic, the writer's obligation. It is like a road sign with pointers in two directions—"Salt Lake City 525 miles, San Francisco 235 miles." It tells you where you have been and where you are going. We think of this sentence also as making a *commitment,* to which the remainder of the paragraph, or of the essay, will be a *response.*

This opening sentence commits us to explain the writer's obligations in the writer-reader contract, and it tells the reader to expect such explanation. The remainder of the paragraph—and most of this introduction—respond to that commitment, saying more about the writer's obligation and moving toward a more specific part of that obligation: to provide clear organization.

The second sentence begins the response by restricting the general topic of the opening. In the first part it reminds the reader of the part of the writer's obligation that has already been considered in the previous section, the writer's stance, and it specifies the part to be introduced here, that "you have to try to be understood." This second sentence also makes a commitment—to say more about being understood—and the third sentence responds with a comment, that it is not easy. It also makes a commitment, to tell why. The final three sentences respond, listing difficulties of being understood, but coming finally to focus on the more specific topic of this section, organization.

Not all paragraphs are like this one; in fact, no two paragraphs are exactly alike. The pattern is flexible. The topic sentence may not be first; it may not be recorded at all if the sentences hang together without it. The topical material may need only part of a sentence, or it may spread over more than one sentence. The paragraph may break into parts, each defined with a subtopic sentence. There may be a clear conclusion or none at all. Length may vary from a sentence or two to more than a page. But the main scheme is likely to be there: a general statement that makes a commitment and a response that is in one way or another concrete and specific. And within the response, there are likely to be more commitment-response units.

Sentences within the response make commitments, which require responses, and so on. The paragraphs in the selections that follow illustrate many variations from this pattern, but in analyzing them you can profitably look for the underlying commitment-response scheme.

You can approach segments of prose longer than a paragraph in the same way, looking for patterns of commitments and responses. The two opening sentences of Pattison's essay, for instance, make an obvious commitment, even indicating that the essay will provide thirteen principles for writing an "F" paper. The thirteen principles provide the response. But the writer goes farther to help the reader, dividing the thirteen principles into three groups, each marked with a subhead. Van Doren's essay is much more complex, but the same basic pattern is there, a commitment to discuss justice and a series of responses that explore the topic point by point.

BRIEF UNITS

37

The following are units of writing, from a very brief paragraph, to what is sometimes called a stadium, *a unit of development like a paragraph, divided by indentation into subunits:* **a.** *the first item is taken from "What's Wrong with Our Press?" by* **Marya Mannes** *who started as a journalist reporting the daily news, but now is best known as a lover of New York and the author of penetrating essays and nonfiction books;* **b.** *the next paragraph is from "The Visitor" in* Switch Bitch *(1974) by* **Roald Dahl,** *a Welsh-born Londoner; it concerns a hero of many affairs, who is waiting for either his host's wife or daughter to come to his bedroom;* **c.** *the excerpt by* **Joseph Epstein** *comes from an article in* Harper's, *"Obsessed with Sport";* **d.** *the paragraph by* **Elliot Liebow** *is from* Tally's Corner, *a study of current American life;* **e. Eric Sevareid,** *after long apprenticeship as a reporter and editor, is now best known as a television commentator; the selection is from his autobiographical* Not So Wild a Dream *(1946);* **f.** *the next example is from "A Note on Comparative Pornography," by* **Norman Mailer,** *who started a notable reputation with* The Naked and the Dead, *a war novel based on his experience in the South Pacific;* **g. J. B. S. Haldane,** *Professor of genetics at the University of London, discusses the advantages of being the right size, in* Possible Worlds *(1928);* **h.** *next is a famous paragraph from* Les Miserables *(1862) by the French novelist* **Victor Hugo; i.** *the* **Jacques Barzun** *selection is from* Teacher in America *(1944), a penetrating survey of education by a highly literate dean at Columbia University;* **j.** *the final excerpt is from the distinguished British bibliographical scholar,* **W. W. Greg,** *writing in* Neophilologus *(1932).*

NEWSPAPERS have two great advantages over television. They can be used by men as barriers against their wives. It is still the only effective screen against the morning features of the loved one, and, as such, performs a unique human service. The second advantage is that you can't line a garbage pail with a television set—it's usually the other way around.

I was just beginning to doze off when I heard some tiny sounds. I recognized them at once. They were sounds that I had heard many times before in my life, and yet they were still, for me, the most thrilling and evocative in the whole world. They consisted of a series of little soft metallic noises, of metal grating gently against metal, and they were made, they were always made by somebody who was very slowly, very cautiously, turning the handle of one's door from the outside. Instantly, I became wide awake. But I did not move. I simply opened my eyes and stared in the direction of the door; and I can remember wishing at that moment for a gap in the curtain, for just a small thin shaft of moonlight to come in from outside so that I could at least catch a glimpse of the shadow of the lovely form that was about to enter. But the room was as dark as a dungeon.

I cannot remember when I was not surrounded by sports, when talk of sports was not in the air, when I did not care passionately about sports. As a boy in Chicago in the late Forties, I lived in the same building as the sister and brother-in-law of Barney Ross, the welterweight champion. Half a block away, down near the lake, the Sullivan High School football team worked out in the spring and autumn. Summers the same field was given over to baseball and men's softball on Sundays. A few blocks to the north was the Touhy Avenue Fieldhouse, where basketball was played, and lifeguards trained, and behind which, in a softball field frozen over in winter, crack-the-whip, hockey, and speed skating took over. To the west, a block or so up Morse Avenue, was the Morse Avenue "L" Recreations, a combined pool hall and bowling alley. Life, in short, was games.

d.   Elliot Liebow

FOR those who hang out there, the Carry-out offers a wide array of sounds, sights, smells, tastes, and tactile experiences which titillate and sometimes assault the five senses. The air is warmed by smells from the coffee urns and grill and thickened with fat from the deep-fry basket. The jukebox offers up a wide variety of frenetic and lazy rhythms. The pinball machine is a standing challenge to one's manipulative skill or ability to will the ball into one or another hole. Flashing lights, bells and buzzers report progress or announce failure. Colorful signs exhort customers to drink Royal Crown Cola and eat Bond Bread. On the wall, above the telephone, a long-legged blond in shorts and halter smiles a fixed wet-lipped smile of unutterable delight at her Chesterfield cigarette, her visage unmarred by a mustache or scribbled obscenities. In the background, a sleek ocean liner rides a flat blue sea to an unknown destination.

e.   Eric Sevareid

THE financial editor worked at a desk directly behind my own. One night when I was working exceptionally late, he came in slightly unsteady from drinking. He emptied into a suitcase the contents of his locker, a few books, a batch of clippings, a pair of golf shoes. I asked in surprise if he was leaving. He said: "I've been on this paper eighteen years, son. I've just been fired by a guy I used to teach where to put commas." He staggered out, leaving me with a sick, hollow feeling in the pit of my stomach and a dark light dawning in my head. Innocence departed. Life, it seemed, was a relentless, never-ending battle; one never "arrived"; loyalty, achievement, could be forgotten in a moment; a single man's whim could ruin one. I began to take stock of the situation and discovered that the men who got to the top, no matter how long they stayed there, were nearly all men who had studied in universities, who knew something besides the routine of their own desks. It was fear as much as anything else that drove me to college, purely personal ambition as much as curiosity about the world I lived in and what had made it the way I found it to be.

f.   Norman Mailer

TALK of pornography ought to begin at the modern root: *advertising*. Ten years ago the advertisements sold the girl with the car—the not altogether unfair connection of the unconscious mind was that the owner of a new convertible was on the way to getting a new girl. Today the girl means less than the machine. A car is sold not because it will help one to get a girl, but because it is already a girl. The leather of its seats is worked to a near-skin, the color is lipstick-pink, or a blonde's pale-green, the taillights are cloacal, the rear is split like the cheeks of a drum majorette.

g.   John Burdon Sanderson Haldane

LET us take the most obvious of possible cases, and consider a giant man of sixty feet high—about the height of Giant Pope and Giant Pagan in the illustrated *Pilgrim's Progress* of my childhood. These monsters were not only ten times as high as Christian, but ten times as wide and ten times as thick, so that their total weight was a thousand times his, or about eighty to ninety tons. Unfortunately, the cross sections of their bones were only a hundred times those of Christian, so that every square inch of giant bone had to support ten times the weight borne by a square inch of human bone. As the human thigh-bone breaks under about ten times the human weight, Pope and Pagan would have broken their thighs every time they took a step. This was doubtless why they were sitting down in the picture I remember. But it lessens one's respect for Christian and Jack the Giant Killer.

h.   Victor Hugo

THOSE who would get a clear idea of the battlefield of Waterloo have only to imagine a capital A. The left side of the A is the road from Nivelles, the right the road from Genappe, the crossbar the sunken road from Chain to Braine-l'Alleud. Wellington is at the apex of the A, at Mont St. Jean; Reille and Jerome Bonaparte are in Hougemont at the bottom toward the left, and Napoleon is near La Haie Sainte at the bottom toward the right. At the middle of the crossbar is the precise point where the final battle word was spoken, and there the lion is placed, the involuntary symbol of the supreme heroism of the imperial guard. The triangle contained within the upper portion of the A, between the slanting sides and the crossbar, is the plateau of Mont St. Jean. The whole battle was a fight for this plateau.

i.   Jacques Barzun

THIS angry confusion about the history of science is dense but not impenetrable. Three things may be distinguished. First there is historical research into the beginnings of science—Greek or Arabic or Medieval. This goes on as advanced study and concerns undergraduates only in the form of broad tested conclusions. Then there is the biography of scientists, which is of immense educational importance—whatever laboratory men may say. Biography does not mean recounting Newton's imaginary embroilments with women or Lavoisier's perfectly real ones with public finance. It means finding out from the lives of great scientific creators what they worked at and how their minds functioned. How tiresome it is to hear nothing from our scientific departments but Sunday-school homilies on the gameness of Galileo, the patience of Pasteur, and the carefulness of Madame Curie. And how uninstructive! Any man who accomplishes anything in any field is as patient as he has to be, and even little boys know that glass being breakable, you have to be careful.

j.   W. W. Greg

LITERARY criticism may, I think, be divided, conveniently if perhaps a little arbitrarily, into three main branches. There is, to begin with, aesthetic and historical criticism, the criticism that seeks to apprize a work of literature, to define its particular quality and value, to set it in historical perspective, and to show, so far as can be shown from external circumstances, how it came to be, in the words of Bishop Butler, "what it is and not another thing." No doubt, there are here two distinct lines of approach, and many critics would insist vehemently on their being kept apart. But I think that most of you will agree with me that they are in fact closely bound up with one another, and that aesthetic criticism is always soundest and most vital when brought into touch with historical environment.

The second branch, into which the first, I must admit, insensibly merges, is interpretation or exegetical criticism, the attempt to discover and expound an author's meaning in what he wrote, both as regards his general intention and as regards particular allusions and the sense of individual phrases.

The third branch—and again there is an obvious bridge—is textual criticism, the attempt to establish the actual words of the author, first by the collecting and sifting of documentary evidence, and afterwards by selection from the readings thus afforded, or if necessary by original emendation. It should be added that the task of textual criticism is not only to establish the true original text, but likewise to trace throughout the history of its transmission. Indeed—and this we shall see is an important point in the view I have to put before you—it is only through the second of these tasks that the first can be accomplished.

Writing Techniques

1. Analyze the pattern of each of the paragraphs. One device for doing so is an informal outline. Paragraph **a,** for example, could be described in a simple outline: a topic sentence suggesting the structure by anticipating two advantages; a second sentence mentioning the first advantage, which is specified in the third sentence of the excerpt; and a third sentence introducing the second advantage, which is the fourth sentence of the paragraph. Or paragraph **d** is a topic sentence followed by a series of specific examples in each sentence, illustrating the five senses introduced in the opening sentence.

2. How does the pattern of paragraph **c** compare with that of **d**?

3. Paragraph **e** uses narrative for its development, recounting an incident in some detail. How does Sevareid use the incident? Which sentence is the topic sentence, if the paragraph has one?

4. Paragraph **f** develops with contrast, supporting the opening topic sentence by describing what was common ten years ago and then describing the present. Do the details supply convincing support?

5. The first two sentences of paragraph **i** introduce a topic and suggest an organization for the paragraph. Does the paragraph meet the commitment of the second sentence?

6. Selection **j** is divided into three paragraphs. Could it have been written as a single paragraph? How is its pattern similar to that of paragraph **i**?

Suggestions for Writing

Paragraph **h,** a famous description by Victor Hugo, develops by analogy. The paragraph becomes almost a description of a map. Write a paragraph describing a scene using the same general technique, organizing the details spatially.

HOW TO WRITE AN "F" PAPER: FRESH ADVICE FOR STUDENTS OF FRESHMAN ENGLISH
Joseph C. Pattison

38

Professor **Joseph C. Pattison,** *a scholar-critic who writes on Nathaniel Hawthorne, teaches composition and literature at Sacramento State University. This selection is from* College English.

WRITING an "F" paper is admittedly not an easy task, but one can learn to do it by grasp of the principles to use. The thirteen below, if practiced at all diligently, should lead any student to that fortune in his writing.

Obscure the ideas:

1. Select a topic that is big enough to let you wander around the main idea without ever being forced to state it precisely. If an assigned topic has been limited for you, take a detour that will allow you to amble away from it for a while.

2. Pad! Pad! Pad! Do not develop your ideas. Simply restate them in safe, spongy generalizations to avoid the need to find evidence to support what you say. Always point out repetition with the phrase, "As previously noted. . . ." Better yet, repeat word-for-word at least one or two of your statements.

3. Disorganize your discussion. For example, if you are using the time order to present your material, keep the reader alert by making a jump from the past to the present only to spring back into the past preparatory to a leap into the future preceding a return hop into

the present just before the finish of the point about the past. Devise comparable strategems to use with such other principles for organizing a discussion as space, contrast, cause-effect, and climax.

4. Begin a new paragraph every sentence or two.

By generous use of white space, make the reader aware that he is looking at a page blank of sustained thought.

Like this.

Mangle the sentences:

5. Fill all the areas of your sentences with deadwood. Incidentally, "the area of" will deaden almost any sentence, and it is particularly flat when displayed prominently at the beginning of a sentence.

6. Using fragments and run-on or comma-spliced sentences. Do not use a main subject and a main verb, for the reader will get the complete thought too easily. Just toss him part of the idea at a time, as in "Using fragments. . . ." To gain sentence variety, throw in an occasional run-on sentence thus the reader will have to read slowly and carefully to get the idea.

7. Your sentence order invert for statement of the least important matters. That will force the reader to be attentive to understand even the simplest points you make.

8. You, in the introduction, body, and conclusion of your paper, to show that you can contrive ornate, graceful sentences, should use involution. Frequent separation of subjects from verbs by insertion of involved phrases and clauses will prove that you know what can be done to a sentence.

Slovenize the diction:

9. Add the popular "-wise" and "-ize" endings to words. Say, "Timewise, it is fastest to go by U.S. 40," rather than simply, "It is fastest to go by U.S. 40." Choose "circularize" in preference to "circulate." Practice will smartenize your style.

10. Use vague words in place of precise ones. From the start, establish vagueness of tone by saying, "The thing is . . ." instead of, "The issue is. . . ." Make the reader be imaginative throughout his reading of your paper.

11. Employ lengthy Latinate locutions wherever possible. Shun the simplicity of style that comes from apt use of short, old, familiar words, especially those of Anglo-Saxon origin. Show that you can get the *maximum* (L.), not merely the *most* (AS.), from every word choice you make.

12. Inject humor into your writing by using the wrong word oc-

casionally. Write "then" when you mean "than" or "to" when you mean "too." Every reader likes to laugh.

13. Find a "tried and true" phrase to use to clinch a point. It will have a comfortingly folksy sound for the reader. Best of all, since you want to end in a conversational and friendly way, sprinkle your conclusions with cliches. "Put a little frosting on the cake," as the saying goes.

Well, to ensconce this whole business in a nutshell, you, above all, an erudite discourse on nothing in the field of your topic should pen. Thereby gaining the reader's credence in what you say.

Suggestion-wise, one last thing: file-ize this list for handy reference the next time you a paper write.

Reading and Interpreting

1. Point out half a dozen instances in which Pattison manages to follow the admonitions he is pretending to recommend. List the blunders exemplified in the last two paragraphs.

2. Did Pattison miss any blunders that will help to produce "F" papers?

Writing Techniques

1. Although Pattison, in principle 3, suggests bad organization, he does not illustrate it in his own writing. Why not? He organizes his material in an almost formal pattern providing regular guidelines for the reader. Make a brief outline of the main divisions and subdivisions of the selection.

2. What is the limited audience Pattison is addressing? Describe the tone of the piece.

Suggestions for Writing

Try using Pattison's techniques, writing a paper by taking a topic and turning it backward or upside down—for example, "How to Prepare a Flunking Chem Lab Notebook," "How Not to Get a Date," "How to Avoid Getting a Second Invitation to Dinner," "How Not to Get Elected to a Student Office."

LET ME SHOW YOU HOW TO WRITE GOOD
39
Michael O'Donoghue

Michael O'Donoghue *is a free-lance writer who lives in New York. He wrote the following essay while he was on the staff of the* National Lampoon.

"If I could not earn a penny from my writing, I would earn my livelihood at something else and continue to write at night." Irving Wallace

"Financial success is not the only reward of good writing. It brings to the writer rich inner satisfactions as well." Elliot Foster, Director of Admissions, Famous Writers School

Introduction

A long time ago, when I was just starting out, I had the good fortune to meet the great Willa Cather. With all the audacity of youth, I asked her what advice she would give the would-be-writer and she replied:

> "My advice to the would-be-writer is that he start slowly, writing short un-demanding things, things such as telegrams, flip-books, crank letters, signature scarves, spot quizzes, capsule summaries, fortune cookies and errata. Then, when he feels he's ready, move up to the more challenging items such as mandates, objective correlatives, passion plays, pointless diatribes, minor classics, manifestos, mezzotints, oxymora, exposés, broadsides and papal bulls.
>
> And above all, never forget the pen is mightier than the plowshare. By this I mean that writing, all in all, is a hell of a lot more fun than farming. For one thing, writers seldom, if ever, have to get up at five o'clock in the morning and shovel manure. As far as I'm concerned, that gives them the edge right there."

She went on to tell me many things, both wonderful and wise, probing the secrets of her craft, showing how to weave a net of words and capture the fleeting stuff of life. Unfortunately, I've forgotten every bit of it.

I do recall, however, her answer when I asked "If you could only give me one rule to follow, what would it be?" She paused, looked down for a moment, and finally said, "Never wear brown shoes with a blue suit."

There's very little I could add to that except to say "Go to it and good luck."

Lesson 1 — The Grabber

The "grabber" is the initial sentence of a novel or short story designed to jolt the reader out of his complacency and arouse his curiosity, forcing him to press onward. For example:

> "It's no good, Alex," she rejoined, "Even if I did love you, my father would never let me marry an alligator."

The reader is immediately bombarded with questions, questions such as: "Why won't her father let her marry an alligator?" "How come she doesn't love him?" and "Can she learn to love him in time?" The reader's interest has been "grabbed"!

Just so they'll be no misunderstanding about grabbers, I've listed a few more below:

> "I'm afraid you're too late," sneered Zoltan. "The fireplace has already flown south for the winter!"

> Sylvia lay sick among the silverware . . .

> "Chinese vegetables mean more to me than you do, my dear," Charles remarked to his wife, adding injury to insult by lodging a grapefruit knife in her neck.

> One morning Egor Samba awoke from uneasy dreams to find himself transformed into a gigantic Volkswagen.

> "I have in my hands," Professor Willowbee exclaimed, clutching a sheaf of papers in his trembling fingers and pacing in circles about the carpet while I stood at the window, barely able to make out the Capitol dome through the thick, churning fog that rolled in off the Potomac, wondering to myself what matter could possibly be so urgent as to bring the distinguished historian bursting into my State Department office at this unseemly hour, "definitive proof that Abraham Lincoln was a homo!"

These are just a handful of the possible grabbers. Needless to say there are thousands of others, but if you fail to think of them, feel free to use any or all of these.

Lesson 2 — The Ending

All too often, the budding author finds that his tale has run its course and yet he sees no way to satisfactorily end it, or, in literary parlance, "wrap it up." Observe how easily I resolve this problem.

> Suddenly, everyone was run over by a truck.
>   — the end —

If the story happens to be set in England, use the same ending, slightly modified:

> Suddenly, everyone was run over by a lorry.
>   — the end —

If set in France:

> Soudainement, tout le monde était écrasé par un camion.
>   — finis —

You'll be surprised at how many different settings and situations this ending applies to. For instance, if you were writing a story about ants, it would end "Suddenly, everyone was run over by a centipede." In fact, this is the only ending you ever need use.*

> * Warning—If you are writing a story about trucks, do *not* have the trucks run over by a truck. Have the trucks run over by a *mammoth* truck.

Lesson 3—Choosing a Title

A friend of mine recently had a bunch of articles rejected by the *Reader's Digest* and, unable to understand why, he turned to me for advice. I spotted the problem at a glance. His titles were all wrong. By calling his pieces such things as "Unwed Mothers—A Head Start on Life," "Cancer—The Incurable Disease," "A Leading Psychologist Explains Why There Should Be More Violence on Television," "Dognappers I Have Known and Loved," "My Baby Was Born Dead and I Couldn't Care Less" and "Pleasantville—Last of the Wide-Open Towns," he had seriously misjudged his market. To steer him straight, I drew up this list of all-purpose, surefire titles:

> _____ *at the Crossroads*
> *The Case for* _____
> *The Role of* _____
> *Coping with Changing*_____
> *A Realistic Look at* _____
> *The* _____ *Experience*
> *Bridging the* _____ *Gap*
> *A* _____ *for All Seasons*

Simply fill in the blanks with the topic of your choice and, if that doesn't work, you can always resort to the one title that never fails: *South America, the Sleeping Giant on Our Doorstep. . . .*

Lesson 5—Finding the Raw Material

As any professional writer will tell you, the richest source of material is one's relatives, one's neighbors and, more often than not, total strangers. A day doesn't go by without at least one person, upon learning that I'm a professional writer, offering me some terrific idea for a story. And I'm sure it will come as no shock when I say that most of the ideas are pretty damn good!

Only last week, a pipe-fitter of my acquaintance came up with a surprise ending guaranteed to unnerve the most jaded reader. What you do is tell this really weird story that keeps on getting weirder and weirder until just when the reader is muttering, "How in the heck is he going to get himself out of this one? He's really painted himself into a corner!" you spring the "mind-blower": "But then he woke up. It had all been a dream!" [which I, professional writer that I am, honed down to: "But then the alarm clock rang. It had all been a dream!"] And this came from a common, run-of-the-mill pipe-fitter! For free!

Cabdrivers, another great wealth of material, will often remark, "Boy, lemme tell ya'! Some of the characters I get in this cab would fill a book! Real kooks, ya' know what I mean?" And then, without my having to coax even the slightest, they tell me about them, and they *would* fill a book. Perhaps two or three books. In addition, if you're at all interested in social science, cabdrivers are able to provide countless examples of the failures of the welfare state.

To illustrate just how valid these unsolicited suggestions can be, I shall print a few lines from a newly completed play inspired by my aunt, who had the idea as far back as when she was attending grade school. It's called *If an Old House Could Talk, What Tales It Would Tell:*

> The Floor: Do you remember the time the middle-aged lady who always wore the stiletto heels tripped over an extension cord while running to answer the phone and spilled the Ovaltine all over me and they spent the next 20 minutes mopping it up?
> The Wall: No.

Of course, I can't print too much here because I don't want to spoil the ending (although I will give you a hint: it involves a truck . . .), I just wanted to show you how much the world would have missed had I rejected my aunt's suggestion out of hand simply because she is not a professional writer like myself.

Lesson 6 — Quoting Other Authors

If placed in a situation where you must quote another author, always write "[sic]" after any word that may be misspelled or looks the least bit questionable in any way. If there are no misspellings or curious words, toss in a few "[sic]"'s just to break up the flow. By doing this, you will appear to be knowledgeable and "on your toes," while the one quoted will seem suspect and vaguely discredited. . . . Two examples will suffice:

"O Sleepless as the river under thee,
Vaulting the sea, the prairies' dreaming sod,
Unto us lowiest sometime sweep, descend
And of the curveship [sic] lend a myth to God."

HART CRANE

"Beauty is but a flowre [sic],
Which wrinckles [sic] will devoure [sic],
Brightnesse [sic] falls from the ayre [sic],
Queenes [sic] have died yong [sic] and faire [sic]
Dust hath closde [sic] *Helens* [sic] eye [sic].
I am sick [sic], I must dye [sic]:
    Lord, have mercy on us."

THOMAS NASHE

Note how only one small "[sic]" makes Crane's entire stanza seem
trivial and worthless, which, in his case, takes less doing than most.
Nashe, on the other hand, has been rendered virtually unreadable.
Anyone having to choose between you and Nashe would pick you
every time! And, when it's all said and done, isn't that the name of
the game? . . .

Lesson 9 — Tricks of the Trade

Just as homemakers have their hints (e.g. a ball of cotton,
dipped in vanilla extract and placed in the refrigerator, will absorb
food odors), writers have their own bag of tricks, a bag of tricks, I
might hasten to point out, you won't learn at any Bread Loaf Conference. Most writers, ivory tower idealists that they are, prefer to play
up the mystique of their "art" (visitations from the Muse, *l'ecriture
automatique,* talking in tongues, et cetera, et cetera), and sweep the
hard-nosed practicalities under the rug. Keeping in mind, however,
that a good workman doesn't curse his tools, I am now going to
make public these long suppressed tricks of the trade.

Suppose you've written a dreadful chapter (we'll dub it Chapter
Six for our purposes here), utterly without merit, tedious and boring
beyond belief, and you just can't find the energy to re-write it. Since
it's obvious that the reader, once he realizes how dull and shoddy
Chapter Six really is, will refuse to read any further, you must provide some strong ulterior motive for completing the chapter. I've always found lust effective:

> Artfully concealed within the next chapter is the astounding secret of
> an ancient Bhutanese love cult that will increase your sexual satis-
> faction by at least 60% and possibly more —

(Print Chapter Six.)

Pretty wild, huh? Bet you can hardly wait to try it! And don't forget to show your appreciation by reading Chapter Seven!*

Fear also works:

> DEAR READER,
>
> THIS MESSAGE IS PRINTED ON *CHINESE POISON PAPER* WHICH IS MADE FROM DEADLY HERBS THAT ARE INSTANTLY ABSORBED BY THE FINGERTIPS SO IT WON'T DO ANY GOOD TO WASH YOUR HANDS BECAUSE YOU WILL DIE A HORRIBLE AND LINGERING DEATH IN ABOUT AN HOUR UNLESS YOU TAKE THE SPECIAL ANTIDOTE WHICH IS REVEALED IN *CHAPTER SIX* AND YOU'LL BE SAVED.
>
> > SINCERELY,
> > (Your Name)

Or even:

> DEAR READER,
>
> YOU ARE OBVIOUSLY ONE OF THOSE RARE PEOPLE WHO ARE IMMUNE TO CHINESE POISON PAPER SO THIS MESSAGE IS PRINTED ON *BAVARIAN POISON PAPER* WHICH IS ABOUT A HUNDRED THOUSAND TIMES MORE POWERFUL AND EVEN IF YOU'RE WEARING GLOVES YOU'RE DEAD FOR SURE UNLESS YOU READ *CHAPTER SIX* VERY CAREFULLY AND FIND THE SPECIAL ANTIDOTE.
>
> > SINCERELY,
> > (Your Name)

Appealing to vanity, greed, sloth and whatever, you can keep this up, chapter by chapter, until they finish the book. In fact, the number of appeals is limited only by human frailty itself. . . .

Lesson 10 — More Writing Hints

There are many more writing hints I could share with you, but suddenly I am run over by a truck.

— the end —

Reading and Interpreting

1. Both this and the article by Pattison work by making what they pretend to advocate so absurd that the reader realizes the author

---

* This insures that the reader reads Chapter Six not once but several times. Possibly, he may even read Chapter Seven.

is advocating the opposite of what he says. It is possible to identify from the Pattison article specific writing blunders to be avoided. Can you do the same for the O'Donoghue article? Which article is more useful as advice for writers?

2. The article is obviously intended to be humorous. Is it funny? What devices does O'Donoghue use to provide humor?

Writing Techniques

1. Describe the organization of the O'Donoghue article. Is it more or less carefully organized than Pattison's article? Pattison's organization depends on analysis (see Section IX). Does O'Donoghue make more or less use of analysis?

2. Toward what kind of audience does the O'Donoghue piece seem directed? Is its audience more or less limited than Pattison's? Describe the tone of the O'Donoghue article. What are some of the characteristics of the writing that reveal the tone?

3. What kind of stance is the author assuming in this section? Describe the character of the person in the role of the speaker.

4. Does the section labeled "Introduction" introduce? If so, what does it introduce? Does the article have a conclusion? In what sense is the final section a conclusion?

Word Study

The following words appear in the Introduction of the selection: *audacity, capsule, errata, correlatives, diatribes, manifestos, oxymora, bulls.* Look each one up in a dictionary and write a definition of it. *Errata* and *oxymora* are plurals; what are the singular forms?

Suggestions for Writing

1. Among the passages that have been omitted are Lesson 4 on Exposition and Lesson 8 on Covering the News. Endeavor to write advice on these two subjects in the manner of O'Donoghue, perhaps using some of his tricks. (Your instructor will have O'Donoghue's version.)

2. As has been suggested above, humor is hard to assign, but you might notice that O'Donoghue has a section "Tricks of the Trade." Could you write something about the tricks of trying to be funny about the trade?

3. One of O'Donoghue's more obvious ways of being funny is to pretend to write about one subject while writing about another. If you do not feel like being funny, better not try, but if you do feel the urge, "Let Me Tell You How to Be a Swell Physicist," and "Inside Dope on Being a A-Student" are possibilities.

A SIN OR A RIGHT?   **40**
Helen Epstein

Helen Epstein, *a free-lance writer with a background in journalism, teaches that subject at New York University. This piece she contributed to* the New York Times Magazine.

About once an hour, the telephone rings at New York's Save-A-Life League. The caller may start talking or burst into tears, or say nothing at all. Sometimes there is a challenge: *"I've got these pills here and I'm going to take them unless you tell me why I should live."* Or questions: *"How much Valium is lethal? How long does it take the gas to work?"* Other times there is awkwardness and embarrassment: *'I've never called you before; how do I start?"*

Facts as introduction.

The calls come from men and women, old and young, black and white, homosexual and heterosexual, rich and poor. Six thousand people each year call Save-A-Life; 10,000 call the Los Angeles Suicide Prevention Center; 20,000 call San Francisco Suicide Prevention — and these are only three of nearly 200 such facilities in the United States. "Six of every 10 callers we get will go on and try to commit suicide," says Harry Warren, director of Save-A-Life, whose Baptist minister father founded the organization in 1906.

Is there any clear statement of a theme idea?

Over the last few years, the Holiday Inn motel chain has been engaging chaplains to be on call in the event their guests try to kill themselves; universities and churches have established crisis-intervention centers; and radio stations have broadcast community alerts to the problems of suicide. In San Francisco, where over 510 people have jumped to death from the Golden Gate Bridge, the "right to suicide" has become a political issue. Researchers grind out over 500 studies each year correlating suicide to factors so varied as poverty, pregnancy, homosexuality and Pacific tidal patterns, yet the phenomenon continues to elude scientific comprehension.

In the last decade, however, suicide rates throughout the world have undergone a change. Youth rates are rising and, in America, suicide now takes second place only to accidents as the leading cause of death among young people. The gap between male and female

Why is the *however* needed here?

rates is narrowing and black suicide is rising. Puerto Ricans in jails, Vietnam War veterans, students and women doctors have especially high rates. Lawyers commit suicide five times as often as the general populace; dentists and physicians, six times as often; psychiatrists 10 times as often. It should be noted, however, that professional organizations take pride in procuring figures like these; no one knows how many cleaning women or sanitation workers do or do not kill themselves.

Notice this qualification.

Each year twice as many Americans kill themselves as kill each other. Experts estimate the number of suicides in America from 25,000 to 60,000 yearly and at least 200,000 more people in this country try to kill themselves and fail. It is on the basis of these statistics that the World Health Organization places the United States far behind world suicide leaders Hungary, Austria, Czechoslovakia, Sweden, Denmark and West Germany, but it qualifies this placement by noting that these countries may simply be keeping the most unbiased and accurate records.

Frustration and rage are thought to be basic to all suicidal groups, although they can be masked by ostensible tranquillity and deadness. This Hendin found particularly true of suicidal students at Columbia and Barnard Colleges, whom he has been studying for the last five years. "Student suicide has traditionally been attributed to a concern with achievement, and in America the theory has been that parents pressured their children to perform," he says. "But, in the students I saw, this pressure was not a crucial factor in their being suicidal. Rather, the child's relationship with his family involved developing an emotional deadness as a kind of protection against life. Their parents wanted quiescent children; they were fairly egocentric — and I think that's true of the whole culture.

Something different begins here.

"Another thing is that students have enormous difficulty relating to the opposite sex. Women are afraid to be victims; men are afraid to be victimizers — and this results in extreme polarization. When I was growing up, social scientists were concerned with alienation. Now it's far beyond that. These young people often don't want to be in touch. They conceive of a life lived in tune with their emotions as extremely painful and dangerous. They almost envy machines for their efficiency. This is a society that puts function above feeling, and I think that's particularly true of young people."

The study of suicide among various groups in America has not been systematic and research regarding women had not received much coverage until the women's movement (and glorification of suicides Virginia Woolf and Sylvia Plath) attracted sufficient attention. In California last year, a state study (conducted by a woman) found that the male-female suicide ratio had narrowed to less than 2 to 1 for the first time in that state's history, with the highest increase at-

Another change in direction.

tributed to black women between the ages of 20 and 24. In New York City, another study confirmed these findings but experts are reluctant to speculate on their significance.

"In general, the rate for men is still higher than the rate for women," says Norman Farberow. "Although the change in the suicide rate for women has occurred concurrently with the development of women's lib, it is inappropriate at the moment to correlate the two. Suicide is far too complex a phenomenon, although women's lib may be contributing to feelings of loneliness, lack of security and the changing nature of formerly stable social elements."

Why does the author rely so much on quotations?

"I'd say the same factors apply to women as apply to blacks," says Dr. Howard Bogard, a psychologist who trains people in crisis intervention. "Many women have begun to redefine their roles in Western culture. The role redefinition leads to confrontations; confrontations result in frustration; frustration leads to anger, rage, depression, and suicide. *If* the statistics are correct about women. It may be that coroners have traditionally been chauvinistic and simply did not accept that women were capable of committing suicide. Or maybe they've suddenly gone the other way. The coroner may now think: I'll fix them. I'll treat them the same way I do men. They're suicides."

Everyone who researches suicide, says Bogard, does so in terms of his own personal and professional needs, and it is often more enlightening to read poets like John Donne, statesmen like Thomas Masaryk, novelists like Albert Camus or critics like A. Alvarez for insights into the subject. Philosophers, clerics and other wise people were pondering suicide for centuries before sociologist Emile Durkheim wrote what is considered to be the classic, "scientific" work on the subject, in 1897. He saw suicide as a factor of social deprivation; Freud attributed it to the death instinct; for Jung, it was an expression of longing for rebirth. Current theory attempts to synthesize the sociological and psychological approaches in the manner of Dr. Ari Kiev.

◄An indirect quotation as a topic sentence.

"The suicide rate reflects the stimulus overload in our society," he says. "We have a high degree of freedom and a multiplicity of choices to make. At the same time, traditional mechanisms like religion and custom—which served to screen out the stimuli—have been lost and the individual has no framework within which to make choices.

"The stimulus overload makes it difficult for *anyone* to make decisions. The depressed person has great difficulties in saying no to the pressures placed on him, in disappointing other people's expectations. When he does so, he feels guilty, worthless, confused and even more indecisive. Suicide can seem a way of asserting control over one's life."

This is a view grounded in current affairs, an explanation with geographic and social limits. The phenomenon of suicide is clearly too old and too mysterious to yield quickly to a generation of scientists impatient for definitive answers. A. Alvarez, a failed suicide whose book "The Savage God" deserves to be placed alongside Durkheim's classic, concludes his discussion of suicide this way:

◀Does the conclusion begin here?

"The sociologists and psychologists who talk of it as a disease puzzle me now as much as the Catholics and Moslems who call it the most deadly of mortal sins. It seems to me to be somehow as much beyond social or psychic prophylaxis as it is beyond morality, a terrible but utterly natural reaction to the necessities we sometimes create for ourselves. And it is not for me. Perhaps I am no longer optimistic enough. I assume now that death, when it finally comes, will probably be nastier than suicide, and certainly a great deal less convenient."

Reading and Interpreting

1. Does Epstein answer the question of the title? The article is primarily a journalistic report, recording facts and opinions on the subject. Does the author's attitude ever emerge?

2. Consider implications of Epstein's facts. Do they have any special significance for students?

3. Since Epstein wrote her article, cases have been reported in the news in which a person with a hopeless terminal illness was being kept alive by a machine. Either the patient or relatives wanted the machine turned off. Do the considerations in Epstein's essay apply to situations like this? Does the patient have a right to turn off the machine, or would turning it off be a sin? Or a crime?

Writing Techniques

1. Consider Epstein's stance. You probably concluded that she means to be objective. That is part of her professional duty as a trained journalist. How does she maintain this stance? Notice the material she uses to develop the first few paragraphs. How would you characterize it? Does it change, so that in the later paragraphs she is relying on other sorts of evidence?

2. Study the organization. What kind of introduction does she use? What sort of conclusion? What about topic sentences? You will notice that paragraph 4 has a standard topic sentence. But several paragraphs do not. Why not? Can you find any paragraphs in which Epstein seems to be saying, in effect, "Keep going. The topic has not changed. This indentation marks only a subdivision of the topic I have already introduced, as you will see if you keep on reading." Do you ever find her using "commitment and response," but no conventional topic sentence?

Suggestions for Writing

1. Write a discussion of some topic suggested by the information in Epstein's essay. You might want to express your own views on whether suicide is justifiable, whether it is a moral or a social problem, whether either suicide or mercy killings are justifiable, or a similar question. You could make a case for everybody's right to determine his own destiny, to destroy his life if he wants to. Or you might make the opposite case. Do you have some obligation to society to contribute to it? And do you have any obligation not to hurt people who love you—even though you may have done nothing consciously to induce their love?

2. You may wish to speculate on the long-range implications of a growing suicide rate for society as a whole. You might wish to report on information you have about persons you have known who have committed suicide or contemplated it.

3. Do you have any ideas about ways to prevent the waste of suicide, which can affect all kinds of people? Do you know of suicide centers like the one Epstein describes? Should more such centers be provided?

WHAT I BELIEVE   **41**
Mark Van Doren

The late **Mark Van Doren,** *younger brother of Carl Van Doren, is most widely remembered as a poet, although he was also critic, editor, fiction writer, playwright, and for generations the idol of students in Columbia College. This piece is from the* Saturday Review.

I believe that justice is the most beautiful thing on earth, or if not on earth, then in heaven. It is seldom if ever encountered on earth, though it is our habit to seek it there, and sometimes it is our fancy that we have found it—or not found it where we thought we would, where it should have been, and then we are angry or sad. No habit is more powerful than this, and no fancy is more familiar. No dream is dearer than the dream that we shall one day drive the truth into a corner—the whole truth, and nothing but the truth—and force it, gently or otherwise, to show its face. For justice and truth are sister goddesses; are twins, in fact; and their being goddesses does not prevent us from having the illusion that we can order them about. Mortals, as it happens, do not possess that power.

The commonest illusion about justice, and the most natural, the most understandable one, is that it means getting what we deserve, what is our due. The only trouble is, there are certain to be those who will deny that our deserts are what *we* think they are, and who may actually be so unpleasant as to define them as punishments rather than rewards. "He got what was coming to him"—such words do not suggest that he wanted it to come, though they do suggest that it was already on its way, was inevitable, and therefore true and just. "He asked for it"—that is harsher still, implying as it does that it was asked for in ignorance of its true nature. Perhaps he asked for justice—only justice—and now he is being told that he shouldn't have been so rash, because he got it, and see how little he enjoys it. There are folk sayings that warn us not to ask for justice because we may get it in the neck. And there is Hamlet's famous outburst when poor old Polonius promises to treat the players "according to their desert": "God's bodykins, man, much better. Use every man after his desert, and who should 'scape whipping? Use them after your own honour and dignity; the less they deserve, the more merit is in your bounty." Be godlike, Hamlet seems to be saying, for in the eyes of the gods all men are imperfect, and to love them is to love them all alike, little as any of them merits such attention.

Why is so little link to the previous paragraph needed?

The law is no respecter of persons; it has the same high opinion of us all—or the same low opinion, according as we view the matter. Justice is blindfold in order that she may decide impersonally which of us is right and which is wrong; to see us might be to like our looks—or dislike them—and our looks are irrelevant to her prime concern, which is what we are behind our faces. Nor does she listen to our special pleas. She is terrible in her impartiality, in the abstractness of her gaze. Whoever first said that there are three sides to every question, my side, your side, and the right side, was looking straight at Justice as he spoke, and what he saw must have chilled him, for the person he saw was not a person after all: was neither man nor woman, neither young nor old, neither fair nor foul, neither kind nor unkind, neither merciless nor merciful.

Notice the parts of this paragraph.

For what *is* the right side? What is rightness? Systems of law are embarrassed by such questions, and ask them as seldom as possible. Beginning students in law schools are likely to be cast down because they never hear their teachers speak of justice; winning cases is the thing. And what is more natural, when law is viewed as a profession? My own view, either of justice or of the law, is so far from being professional that I now must repeat my opening statement— Justice is beautiful—and turn to an altogether different aspect of the theme, an aspect having nothing to do with right or wrong, innocent or guilty, desert or undesert.

Justice is beautiful—more beautiful than any other human thing—because the very thought of it brings peace. To think of it is to think of everything else also. To imagine it is to imagine all the parts of the world serenely in place as on the day of their creation: fitting together, never to be disjoined. To keep on thinking of it is to look at, and listen to, a stupendous work of art: not a noisy one, not even a huge one, but one whose quiet force can be felt forever. Justice thus conceived is the sum of all goods, the crown of all felicities.

> Does this mark a major division?

Which, I grant, is an extravagant way of recognizing Socrates' contribution to the discussion. In Plato's *Republic,* the masterpiece among all books about justice, Socrates works his way through several unsatisfactory definitions of justice and arrives not so much at a better definition as at a position from which he can see justice in relation to three virtues on which its own existence depends. These three are courage, temperance, and wisdom, which first of all depend upon one another, since none of them can be possessed unless the others are, but which in combination produce the possibility of justice, either in an individual or in a state. Justice, finally, is the harmony that results when all the other goods are present in the right proportions; it is the binding good, the ultimate virtue, the thought of which brings peace. Now all talk of my side and your side suddenly seems childish; the figure emerges, if only in one's imagination, of a person so anchored in reality, so aware of all the things that are, so wise, so temperate, so courageous, that he is free not only from others but from himself. He is of course an ideal person. But so is justice an ideal, a thing not to be looked for in either time or place: a thing, in other words, of heaven.

> Another good example of divisions within a paragraph.

We are not to think, then, of just acts—single just acts, or single just decisions—but rather of the person whose disposition, whose genius, is just, whose habits of mind are generous, patient, and farseeing, who waits before he acts, and perhaps in the end does not act at all, though when action is necessary proves capable of it without hesitation. I have always been interested in the last three lines of a poem by Thoreau, a poem called "Mist":

> Could you call this a preconclusion?

> Spirit of lakes and seas and rivers,
> Bear only perfumes and the scent
> Of healing herbs to just men's fields.

Justice itself hangs like a perfume, a healing scent, above the world of this poem—a world that for all we know has many just men in it, men who live quietly, representing in their lives the essence of wisdom and peace.

Such persons may constitute a secret society within the larger society that contains them—a secret society whose members do not know one another, who never meet, but whose influence nevertheless is somehow mutual. And such a society might be larger than we think; and the name of the substance that binds them together might be justice. I have never been able to interest any linguist in what for me is a fascinating fact, namely, that the word *ius* in Latin meant two apparently unrelated things: *justice* and *juice.* Sauce is a better version of the second term, which still may seem ridiculously different from the first. Yet what if in the Sanskrit source of both words there was sameness instead of difference, so that justice could be seen, even tasted, as the juice of a state, as the thing that bound its parts together, making them finally all one, giving all of them a single savor, a single character, a single understanding of what the state was founded for? Linguists laugh when I ask this question, but I hold out for a possible connection between the idea of something that makes all the portions of a dish taste good and the idea of something that makes all the members of a society aware of what they belong to, and happy to be so aware. If ever justice rules the earth, it may be like that.

A rapid transition and preparation for a conclusion.

A succinct concluding sentence.

Reading and Interpreting

1. Summarize Van Doren's belief about justice. Does he provide a clear definition? How is his view related to Plato's attempts at definition? Can you subscribe to his beliefs?

2. Is what Van Doren calls the "commonest illusion" about justice actually an illusion? Do you agree with his objections to it?

3. How does Van Doren come to the view, in the next to the last paragraph, that "we are not to think of just acts"? Can you think of persons who might belong to his "secret society"?

Writing Techniques

1. Assume that Van Doren's essay approaches being a model for orderly organization. Check it for the following:

a. Is there a clear, formally stated introduction? Is there a similar clear, identifiable conclusion? Does it conclude?

b. Does every paragraph have a precise, recognizable topic sentence? Is it the first sentence? If not, where is it? Why?

    c. Is every paragraph but the first clearly linked by transition to an earlier paragraph or paragraphs?

    d. Is every paragraph adequately developed, not cluttered with useless matter, but sufficiently built to make its point?

    e. Is every paragraph constructed in accordance with some apparent plan?

    f. Does the writing gain continuity through "commitment and response"? That is, do sentences develop from preceding sentences?

    2. Try to describe Van Doren's stance. How would you contrast it with Epstein's stance?

Suggestions for Writing

    1. The most obvious suggestion is to take a title like Van Doren's, "What I Believe," and do what you can with it.

    2. An easier assignment would be to work with an example of justice or injustice: "I Encounter Injustice" or "I Caught a Glimpse of Justice."

Prose Strategies: The Writer's Building Blocks

Development: Details, Examples

This book is divided into three main parts because writing works at least three ways at once. In Part One we considered the purpose of writing, examining the so-called "four forms of discourse": narration, description, argument, and exposition. In Part Two we examined writing as social communication, as the interplay between audience and author. In Part Three we shall look into development, the way a topic grows, and to be practical, we shall consider specific devices for making topics grow, weighing them one by one. Of course in practice neither writing nor reading is a one-by-one activity, and even in developing an idea a writer seldom uses only one strategy. When we write or speak, read or listen, we have to deal with wholes, but when we study the use of language, we can learn something by looking at the parts.

The most common, the workhorse method of expanding an idea, is to provide details. If you will think back over the examples in this book, you will notice that all the authors used details. Even a highly specialized device like analogy required details. You will recall that in the description of the battlefield at Waterloo the author compared the terrain to a capital letter A, but having set up this analogy he had at once to start providing details, or the analogy would have had little meaning.

And the editors of this book had to use details writing the introductions. You may recall the first of them, in which you were asked to imagine you had been in an accident, and your friends asked you what happened. You started a narrative, but the narrative was made up of details, what you and other people had done. Similarly, details filled up the other forms of discourse; description was sometimes little more than the ordering of details. Arguments and explanations required details.

Of course not all details are of one kind, and you will want to ask yourself, which sorts of details work best for various kinds of writing? One answer you have probably heard is that telling details are those that can be described as *concrete, precise, specific, exact, vivid, sensuous, colorful, factual,* and the like. You may have heard this question talked about under the heading *levels of specificity,* with the implication that the more specificity—the more details are specific—the better.

You may care to pursue this question of specificity. Check through the group of readings following, in "Brief Examples of Detail." Most of these pieces would be rated as having "a high level of specificity." Then check through some of the earlier collections of brief selections, number *13,* "Brief Arguments," or number *19,* "Brief Expositions," for example. You will find specific, concrete details in all of them. The authors are all skillful writers, but the level of specificity will be lower in some than in others. Or compare the detail in number *42* of this section with the detail in some of your own writing. Can you match these professionals in the detail you use? Probably not, at least not all the time, but you ought to sometimes. Or try to think back over the selections you have read, to see which contained detail so vivid or telling that you remember them. Perhaps the little incident involving Le Pirate (*9*), or the piece about the baby whale (*5*)?

Similar to details are *examples.* In fact, the two blend into one another enough so that you may have thought of them as the same thing. They are so similar that writers commonly associate them, also, and you need not distinguish sharply between them in order to use them well. But the distinction is worth noticing. A detail is part of something. In the hypothetical motorcycle accident mentioned above, we noticed details, the parts of the accident, the people, the actions, the physical things involved. The same accident could have been used as an example.

Suppose somebody has complained, "My mother said motorcycles are dangerous. That's silly!" Now assume you reply, admitting that riding a motorcycle can be fun, and it can be handled so that it is not dangerous, but on the whole they are more dangerous than are some other means of transportation. Then you might recount the accident you had, and use it to illustrate how riding motorcycles can be or need not be dangerous. Your account of the accident will be made up of details. The whole will be used as an example to illustrate the thesis you have adopted.

In the selections that follow you will find use of both details and examples. You might compare two of the longer pieces: would it be judicious to say that Mirsky uses more detail than does Orwell, but Orwell uses more examples than does Mirsky? Would it be correct to say that Middleton starts with details and works toward examples, but that Lehman starts mainly with examples and shifts so that he uses more details?

BRIEF EXAMPLES OF DETAIL   **42**

Detail is so essential to development, that almost every selection in this book provides examples. The following pieces, however, illustrate particularly how writing can progress as a series of related details. **a. Joseph Conrad,** *was a Pole who became a British sea captain, and at length one of England's leading novelist; this excerpt is from* Victory *(1915);* **b.** *Islands in the Stream (1970), from which this was taken, is a posthumously published novel of Nobel Prize winner* **Ernest Hemingway;** **c.** *the selection is from a comic novel about former President Richard Nixon and his associates,* Our Gang *(1971) by* **Philip Roth;** **d.** *the next excerpt comes from the American classic,* The Red Badge of Courage *(1895) by* **Stephen Crane;** **e.** *Noble Prize winner* **John Steinbeck** *recounts an incident in* Cannery Row, *one of the novels set near Monterey, California;* **f.** *the* **Truman Capote** *piece is from* In Cold Blood *(1965), one of a recent spate of books that blend journalistic reporting with fiction;* **g. Vladimir Nabokov,** *a Russian emigré who has lived in the United States, Switzerland, and elsewhere, is one of the leading international literary figures; the selection is from* Ada *(1969).*

a.   Joseph Conrad

MR. JONES, the front of his soiled white tunic soaked and plastered against his breast-bone, staggered away from the water-pipe. Steadying himself on Ricardo's shoulder, he drew a long breath, raised his dripping head, and produced a smile of ghastly amiability, which was lost upon the thoughtful Heyst. Behind his back the sun, touching the water, was like a disc of iron cooled to a dull red glow, ready to start rolling round the circular steel plate of the sea, which, under the darkening sky, looked more solid than the high ridge of Samburan: more solid than the point, whose long outlined slope melted into its own unfathomable shadow blurring the dim sheen on the bay. The forceful stream from the pipe broke like shattered glass on the boat's gunwale. Its loud, fitful, and persistent splashing revealed the depth of the world's silence.

b.   Ernest Hemingway

THOMAS HUDSON shot again and was behind with another spurt of water. He felt sick at his stomach, as though something had hold of him inside and was gripping him there, and he shot again; as carefully and steady as he could; knowing fully what the shot meant; and the spurt of water was ahead of the fin. The fin kept right on with the same awful motion. He had one shot now, no extra shells, and the shark was about thirty yards from the boy, coming in with the same slicing motion. David had the fish off the spear and in his hand, the mask was up on his forehead, and he was looking steadily toward the shark coming.

c.   Philip Roth

LET'S begin here, with the smallest of the four blades. In the language of those who employ such weapons, it is known as "the bottle opener." I'll tell you how it got that name in a moment. You will observe that it is hook-shaped at the end, and measures one inch and one-eighth. It is employed during the interrogation of prisoners primarily to gouge out one or both of the eyes. It is also used on the soles of the feet, which are sliced open, like so, with the point of the hook. Last, but not least, it is sometimes inserted into the mouth of a prisoner who will not talk, in order to slit the flesh at the upper part of the larynx, between the vocal cords. That opening up there is called the glottis, and "bottle opener" is derived from "glottal opener," the pet name originally attached to the blade by its most cold-blooded practitioners.

d. Stephen Crane

BUT there was a frenzy made from this furious rush. The men, pitching forward insanely, had burst into cheerings, moblike and barbaric, but tuned in strange keys that can arouse the dullard and the stoic. It made a mad enthusiasm that, it seemed, would be incapable of checking itself before granite and brass. There was the delirium that encounters despair and death, and is heedless and blind to the odds. It is a temporary but sublime absence of selfishness. And because it was of this order was the reason, perhaps, why the youth wondered, afterward, what reasons he could have had for being there.

e. John Steinbeck

DURING the millennia that frogs and men have lived in the same world, it is probable that men have hunted frogs. And during that time a pattern of hunt and parry has developed. The man with net or bow or lance or gun creeps noiselessly, as he thinks, toward the frog. The pattern requires that the frog sit still, sit very still and wait. The rules of the game require the frog to wait until the final flicker of a second, when the net is descending, when the lance is in the air, when the finger squeezes the trigger, then the frog jumps, plops into the water, swims to the bottom and waits until the man goes away. That is the way it is done, the way it has always been done. Frogs have every right to expect it will always be done that way. Now and then the net is too quick, the lance pierces, the gun flicks and that frog is gone, but it is all fair and in the framework. Frogs don't resent that. But how could they have anticipated Mack's new method? How could they have foreseen the horror that followed? The sudden flashing of lights, the shouting and squealing of men, the rush of feet. Every frog leaped, plopped into the pool, and swam frantically to the bottom. Then into the pool plunged the line of men, stamping, churning, moving in a crazy line up the pool, flinging their feet about. Hysterically the frogs displaced from their placid spots swam ahead of the crazy thrashing feet and the feet came on. Frogs are good swimmers but they haven't much endurance. Down the pool they went until finally they were bunched and crowded against the end. And the feet and wildly plunging bodies followed them. A few frogs lost their heads and floundered among the feet and got through and these were saved. But the majority decided to leave this pool forever, to find a new home in a new country where this kind of thing didn't happen. A wave of frantic, frustrated frogs, big ones, little ones, brown ones, green ones, men frogs and women frogs, a wave of them broke over the bank, crawled, leaped, scrambled. They clambered up the grass, they clutched at each other, little ones rode on big ones. And then—horror on horror—the flashlights found them. Two men gathered them like berries. The line came out of the water and closed in on their rear and gathered them like potatoes. Tens and fifties of them were flung into the gunny sacks, and the sacks filled with tired, frightened, and disillusioned frogs, with dripping, whimpering frogs. Some got away, of course, and some had been saved in the pool. But never in frog history had such an execution taken place. Frogs by the pound, by the fifty pounds. They weren't counted but there must have been six or seven hundred. Then happily Mack tied up the necks of the sacks. They were soaking, dripping wet and the air was cool. They had a short one in the grass before they went back to the house so they wouldn't catch cold.

f.   Truman Capote

MRS. CLARE is a famous figure in Finney County. Her celebrity derives not from her present occupation but a previous one—dance-hall hostess, an incarnation not indicated by her appearance. She is a gaunt, trouser-wearing, woolen-skirted, cowboy-booted, ginger-colored, gingerly-tempered woman of unrevealed age ("That's for me to know, and you to guess") but promptly revealed opinions, most of which are announced in a voice of rooster-crow altitude and penetration. Until 1955 she and her late husband operated the Holcomb Dance Pavilion, an enterprise that owing to its uniqueness in the area, attracted from a hundred miles around a fast-drinking, fancy-stepping clientele, whose behavior, in turn, attracted the interest of the sheriff now and then. "We had some tough times, all right," says Mrs. Clare, reminiscing. "Some of those bowlegged boys, you give 'em a little hooch and they're like redskins—want to scalp everything in sight. Course, we only sold setups, never the hard stuff itself. Wouldn't have, even if it was legal. My husband, Homer Clare, he didn't hold with it; neither did I. One day Homer Clare—he passed on seven months and twelve days ago today, after a five-hour operation out in Oregon—he said to me, 'Myrt, we've lived all our lives in hell, now we're going to die in heaven.' The next day we closed the dance hall. I've never regretted it. Oh, along at first I missed being a night owl—the tunes, the jollity. But now that Homer's gone, I'm just glad to do my work here at the Federal Building. Sit a spell. Drink a cup of coffee."

g. Vladimir Nabokov

WAS she really beautiful? Was she at least what they call attractive? She was exasperation, she was torture. The silly girl had heaped her hair under a rubber cap, and this gave an unfamiliar, vaguely clinical look to her neck, with its odd dark wisps and strags, as if she had obtained a nurse's job and would never dance again. Her faded, bluish-gray, one-piece swimsuit had a spot of grease and a hole above one hip—nibbled through, one might conjecture, by a tallow-starved larva—and seemed much too short for careless comfort. She smelled of damp cotton, axillary tufts, and nenuphars, like mad Ophelia. None of those minor matters would have annoyed Van, had she and he been alone together; but the presence of the all-male actor made everything obscene, drab and insupportable. We move back to the lip of the pool.

Writing Techniques

1. A writer using details must always select from hundreds of possibilities in order to produce a particular impression. Try to decide for each selection why the writer has chosen a particular set of details. For example, how is Conrad's final sentence related to his selection of details?

2. Try summarizing the Philip Roth paragraph in a single sentence. Then consider why you cannot write a summary sentence that produces a sense of horror as sharply as the collection of matter-of-fact concrete details.

3. How does the point of view in the Steinbeck piece—which considers, partly whimsically, the attitudes of the frogs—affect the choice of details?

4. How does Capote's use of direct quotations clarify the reader's impression of the character he is describing? What does the reader learn from the manner of her speech as well as its content?

5. Nabokov uses a series of unusual specific details to characterize a girl. Do they give an impression of the girl as clearly as would more general descriptive statements? How does the selection of detail relate to the next to the last sentence? Compare this description with that of Capote.

Suggestions for Writing

Write either a description of a brief incident or of a character, by listing specific details, following one of the models above in any way you find useful.

SANITY NOTE: WE CAN STILL LAUGH AT GOVERNMENT   **43**
Maxwell Lehman

Professor **Maxwell Lehman,** *of Fairfield University has published two books on government and society; he was formerly an administrator of New York City. This article was published in* Human Communications *(1974).*

RECENT public opinion polls indicate that confidence in political and governmental institutions has fallen, as one newspaper headline tells us, "to an all-time low."

Not so. The deterioration of confidence did not begin with Watergate; it has always been low. The American people take a jaundiced view of their political systems, observing with a healthy and often delightful cynicism the pomposities, pretentions, posturings and antics of their officialdom. The attitude expresses itself in political humor, a form of communication that has been in continuous currency since colonial times.

Benjamin Franklin, reflecting eighteenth-century public attitudes, said: "Keep the pay of public officials low, because they'll get it anyhow."

Alben Barkley, Harry Truman's Vice President, told this story of a public execution scene in the early nineteenth century. Turning to the prisoner about to be hanged, the executioner said:

"Under the law you have five minutes to make a statement to the audience."

"No," replied the prisoner, "I don't need to make a statement."

From the audience a man came dashing to the scaffold, huffing and puffing, and addressed the condemned man. "Mister, mister, I'm running for the assembly. Can I have your five minutes?"

Technically, not so is a fragment. Why is it not troublesome here?

"It's O.K. with me," replied the prisoner, "but would you mind if they hang me first?"

Political office-holders are usually held in decent respect by Americans. But the definitions of a politician as communicated via American folklore reveal more incisively what the people really feel about this breed.

Here are a few examples, gathered from various sections of the United States.

"A politician is a man who sits on a fence while keeping both ears to the ground."

"A politician is a man who stands for what he thinks others will fall for."

Definitions as comic examples.

"A politician is a man who divides his time between running for office and running for cover."

"Some politicians repair their fences while hedging."

"A hat is something a man covers his head with, the beggar passes around, the politician tosses into the ring and talks through."

"There was a politician in Indiana who was really honest. When he was bought, he stayed bought."

In a more bitter vein, Thomas Jefferson once said: "Whenever a man has cast a longing eye on offices, a rottenness begins in his conduct."

So pervasive is the distrust of politicians that Webster's Biographical Dictionary has an explanatory note which reads: "It should be noted that the word 'politician' is used in the Dictionary in the general meaning of a person engaged in politics and has no derogatory implications."

Political patronage and nepotism, although condemned by reform and "good government" groups, have from the beginning been a way of life in the day-to-day job-filling aspects of government. The process of placing relatives or less-than-competent persons into appointive posts has entered the folklore stream.

Would you call this an example?

A story that made the rounds in New York's Tammany Hall in the early years of the twentieth century told of the hard-working, small-time political club functionary who assiduously knocked on doors and helped round up votes to elect the mayor. After the victory celebration, he approached the local district leader. "Boss," he said, "you promised that if we won the election I would get appointed to a job."

"What job did you have in mind, Joe?" asked the boss.

"I want to be Water Commissioner."

"What!" exclaimed the leader, "Water Commissioner? You're out of your mind! You can't read or write."

To this, Joe replied angrily: "I told you I want to be commissioner, not deputy commissioner."

And in this category belongs also another story testifying to the shoulder-shrugging cynicism that Americans traditionally maintain toward public office. The story goes like this:

A political sachem brings his son into the office of a newly elected official. "Mike," he says to the official, "my boy would like a job in your department."

The official regarded the boy dubiously. "What can he do?"

"Nothing," was the frank response.

"Oh, that simplifies it," beamed the office-holder. "Then we won't have to break him in."

And there's the story of the youngster whose parents were undecided about what he would do when he became an adult. They struck on a plan. They placed before the child an apple, a prayer book and a dollar bill. The apple represented farming, the prayer book clergy, the dollar bill banking. They waited to see which of these objects the child would reach for. He ate the apple, read the prayer book, and put the dollar bill in his pocket. The parents decided he would be a politician.

Does this paragraph develop by detail?

Throughout American history, the cynicism continues. It applies to the intricacies of congressional maneuvering as well as to executive hanky-panky.

Derisive tales about Congress abound in the political literature. Nearly all of these stories have the same oddly suspicious yet affectionate view with which Americans regard their decision-makers.

An actor visited the spectators' gallery of the House of Representatives. "Congress is so strange," he reported afterward. "A man gets up to speak and says nothing. Nobody listens — and then everybody disagrees."

And this: A father took his small son to the visitor's gallery of the Senate.

"Father, who is that gentleman?" asked the boy, pointing to the chaplain.

"That, my son, is the man who prays," replied the father.

"Does he pray for the Senators?" asked the boy.

"No, my son, when he looks around and sees the Senators sitting there, he prays for the country."

Conversation as detail.

John Mason Brown, an acute observer of the public scene, in his book *Through These Men*, put it this way: "The more I observed Washington, the more frequently I visited it, and the more people I interviewed there, the more I understood how prophetic L'Enfant was when he laid it out as a city that goes around in circles."

The cynicism which attaches to politics is reflected in attitudes toward government and government bureaucracy. Considering the grumbling that is a constant about the cost of government, there is perhaps some elemental wisdom in the old saw, "There is one fixed

What is this as organization?

rule about government—the less it's worth the more it costs."

And: "All of us are working for the government. The trick is to get paid for it."

Americans have the saving grace of being able to laugh at themselves. Within the precincts of government, the much-maligned bureaucrats have a humor and a language of their own. Here are a few examples:

"Mr. Wampus, I fear you are ignoring our efficiency system."

"Maybe so, Mr. Grump, but somebody has to get the work done."

And this one:

Efficiency expert says: "I'm gratified to see how many new men you have taken on since I installed my new system."

"Yes, I hired 'em to take care of the system."

There's a certain grim humor in the bureaucrat's definitions. Take that word "expert." You know its common dictionary definition, but to government people, weary of consultants who come in and disrupt their neat routines, the word "expert" has this meaning: "Somebody from out of town." If he smokes a pipe, he's a bigger expert.

Do definitions here become a sort of detail?

Other definitions, some of them self-deprecating, heard in government offices:

Civic organization—A group of two or more people with access to a Xerox machine.

Personnel administration—A scientific means for protecting the rights and privileges of the bureaucracy.

Bureaucracy—A group of people holding public jobs whose major activity is holding up public action.

Civil service—A commodity formerly obtainable in restaurants.

Systems analysis—An astrological term; casting horoscopes by means of the computer.

Computer—An inscrutable machine in which, when anything goes wrong, which is always, it can never be made right again. *Alt.*—A mechanism for delaying public business.

Work simplification—A method of getting less work done by more people at higher cost after a survey. Related to Parkinson's Law.

Decision-making—A process which, when children do it, is called blind man's bluff.

Each of these stories and definitions has an element of truth in it. Each betrays a refusal to accept at face value what is spoon-fed, a healthy suspiciousness deeply entrenched in the American psyche about government and the political process.

American political word usage is brilliantly incisive, earthy, and often funny. A phrase or a single word can make even abstract concepts vividly clear. For example: *He suffers from foot-in-mouth disease*

◀Is this topic sentence adequate?

to describe an inept orator. Or *red herring* to delineate a phony political issue. Or the single word *backlash* to depict a whole plethora of deep-seated social attitudes. A *hatchetman* is the tough guy who performs onerous political tasks. A party leader in a legislative body is the *whip,* a word that colorfully tells us what his job is—to get the party members to vote the way the leadership wants them to vote. The ordinary citizen's disillusion with slick campaign literature is expressed in the sarcastic phrase *Madison Avenue techniques.*

William Safire, once President Nixon's speechwriter and now a *New York Times* columnist, has compiled an interesting collection in his book, *The New Language of Politics.* Safire points out: The lexicon delights in disaster: *landslides, prairie fires, tidalwaves,* and *avalanches* are the goals of *whirlwind campaigns.* Politicians pray that *lightning may strike* . . . An anonymous voice becomes a *voice from the sewer,* a bigot an *apostle of hate,* a pessimist a *prophet of gloom and doom,* a censor a *bookburner.*

The list of short, vivid phrases or single-word descriptions of complex ideas is endless. There is the word *lulu,* for political expense accounts; *gutfighter* for the ruthless political candidate; *shoo-in* for what appears to be a clear victory at the polls; *lame duck* for an office-holder who has not been re-elected but still has some time to serve; *dark horse* for an unexpected candidate. Animals, in fact, figure prominently in political folklore. A *wheelhorse* is one who does drudge work in campaigns. A political character who has *made a boo-boo* (a mistake) and publicly regrets it *eats crow.* Rich contributors are *fat cats.*

The wry humor with which Americans view their institutions is evidence of democratic strength. In a dictatorship, one jests about government and politics only at one's peril; such jokes as are made can be only surreptitious. In most countries, public officialdom wears haloes, whether by awe or tradition-hallowed. Americans, on the other hand, question everything; they are neither awed nor cowed. Their humor, reflecting their basic attitudes, is a leavening influence on the political process. The great lawyer Clarence Darrow once said: "When I was a boy I was told anybody could become President; I'm beginning to believe it." Perhaps more pertinent today is the line uttered by comedian Joey Adams: "Every American has a chance to be President. That's a risk, he has to take."

[margin note: A long conclusion. Is it worth the space?]

Reading and Interpreting

What is the main idea of this piece? Does the idea expressed in the introduction differ in any way from that expressed in the conclusion?

Writing Techniques

1. The essay is organized mainly through classification of examples into groups (for more on classification, see Section IX). Identify the main divisions of the essay, the main groups into which the details are classified.

2. Indicate the basis on which each group of details is collected. Do all the details seem logically to belong in the groups to which they are assigned? Consider the topic sentences that control each group of details. To what does each commit the writer?

3. Consider Lehman's use of quotations. When does he quote, and when does he summarize?

Suggestions for Writing

Try using Lehman's method for a paper on student humor, collecting examples, making a generalization about them and then developing the commitment of the generalization with examples classified into groups. Consider whether students do laugh at themselves, at the faculty, at examinations, grades, credits, education generally.

WHO SAYS SO?   **44**
Thomas H. Middleton

Thomas H. Middleton *writes a column for* Saturday Review *called "Light Refractions." This was his refraction for the issue of October 5, 1974.*

IN a column called "Linguistic Inanities" (SR/W, July 13), I suggested that there was nothing wrong with "aren't I?" as a colloquial substitute for "am I not?" — little knowing that I was attacking quasi-religious dogma by doing so. All hell broke loose, and I felt the slings and arrows of outraged purists. Dozens of them.

One lady asked, "Have you ever in your pseudo-democratic life heard *anyone* say, 'I are not'? I doubt it. Then why on earth should anyone say, 'Aren't I?' Such a senseless, 'inane' manufacture has no justification in logic, grammar, clarity, or colloquiality.

"Whatever you say, 'aren't I?' is certainly *not* almost universal. I've never said it in my puff, never expect to, and never remember anyone saying it. I was surprised to see you dub it 'colloquially respectable.' "

I'm puzzled by that use of "puff," but let it pass. And I won't pick on "never remember anyone saying it," except to suggest that if the lady really doesn't remember hearing "aren't I?" she, as a self-styled "intelligent, college-educated, well-read, lively, middle-aged woman," either has a faulty memory or has led a very sheltered, however lively, life. And it wasn't I, but H. W. Fowler in *Modern English Usage,* who said "aren't I?" was "almost universal" and who dubbed it "colloquially respectable." He and I agree, but the words are his.

A correspondent from Indiana says, " 'Aren't I?' . . . may sound smoother because we are used to it, but wrong it is.

"Neither Webster nor Fowler is an authority on what is 'right' in English. They, the lexicographers, have no judicial powers. Webster and Fowler are reporters. That is right to them which is used by a majority."

I get the impression that many people who can't accept "aren't I?" feel quite at home with sentences like "That is right to them which is used by a majority." *De gustibus. . . .*

But this gentleman has hit upon the crux of the matter: "They, the lexicographers, have no judicial powers."

Who *has* judicial powers?

I think I first wondered about who decided what was "good" English and what was "bad" English when I was taught that we should say "I shall" and "you will" except when there's volition implied, when it becomes "I will" and "you shall."

That struck me as being at once very arbitrary and very fuzzy — a combination that made me uneasy. It wasn't that I was going to worry about what to say; as a practical matter, I was going to say "I'll," except in response to questions such as "Who'll finish up the ice cream?" — in which case I'd say, will." But the "I shall, you will"– "I will, you shall" problem nagged me, partly because I knew I could never bring myself to say, "I shan't," but, more important, because of the honorable principle of "Who says so?"

Fowler knew that while it has its logic, the English language is not a logical system and is affected by the winds and tides of human behavior.

"Aren't I?" may not be logical, but neither is the verb *to be* logical. In fact, the *Oxford English Dictionary*'s opening shot at the verb *be* goes "an irregular and defective verb." The fact is that *be, am, is, are, was,* and *were* came from different parts of the world and found themselves huddled together in the super-accommodating arms of the English language.

"Aren't" is as logical and as illogical for "am not" as "won't" is for "will not." The point is that logic has nothing to do with the case. Sometimes the language is logical, and sometimes it isn't. It's possible for it to be "good-logical" and ugly or "bad-illogical" and beautiful. Every educated person knows that "more perfect" is illogical, "bad" English. But if the Preamble to the Constitution said, "We, the People of the United States, in order to form a more nearly perfect union," I think we'd have lost something.

As with so many questions of language, appropriateness is the key. "Am I not to be accorded the rights and privileges of citizenship as well as its obligations" is much better than "Aren't I to be accorded . . . "; but if you're in a crowd before the deli counter, "I'm after you, aren't I?" is much more fitting than "I'm after you, am I not?"

Asked why, I'm reminded of Louis Armstrong, who, when asked, "What is jazz?" answered, "If you gotta ask what is it, you ain't never gonna know."

If there's one unshakably valid grammatical rule based on logic, it's the one against the double negative, but it's my feeling, probably unverifiable, that the more you know about the English language, the more beautiful you'll find Louis Armstrong's answer, illogical and ungrammatical though it is.

Reading and Interpreting

1. What is the main point of Middleton's column? How does he use "aren't I" in developing that main idea?

2. Middleton calls the prohibition of the double negative "one unshakably valid grammatical rule based on logic." Check dictionaries and books of usage for attitudes on this rule.

3. The third paragraph from the end offers a "key" to questions of language. Is it a key that will unlock anything?

Writing Techniques

1. Middleton develops his column mainly through one example of a disputed usage. How does he develop this example? What use does he make of details within that example?

2. How adequate is the final paragraph as a conclusion? Does it provide an answer to the questions raised in the column, or imply an answer?

Suggestions for Writing

Write a paper centering on some disputed usage item — *ain't, it's me, more unique, everybody put on their coats.* You might try getting details for development by collecting views on the usage from friends.

LEARNED, PROFESSIONAL, AND OFFICIAL TURGIDITY
Charlton Laird

45

Charlton Laird, *Professor Emeritus at the University of Nevada, one of the editors of this book, is responsible for several volumes, of which the best known is* The Miracle of Language *(1953). The following selection is from* Language in America.

Another socially oriented use of language is more pervasive but harder to detect and describe. I refer to the solemn turgidity charactertistic of much learned, professional, and official prose. . . .

The following tale may be apocryphal, but it has analogues. A government bureau received a telegram inquiring if hydrochloric acid could safely be used to clean a boiler tube. The bureau replied "Uncertainties of reactive processes make use of hydrochloric acid undesirable when alkalinity is involved." The bureau then received a letter of thanks which added that the writer would now clean his boiler with the acid. The bureau wired back, "Regrettable decision involves uncertainties. Hydrochloric will produce submuriate invalidating reactions." Again the recipient thanked the bureau for assuring him that the acid was a safe cleanser. At that the bureau abandoned jargon, and wired, "Hydrochloric acid will eat hell out of your tube." Less amusing but equally terrifying evidence could be multiplied; the following from a military officer was submitted by Representative James A. Quigley of Pennsylvania as creeping federalese:

> . . . The Board of Commissioners took the position that as the Secretary of the Army necessarily would consider the board's recommendation against the legislation and the board's reasons for its action, in connection with both references, the advising you of the board's views and recommendations should be delayed until final action by the Secretary of the Army on your reference to the Department of Defense.

Meanwhile, a representative of the Pentagon offered the following definition: "Overkill equals total nonsurviveability plus." The president of a large corporation, reporting a bad year, pointed to "the

What does this example illustrate? Is the word apocryphal *appropriate?*

slowdown in order activity," in part because of a "dollar factor increase," and in part because of "the inertia of reactivating" programs which had never been activated. Nonetheless, he was optimistic, asserting that "With relatively limited exposure to date our superior performance capabilities and adaptability to a wide range of portable, mobile, and airborne environments have generated rapid and far-reaching customer acceptance," with which "we expect to steadily increase our penetration in this market."

Doubtless this endemic jargonitis flourishes in our nouveau riche country more than in most societies, but anyone who supposes that the same virus is not spreading should read Sir Ernest Gowers' *Plain Words: Their ABC*,[1] an attempt "to help officials in their use of written English." Gowers wisely observes, "I suspect that this project may be received by many of them [the officials] without any marked enthusiasm or gratitude." He notes that the following were "all written for plain men," and wonders what plain men made of them:

> Prices are basis prices per ton for the representative-basis-pricing specification and size and quantity.

England has its problems too.

> Where particulars of a partnership are disclosed to the Executive Council the remuneration of the individual partner for superannuation purposes will be deemed to be such proportions of the total remuneration of such practitioners as the proportion of his share in partnership profits bears to the total proportions of the shares of such practitioner in those profits.

> The treatment of this loan interest from the date of the first payment has been correct — i.e. tax charged at full standard rate on Mr. X and treated in your hands as liability satisfied before receipt.

Gowers, like observers on the western side of the Atlantic finds that scientists resemble bureaucrats in their addiction to involuted prose:

> Reserves that are occupied in continuous uni-directional adjustment of a disorder are no longer available for use in the ever-varying interplay of organism and environment in the spontaneity of mutual synthesis.

Jargon breeds jargon, apparently, on both sides of the Atlantic; in the following British exchange, the first comes from departmental regulations:

> Every woman by whom . . . a claim for maternity benefit is made shall furnish evidence that she has been, or that it is expected that she will

[1] New York; Knopf, 1955, pp. 126, 128, 148, 182, etc.; originally published as *The Complete Plain Words* (London: the Controller of Her Brittanic Majesty's Stationery Office, 1954).

be, confined by means of a certificate given in accordance with the rules . . .

One woman replied as follows:

> In accordance with your instructions I have given birth to twins in the enclosed envelope.

Similarly, on both sides of the Atlantic, jargon has sprung from the use of old figures of speech when metaphorical language has become so familiar as to be used without awareness of its figurative quality. Gowers, intrigued by the implications of *breakdown* when it implies classification, collected the following:

◄Does this topic sentence signal any change in the examples?

> Care should be taken that the breakdown of patients by the department under whose care they were immediately before discharge is strictly followed.

> Unfortunately a complete breakdown of British trade is not possible.

> Statistics have been issued of the population of the United States, broken down by age and sex.

A Mr. Henry Strauss, writing in the London *Times,* has noticed that the jargonic development of *bottleneck* provides "the biggest bottleneck in housing," "bottlenecks must be ironed out," "bottlenecks ahead," "bottlenecks in bottles," "the most drastic bottlenecks," "bottleneck . . . which is particularly far-reaching and decisive," "the overriding bottleneck," and "What is planned is actually a series of bottlenecks." The word reaches its inevitable development in the "worldwide bottleneck" and the "vicious circle of interdependent bottlenecks." Contemplating such marvels, Gowers understandably wonders, "What barnacular song do the puddering sirens sing to lure the writer into the land of Jargantua?"

The speech of smalltime American politicians is not more literate, but it is sometimes more picturesque. The following were heard on the floor of the Wisconsin State Senate, and could doubtless be paralleled in other legislatures:[2]

◄A transition relies on both analysis and contrast.

> The bankers' pockets are bulging with the sweat of honest workingmen.
>
> My integrity was imposed upon.
>
> I know there is a beautiful maximum behind the scenes that I'll never catch up with.
>
> This is a bill for accountants, figureheads, and whatnots.
>
> This is enough to make your head stand on end.
>
> Milwaukee is the golden egg that the rest of the state wants to milk.

[2] *The New Yorker,* (Oct. 14, 1961), p. 184.

I will defend anyone's right to agree with me.

He was absolutely right to a certain extent.

When we get to the bridge we'll jump.

None of them facts are factual facts.

We put out no false misinformation.

You've got to consider egress and degress from the building.

This guy was down in Illinois under a consumed name.

This program is absolutely essential. What's more, it's necessary.

In this connection we might note that a collection of set phrases has developed among politicians without which many public figures would be left speechless. They send up *trial balloons,* and they fear *boomerangs that may backfire.* They deprecate *changing horses in midstream, rocking the boat,* and *killing the goose that laid the golden egg,* while accusing their opponents of being *ostriches that hide their heads in the sand,* of *dragging red herrings, of being out of step,* of *emitting half truths,* and of *straining at a gnat but swallowing a camel.* They fear *hot potatoes* and deplore *political footballs.* As one of them put it, "I didn't want to jump the gun and be left on a limb." They like to *get off the hook,* to be sure *the door is left open,* and that the *cards are laid on the table.* The more literate jargonists are now beginning to speak of *throwing the baby out with the bath.* As I write this, one of the growing clichés is *guidelines;* here was a useful figure of speech, and executives first spoke of laying guidelines down, or drawing them up. Now they talk about carrying them out; a literal minded person might wonder where they expect to dump them. Whatever the reason for the popularity of such phrases, one can scarcely fail to notice that they embody simple figures of the sort beloved of the more conventional cartoonists. That ostriches do not hide their heads in the sand does not deter a politician from using *ostrich* as a verb, and people who could not distinguish a red herring from any other sort, who would not know why it should or should not be dragged, delight in commanding such eloquence.

A paragraph developed with details.

We are probably in the presence here of something subtle and pervading in man's mind and in his use of language. We love these phrases and we do not wish to lose them. More than a quarter of a century ago a research worker discovered and published the fact that Voltaire did not say, "I disagree with everything you say and will defend to the death your right to say it." In my youthful innocence I confidently expected that this discovery would attract wide attention and lead to the correction of the error. The report has remained undisturbed in a scholarly journal, and probably no day passes without some American quoting Voltaire for what he did not say. The misquotation is too good to lose. . . .

The style shifts here. Why?

A yearning for inept elegance, which inspires much turgid

prose, has gone so far as to corrupt even the honest cop, who is developing what has been aptly termed "the constabulary style."[3] The modern officer, whether because of the dignity of the law he enforces or the echoes of the police school he attended, can now adorn a police blotter with rhetoric like the following: "The car had backed into the house siding, leaving somewhat a state of collapse." "The complainant talked in riddles constantly and this officer's opinion is that everything she said was made-up of quite a few fabrications." "Upon entering the establishment, found the suspect in a heated argument with the bartender using profane language as punctuation." "The suspect beat a hasty but lawful retreat." "Mrs. J—— stated that she wished to commit herself to the state hospital for alcoholism. She was advised that she could do so after she sobered up. She agreed to this. Mr. J—— declined to sober up at this time." "The undersigned contacted the complainant who had been drinking to excess. She stated that the subject started the argument and told her that he was leaving the apartment and was taking the fifth of whisky, which both had been drinking out of, with him. He ended up getting struck over the head with the bottle, which broke." "While conferring in reference to the situation, it was soon discovered that the subject had departed his state of detention, along with the evidence, running from the establishment." "Upon arrival observed the subject being held to his feet by a passing male citizen to refrain him from falling down. Subject was cooperative, polite and denounced himself for drinking too much. Due to subject's attitude, he was transported home to the waiting arms of his wife." "The subjects were contacted at the above address and it was learned that Mr. and Mrs. L—— were having a disagreement and it seemed that they traded blows to each other's eyes." "By the suspect's own admission to drinking during the prior hours, the smell of intoxication on his breath and his bloodshot eyes all to subordinate the state of drunkenness. The suspect was warned by this officer on their first meeting what consequences might be if he were to violate the ordinances spoken about."

> Another developed example. What does it illustrate?

Officers are apparently developing their own narrative styles. One wrote as follows: "Mr. Y—— was observed by reporting officer attempting to get into his car. After several attempts, which extended from the hood to the trunk, Mr. Y—— finally found the door and fell into the front seat. Such actions necessitated investigative action by this officer, and Mr. Y—— was approached, and upon being properly identified, he greeted the officer with, 'Here, my friend, take the keys to my car,' thus handing the officer his house keys. Such cleverness and display of good sense was rewarded by officer taking Mr.

> Are details or examples used here, or both?

[3] Carleton Williams, "The Constabulary Style," *Esquire* (November, 1964), 106–107, 166.

Y—— to his residence and depositing him therein." Another, with an experimental flair, is developing economy in reporting conversation, as follows: "At the above location, this officer observed G—— slumped over the wheel of his vehicle. The officer asked G—— what seemed to be his problem. G—— stated that he was waiting, oh. He was then asked what he was waiting for. G—— then stated that he was just waiting, oh. He was then taken to the office to be booked. While at the booking desk, G—— became very belligerent and used profane language toward the arresting officers, etc. The etc. was meant to be the matron."

Along with expanding vocabulary that patently falls within some determinably changing pattern of life are words whose growth is less explicable. On the analogy of astronomy we might call them "nova" words, since they flare into sudden prominence, and if not inexplicably, seemingly outside the main patterns of linguistic change. Sometimes they are revivals; I should estimate that the word *presently* is presently used most frequently in the United States—although probably not in England—as I have just used it in this sentence. Some hundreds of years ago this was the common use, but this meaning declined so much that dictionaries edited a few decades ago labeled it "obsolete or dialectal." Other expanding words involve recently developed uses of old terms or sudden expansions of uses that had previously enjoyed only moderate currency. Consider *state* as a verb; the *Century* dictionary, edited shortly before 1900, recognized four uses as follows: To establish, to bestow upon, "to express the particulars of," and to allege. Most professional writers still use this word with restraint, but the great body of amateurs, if those who have passed through my classes are exemplary, use this word as some of us still employ the word *say*.

Some apparent nova are new coinages; *brainwashed* was probably popularized through defectors in the Korean police action, but it has grown so rapidly that at this writing a prospective presidential candidate finds himself much embarrassed at having asserted he had been brainwashed. Apparently he meant to say in vigorous language that he had been misinformed, but this particular nova seems not to have generalized so fast as he had assumed. Similarly, *critical* is growing, and in other senses than those concerned with criticism, as in the headlines: INJURED WOMAN SAID NOT CRITICAL. Of course these nova presumably do have an explanation, or several explanations. Some of these new uses represent reversals of older meanings; *literally* is now frequently used to mean figuratively; the following is taken from an international dispatch reporting a trial in which a prostitute was obviously lying when she said she could not remember the names of politically important customers: "Justice Marshall leaned over backwards, literally, to help her remember." If the state-

[margin note:] Changing meanings and words.

[margin note:] Can you distinguish between details and examples? Does Laird try to distinguish?

ment is to be taken literally—in the older sense—this was remarkable juridical conduct.

One has the feeling that a political campaign could not be planned without the word *boomerang;* no doubt this popularity stems from several causes, including political love of figurative language and the complexity of modern vote-getting. Among the rapidly growing words that I have observed are *relative, circumstances, factor,* and *conditions,* all in senses more general than those that were formerly most used. Have these words ballooned because we have become more discussional, and more publicly so, than our ancestors? Or are they separate growths, nova in the language? The answer might not be easy.

Reading and Interpreting

1. The book from which this selection is taken asserts that man has done things to language and language has done things to man. Does this sample provide evidence for the truth of either?

2. Does Laird's inclusion of some examples from England add anything to the general significance of his observations?

Writing Techniques

1. Since the author of this piece is also an editor of this book, his view of his audience can be determined. He says he was trying to deal with serious thinking and research about language but to present it in a readable way, to popularize knowledge. He therefore had to consider a general audience, including especially three groups: (1) people who work with language and have a practical interest in it; (2) people who believe that knowing about language will be good for them; and (3) people who find reading about language generally interesting, especially if they can get a little fun while they read. How accurately does the selection seem directed at this kind of audience? Has the author anticipated the right audience and written appropriately?

2. Both philosophically and rhetorically, details differ from examples, although as a writer uses them they may blend into each other. Can you distinguish between them by defining each? Can you divide Laird's concrete evidence into two groups, one all details and the other all examples? Can you find any evidence that Laird was conscious of the distinction as he wrote, and deliberately used one as against the other?

Suggestions for Writing

Write a paragraph or a longer paper using Laird's method to develop a generalization about some language usage. Collect or recall examples and details—of college slang, political campaign speeches, sports columns, or television news programs, or of the talk of athletes, automobile mechanics, gamblers, small children, or any group you know something about. Then frame a generalization about the talk and use the examples and details to illustrate it.

POLITICS AND THE ENGLISH LANGUAGE
George Orwell

46

George Orwell *(whose real name was Eric Blair) was an English satirist, best known for his novels* Animal Farm *and* 1984. *This essay is from* Shooting an Elephant and Other Essays *(1945).*

MOST people who bother with the matter at all would admit that the English language is in a bad way, but it is generally assumed that we cannot by conscious action do anything about it. Our civilization is decadent and our language—so the argument runs—must inevitably share in the general collapse. It follows that any struggle against the abuse of language is a sentimental archaism, like preferring candles to electric light or hansom cabs to aeroplanes. Underneath this lies the half-conscious belief that language is a natural growth and not an instrument which we shape for our own purposes.

Now, it is clear that the decline of a language must ultimately have political and economic causes; it is not due simply to the bad influence of this or that individual writer. But an effect can become a cause, reinforcing the original cause and producing the same effect in an intensified form and so on indefinitely. A man may take to drink because he feels himself to be a failure, and then fail all the more completely because he drinks. It is rather the same thing that is happening to the English language. It becomes ugly and inaccurate because our thoughts are foolish, but the slovenliness of our language makes it easier for us to have foolish thoughts. The point is that the process is reversible. Modern English, especially written English, is full of bad habits which spread by imitation and which can be avoided if one is willing to take the necessary trouble. If one gets rid

Basic assumptions about language.

of these habits one can think more clearly, and to think clearly is a necessary first step toward political regeneration: so that the fight against bad English is not frivolous and is not the exclusive concern of professional writers. . . .

Each of these passages [here omitted] has faults of its own, but, quite apart from avoidable ugliness, two qualities are common to all of them. The first is staleness of imagery; the other is lack of precision. The writer either has a meaning and cannot express it, or he inadvertently says something else, or he is almost indifferent as to whether his words mean anything or not. This mixture of vagueness and sheer incompetence is the most marked characteristic of modern English prose, and especially of any kind of political writing. As soon as certain topics are raised, the concrete melts into the abstract and no one seems able to think of turns of speech that are not hackneyed: prose consists less and less of *words* chosen for the sake of their meaning, and more and more of *phrases* tacked together like the sections of a prefabricated henhouse. I list below, with notes and examples, various of the tricks by means of which the work of prose-construction is habitually dodged:

A topic sentence plus a subtopic sentence?

Dying metaphors. A newly invented metaphor assists thought by evoking a visual image, while on the other hand a metaphor which is technically "dead" (e.g, *iron resolution*) has in effect reverted to being an ordinary word and can generally be used without loss of vividness. But in between these two classes there is a huge dump of worn-out metaphors which have lost all evocative power and are merely used because they save people the trouble of inventing phrases for themselves. Examples are: *Ring the changes on, take up cudgels for, toe the line, ride roughshod over, stand shoulder to shoulder with, play into the hands of, no axe to grind, grist to the mill, fishing in troubled waters, on the order of the day, Achilles' heel, swan song, hotbed.* Many of these are used without knowledge of their meaning . . . and incompatible metaphors are frequently mixed, a sure sign that the writer is not interested in what he is saying. Some metaphors now current have been twisted out of their original meaning without those who use them even being aware of the fact. For example, *toe the line* is sometimes written *tow the line*. Another example is *the hammer and the anvil,* now always used with the implication that the anvil gets the worst of it. In real life it is always the anvil that breaks the hammer, never the other way about: a writer who stopped to think what he was saying would be aware of this, and would avoid perverting the original phrase.

Orwell labels them examples.

Operators or *verbal false limbs.* These save the trouble of picking out appropriate verbs and nouns, and at the same time pad each sentence with extra syllables which give it an appearance of symmetry.

Characteristic phrases are *render inoperative, militate against, make contact with, be subjected to, give rise to, give grounds for, have the effect of, play a leading part (role) in, make itself felt, take effect, exhibit a tendency to, serve the purpose of,* etc. etc. The keynote is the elimination of simple verbs. Instead of being a single word, such as *break, stop, spoil, mend, kill,* a verb becomes a *phrase,* made up of a noun or adjective tacked on to some general-purpose verb such as *prove, serve, form, play, render.* In addition, the passive voice is wherever possible used in preference to the active, and noun constructions are used instead of gerunds *(by examination of* instead of *by examining).* The range of verbs is further cut down by means of the *-ize* and *de-* formations, and the banal statements are given an appearance of profundity by means of the *not un-* formation. Simple conjunctions and prepositions are replaced by such phrases as *with respect to, having regard to, the fact that, by dint of, in view of, in the interests of, on the hypothesis that;* and the ends of sentences are saved for anticlimax by such resounding commonplaces as *greatly to be desired, cannot be left out of account, a development to be expected in the near future, deserving of serious consideration, brought to a satisfactory conclusion,* and so on and so forth.

> He does not label these, but are they details?

Pretentious diction. Words like *phenomenon, element, individual* (as noun), *objective, categorical, effective, virtual, basic, primary, promote, constitute, exhibit, exploit, utilize, eliminate, liquidate,* are used to dress up simple statements and give an air of scientific impartiality to biased judgments. Adjectives like *epoch-making, epic, historic, unforgettable, triumphant, age-old, inevitable, inexorable, veritable,* are used to dignify the sordid processes of international politics, while writing that aims at glorifying war usually takes on an archaic color, its characteristic words being: *realm, throne, chariot, mailed fist, trident, sword, shield, buckler, banner, jackboot, elarion.* Foreign words and expressions such as *cul de sac, ancien régime, deus ex machina, mutatis mutandis, status quo, gleichschaltung, weltanschauung,* are used to give an air of culture and elegance. Except for the useful abbreviations *i.e., e.g.,* and *etc.,* there is no real need for any of the hundreds of foreign phrases now current in English. Bad writers, and especially scientific, political and sociological writers, are nearly always haunted by the notion that Latin or Greek words are grander than Saxon ones, and unnecessary words like *expedite, ameliorate, predict, extraneous, deracinated, clandestine, subaqueous,* and hundreds of others constantly gain ground from their Anglo-Saxon opposite numbers. The jargon peculiar to Marxist writing *(hyena, hangman, cannibal, petty bourgeois, these gentry, lackey, flunkey, mad dog, White Guard,* etc.) consists largely of words and phrases translated from Russian, German, or French; but the normal way of coining a new word is to use a Latin or Greek root with the appropriate affix and, where necessary, the *-ize* formation. It

> Can you defend the use of any foreign words?

is often easier to make up words of this kind (*deregionalize, impermissible, extramarital, nonfragmentary,* and so forth) than to think up the English words that will cover one's meaning. The result, in general, is an increase in slovenliness and vagueness.

Meaningless words. In certain kinds of writing, particularly in art criticism and literary criticism, it is normal to come across long passages which are almost completely lacking in meaning. Words like *romantic, plastic, values, human, dead, sentimental, natural, vitality,* as used in art criticism, are strictly meaningless, in the sense that they not only do not point to any discoverable object, but are hardly ever expected to do so by the reader. When one critic writes, "The outstanding feature of Mr. X's work is its living quality," while another writes, "The immediately striking thing about Mr. X's work is its peculiar deadness," the reader accepts this as a simple difference of opinion. If words like *black* and *white* were involved, instead of the jargon words *dead* and *living,* he would see at once that language was being used in an improper way. Many political words are similarly abused. The word *Fascism* has now no meaning except in so far as it signifies "someting not desirable." The words *democracy, socialism, freedom, patriotic, realistic, justice,* have each of them several different meanings which cannot be reconciled with one another. In the case of a word like *democracy,* not only is there no agreed definition, but the attempt to make one is resisted from all sides. It is almost universally felt that when we call a country democratic we are praising it: consequently the defenders of every kind of regime claim that it is a democracy, and fear that they might have to stop using the word if it were tied down to any one meaning. Words of this kind are often used in a consciously dishonest way. That is, the person who uses them has his own private definition, but allows his hearer to think he means something quite different. Statements like *Marshal Petain was a true patriot, The Soviet press is the freest in the world, The Catholic Church is opposed to persecution,* are almost always made with intent to deceive. Other words used in variable meanings, in most cases more or less dishonestly, are: *class, totalitarian, science, progressive, reactionary, bourgeois, equality.*

Now that I have made this catalogue of swindles and perversions, let me give another example of the kind of writing that they lead to. This time it must of its nature be an imaginary one. I am going to translate a passage of good English into modern English of the worst sort. Here is a well-known verse from *Ecclesiastes:*

> I returned and saw under the sun, that the race is not to the swift, nor the battle to the strong, neither yet bread to the wise, nor yet riches to men of understanding, nor yet favour to men of skill; but time and chance happeneth to them all.

Margin notes:

Is "normal to come across" jargon?

Are examples here mingled with details?

Analysis of a parody to summarize.

Here it is in modern English:

> Objective consideration of contemporary phenomena compels the con-
> clusion that success or failure in competitive activities exhibits no ten-
> dency to be commensurate with innate capacity, but that a consid-
> erable element of the unpredictable must invariably be taken into
> account.

This is a parody, but not a very gross one. . . . It will be seen
that I have not made a full translation. The beginning and ending of
the sentence follow the original meaning fairly closely, but in the
middle the concrete illustrations — race, battle, bread — dissolve into
the vague phrase "success or failure in competitive activities." This
had to be so, because no modern writer of the kind I am discussing — no one capable of using phrases like "objective consideration of contemporary phenomena" — would ever tabulate his
thoughts in that precise and detailed way. The whole tendency of
modern prose is away from concreteness. Now analyze these two
sentences a little more closely. The first contains forty-nine words but
only sixty syllables, and all its words are those of everyday life. The
second contains thirty-eight words of ninety syllables: eighteen of its
words are from Latin roots, and one from Greek. The first sentence
contains six vivid images, and only one phrase ("time and chance")
that could be called vague. The second contains not a single fresh, arresting phrase, and in spite of its ninety syllables it gives only a
shortened version of the meaning contained in the first. Yet without
a doubt it is the second kind of sentence that is gaining ground in
modern English. I do not want to exaggerate. This kind of writing is
not yet universal, and outcrops of simplicity will occur here and there
in the worst-written page. Still, if you or I were told to write a few
lines on the uncertainty of human fortunes, we should probably
come much nearer to my imaginary sentence than to the one from
Ecclesiastes.

As I have tried to show, modern writing at its worst does not
consist in picking out words for the sake of their meaning and inventing images in order to make the meaning clearer. It consists in
gumming together long strips of words which have already been set
in order by someone else, and making the results presentable by
sheer humbug. The attraction of this way of writing is that it is easy.
It is easier — even quicker, once you have the habit — to say *In my
opinion it is not an unjustifiable assumption that* than to say *I think*. If
you use ready-made phrases, you not only don't have to hunt about
for words; you also don't have to bother with the rhythms of your
sentences, since these phrases are generally so arranged as to be
more or less euphonious. When you are composing in a hurry — when
you are dictating to a stenographer, for instance, or making a public

When does
Orwell write
in the first
person?

◄Orwell is
signaling
something here.
What?

speech—it is natural to fall into a pretentious, Latinized style. Tags like *a consideration which we should do well to bear in mind* or *a conclusion to which all of us would readily assent* will save many a sentence from coming down with a bump. By using stale metaphors, similes, and idioms, you save much mental effort at the cost of leaving your meaning vague, not only for your reader but for yourself. This is the significance of mixed metaphors. The sole aim of a metaphor is to call up a visual image. When these images clash—as in *The Fascist octopus has sung its swan song, the jackboot is thrown into the melting pot*—it can be taken as certain that the writer is not seeing a mental image of the objects he is naming; in other words he is not really thinking. . . .

Orwell on figurative writing.

A scrupulous writer, in every sentence that he writes, will ask himself at least four questions, thus: What am I trying to say? What words will express it? What image or idiom will make it clearer? Is this image fresh enough to have an effect? And he will probably ask himself two more: Could I put it more shortly? Have I said anything that is avoidably ugly? But you are not obliged to go to all this trouble. You can shirk it by simply throwing your mind open and letting the ready-made phrases come crowding in. They will construct your sentences for you—even think your thoughts for you, to a certain extent—and at need they will perform the important service of partially concealing your meaning even from yourself. It is at this point that the special connection between politics and the debasement of languages becomes clear.

Is this a topic sentence or more than a topic sentence?

In our time it is broadly true that political writing is bad writing. Where it is not true, it will generally be found that the writer is some kind of rebel, expressing his private opinions and not a "party line." Orthodoxy, of whatever color, seems to demand a lifeless, imitative style. The political dialects to be found in pamphlets, leading articles, manifestoes, White Papers and the speeches of undersecretaries do, of course, vary from party to party, but they are all alike in that one almost never finds in them a fresh, vivid, home-made turn of speech. When one watches some tired hack on the platform mechanically repeating the familiar phrases—*bestial atrocities, iron heel, bloodstained tyranny, free peoples of the world, stand shoulder to shoulder*—one often has a curious feeling that one is not watching a live human being but some kind of dummy: a feeling which suddenly becomes stronger at moments when the light catches the speaker's spectacles and turns them into blank discs which seem to have no eyes behind them. And this is not altogether fanciful. A speaker who uses that kind of phraseology has gone some distance toward turning himself into a machine. The appropriate noises are coming out of his larynx, but his brain is not involved as it would be if he were choosing his words for himself. If the speech he is making

Is this generalization substantiated?

is one that he is accustomed to make over and over again, he may be almost unconscious of what he is saying, as one is when one utters the responses in church. And this reduced state of consciousness, if not indispensable, is at any rate favorable to political conformity.

In our time, political speech and writing are largely the defense of the indefensible. Things like the continuance of British rule in India, the Russian purges and deportations, the dropping of the atom bombs on Japan, can indeed be defended, but only by arguments which are too brutal for most people to face, and which do not square with the professed aims of political parties. Thus political language has to consist largely of euphemism, question-begging and sheer cloudy vagueness. Defenseless villages are bombarded from the air, the inhabitants driven out into the countryside, the cattle machine-gunned, the huts set on fire with incendiary bullets: this is called *pacification*. Millions of peasants are robbed of their farms and sent trudging along the roads with no more than they carry; this is called *transfer of population* or *rectification of frontiers*. People are imprisoned for years without trial, or shot in the back of the neck or sent to die of scurvy in Arctic lumber camps: this is called *elimination of unreliable elements*. Such phraseology is needed if one wants to name things without calling up mental pictures of them. Consider for instance some comfortable English professor defending Russian totalitarianism. He cannot say outright, "I believe in killing off your opponents when you can get good results by doing so." Probably, therefore, he will say something like this:

> "While freely conceding that the Soviet regime exhibits certain features which the humanitarian may be inclined to deplore, we must, I think, agree that a certain curtailment of the right to political opposition is an unavoidable concomitant of transitional periods, and that the rigors which the Russian people have been called upon to undergo have been amply justified in the sphere of concrete achievement."

The inflated style is itself a kind of euphemism. A mass of Latin words falls upon the facts like soft snow, blurring the outlines and covering up all the details. The great enemy of clear language is insincerity. When there is a gap between one's real and one's declared aims, one turns as it were instinctively to long words and exhausted idioms, like a cuttlefish squirting out ink. In our age there is no such thing as "keeping out of politics." All issues are political issues, and politics itself is a mass of lies, evasions, folly, hatred, and schizophrenia. When the general atmosphere is bad, language must suffer. I should expect to find—this is a guess which I have not sufficient knowledge to verify—that the German, Russian and Italian languages have all deteriorated in the last ten or fifteen years, as a result of dictatorship.

Have some of these euphemisms survived?

Notice that Orwell knows how to use a short topic sentence.

But if thought corrupts language, language can also corrupt thought. A bad usage can spread by tradition and imitation, even among people who should and do know better. The debased language that I have been discussing is in some ways very convenient. Phrases like *a not unjustifiable assumption, leaves much to be desired, would serve no good purpose, a consideration which we should do well to bear in mind,* are a continuous temptation, a packet of aspirins always at one's elbow. Look back through this essay, and for certain you will find that I have again and again committed the very faults I am protesting against. By this morning's post I have received a pamphlet dealing with conditions in Germany. The author tells me that he "felt impelled" to write it. I open it at random, and here is almost the first sentence that I see: "[The Allies] have an opportunity not only of achieving a radical transformation of Germany's social and political structure in such a way as to avoid a nationalistic reaction in Germany itself, but at the same time of laying the foundations of a cooperative and unified Europe." You see, he "feels impelled" to write—feels, presumably, that he has something new to say—and yet his words, like cavalry horses answering the bugle, group themselves automatically into the familiar dreary pattern. This invasion of one's mind by ready-made phrases (*lay the foundations, achieve radical transformation*) can only be prevented if one is constantly on guard against them, and every such phrase anaesthetizes a portion of one's brain.

I said earlier that the decadence of our language is probably curable. Those who deny this would argue, if they produced an argument at all, that language merely reflects existing social conditions, and that we cannot influence its development by any direct tinkering with words and constructions. So far as the general tone or spirit of a language goes, this may be true, but it is not true in detail. Silly words and expressions have often disappeared, not through any evolutionary process but owing to the conscious action of a minority. Two recent examples were *explore every avenue* and *leave no stone unturned,* which were killed by the jeers of a few journalists. There is a long list of flyblown metaphors which could similarly be got rid of if enough people would interest themselves in the job; and it should also be possible to laugh the *not un-* formation out of existence,[1] to reduce the amount of Latin and Greek in the average sentence, to drive out foreign phrases and strayed scientific words, and, in general, to make pretentiousness unfashionable. But all these are minor points. The defense of the English language implies more than this,

> Balanced construction permits a deft transition and a terse topic sentence.

> How does language change?

---

[1] One can cure oneself of the *not un-* formation by memorizing this sentence. *A not unblack dog was chasing a not unsmall rabbit across a not ungreen field.*

and perhaps it is best to start by saying what it does *not* imply.

To begin with it has nothing to do with archaism, with the salvaging of obsolete words and turns of speech, or with the setting up of a "standard English" which must never be departed from. On the contrary, it is especially concerned with the scrapping of every word or idiom which has outworn its usefulness. It has nothing to do with correct grammar and syntax, which are of no importance so long as one makes one's meaning clear, or with the avoidance of Americanisms, or with having what is called a "good prose style." On the other hand it is not concerned with fake simplicity and the attempt to make written English colloquial. Nor does it even imply in every case preferring the Saxon word to the Latin one, though it does imply using the fewest and shortest words that will cover one's meaning. What is above all needed is to let the meaning choose the word, and not the other way about. In prose, the worst thing one can do with words is to surrender to them. When you think of a concrete object, you think wordlessly, and then, if you want to describe the thing you have been visualizing you probably hunt about till you find the exact words that seem to fit it. When you think of something abstract you are more inclined to use words from the start, and unless you make a conscious effort to prevent it, the existing dialect will come rushing in and do the job for you, at the expense of blurring or even changing your meaning. Probably it is better to put off using words as long as possible and get one's meaning as clear as one can through pictures or sensations. Afterward one can choose—not simply *accept*—the phrases that will best cover the meaning, and then switch round and decide what impression one's words are likely to make on another person. This last effort of the mind cuts out all stale or mixed images, all prefabricated phrases, needless repetitions, and humbug and vagueness generally. But one can often be in doubt about the effect of a word or a phrase, and one needs rules that one can rely on when instinct fails. I think the following rules will cover most cases:

> A long paragraph. Does it utilize more than one sort of development?

(i) Never use a metaphor, simile, or other figure of speech which you are used to seeing in print.

(ii) Never use a long word where a short one will do.

(iii) If it is possible to cut a word out, always cut it out.

(iv) Never use the passive where you can use the active.

(v) Never use a foreign phrase, a scientific word, or a jargon word if you can think of an everyday English equivalent.

(vi) Break any of these rules sooner than say anything outright barbarous.

> A shift to a negative approach.

These rules sound elementary, and so they are, but they demand a deep change of attitude in anyone who has grown used to writing in the style now fashionable.

Reading and Interpreting

1. Is Orwell talking about changes in language or changes in the way people are using language? Is there any difference between these two ways of looking at his examples?

2. Orwell's essay was written more than thirty years ago. Are his observations still applicable?

3. According to Orwell, what are the dangers of what he calls "political language"?

Writing Techniques

1. Orwell writes many rather long paragraphs. Can you deduce any reasons why? Would they be easier to read if he broke them up? What would he have to do if he did?

2. Orwell uses many details and examples. Does he use any other strategies for development at the same time? For example, after the third paragraph he has four paragraphs with subheads. What process is behind the development here (see Section IX)?

3. This is a complicated essay, composed of several parts. Identify these. Then notice what Orwell does to guide you from one part to the next.

4. Orwell's topic sentences are worth study. Some are short, ten words or fewer. But some are long, notably made up of two main parts. Why? Do they consistently follow a standard pattern for topic sentences? That is, do they (1) usually stand at the beginning of the paragraph? (2) provide any necessary transition? (3) provide commitment adequate for the development of the remainder of the paragraph?

Suggestions for Writing

Look at some current prose—letters to the editor, newspaper reports of speeches, editorials, columns, and so on, and then write your own comment on political writing. You may want to disagree with Orwell or to confirm his views.

DESTROYERS OF THE DREAM
Mark J. Mirsky

47

Mark Jay Mirsky, *B.A. Harvard University* magna cum laude, *teacher and writer, has produced long and short fiction, including* Thou Worm Jacob *(1967). This piece appeared in* The Progressive.

ARCHITECTS are the mass murderers of the Twentieth Century. In a fit of romantic pique, Hitler drove the Bauhaus from Germany, not realizing that it shared his fanatical preoccupation with purity of line and efficiency and that long after his tawdry dreams would lie in ashes, a totalitarian shadow would be cast in concrete bunker on every major and minor city of the industrial world. We, all of us city dwellers, are living in death camps. The architecture which ought to point us toward mystery, which ought to inspire dreams and vanities, pomp and pride, confines us instead to the smallest plot and space practical.

I walk about Boston in shock; I still can't believe what has been done to this New England city. My palms sweat and beads break out of my forehead when I behold that tasteless horror, the Government Center, and especially its brick lavatory, the new City Hall, a set of concrete stalls evacuating red clay. It is an offense in itself, but think of what it replaced: classic theaters like the Old Howard, the ring of fine, weather-burnished brick warehouse and granite setting Faneuil Hall off so perfectly that when you came down Corn Hill you could imagine Sam Adams rabble rousing in the midst of Eighteenth Century Boston, setting fire to the hearts of the massacre crowd.

Examples to illustrate.

The old, mangled souls of civil servants in the new City Hall, displaced from the Corinthian capitals and pillars of their former haunt—a baroque post-Civil War structure that echoed the Greek dream of city-state and ennobled service and patronage alike—they know what has been done to them. "Mirsky, it's a garage," they whine to my father, a retired politician. "Who the hell wants to work in a fuckin' garage?"

But here is the comment of an expert, Ada Louise Huxtable, architecture critic of *The New York Times:* "The scheme has produced one of the best urban spaces of the Twentieth Century and that is no insignificant achievement . . . the vast nine-acre City Hall Plaza that is the urban and esthetic glue that holds the whole thing together." *This* in description of a sprawling sixty-acre plot without a single interesting avenue of light or shadow, a hodgepodge of concrete eggshell crates set in no discernible relationship to one another, relating

A different kind of evidence.

in no way to the terrain in which they are placed, either hill or vale (and they are between two of the historic mountains of Boston).

"With the plaza and specifically because of it, the Boston Government Center can now take its place among the world's great city spaces," Huxtable continues. "Roughly the size of St. Peter's Square in Rome, it lends a unity and style and sense of logical and rewarding spatial relationships to the complex that are a clear illustration of the best and most basic principles of urban design. It is in the direct tradition of historic Italian plazas and European squares."

"The Emperor is naked!" I want to cry, staring into this bleak boneyard, as dreadful as a concrete playground. Even the barest relation to any of the European plazas with their formal organization of arches, park space, fountains, restaurants, escapes me. There was a plaza here before, Scollay Square, not a wide, paved-over cemetery.

Do you know the reference? What good are such references?

No language is extreme enough to express the outrage of the living dead, of tearing out the raffish Boston, Kerry Village, the old West End, Dover Street—ay, even Dover, with its whores and winos. (Did you never read Villon and Rabelais, do you have only dirt under your nails under the lawn at Mount Hope, New Calvary, Sharon?) Finally Scollay, that marvelous, tumble-down, stone and brick town spilling over the shady side of Beacon Hill in uninterrupted, unprettified antiquity to river and harbor.

Under the slogan of *progress,* a curse which has a most stupefying effect on common sense beyond the wildest hope of any magician's mumbo jumbo, a combination of arrogant bankers, corrupt politicians, and seedy contracting interests (the adjectives are interchangeable) has bilked and milked millions from the Commonwealth and the City. Leveling Scollay Square and the West End, chasing the Flower Market from Dover Street, drawing an elevated highway through the harbor access, putting high rises on the Atlantic Avenue docks—this isn't funny business which we subsidize, like television, with pennies hidden in the cost of living; it is an attack on history.

All this deprives the average Bostonian of the hallowed, strange sense of walking through his town's annals. It stills the echo of Eighteenth and Nineteenth Century music and light that softened the harsh features of the downtown businessman, gave him a unique eye and ear akin to those of the townsmen of London and Dublin, an eccentricity of accent and humor bound up not only in the cruel parochialisms of family and church but in the sweet private voice of the city, its winding alleys, out-of-the-way restaurants, weathered fronts, and high windows. What have we in exchange for Eighteenth Century courtyards, Nineteenth Century cornices floating on the warehouse tops, streets like tunnels bowing under arches, an elegant profile no matter how seedy or shabby it showed through at the elbows? . . .

This reads like a conclusion. What does it conclude?

History gives us noble dreams. Boston has turned on her history and I despise her for it. The bankers, contractors, politicians may wonder why their children are lost in a haze of marijuana smoke. I do not. You have removed wonder from around them. You have put them in a garage. They must breathe smoke anyway, why shouldn't it be narcotic?

In Roxbury, the Shirley Mansion stands rotting. Millions are poured into the parking space beneath the Common. Kerry Village, the fascinating collection of tiny brick cottages, home of freed-slave Boston, is edged off our map by bulldozers. With the turnpike extension, it is now possible to drive through the city without seeing it. Boston, like all the other metropolises of America, has become a ghost. We step in it without looking, without rubbing our backs against brick and iron lacework.

What is the consequence of being forced off our space, penned in? It is to live in heightened anxiety, in terror. We are in a state of shock, running, standing still, doping ourselves, suicidal finally because the time we acquire has no meaning.

Why has the author started asking questions?

This instance on a progress which annihilates the past, is it not a deep sickness—patricide?

We have lifted our hands against the father. There is an insane craving to wipe the memory of our fathers off the earth. The impiety which is the high social crime of both Greek and Hebrew tradition has become institutionalized, banalized, mechanized in the squat offices and restaurants of every modern small-town shopping center. And in the large cities, a more appalling spectacle arises: the vanity of mediocrity, a willful display of the ultimate in our worship of cost cut and small mind; in New York City the shattering aluminum foil of the Tishman Building; in Boston, the pure vulgarity of the State Street Bank advertising itself from a blunt steeple as if the Gullivers of Finance were lowering their drawers to piss publicly on the diminished citizenry.

Examples illustrate.

Of course there are exceptions: the Ford Foundation building, whose lofty glassed-in garden on the ground floor makes a fairy tale ending to its tedious block of New York concrete; the CBS skyscraper which subtly, almost humorously, mocks the steel white sounding blues of the rest of Sixth Avenue; the Carpenter Center in Cambridge, set in a decorous street of old lady edifice. But these are fine things in isolation. When architects get together, as in the Government Center, the result is desolate pandemonium. Boston, the city on seven hills, dwindles down to a massive, reinforced gulch.

Say me nay? Stand, citizen, on the flank of Beacon Hill. Look up to the gold of Bullfinch's dome on the State House; then stare down at the ribs of masonry, the repetition of window without reference to light, the brick pile oblivious to the catacombs of snow or summer haze, and tell me, truly, is the Emperor not naked?

Is this second conclusion more telling than the first?

Is a humane architecture possible? What is humane archi- Is the conclusion supported? tecture? It is a house, building, aggregate, which gives dignity to man and his tasks. The sun, wind, water by which we used to set the reference of our architecture did not make man seem smaller than himself but rather endowed him with a sense of his mystery against the natural elements. We need to orient our buildings to the phenomena and magic of the external world—light, water, wind—and of the internal world, our toys, our dreams.

Let us rip out those hideous brick and cement piles of the last twenty years, and construct cities that will inspire our grandchildren to sigh after our lives.

Reading and Interpreting

1. In what sense does Mirsky mean that we "are living in death camps"? In what sense are architects mass murderers?

2. What does Mirsky think architecture should be? Does he provide a clearer picture of what he considers good or what he considers bad?

3. Describe as precisely as you can what Mirsky objects to in modern architecture.

Writing Techniques

1. Mirsky relies heavily on strong statements and loaded words. Does he provide sufficient evidence to support his contentions?

2. Is Mirsky's specific evidence adequate to make his case? Does it require special knowledge of the reader? Are any of the illustrations inappropriate or not very helpful? Does he tend to use details or examples?

3. Is the first paragraph a statement of the theme of the piece? Does the remainder of the paragraph alter the significance of the first sentence?

Suggestions for Writing

1. You might try a defense of modern architecture, or of some of it, using details as Mirsky does to support your view. Or you might do a short piece supporting Mirsky's view but using your own illustrations.

2. You might try a criticism of some other development of our society, making use of examples to support a view. Possibilities are chain restaurants, trailer parks, condominium complexes, monopolies like Exxon or General Motors, highway billboards.

Classification and Analysis

Here are two ways of developing that work together. You can scarcely use one without the other, and once either is set up, the other may be almost obvious. Both rely on how things are similar and how they are different.

Consider people. In some ways they are alike: Unless they have been unlucky, they have each two hands and two feet; they live by eating food, drinking liquids, and breathing; they all have good brains, at least compared with those of mosquitoes and dodos. They also differ: Some are male, some female; some are tall, some short; some have blue eyes and some do not.

Using such similarities and differences, we can make an analysis. We have one broad category of things or creatures, people, and we can establish criteria for subdividing it, breaking it into parts: sex, tallness or shortness, color of eyes, brain power, and the like. Theoretically, we could set up so many and such minute criteria that only one person would land in each subdivision. When you use sex as a basis for analysis you get only two groups, one with about half the human race, the males, and the other with the other half, the females. Then the females could be analyzed again on the basis of height into tall and short, or even into hundreds of groups, for example, those that are 62 inches tall separated from those that are 63 inches tall. And those that are 62 inches tall could be analyzed again, distinguishing those with an IQ of 100 from those with a score of 90. And this could go on, distinguishing those that like pink better than red from those that like red better than pink, those that can play a musical instrument from those who cannot, *ad infinitum.*

Of course analysis so detailed and so extensive has little part in writing. Complete analysis would be both wasteful and boring. And at the other end of the scale, very simple analysis has not much use, either. You need no elaborate rhetorical machinery to tell you there are two sexes. But breaking anything complicated into its parts, identifying those parts, and comparing them with one another and to the whole is a good way to think, and if it is a good way to think it will be a good way, also, to write. If you want to discuss the question of whether there should be more community and junior colleges, and which courses such institutions should teach, you may want to analyze the reasons that individuals continue their education after high school. Such an analysis would not be simple-minded like the male-female distinction, and it would not need to be complete, but it would be helpful in deciding what higher education should be. In fact, one wonders how we could think or talk intelligently about the subject without making such an analysis.

If an analysis has been made, and categories set up, classification may be obvious. If you have determined that one category is height, and you have before you a basketball player seven feet six inches tall and a midget three feet six, you will know which should go in the tall group and which in the short. Not all classification is so simple; if you are dealing with baby rabbits you may have difficulty knowing which is male and which female. Likewise, could you objectively classify a given belief as populism or Jacksonian democracy? All activity becomes complicated, especially mental activity.

Without trying to settle such questions, we can notice that analysis and classification work together. Once we have analyzed a subject and know its parts, we have made a good start toward bringing like things together. And if we have like things together, by putting them into classes, we have made a good start toward analysis. Analysis and classification are so intimately interrelated that you need not even try to decide which one you are using.

But you do need to know what this tool is good for and how to use it. You need, for instance, to know when your analysis is complete, when it accounts for all parts. An analysis of people as redheads and brunettes has obvious inadequacy. And you need to avoid classifying on more than one basis at a time, grouping people as redheads, brunettes, and tall. The selections that follow use analysis and classification in more complex ways primarily as a basis for organization. Max Lerner's discussion, for instance, is an analysis of American people into types. Is the analysis complete? How does he use it to organize his essay? Bacon in his second paragraph summarizes his analysis directly, giving order to a set of difficult concepts.

AMERICAN TYPES   **48**
Max Lerner

For more than a half century **Max Lerner** *has used both the classroom and the editorial desk to make thousands of observations on the current scene, with suggestions for a better future, via columns, editorials, articles, broadcasts, and a number of books, including* America as Civilization *(1957), from which the following is taken.*

SEVENTEENTH-CENTURY England produced a number of books on *Characters* depicting English society through the typical personality patterns of the era. Trying something of the same sort for contemporary America, the first fact one encounters is the slighter emphasis on a number of character types than stand out elsewhere in Western society: to be sure, they are to be found in America as well, but they are not characteristically American. One thinks of the scholar, the aesthete, the priest or "parson," the "aristocratic" Army officer, the revolutionary student, the civil servant, the male schoolteacher, the marriage broker, the courtesan, the mystic, the saint. Anyone familiar with European literature will recognize these characters as stock literary types and therefore as social types. Each of them represents a point of convergence for character and society. Anyone familiar with American literature will know that it contains stock portraits of its own which express social types. I want to use these traditional types as backdrops and stress some of the social roles that are new and still in process of formation.

The introduction prepares for division into classes.

Thus there is the *fixer,* who seems an organic product of a society in which the middleman function eats away the productive one. He may be public-relations man or influence peddler; he may get your traffic fine settled, or he may be able—whatever the commodity—to "get it for you wholesale." He is contemptuous of those who take the formal rules seriously; he knows how to cut corners—financial, political, administrative, or moral. At best there is something of the iconoclast in him, an unfooled quality far removed from the European personality types that always obey authority. At worst he becomes what the English call a "spiv" or cultural procurer.

Related to the fixer is the *inside dopester,* as Riesman has termed him. He is oriented not so much toward getting things fixed as toward being "in the know" and "wised up" about things that innocents take at face value. He is not disillusioned because he has never allowed himself the luxury of illusions. In the 1920s and 1930s he consumed the literature of "debunking"; in the current era he knows everything that takes place in the financial centers of Wall Street, the political centers of Capitol Hill, and the communications centers of Madison Avenue—yet among all the things he knows there is little he believes in. His skepticism is not the wisdom which deflates pretentiousness but that of the rejecting man who knows ahead of time that there is "nothing in it" whatever the "it" may be. In short, he is "hep."

Another link leads to the *neutral* man. He expresses the devaluing tendency in a culture that tries to avoid commitments. Fearful of being caught in the crosscurrents of conflict that may endanger his safety or status, he has a horror of what he calls "controversial figures"—and anyone becomes "controversial" if he is attacked. As the fixer and the inside dopester are the products of a middleman's society, so the neutral man is the product of a technological one. The technician's detachment from everything except effective results becomes—in the realm of character—an ethical vacuum that strips the results of much of their meaning.

From the neutral man to the *conformist* is a short step. Although he is not neutral—in fact, he may be militantly partisan—his partisanship is on the side of the big battalions. He lives in terror of being caught in a minority where his insecurity will be conspicuous. He gains a sense of stature by joining the dominant group, as he gains security by making himself indistinguishable from that group. Anxious to efface any unique traits of his own, he exacts conformity from others. He fears ideas whose newness means they are not yet accepted, but once they are firmly established he fights for them with a courage born of the knowledge that there is no danger in championing them. He hates foreigners and immigrants. When he talks of the "American way," he sees a world in which other cultures have become replicas of his own.

Topic sentences label each class.

Does this paragraph develop by definition?

It is often hard to distinguish the conformist from the *routineer.* Essentially he is a man in uniform, sometimes literally, always symbolically. The big public-service corporations — railroads, air lines, public utilities — require their employees to wear uniforms that will imprint a common image of the enterprise as a whole. City employees, such as policemen and firemen, wear uniforms. Gas-station attendants, hotel clerks, bellhops, must similarly keep their appearance within prescribed limits. Even the sales force in big department stores or the typists and stenographers in big corporations tend toward the same uniformity. There are very few young Americans who are likely to escape the uniform of the Armed Services. With the uniform goes an urge toward pride of status and a routineering habit of mind. There is the confidence that comes of belonging to a large organization and sharing symbolically in its bigness and power. There is a sense of security in having grooves with which to move. This is true on every level of corporate business enterprise, from the white-collar employee to "the man in the gray flannel suit," although it stops short of the top executives who create the uniforms instead of wearing them. Even outside the government and corporate bureaus there are signs of American life becoming bureaucratized, in a stress on forms and routines, on "going through channels."

What does it mean to be symbolically in uniform?

Unlike the conformist or routineer, the *status seeker* may possess a resourceful energy and even originality, but he directs these qualities toward gaining status. What he wants is a secure niche in a society whose men are constantly being pulled upward or trodden down. Scott Fitzgerald has portrayed a heartbreaking case history of this character type in *The Great Gatsby,* whose charm and energy are invested fruitlessly in an effort to achieve social position. The novels of J. P. Marquand are embroideries of a similar theme, narrated through the mind of one who already has status and is confronted by the risk of losing it. At various social levels the status seeker becomes a "joiner" of associations which give him symbolic standing.

Having defined his classifications, Lerner has laid a foundation for further writing.

Reading and Interpreting

1. Lerner described these several types of Americans in 1957. Do they still exist? Do you know people who would fit into his categories?

2. Are Lerner's types an accurate description of American society? Should others be added? Should some be deleted?

3. Does Lerner's selection of types and his descriptions of them imply some general criticism of American society?

Writing Techniques

1. The selection from Lerner provides an obvious example of organization and development by analysis. What is the subject that Lerner is analyzing, dividing into parts? Is the analysis complete; that is, do the categories include all of the subject?

2. Analysis produces the main divisions of the selection. How are the divisions indicated to the reader? How is classification used?

3. Study Lerner's essay for varieties of development. He uses analysis and classification. Within this strategy he uses definition. Does he use any others?

Word Study

Lerner offers his own definition of *fixer, inside dopester, neutral man, conformist, routineer,* and *status seeker.* Which of these are clearly defined in your dictionary. Which can be somewhat inferred from more general terms? How do Lerner's definitions differ from those in your dictionary?

Suggestions for Writing

Use analysis to divide some subject into parts and then classify details in each part to develop the topic. One possibility is to divide some collection into types and then classify characteristics of each type under the headings you produce—for example, types of students, types of professors, types of television programs, types of automobiles, types of bridge players. The analysis need not be complete. It may, like Lerner's, deal with *some* types, but the reader should understand that you are deliberately not being exhaustive.

ANALYSIS OF A POEM   **49**
Cleanth Brooks and Robert Penn Warren

Cleanth Brooks *and* **Robert Penn Warren,** *Professors Emeritus at Yale, are among America's most distinguished critics. The selection is from one of their important textbooks,* Understanding Poetry. *E. E. Cummings was a young innovative poet in 1926 when "Portrait" was published.*

PORTRAIT
E. E. Cummings

Buffalo Bill's
defunct
      who used to
      ride a watersmooth-silver
                  stallion
and break onetwothreefourfive pigeonsjustlikethat
                          Jesus
he was a handsome man
                and what i want to know is
how do you like your blueeyed boy
Mister Death

This poem deals with what is a rather common theme, and treats that theme simply. Death claims all men, even the strongest and most glamorous. How does the poet in treating such a common theme manage to give a fresh and strong impression of it? He might, of course, have achieved this effect in a number of different ways, and as a matter of fact, the general device which he employs is not simply one device: it is complex. In this case, however, the most prominent element is the unconventional attitude which he takes toward a conventional subject, and in this particular poem, the matter of tone is isolated sufficiently for us to examine it rather easily (though we must not forget either that there are other matters to be examined in this poem or that tone is a factor in every poem).

In the first place, what is the difference between writing

          Buffalo Bill's
          defunct

and

          Buffalo Bill's
          dead?

The first carries something of a tone of conscious irreverence. The poet here does not approach the idea of death with the usual and expected respect for the dead. He is matter-of-fact, unawed, and even somewhat flippant and joking. But the things which he picks out to comment on in Buffalo Bill make a strong contrast with the idea of death. The picture called up is one of tremendous vitality and speed: for example, the stallion is mentioned and is described as "watersmooth-silver." The adjective contains not only a visual description of the horse which Buffalo Bill rode but a kinetic description is implied too. How was the horse "watersmooth"? Smooth, graceful in action. (The poet by running the words together in the next line is perhaps telling us how to read the line, running the words together to give the effect of speed. The way the poem is printed on the page is designed probably to serve the same purpose, the line divisions being intended as a kind of arrangement for punctuation and emphasis. But the odd typography is not of fundamental importance.) The "portrait" of Buffalo Bill given here after the statement that he is "defunct" is a glimpse of him in action breaking five claypigeons in rapid succession as he flashes by on his stallion—the sort of glimpse which one might remember from the performance of the Wild West show in which Buffalo Bill used to star. The exclamation which follows is exactly the sort of burst of boyish approval which might be struck from a boy seeing him in action or remembering him as he saw him. And the quality of "handsome" applies, one feels, not merely to his face but to his whole figure in action.

The next lines carry on the tone of unabashed, unawed, slangy irreverence toward death. Death becomes "Mister Death." The implied figure of the spectator at a performance of the Wild West show helps justify the language and manner of expression used here, making us feel that it is in character. But the question as asked here strikes us on another level. It is a question which no boy would ask; it is indeed one of the old unanswerable questions. But here it is transformed by the tone into something fresh and startling. Moreover, the dashing, glamorous character of the old Indian fighter gets a sharp emphasis. The question may be paraphrased like this: Death, you don't get lads like him every day, do you? The way the question is put implies several things. First, it implies the pathos at the fact that even a man who had such enormous vitality and unfailing youthfulness had to die. But this pathos is not insisted upon; rather, it is presented indirectly and ironically because of the bantering and flippant attitude given in the question, especially in the phrases "Mister Death" and "blueeyed boy." And in the question, which sums up the whole poem, we also are given the impression that death is not terrible for Buffalo Bill—it is "Mister Death" who stands in some sort of fatherly and prideful relation to the "blueeyed boy."

In attempting to state what the tone is in this poem, we have, no doubt, somewhat distorted it. Moreover, we have certainly not given an exhaustive account of the tone of this poem. But what has been said above may perhaps let us see how important an element the tone inevitably is. In this case—a case in which, as we have already noted, it is easy to deal with the tone in some isolation—it is the *tone* which transforms what might easily be a hackneyed and dead poem into something fresh and startling.

Reading and Interpreting

1. After reading the Cummings poem, do you agree with the critics' statement about the general theme of the poem?

2. As the critics observe, the style of the poem is unconventional in several ways. Mention specific ways in which it is different. Can you suggest reasons for the differences beyond those cited by Brooks and Warren?

Writing Techniques

1. How does the parenthetical clause at the end of the first paragraph imply that there has been an analysis of the subjects that might be considered in a criticism of the poem? From that analysis what topic has been selected for emphasis?

2. What is the basis for the organization of the criticism after the opening paragraph?

Word Study

The authors admit they may have "somewhat distorted" the tone of the poem. If so, the distortion probably appears in certain vigorous words. Look up the following in the paragraph second from the last, and try to decide whether they do or do not exaggerate the tone of the poem: *unabashed, unawed, irreverence, transformed, glamorous, vitality, flippant, terrible.*

Suggestions for Writing

Using this selection for suggestions on method, write a brief criticism of a poem or story or film that has interested you. Do not try to discuss every topic that might be of interest in criticizing the work; rather, follow the lead of Brooks and Warren and limit your criticism. For example, you might focus on the diction of a poem or the imagery or the rhythmic patterns or the development of the theme. You might consider the plot or the theme or the characterization in a story or film.

FENIMORE COOPER'S LITERARY OFFENCES
Mark Twain

Samuel L. Clemens, who wrote under the pseudonym **Mark Twain,** *was one of America's greatest novelists and humorists, best known for* Huckleberry Finn *and* The Adventures of Tom Sawyer. *He published this essay in 1892.*

> *The Pathfinder* and *The Deerslayer* stand at the head of Cooper's novels as artistic creations. There are others of his works which contain parts as perfect as are to be found in these, and scenes even more thrilling. Not one can be compared with either of them as a finished whole.
> The defects in both of these tales are comparatively slight.
> They were pure works of art. PROF. LOUNSBURY
> The five tales reveal an extraordinary fulness of invention.
> . . . One of the very greatest characters in fiction, Natty Bumppo. . . .
> The craft of the woodsman, the tricks of the trapper, all the delicate art of the forest, were familiar to Cooper from his youth up.
> PROF. BRANDER MATTHEWS
>
> Cooper is the greatest artist in the domain of romantic fiction yet produced by America. WILKIE COLLINS

It seems to me that it was far from right for the Professor of English Literature in Yale, the Professor of English Literature in Columbia, and Wilkie Collins to deliver opinions on Cooper's literature without having read some of it. It would have been much more decorous to keep silent and let persons talk who have read Cooper.

Cooper's art has some defects. In one place in *Deerslayer,* and in the restricted space of two-thirds of a page, Cooper has scored 114 offences against literary art out of a possible 115. It breaks the record.

There are nineteen rules governing literary art in the domain of romantic fiction—some say twenty-two. In *Deerslayer* Cooper violated eighteen of them. These eighteen require:

Is Twain making fun of classifications of rules?

1. That a tale shall accomplish something and arrive somewhere. But the *Deerslayer* tale accomplishes nothing and arrives in the air.

2. They require that the episodes of a tale shall be necessary parts of the tale, and shall help to develop it. But as the *Deerslayer* tale is not a tale, and accomplishes nothing and arrives nowhere, the episodes have no rightful place in the work, since there was nothing for them to develop.

Do these sound like standard rules for writing?

3. They require that the personages in a tale shall be alive, except in the case of corpses, and that always the reader shall be able to

tell the corpses from the others. But this detail has often been over-looked in the *Deerslayer* tale.

How is Twain using "detail"?

4. They require that the personages in a tale, both dead and alive, shall exhibit a sufficient excuse for being there. But this detail also has been overlooked in the *Deerslayer* tale.

5. They require that when the personages of a tale deal in con-versation, the talk shall sound like human talk, and be talk such as human beings would be likely to talk in the given circumstances, and have a discoverable meaning, also a discoverable purpose, and a show of relevancy, and remain in the neighborhood of the subject in hand, and be interesting to the reader, and help out the tale, and stop when the people cannot think of anything more to say. But this requirement has been ignored from the beginning of the *Deerslayer* tale to the end of it.

6. They require that when the author describes the character of a personage in his tale, the conduct and conversation of that person-age shall justify said description. But this law gets little or no atten-tion in the *Deerslayer* tale, as Natty Bumppo's case will amply prove.

7. They require that when a personage talks like an illustrated, gilt-edged, tree-calf, hand-tooled, seven-dollar Friendship's Offering in the beginning of a paragraph, he shall not talk like a negro min-strel in the end of it. But this rule is flung down and danced upon in the *Deerslayer* tale.

8. They require that crass stupidities shall not be played upon the reader as "the craft of the woodsman, the delicate art of the for-est," by either the author or the people in the tale. But this role is persistently violated in the *Deerslayer* tale.

Is this rule made up especially for Cooper?

9. They require that the personages of a tale shall confine themselves to possibilities and let miracles alone; or, if they venture a miracle, the author must so plausibly set forth as to make it look pos-sible and reasonable. But these rules are not respected in the *Deer-slayer* tale.

10. They require that the author shall make the reader feel a deep interest in the personages of his tale and in their fate; and that he shall make the reader love the good people in the tale and hate the bad ones. But the reader of the *Deerslayer* tale dislikes the good people in it, is indifferent to the others, and wishes they would all get drowned together.

11. They require that the characters in a tale shall be so clearly defined that the reader can tell beforehand what each will do in a given emergency. But in the *Deerslayer* tale this rule is vacated.

How many of these violations are illustrated in the discussion following them?

In addition to these large rules there are some little ones. These require that the author shall

12. *Say* what he is proposing to say, not merely come near it.

13. Use the right word, not its second cousin.

14. Eschew surplusage.
15. Not omit necessary details.
16. Avoid slovenliness of form.
17. Use good grammar.
18. Employ a simple and straightforward style.

Even these seven are coldly and persistently violated in the *Deerslayer* tale.

Cooper's gift in the way of invention was not a rich endowment; but such as it was he liked to work it, he was pleased with the effects, and indeed he did some quite sweet things with it. In his little box of stage properties he kept six or eight cunning devices, tricks, artifices for his savages and woodsmen to deceive and circumvent each other with, and he was never so happy as when he was working these innocent things and seeing them go. A favorite one was to make a moccasined person tread in the tracks of the moccasined enemy, and thus hide his own trail. Cooper wore out barrels and barrels of moccasins in working that trick. Another stage-property that he pulled out of his box pretty frequently was his broken twig. He prized his broken twig above all the rest of his effects, and worked it the hardest. It is a restful chapter in any book of his when somebody doesn't step on a dry twig and alarm all the reds and whites for two hundred yards around. Every time a Cooper person is in peril, and absolute silence is worth four dollars a minute, he is sure to step on a dry twig. There may be a hundred handier things to step on, but that wouldn't satisfy Cooper. Cooper requires him to turn out and find a dry twig; and if he can't do it, go and borrow one. In fact, the Leather Stocking Series ought to have been called the Broken Twig Series.

Irony?

I am sorry there is not room to put in a few dozen instances of the delicate art of the forest, as practised by Natty Bumppo and some of the other Cooperian experts. Perhaps we may venture two or three samples. Cooper was a sailor—a naval officer; yet he gravely tells us how a vessel, driving towards a lee shore in a gale, is steered for a particular spot by her skipper because he knows of an *undertow* there which will hold her back against the gale and save her. For just pure woodcraft, or sailorcraft, or whatever it is, isn't that neat? For several years Cooper was daily in the society of artillery, and he ought to have noticed that when a cannon-ball strikes the ground it either buries itself or skips a hundred feet or so; skips again a hundred feet of so—and so on, till finally it gets tired and rolls. Now in one place he loses some "females"—as he always calls women—in the edge of a wood near a plain at night in a fog, on purpose to give Bumppo a chance to show off the delicate art of the forest before the reader. These mislaid people are hunting for a fort. They hear a cannonblast, and a cannon-ball presently comes rolling into the wood and stops at

A paragraph developed with examples.

their feet. To the females this suggests nothing. The case is very different with the admirable Bumppo. I wish I may never know peace again if he doesn't strike out promptly and *follow the track* of that cannon-ball across the plain through the dense fog and find the fort. Isn't it a daisy? If Cooper had any real knowledge of Nature's ways of doing things, he had almost delicate art in concealing the fact. For instance: one of his acute Indian experts, Chingachgook (pronounced Chicago, I think), has lost the trail of a person he is tracking through the forest. Apparently that trail is hopelessly lost. Neither you nor I could ever have guessed out the way to find it. It was very different with Chicago. Chicago was not stumped for long. He turned a running stream out of its course, and there, in the slush in its old bed, were that person's moccasin-tracks. The current did not wash them away, as it would have done in all other like cases—no, even the eternal laws of Nature have to vacate when Cooper wants to put up a delicate job of woodcraft on the reader.

Notice Twain's choice of words. How much does he rely on a simple, familiar vocabulary?

We must be a little wary when Brander Matthews tells us that Cooper's books "reveal an extraordinary fulness of invention." As a rule, I am quite willing to accept Brander Matthews's literary judgments and applaud his lucid and graceful phrasing of them; but that particular statement needs to be taken with a few tons of salt. Bless your heart, Cooper hadn't any more invention than a horse; and I don't mean a high-class horse, either; I mean a clotheshorse. It would be very difficult to find a really clever "situation" in Cooper's books, and still more difficult to find one of any kind which he has failed to render absurd by his handling of it. Look at the episodes of "the caves"; and at the celebrated scuffle between Maqua and those others on the table-land a few days later; and at Hurry Harry's queer water-transit from the castle to the ark; and at Deerslayer's half-hour with his first corpse, and at the quarrel between Hurry Harry and Deerslayer later; and at—but choose for yourself; you can't go amiss.

If Cooper had been an observer his inventive faculty would have worked better; not more interestingly, but more rationally, more plausibly. Cooper's proudest creations in the way of "situations" suffer noticeably from the absence of the observer's protecting gift. Cooper's eye was splendidly inaccurate. Cooper seldom saw anything correctly. He saw nearly all things as through a glass eye, darkly. Of course a man who cannot see the commonest little every-day matters accurately is working at a disadvantage when he is constructing a "situation." In the *Deerslayer* tale Cooper has a stream which is fifty feet wide where it flows out of a lake; it presently narrows to twenty as it meanders along for no given reason, and yet when a stream acts like that it ought to be required to explain itself. Fourteen pages later the width of the brook's outlet from the lake has suddenly shrunk thirty feet, and become "the narrowest part of the stream." This

What point is Twain making in the river example?

shrinkage is not accounted for. The stream has bends in it, a sure indication that it has alluvial banks and cuts them; yet these bends are only thirty and fifty feet long. If Cooper had been a nice and punctilious observer he would have noticed that the bends were oftener nine hundred feet long than short of it.

Cooper made the exit of the stream fifty feet wide, in the first place, for no particular reason; in the second place, he narrowed it to less than twenty to accommodate some Indians. He bends a "sapling" to the form of an arch over this narrow passage, and conceals six Indians in its foliage. They are "laying" for a settler's scow or ark which is coming up the stream on its way to the lake; it is being hauled against the stiff current by a rope whose stationary end is anchored in the lake; its rate of progress cannot be more than a mile an hour. Cooper describes the ark, but pretty obscurely. In the matter of dimensions "it was little more than a modern canal-boat." Let us guess, then, that it was about one hundred and forty feet long. It was of "greater breadth than common." Let us guess, then, that it was about sixteen feet wide. This leviathan had been prowling down bends which were but a third as long as itself, and scraping between banks where it had only two feet of space to spare on each side. We cannot too much admire this miracle. A low-roofed log dwelling occupies "two-thirds of the ark's length"—A dwelling ninety feet long and sixteen feet wide, let us say—a kind of vestibule train. The dwelling has two rooms—each forty-five feet long and sixteen feet wide, let us guess. One of them is the bedroom of the Hutter girls, Judith and Hetty; the other is the parlor in the daytime, at night it is papa's bedchamber. The ark is arriving at the stream's exit now, whose width has been reduced to less than twenty feet to accommodate the Indians—say to eighteen. There is a foot to spare on each side of the boat. Did the Indians notice that there was going to be a tight squeeze there? Did they notice that they could make money by climbing down out of that arched sapling and just stepping aboard when the ark scraped by? No, other Indians would have noticed these things, but Cooper's Indians never notice anything. Cooper thinks they are marvelous creatures for noticing, but he was almost always in error about his Indians. There was seldom a sane one among them.

The ark is one hundred and forty feet long; the dwelling is ninety feet long. The idea of the Indians is to drop softly and secretly from the arched sapling to the dwelling as the ark creeps along under it at the rate of a mile an hour, and butcher the family. It will take the ark a minute and a half to pass under. It will take the ninety foot dwelling a minute to pass under. Now, then, what did the six Indians do? It would take you thirty years to guess, and even then you would have to give it up, I believe. Therefore, I will tell you what the

Are Twain's calculations accurate?

Is Twain using satire? Even ridicule?

Humor from specific, concrete details.

Indians did. Their chief, a person of quite extraordinary intellect for a Cooper Indian, warily watched the canal-boat as it squeezed along under him, and when he had got his calculations fined down to exactly the right shade, as he judged, he let go and dropped. And *missed the house!* That is actually what he did. He missed the house, and landed in the stern of the scow. It was not much of a fall, yet it knocked him silly. He lay there unconscious. If the house had been ninety-seven feet long he would have made the trip. The fault was Cooper's, not his. The error lay in the construction of the house. Cooper was no architect.

There still remained in the roost five Indians. The boat has passed under and is now out of their reach. Let me explain what the five did — you would not be able to reason it out for yourself. No. 1 jumped for the boat, but fell in the water astern of it. Then No. 2 jumped for the boat, but fell in the water still farther astern of it. Then No. 3 jumped for the boat, and fell a good way astern of it. Then No. 4 jumped for the boat, and fell in the water *away* astern. Then even No. 5 made a jump for the boat — for he was a Cooper Indian. In the matter of intellect, the difference between a Cooper Indian and the Indian that stands in front of the cigar-shop is not spacious. The scow episode is really a sublime burst of invention; but it does not thrill, because the inaccuracy of the details throws a sort of air of fictitiousness and general improbability over it. This comes of Cooper's inadequacy as an observer.

Why is repetition funny here, but often is dull?

Reading and Interpreting

1. Mark Twain is obviously not totally serious, but how many of his criticisms do sound like valid objections to Cooper's writing? If you have read *The Deerslayer* or other Cooper novels, comment on how much Twain is exaggerating.

2. Summarize Twain's main objections to Cooper's writing.

Writing Techniques

1. Analysis and classification can be useful for humorous as well as serious writing. Is Twain, in part, parodying the obvious uses of classification, especially in his list of eighteen violations of nineteen rules? Are the "rules" genuine subdivisions of principles of literary art?

2. Although the use of classification is most obvious in the first part of the essay in the list of rules, it also operates for the remainder of the review. Indicate the subdivisions in the last two-thirds of the essay under which Twain classifies his examples and other details.

Suggestions for Writing

Humorous writing is not easy, and Mark Twain is hard to imitate, but you might try your own style on a criticism pointing out absurdities in a film or television show. Westerns, soap operas, police or detective shows are good possibilities.

IDOLS OF THE MIND   **51**
Francis Bacon

Francis Bacon, *early seventeenth-century lawyer, philosopher, scientist, and high government official, attempted a new system of knowledge based on a right interpretation of nature. The selection is from his* Novum Organum, *Book 1. Bacon's vocabulary is not easy, partly because he was writing for a learned audience who would be well read, and partly because some of the words he uses have changed since his time, or the use he employs is no longer the most common. Before you read the essay, look up the Word Study at the end of the selection.*

THE idols and false notions which are now in possession of the human understanding, and have taken deep root therein, not only so beset men's minds that truth can hardly find entrance, but even after entrance obtained, they will again in the very instauration of the sciences meet and trouble us, unless men being forewarned of the danger fortify themselves as far as may be against their assaults.

entrance
instauration

There are four classes of Idols which beset men's minds. To these for distinction's sake I have assigned names,—calling the first class *Idols of the Tribe;* the second, *Idols of the Cave;* the third, *Idols of the Marketplace;* the fourth, *Idols of the Theatre.*

Analysis breaks the topic into parts.

The formation of ideas and axioms by true induction is no doubt the proper remedy to be applied for the keeping off and clearing away of idols. To point them out, however, is of great use; for the doctrine of Idols is to the Interpretation of Nature what the doctrine of the refutation of Sophisms is to common Logic.

Sophisms

The Idols of the Tribe have their foundation in human nature itself, and in the tribe or race of men. For it is a false assertion that the sense of man is the measure of things. On the contrary, all perceptions as well of the sense as of the mind are according to the measure of the individual and not according to the measure of the universe. And the human understanding is like a false mirror, which, receiving rays irregularly, distorts and discolours the nature of things by mingling its own nature with it.

The Idols of the Cave are the idols of the individual man. For every one (besides the errors common to human nature in general) has a cave or den of his own, which refracts and discolours the light of nature; owing either to his own proper and peculiar nature, or to his education and conversation with others; or to the reading of books, and the authority of those whom he esteems and admires; or to the differences of impressions, accordingly as they take place in a mind preoccupied and predisposed or in a mind indifferent and settled; or the like: So that the spirit of man (according as it is meted out to different individuals) is in fact a thing variable and full of perturbation, and governed as it were by chance. Whence it was well observed by Heraclitus that men look for sciences in their own lesser worlds, and not in the greater or common world.

Brief summaries of each class.

perturbation

There are also Idols formed by the intercourse and association of men with each other, which I call Idols of the Marketplace, on account of the commerce and consort of men there. For it is by discourse that men associate; and words are imposed according to the apprehension of the vulgar. And therefore the ill and unfit choice of words wonderfully obstructs the understanding. Nor do the definitions or explanations wherewith in some things learned men are wont to guard and defend themselves, by any means set the matter right. But words plainly force and overrule the understanding, and throw all into confusion, and lead men away into numberless empty controversies and idle fancies.

commerce consort

Lastly, there are Idols which have immigrated into men's minds from the various dogmas of philosophies, and also from wrong laws of demonstration. These I call Idols of the Theatre; because in my judgment all the received systems are but so many stage-plays, representing worlds of their own creation after an unreal and scenic fashion. Nor is it only of the systems now in vogue, or only of the ancient sects and philosophies, that I speak; for many more plays of the same kind may be composed and in like artificial manner set forth; seeing that errors the most widely different have nevertheless causes for the most part alike. Neither again do I mean this only of entire systems, but also of many principles and axioms in science, which by tradition, credulity, and negligence have come to be received.

credulity

But of these several kinds of Idols I must speak more largely and exactly, that the understanding may be duly cautioned.

The human understanding is of its own nature prone to suppose the existence of more order and regularity in the world than it finds. And though there be many things in nature which are singular and unmatched, yet it devises for them parallels and conjugates and relatives which do not exist. Hence the fiction that all celestial bodies

Futher analysis of the first idol.

conjugates

move in perfect circles; spirals and dragons being (except in name) utterly rejected. Hence too the element of Fire with its orb is brought in, to make up the square with the other three which the sense perceives. Hence also the ratio of density of the so-called elements is arbitrarily fixed at ten to one. And so on of other dreams. And these fancies affect not dogmas only, but simple notions also.

The human understanding when it has once adopted an opinion (either as being the received opinion or as being agreeable to itself) draws all things else to support and agree with it. And though there be a greater number and weight of instances to be found on the other side, yet these it either neglects and despises, or else by some distinction sets aside and rejects; in order that by this great and pernicious predetermination the authority of its former conclusions may remain inviolate. And therefore it was a good answer that was made by one who when they showed him hanging in a temple a picture of those who had paid their vows as having escaped shipwreck, and would have him say whether he did not now acknowledge the power of the gods,—"Aye," asked he again, "but where are they painted that were drowned after their vows?" And such is the way of all superstition, whether in astrology, dreams, omens, divine judgments, or the like; wherein men, having a delight in such vanities, mark the events where they are fulfilled, but where they fail, though this happens much oftener, neglect and pass them by. But with far more subtlety does this mischief insinuate itself into philosophy and the sciences; in which the first conclusion colours and brings into conformity with itself all that come after, though far sounder and better. Besides, independently of that delight and vanity which I have described, it is the peculiar and perpetual error of the human intellect to be more moved and excited by affirmatives than by negatives; whereas it ought properly to hold itself indifferently disposed towards both alike. Indeed in the establishment of any true axiom, the negative instance is the more forcible of the two.

pernicious
predetermination
inviolate

insinuate itself

The human understanding is divided into different characteristics.

The human understanding is moved by those things most which strike and enter the mind simultaneously and suddenly, and so fill the imagination; and then it feigns and supposes all other things to be somehow, though it cannot see how, similar to those few things by which it is surrounded. But for that going to and fro to remote and heterogeneous instances, by which axioms are tried as in the fire, the intellect is altogether slow and unfit, unless it be forced thereto by severe laws and overruling authority.

heterogeneous

The human understanding is unquiet; it cannot stop or rest, and still presses onward, but in vain. Therefore it is that we cannot conceive of any end or limit to the world; but always as of necessity it occurs to us that there is something beyond. Neither again can it be conceived how eternity has flowed down to the present day; for that distinction which is commonly received of infinity in time past and in time to come can by no means hold; for it would thence follow that one infinity is greater than another, and that infinity is wasting away and tending to become finite. The like subtlety arises touching the infinite divisibility of lines from the same inability of thought to stop. But this inability interferes more mischievously in the discovery of causes; for although the most general principles in nature ought to be held merely positive, as they are discovered and cannot with truth be referred to a cause; nevertheless the human understanding being unable to rest still seeks something prior in the order of nature. And then it is that in struggling towards that which is further off it falls back upon that which is more nigh at hand; namely, on final causes: which have relation clearly to the nature of man rather than to the nature of the universe; and from this source have strangely defiled philosophy. But he is no less an unskilled and shallow philosopher who seeks causes of that which is most general, than he who in things subordinate and subaltern omits to do so.

Limits on the human understanding.

subaltern

The human understanding is no dry light, but receives an infusion from the will and affections; whence proceed sciences which may be called "sciences as one would." For what a man had rather were true he more readily believes. Therefore he rejects difficult things from impatience of research; sober things, because they narrow hope; the deeper things of nature, from superstition; the light of experience, from arrogance and pride, lest his mind should seem to be occupied with things mean and transitory; things not commonly believed, out of deference to the opinion of the vulgar. Numberless in short are the ways, and sometimes imperceptible, in which the affections colour and infect the understanding.

Topic sentences summarize characteristics of the human understanding.

transitory

imperceptible

But by far the greatest hindrance and aberration of the human understanding proceeds from the dullness, incompetency, and deceptions of the senses; in that things which strike the sense outweigh things which do not immediately strike it, though they be more important. Hence it is that speculation commonly ceases where sight ceases; insomuch that of things invisible there is little or no observation. Hence all the working of the spirits inclosed in tangible bodies lies hid and unobserved of men. So also all the more subtle changes of form in the parts of coarser substances (which they commonly call alteration, though it is in truth local motion through exceedingly small spaces) is in like manner unobserved. And yet unless these two things just mentioned be searched out and brought to light, nothing great can be achieved in nature, as far as the production of works is concerned. So again the essential nature of our common air, and of all bodies less dense than air (which are very many), is almost unknown. For the sense by itself is a thing infirm and erring; neither can instruments for enlarging or sharpening the senses do much; but

incompetency

Microscopes and telescopes were few and crude in Bacon's day.

all the truer kind of interpretation of nature is effected by instances and experiments fit and apposite; wherein the sense decides touching the experiment only, and the experiment touching the point in nature and the thing itself.

The human understanding is of its own nature prone to abstractions and gives a substance and reality to things which are fleeting. But to resolve nature into abstractions is less to our purpose than to dissect her into parts; as did the school of Democritus, which went further into nature than the rest. Matter rather than forms should be the object of our attention, its configurations and changes of configuration, and simple action, and law of action or motion; for forms are figments of the human mind, unless you will call those laws of action forms.

abstractions

configurations

Such then are the idols which I call *Idols of the Tribe;* and which take their rise either from the homogeneity of the substance of the human spirit, or from its preoccupation, or from its narrowness, or from its restless motion, or from an infusion of the affections, or from the incompetency of the senses, or from the mode of impression.

A summary concludes a subsection.

The *Idols of the Cave* take their rise in the peculiar constitution, mental or bodily, of each individual; and also in education, habit, and accident. Of this kind there is a great number and variety; but I will instance those the pointing out of which contains the most important caution, and which have most effect in disturbing the clearness of the understanding.

Men become attached to certain particular sciences and speculations, either because they fancy themselves the authors and inventories thereof, or because they have bestowed the greatest pains upon them and become most habituated to them. But men of this kind, if they betake themselves to philosophy and contemplations of a general character, distort and colour them in obedience to their former fancies; a thing especially to be noticed in Aristole, who made his natural philosophy a mere bondservant to his logic, thereby rendering it contentious and well nigh useless. The race of chemists again out of a few experiments of the furnace have built up a fantastic philosophy, framed with reference to a few things; and Gilbert also, after he had employed himself most laboriously in the study and observation of the loadstone, proceeded at once to construct an entire system in accordance with his favourite subject.

habituated

bondservant
contentious

Examples support a proposition.

There is one principle and as it were radical distinction between different minds, in respect of philosophy and the sciences; which is this: that some minds are stronger and apter to mark the differences of things, other to mark their resemblances. The steady and acute mind can fix its contemplation and dwell and fasten on the subtlest distinction: the lofty and discursive mind recognises and puts together the finest and most general resemblances. Both kinds however

apter

easily err in excess, by catching the one at gradations the other at shadows.

There are found some minds given to an extreme admiration of antiquity, others to an extreme love and appetite for novelty; but few so duly tempered that they can hold the mean, neither carping at what has been well laid down by the ancients, nor despising what is well introduced by the moderns. This however turns to the great injury of the sciences and philosophy; since these affections of antiquity and novelty are the humours of partisans rather than judgments; and truth is to be sought for not in the felicity of any age, which is an unstable thing, but in the light of nature and experience, which is eternal. These factions therefore must be abjured, and care must be taken that the intellect not be hurried by them into assent.

Does Bacon use balance in his sentence structure here? Elsewhere?

felicity

abjured

Contemplations of nature and of bodies in their simple form break up and distract the understanding, while contemplations of nature and bodies in their composition and configuration overpower and dissolve the understanding: a distinction well seen in the school of Leucippus and Democritus as compared with the other philosophies. For that school is so busied with the particles that it hardly attends to the structure; while the others are so lost in admiration of the structure that they do not penetrate to the simplicity of nature. These kinds of contemplation should therefore be alternated and taken by turns; that so the understanding may be rendered at once penetrating and comprehensive, and the inconveniences above mentioned, with the idols which proceed from them, may be avoided.

Notice the effect of the balance here.

Let such then be our provision and contemplative prudence for keeping off and dislodging the *Idols of the Cave,* which grow for the most part either out of the predominance of a favorite subject, or out of an excessive tendency to compare or to distinguish, or out of partiality for particular ages, or out of the largeness or minuteness of the objects comtemplated. And generally let every student of nature take this as a rule,—that whatever his mind seizes and dwells upon with peculiar satisfaction is to be held in suspicion, and that so much the more care is to be taken in dealing with such questions to keep the understanding even and clear.

Another summary.

But the *Idols of the Marketplace* are the most troublesome of all: idols which have crept into the understanding through the alliances of words and names. For men believe that their reason governs words; but it is also true that words react on the understanding; and this it is that has rendered philosophy and the sciences sophistical and inactive. Now words, being commonly framed and applied acording to the capacity of the vulgar, follow those lines of division which are most obvious to the vulgar understanding. And whenever an understanding of greater acuteness or a more diligent observation would alter those lines to suit the true divisions of nature, words

sophistical

◄In Bacon's time such statements were radical in the extreme.

stand in the way and resist the change. Whence it comes to pass that the high and formal discussions of learned men end oftentimes in disputes about words and names; with which (according to the use and wisdom of the mathematicians) it would be more prudent to begin, and so by means of definitions reduce them to order. Yet even definitions cannot cure this evil in dealing with natural and material things; since the definitions themselves consist of words, and those words beget others: so that it is necessary to recur to individual instances, and those in due series and order; as I shall say presently when I come to the method and scheme for the formation of notions and axioms.

The idols imposed by words on the understanding are of two kinds. They are either names of things which do not exist (for as there are things left unnamed through lack of observation, so likewise are there names which result from fantastic suppositions and to which nothing in reality corresponds), or they are names of things which exist, but yet confused and ill-defined, and hastily and irregularly derived from realities. Of the former kind are Fortune, the Prime Mover, Planetary Orbits, Element of Fire, and like fictions which owe their origin to false and idle theories. And this class of idols is more easily expelled, because to get rid of them it is only necessary that all theories should be steadily rejected and dismissed as obsolete.

Analysis divides a subtopic into two parts.

But the other class, which springs out of a faulty and unskilful abstraction, is intricate and deeply rooted. Let us take for example such a word as *humid*; and see how far the several things which the word is used to signify agree with each other; and we shall find the word *humid* to be nothing else than a mark loosely and confusedly applied to denote a variety of actions which will not bear to be reduced to any constant meaning. For it both signifies that which easily spreads itself around any other body; and that which in itself is indeterminate and cannot solidise; and that which readily yields in every direction; and that which easily divides and scatters itself; and that which easily unites and collects itself; and that which readily flows and is put in motion; and that which readily clings to another body and wets it; and that which is easily reduced to a liquid, or being solid easily melts. Accordingly when you come to apply the word,—if you take it in one sense flame is humid; if in another, air is not humid; if in another, fine dust is humid; if in another, glass is humid. So that it is easy to see that the notion is taken by abstraction only from water and common and ordinary liquids, without any due verification.

humid

There are however in words certain degrees of distortion and error. One of the least faulty kinds is that of names of substances, especially of lowest species and well-deduced (for the notion of *chalk* and of *mud* is good, of *earth* bad); a more faulty kind is that of ac-

A different treatment of the fourth idol.

tions, as to *generate, to corrupt, to alter;* the most faulty is of qualities (except such as are the immediate objects of the sense) as *heavy, light, rare, dense,* and the like. Yet in all these cases some notions are of necessity a little better than others, in proportion to the greater variety of subjects that fall within the range of the human sense.

generate

But the *Idols of the Theater* are not innate, nor do they steal into the understanding secretly, but are plainly impressed and received into the mind from the play-books of philosophical systems and the perverted rules of demonstration. To attempt refutations in this case would be merely inconsistent with what I have already said: for since we agree neither upon principles nor upon demonstrations there is no place for argument. And this is so far well, inasmuch as it leaves the honour of the ancients untouched. For they are no wise disparaged—the question between them and me being only as to the way. For as the saying is, the lame man who keeps the right road outstrips the runner who takes the wrong one. Nay it is obvious that when a man runs the wrong way, the more active and swift he is the further he will go astray.

Notice the implications of "play-books."

disparaged

But the course I propose for the discovery of sciences is such as leaves but little to the acuteness and strength of wits, but places all wits and understandings nearly on a level. For as in the drawing of a straight line or a perfect circle, much depends on the steadiness and practice of the hand, if it be done by aim of hand only, but if with the aid of rule or compass, little or nothing: so is it exactly with my plan. But though particular confutations would be of no avail, yet touching the sects and general divisions of such systems I must say something, something also touching the external signs which show that they are unsound; and finally something touching the causes of such great infelicity and of such lasting and general agreement in error; that so the access to truth may be made less difficult, and the human understanding may the more willingly submit to its purgation and dismiss its idols.

acuteness

Bacon uses many words derived from Latin. Why?

purgation

Reading and Interpreting

1. Bacon's discussion of idols and false notions was written more than 350 years ago. How much of it seems dated and how much seems pertinent today?

2. Write a brief statement of your own defining each of the idols. (In Bacon's day *idol* meant "a mental fiction, a phantasy.")

3. Compare Bacon's discussions of words and meanings with comments by Orwell (46) and other writers on language.

Writing Techniques

1. Bacon's essay is more complex than the previous two selections, but the use of analysis and classification is generally similar. One difference is that Bacon divides his main subsections by analysis. Identify the parts of his discussion of the human understanding.

2. How much of the essay constitutes the introduction? Could the introduction have been put into a single paragraph?

Word Study

Be sure you know the meaning of the following terms, which are printed in the margins; consult a dictionary when necessary: *entrance, instauration, Sophisms, perturbation, commerce, consort, credulity, conjugate, pernicious, predetermination, inviolate, insinuate itself, heterogeneous, subaltern, transitory, imperceptible, incompetency, abstractions, configuration, habituated, bondservant, contentious, apter, felicity, abjured, sophistical, humid, generate, disparaged, acuteness, purgation.*

Suggestions for Writing

Select one of the idols and try writing a paper relating it to present-day problems. Can your description be analyzed into parts?

Processes: How to Do It

Describing a process, telling somebody how to do something, may seem to be the simplest kind of writing in this book, and the dullest. Telling somebody how to go from the administration building to the gymnasium is not very exciting prose.

But it is very useful. And telling how to is not as easy as it may seem — as anyone can testify who has been given the wrong route to the gymnasium, or tried to follow directions for assembling a child's toy. Clear directions for making or doing something are in constant demand: how to use a bottle of medicine, how to train a hunting dog, how to play the organ in ten easy lessons, how to put English on a billiard ball, how to win at bridge, or more seriously how to study or how to pass the bar examinations in Michigan. A title in your algebra textbook may have read "Quadratic Equations," suggesting exposition, an explanation of what such equations are. But the chapter probably would have been more accurately titled "How to Solve Quadratic Equations" and was actually a "how-to." Hundreds of books have been written, long and difficult books, telling people how to get to heaven.

Usually, however, descriptions of processes are less ambitious and more practical. The novelist Pelham Grenville Wodehouse tells about a dyspeptic lord who liked to go to sleep while his valet read

gourmet recipes out of a cookbook. The poor fellow could no longer
eat anything that had any taste, and thus while he toyed with his
milk toast he delighted in hearing how great chefs prepared elaborate
dishes. But usually descriptions of processes are utilitarian only.
Once the reader knows how to perform the process himself he has no
more use for the "how-to" book or article. Thus the requirements of
such writing may be relatively simple, but they are exacting and
measurable. You may not be able to tell a bad poem from a good
poem, but you can identify a bad description of a process. If the
reader cannot perform the process once he has read the "how-to"
carefully, there is something wrong with either the writing or the
reading.

What makes a description of a process good? How should such
a piece be read? How should it be written? The selections below
should help answer these questions. They fall under two heads. In
the first, various people tell you how to do something. What do these
pieces have in common? How do they differ? Could you, on the basis
of one of these expositions, do the thing yourself? If not, why not?
The answers may be different for the selections by Paul Corey (he
learned to build houses as a way to make a living), by some technical
writers, and by critics Macauley and Lanning. But they must have
something in common. Does any of them have faults—the basic fault,
that the reader would not know how to go about following the
process? In the second selection, a popular novelist uses the "how-
to" approach to organize a chapter.

This may be as good a place as any to repeat what has been
said or implied several times before, that almost no writing develops
by only one strategem at a time. Obviously, each of these "how-to's"
uses details as well as process; in fact, how could anyone describe a
process without going into details? And most of them will include, or
at least presume, some analysis and classification.

BRIEF "HOW-TO'S"

52

*Following are brief samples of writing that make various use of pro-
cess:* **a. George Lang** *is an author, a columnist for* Travel and Leisure,
*writer of the "Gastronomy" and "Restaurant" articles in the new edi-
tion of the* Encyclopaedia Britannica, *and by profession President of an
international restaurant and hotel consulting firm, The George Lang
Corporation.* **b. Paul Corey,** *a free-lance writer, has written novels,
science fiction, many articles, and how-to's, including* Build a Home,
from which this selection is taken; **c.** *The next passage was published in*
Family Medical Guide *and presumably was written by staff writers*

working under the editorship of **Vernon C. Branham,** *M.D., and* **Samuel B. Kutash,** *Ph.D., lecturer in psychotherapy at Brooklyn College;* **d. Robie Macauley** *and* **George Lanning,** *distinguished novelists, were editors of* The Kenyon Review *when they wrote* Technique in Fiction, *from which this passage is taken;* **e. Ernest Hemingway** *needs no introduction to readers of serious American literature; the selection reprinted here is from a news dispatch to the* Toronto Star, *done before Hemingway had graduated into fiction;* **f. Cleveland Amory,** *author of the delightful* The Proper Bostonians, *writes a column for the* Saturday Review — *the selection below is from one of them — that is followed avidly for its wit and humor;* **g. Willy Ley,** *has become known in this country, with volumes like* The Lungfish and the Unicorn *and* The Days of Creation, *as a popularizer of science;* **h.** *Dr.* **Desmond Morris,** *formerly of Oxford University and more recently curator of mammals for the Zoological Society, has published more than fifty scientific articles and several books readable by laymen, including* The Naked Ape *(1967), the source of this selection;* **i. Thor Heyerdahl,** *an intrepid and imaginative Norwegian anthropologist, is known for his writings and for testing possible migrations by floating on the oceans; the passage concerns the making of the* Ra, *which floated from Africa to the Caribbean. See* The Ra Expeditions.

a.   *How to Make a Caesar Salad,* George Lang

ALTHOUGH I discovered at least seven "original" recipes for a Caesar Salad — I don't think anyone really knows the 1927 version. Here is an educated composite:

     1 clove of crushed garlic
    ¾ cup olive oil
     2 cups croutons
   2-3 heads young romaine, broken to pieces
    ½ teaspoon salt
        Pepper to taste
     2 coddled eggs
        Juice of a large lemon
     6 fillets of anchovies
    ½ cup grated Parmesan cheese

Marinate crushed garlic in olive oil for 24 hours. Take sourdough bread which is several days old, dice it and mix with ¼ cup olive oil. Brown it in the oven, making sure it will be stirred several times to have an even golden color. Drain on paper towels. Take a large salad bowl, add freshly crushed pepper and salt and squeeze in the juice of one large or two smaller lemons. Drip ½ cup olive oil with one hand, while whipping with the other to slightly thicken it. When it begins to turn cloudy, break in coddled eggs and continue whipping. Drop in lettuce and toss it until it's completely coated. Add ½ cup freshly grated Parmesan, toss it again and adjust the taste by adding more salt/or lemon juice. Add croutons *at last minute* to make sure they don't become soggy.

Note: *Some experts coat the romaine leaves with the oil first and continue with the rest of the process afterwards.*

b. *How to Frame a Tall A-Frame Alone,* **Paul Corey**

DON'T forget—my plans called for an exaggerated A-roof. From the center of the ends of this unit to the peak would be a rise of sixteen feet—sixteen feet up in the air with nothing to put a ladder against. And the ridgepole would be close to twenty-six feet long which meant that I would have to splice a couple of 2x4s to get such a length. Now how the devil would you get such a structure up alone?

Sky hooks would simplify such operations. You can see why a shed-roof or a flat-roof would be a damned sight easier to build—that's why I recommend them to you.

Anyhow, I went to work on this problem. First, I found the center of the ends of the unit and marked them; then I set a 2x4 on edge, centered on these marks, and marked both sides of the 2x4. Then I fastened a twenty-foot 2x4 upright from the frame so that its edge just touched the edge of the 2x4 mark I'd made on the center of the frame. After getting this 2x4 plumb and firmly braced, I repeated this construction at the opposite end of the unit.

Now, you'll note that these upright 2x4s were longer than the height of the roof and they were placed one-half the thickness of a 2x4 off center. But this construction was only temporary.

The simplest way to have done it would have been to put the upright 2x4s exactly in the center, cut to the exact length which they should be, then two persons with ladders placed against each vertical timber could carry up each end of the ridgepole and set it on top of the two upright 2x4s and fasten it into place.

But there was only one of me, and I had only one ladder. Had I fastened one end of the ridgepole into place atop one of the uprights, while the other end rested on the floor, then moved my ladder to the other upright, I would have found that the end of the ridgepole still on the floor was so far from the foot of the ladder that I wouldn't be able to reach it and carry it up to the top of the other upright.

That was my reason for using twenty-foot 2x4s instead of the correct length timbers, and that was why I didn't put those uprights in the exact center of the ends of the building but beside the position of the future center 2x4s.

After getting the temporary uprights plumb, I measured up to the point which would be the base of the ridgepole on each. Then I spliced two 2x4s together, making a ridgepole longer than I would eventually need—long enough so that when I got one end nailed into position on one upright, the other end, slanting to the floor, would come close enough to the ladder placed against the opposite upright for me to reach it and carry it up to nail into position at that end.

c. *How to Preserve Firearm Evidence*

RECOVERY of the bullet must be done with the utmost care. First, a probe is introduced into the wound in such a way as to give a clear idea of the course of the bullet into the body. This factor, of course, will be correlated with the evidence given by the officer making the initial investigation. The point of entrance of the bullet into the body is carefully examined as to size, shape and possible powder markings on the skin. Due to the fact that the skin is taut by the pressure of the bullet, wounds at the point of entrance are likely to appear much smaller than the actual caliber of the bullet itself. The tissues return to their original position before impact. Points of exit, on the other hand, are much larger than the bullet and are usually torn and ragged due to detritus being carried through the body ahead of the missile. Often shreds of tissue will exude from exit wounds. If possible, the probe should be passed entirely through from entrance to exit which will indicate clearly the line of passage and also notes will be taken as to what structures are encountered by the bullet on its way through the body. Bullets removed from the body or from any object in which they have embedded themselves must be recovered with the utmost care as the marks of any instrument used in such recovery may seriously hinder the process of identification. The examining physician will then put his identifying mark upon the nose of the bullet rather than upon its base or sides since those portions of the bullet are factors of great importance in the examination of marks of identification. If the lethal weapon is held directly against the body as is so often the case in suicides—this is especially true with contact wounds of the head—the point of entry is likely to be quite torn and to give somewhat the effect of the point of exit type of wound. Pressure of the muzzle of the weapon against the skin, the undermining of the tissues immediately beneath due to impedance of expanding gases from the muzzle and other factors will indicate readily the nature of the wound. If the wound is made within a range of 2" to 18", the skin becomes "tattooed" by powder grains being projected into the surface of the skin. Accompanying this is smudging especially if black powder has been used. The caliber of the bullet and the type of powder used give valuable evidence as to the distance the gun was held at the time of firing. Tattooing and smudging are usually not present when the muzzle of the gun was above 18" distant from the point of entrance. The powder grains must be embedded in the skin to constitute tattooing.

d. *How to Plot a Story,* **Robie Macauley and George Lanning**

THE beginning writer is usually wise to follow the traditional principles of construction in writing his first stories or novel. This practice gives him some guidelines that he can follow until he is quite confident of the departures he wants to make and in which ways his originality will best operate. On the other hand, it is hardly necessary or profitable to try to fit his story rigidly into such traditional plot regulations as are outlined below. Some freer version of the plot design, which nevertheless does not abandon the idea of consistent development, is probably the most useful kind of reference.

Introduction of oppositions. In establishing the primary situation of his story, the writer should delineate some opposing forces or ideas in order to produce the essential element of tension. More specific words for this are: conflict, doubt, problem, struggle, division. It may be a matter of conflict within the mind of one person or it may be a more external conflict; the important thing is to make the reader aware that there is a pressure to decide between or among alternatives.

Deepening of the oppositions. If oppositions remain in constant balance, repressed, or latent, there will never be a story. But once set up, they must grow more grave, heading toward a point of intolerance. This part is the development of the fiction and it is here that the tensions are made clearer and more forceful.

The point of intolerance, or crisis. The oppositions reach a stage at which they can no longer exist with each other. They are now fully realized and fully focused and they must reach a showdown in some occurrence.

The resolution. After the crisis, things can never be quite the same. The world of the fiction has changed for better or for worse. It may be that the characters whose part the author has taken have been blessed with success, or half-success. Perhaps they have been deceived by an apparent success and we know better. Perhaps they have failed completely. Or perhaps they have failed in gaining a small objective but have won in a larger sense. These are just a few of the many possibilities the resolution may bring about.

The main thing to observe in constructing a story is that everything should originate in character. It is what impresses the reader—the characters are what he remembers long after the intricacies of the plot have been forgotten.

e.   *Fishing for Trout*, **Ernest Hemingway**

FISHING slowly down the edge of the stream, avoiding the willow trees near the water and the pines that run along the upper edge of what was once the old canal bank with your back cast, you drop the fly on to the water at every likely looking spot. If you are lucky, sooner or later there will be a swirl or a double swirl where the trout strikes and misses and strikes again, and then the old, deathless thrill of the plunge of the rod and the irregular plunging, circling, cutting up stream and shooting into the air fight the big trout puts up, no matter what country he may be in. It is a clear stream and there is no excuse for losing him when he is once hooked, so you tire him by working him against the current and then, when he shows a flash of white belly, slide him up against the bank and snake him up with a hand on the leader.

It is a good walk in to Aigle. There are horse chestnut trees along the road with their flowers that look like wax candles and the air is warm from the heat the earth absorbed from the sun. The road is white and dusty, and I thought of Napoleon's grand army, marching along it through the white dust on the way to the St. Bernard pass and Italy. Napoleon's batman may have gotten up at sun up before the camp and sneaked a trout or two out of the Rhone canal for the Little Corporal's breakfast. And before Napoleon, the Romans came along the valley and built this road and some Helvetian in the road gang probably used to sneak away from the camp in the evening to try for a big one in one of the pools under the willows. In the Roman days the trout perhaps weren't as shy.

So I went along the straight white road to Aigle through the evening and wondered about the grand army and the Romans and the Huns that traveled light and fast, and yet must have had time to try the stream along towards daylight, and very soon I was in Aigle, which is a very good place to be. I have never seen the town of Aigle, it straggles up the hillside, but there is a cafe across the station that has a galloping gold horse on top, a great wisteria vine as thick through as a young tree that branches out and shades the porch with hanging bunches of purple flowers that bees go in and out of all day long and that glisten after a rain; green tables with green chairs, and seventeen per cent dark beer. The beer comes foaming out in great glass mugs that hold a quart and cost forty centimes, and the barmaid smiles and asks about your luck.

Trains are always at least two hours apart in Aigle, and those waiting in the station buffet, this cafe with the golden horse and the wisteria hung porch is a station buffet, mind you, wish they would never come.

f. *Teenagers, Bugs, and Bedrooms,* **Cleveland Amory**

TEENAGERS, we read the other day, can be—and we quote—"sullen, argumentative, lethargic." So what else is new? They're teenagers, aren't they? Anyway, according to Helen Rabichow, executive director of something called Scholarship and Guidance, an agency which counsels troubled teenagers and which, we presume, is a gold mine, you don't have to worry unless your teenager has, and we quote again, "an unrelieved lethargy." An unrelieved lethargy! Let's see now. It's not unrelieved in the morning. Teenagers sleep through it. In the afternoon? Well, it's not really unrelieved—they sit through it. It's the evening that's the problem. Occasionally they do want to get up to go somewhere. But look at it this way. At least most of the time, it's somewhere *else!*

Everyone, says Miss Rabichow, carries inside a certain amount of depression. But most adults have learned to handle it. The reason is, she explains, that our expectations are low. The trouble comes with teenagers who, she says, think all good things are possible. Well, all good things *are* possible. Nobody stays a teenager forever. And it's a lucky thing that nobody does. If you don't believe it, don't look now, but ask yourself whether anything is bugging you these days. We're kidding, of course. Obviously, just about everything is. But what we mean is, literally bugging you. And we don't mean the FBI or CIA either. We mean your own kids.

The point is that there is now in existence—and this time we wish we were kidding—a mail-order firm specializing in kids' bugging sets. For kids to bug—now get this—you. And in your own bedroom, too. The sets are advertised as terrific fun. Furthermore, it takes a diligent search by parents to find these bugs. One couple took 90 days.

Our feeling is that these parents made a big mistake in admitting that they *ever* found the bug. We think that they should have gone right on doing whatever they do in the bedroom and pretending they didn't know about the bug. They should have talked very casually, in normal tones. First, they should have started gently, with lines such as: "No, I don't agree. They're not all bad—there's some good in them." Then, a little stronger: "A fellow at the office told me you can get any kid snatched. They'll hold the kids in a dark cellar for a week if necessary, and all you have to do is pretend to negotiate." And, finally, the clincher: "Well, I don't know, but I do know my old army pal, Ted, put out a contract on *his* kids."

We tell you, after a few conversations like that, the kids would either unplug the bug or call the cops.

g.   *Constructing a Genealogical Tree,* **Willy Ley**

AFTER Darwin had disproved the Linnaean dogma of the stability of species, the German evolutionist Haeckel (in whose mouth we have already ventured to put some remarks on the horseshoe crab) set out to construct "genealogical trees" for the various families of animal life. These first attempts to replace Linnaeus' rigid, fossilized system by one that really explained relationships through actual lines of descent naturally involved much that was only theory or conjecture. The most hotly debated points were those at which the lines of evolution forked, and in the course of these controversies was conceived the idea of "common ancestors" or "missing links." Thus, for example, it was obvious that the living types of horse, donkey, and zebra, though all related, had not evolved directly one from another. All three of them (and a host of extinct horses besides) must have descended from a common ancestor. This particular missing link was finally found (long after *Ceratodus*): tiny *Eohippus* of the early Tertiary Period, extinct for more than five million years, which was only as large as a dog, but which was nevertheless the forefather of all the horses, donkeys, and zebras to come. To this day, however, scientists have not been lucky enough to be able to fill in all the gaps in the outline histories of the more important animals, not to mention the less important types.

h. *Investigating Our Urges,* **Desmond Morris**

IN all exploratory behaviour, whether artistic or scientific, there is the ever-present battle between the neophilic and neophobic urges. The former drives us on to new experiences, makes us crave for novelty. The latter holds us back, makes us take refuge in the familiar. We are constantly in a state of shifting balance between the conflicting attractions of the exciting new stimulus and the friendly old one. If we lost our neophilia we would stagnate. If we lost our neophobia, we would rush headlong into disaster. This state of conflict does not merely account for the more obvious fluctuations in fashions and fads, in hair-styles and clothing, in furniture and cars; it is also the very basis of our whole cultural progression. We explore and we retrench, we investigate and stabilize. Step by step we expand our awareness and understanding both of ourselves and of the complex environment we live in.

Before leaving this topic there is one final, special aspect of exploratory behaviour that cannot go unmentioned. It concerns a critical phase of social play during the infantile period. When it is very young, the infant's social play is directed primarily at the parents, but as it grows the emphasis is shifted from them towards other children of the same age. The child becomes a member of a juvenile "play group." This is a critical step in its development. As an exploratory involvement it has far-reaching effects on the later life of the individual. Of course, all forms of exploration at this tender age have long-term consequences—the child that fails to explore music or painting will find these subjects difficult as an adult—but person-to-person play contacts are even more critical than the rest. An adult coming to music, say, for the first time, without childhood exploration of the subject behind him, may find it difficult, but not impossible. A child that has been severely sheltered from social contact as a member of a play group, on the other hand, will always find himself badly hampered in his adult social interactions. Experiments with monkeys have revealed that not only does isolation in infancy produce a socially withdrawn adult, but it also creates an anti-sexual and anti-parental individual. Monkeys that were reared in isolation from other youngsters failed to participate in play-group activities when exposed to them later, as older juveniles. Although the isolates were physically healthy and had grown well in their solitary states, they were quite incapable of joining in the general rough and tumble. Instead they crouched, immobile, in the corner of the play-room, usually clasping their bodies tightly with their arms, or covering their eyes. When they matured, again as physically healthy specimens, they showed no interest in sexual partners. If forcibly mated, female isolates produced offspring in the normal way, but then proceeded to treat them as though they were huge parasites crawling on their bodies. They attacked them, drove them away, and either killed them or ignored them.

i.   *Making an Ocean-Going Raft,* **Thor Heyerdahl**

THERE was not a day to be lost. It was nearly Christmas. If we were to cross the Atlantic before the hurricane season began on the other side, we must set sail from Africa in May. I was afraid of having the papyrus cut too soon, since the old reed is not so strong, but unless it were cut now we could not be ready to start in May. Cutting two or three hundred thousand papyrus stems would take time, because it was high water in Lake Tana at present and if the reeds were to measure about ten feet long the stem must be cut far below the surface of the water. Afterward the reeds must be properly sun-dried or they would rot in their bundles. Then would come the difficult journey over the mountains and finally up the Red Sea. There was war in the Suez area and all traffic was at a standstill. I would have to fight for special permission to unload cargo in this area. In fact, the inflammable reed must be landed in Suez and transported along blocked roads to rejoin the Nile near Cairo. Before the papyrus load reached the pyramids, a camp with all conveniences including a cook and provisions must be ready in the desert for the necessary guards and labor force. The boatbuilding was to be headed by Buduma Negroes from Chad, who were still living their simple ancestral lives on floating islands in the most out-of-the-way desert corner of Central Africa. When all was set for the building to begin it would be a lenghty process to lash the hundreds of thousands of thin papyrus stems into a compact seagoing vessel forty-five feet long and fifteen feet broad. Also, plans and preparations had to be made in advance for the transport of the finished boat to its launching place at some African port on the Atlantic coast. Sail and rigging, ancient Egyptian steering mechanism, wickerwork cabin, specially made earthenware storage jars and ship's food prepared as in ancient times—there were a thousand things to prepare. And less than six months to do it in.

Reading and Interpreting

1. Are the directions in the various selections equally clear? Would you have trouble following any of them?
2. Does Lang in selection **a** omit any instructions?

Writing Techniques

1. The pieces **a** through **d** are straight "how-to." In general, they trace a process step-by-step from beginning to end. They differ, however, in their approaches to the process. Describe the differences.

2. Beginning with selection **e**, the authors are using process as a strategy in another sort of writing. Hemingway in **e**, a 1922 dispatch to a Toronto paper, is not expecting many of his readers to leave at once to fish for trout in France. What is his purpose? How does he use process to promote it?

3. What is the purpose of selection **f**? What is the process it describes?

4. How much of selection **g** is process? What is the purpose of the paragraph?

5. In selection **h** Morris uses process only by implication. What are the main strategies of the piece?

6. In selection **i** the process is outlined, but obviously not to teach the reader how to build a raft. What is the purpose of the outline of the process?

7. So far as you can observe, what are the qualities of writing most needed in using process as a strategy in writing?

Word Study

Three of the writers are scientists: Ley, Morris, and Heyerdahl. You probably had to look up some words in the piece by Morris. If you did not have to look up words in Ley and Heyerdahl, can you explain how they were able to write about science without sending you to a dictionary? Ley puts some terms within quotation marks and prints some in italic type. Can you explain why he uses different treatment for these terms, and why he leaves some others without either designation?

Suggestions for Writing

If you have ever followed directions for putting together a child's toy or putting together a piece of unassembled furniture, you know that writing directions requires some skill. Write directions for something you know about: how to cook something, how to do a ski turn, how to make a box kite, how to play a game, and so on.

AMPUTATION AS A PROCESS 53
Arthur Hailey

Arthur Hailey, *who lives in Toronto, had a reputation in Canada and the United States for television dramas before he became a successful novelist, specializing in stories with well-developed settings. They include* Hotel *(1965),* Airport *(1968),* Wheels *(1971), which deals with the automobile industry, and* The Final Diagnosis *(1959), which is set in a hospital, and from which this excerpt is taken.*

THE amputation of Vivian's left leg began at 8:30 A.M. precisely. Punctuality in the operating rooms was something that Dr. O'Donnell had insisted on when he first became chief of surgery at Three Counties, and most surgeons complied with the rule.

The procedure was not complicated, and Lucy Grainger anticipated no problems other than routine. She had already planned to amputate the limb fairly high, well above the knee and in the upper part of the femur. At one point she had considered disarticulating at the hip in the belief that this might give a better chance of getting ahead of the spreading malignancy from the knee. But the disadvantage here would be extreme difficulty later on in fitting an artificial limb to the inadequate stump. That was why she had compromised in planning to leave intact a portion of the thigh.

> Planning as the first step.

> *femur*

She had also planned where to cut her flaps so that the flesh would cover the stump adequately. In fact, she had done this last night, sketching out the necessary incisions in her mind, while allowing Vivian to believe that she was making another routine examination.

> Are these paragraphs part of the process?

That had been after she had broken the news to Vivian, of course—a sad, strained session in which the girl at first had been dry-eyed and composed and then, breaking down, had clung to Lucy, her despairing sobs acknowledging that the last barriers of hope had gone. Lucy, although accustomed by training and habit to be clinical and unemotional at such moments, had found herself unusually moved.

The session with the parents subsequently, and later when young Dr. Seddons had come to see her, had been less personal but still troubling. Lucy supposed she would never insulate entirely her own feelings for patients the way some people did, and sometimes she had had to admit to herself that her surface detachment was only a pose, though a necessary one. There was no pose, though, about detachment here in the operating room; that was one place it became essential, and she found herself now, coolly and without personal feelings, assessing the immediate surgical requirements.

The anesthetist, at the head of the operating table, had already given his clearance to proceed. For some minutes now Lucy's assistant—today, one of the hospital interns—had been holding up the leg which was to be removed, so as to allow the blood to drain out as far as possible. Now Lucy began to arrange a pneumatic tourniquet high on the thigh, leaving it, for the moment, loosely in position.

anesthetist

pneumatic tourniquet

Without being asked the scrub nurse handed scissors across the table, and Lucy began to snip off the bandages which had covered the leg since it had been shaved, then prepped with hexachlorophene, the night before. The bandages fell away and the circulating nurse removed them from the floor.

prepped hexachlorophene

Lucy glanced at the clock. The leg had been held up, close to vertical, for five minutes and the flesh appeared pale. The intern changed hands and she asked him, "Arms getting tired?"

The beginning of the operation.

He grinned behind his face mask. "I wouldn't want to do it for an hour."

The anesthetist had moved to the tourniquet and was looking at Lucy inquiringly. She nodded and said, "Yes, please." The anesthetist began to pump air into the rubber tourniquet, cutting off circulation to the leg, and when he had finished the intern lowered the limb until it rested horizontally on the operating table. Together the intern and scrub nurse draped the patient with a sterile green sheet until only the operative portion of the leg remained exposed. Lucy then began the final prepping, painting the surgical area with alcoholic zephiran.

zephiran

There was an audience in the O.R. today—two medical students from the university, and Lucy beckoned them closer. The scrub nurse passed a knife, and Lucy began to scrape the tip of the blade against the exposed flesh of the thigh, talking as she worked.

How does Hailey use the surgeon's teaching to clarify the process?

"You'll notice that I'm marking the level of the flaps by scratching them on first. That's to give us our landmarks." Now she began to cut more deeply, exposing the fascia immediately below the skin, with its layer of yellow fatty tissue. "It's important always to make the front flap longer than the back one, so that afterward the suture line comes a little posterially. In that way the patient won't have a scar right at the end of the stump. If we did leave a scar in that position it could be extremely sore when any weight was put upon it."

fascia

posterially

Now the flesh was cut deeply, the lines of both flaps defined by the blood which had begun to seep out. The effect, front and rear, was rather like two shirttails—one long, one short—which eventually would be brought together and sewn neatly at their edges.

Using a scalpel and working with short, sharp movements, Lucy began to strip back the flesh, upward, exposing the bloody red mass of underlying tissue.

scalpel

"Rake, please!" The scrub nurse passed the instrument and Lucy positioned it, holding back the loose, cut flesh, clear of the next layer below. She signaled to the intern to hold the rake in place, which he did, and she applied herself to cutting deeper, through the first layer of quadriceps muscle.

quadriceps

"In a moment we shall expose the main arteries. Yes, here we are—first the femoral vessel." As Lucy located it the two medical students leaned forward intently. She went on calmly, matching her action to the words. "We'll try to free the vessels as high up as possible, then pull them down and tie off so that they retract well clear of the stump." The needle which the scrub nurse had passed danced in and out. Lucy tied the big vessels twice to be sure they were secure and would remain so; any later hemorrhage in this area could be catastrophic for the patient. Then, holding her hand for scissors, she took them and severed the main artery leading to the lower limb. The first irrevocable step to amputation had now been taken.

The arteries.

The same procedure followed quickly for the other arteries and veins. Then, cutting again through muscle, Lucy reached and exposed the nerve running parallel downward. As her gloved hands ran over it exploringly, Vivian's body stirred suddenly on the table and all eyes switched quickly to the anesthetist at its head. He nodded reassuringly. "The patient's doing fine; no problems." One of his hands was against Vivian's cheek; it was pale, but her breathing was deep and regular. Her eyes were open but unseeing; with her head fully back, untilted to one side or the other, the pockets of her eyes were deep with water—her own tears, shed in unconsciousness.

"We follow the same procedure with the nerve, as with the arteries and veins—pull it down, tie it off as high as possible, then cut and allow it to retract." Lucy was talking almost automatically, the words following her hands, the habit of teaching strong. She went on calmly, "There's always been a lot of discussion among surgeons on the best way to treat nerve ends during amputation. The object, naturally, is to avoid pain afterward at the stump." She deftly tied a knot and nodded to the intern, who snipped off the spare ends of suture. "Quite a few methods have been tried—injection of alcohol; burning the nerve end with an electric cautery; but the method we're following today is still the simplest and most widely used."

The nerve.

Lucy glanced up at the clock on the O.R. wall. It showed 9:15—forty-five minutes so far since they had begun. She returned her eyes by way of the anesthetist.

The checks on the time make the account more dramatic.

"Still all right?"

The anesthetist nodded. "Couldn't be better, Lucy. She's a real healthy girl." Facetiously he asked, "You sure you're taking the leg off the right patient?"

"I'm sure."

Lucy had never enjoyed operating-room jokes about patients on the table, though she had known some surgeons who wisecracked their way from first incision to closure. She supposed it was all in your point of view. Perhaps with some people levity was a means to cover up deeper feelings, perhaps not. At any rate she preferred to change the subject. Beginning to cut the muscles at the back of the leg, she asked the anesthetist, "How's your family?" Lucy paused to use a second rake to hold back the flesh from the new incision.

"They're fine. We're moving into a new house next week."

"Oh, really. Whereabouts?" To the intern she said, "A little higher, please. Try to hold it back right out of the way."

"Somerset Heights. It's a new subdivision in the north end."

The back leg muscles were almost severed. She said, "I think I've heard of it. I expect your wife is pleased."

Now the bone was visible, the whole incision big, red, gaping. The anesthetist answered, "She's in seventh heaven—buying rugs, choosing draperies, all the other things. There's only one problem."

Lucy's fingers went around the leg bone, working up and freeing the surrounding muscles. Speaking for the students' benefit, she said, "You'll notice that I'm pushing the muscles as far out of the way as I can. Then we can sever the bone quite high so that afterward it will be entirely covered with muscle."

The intern was having trouble holding back the overlapping muscles with his two rakes. She helped him position them and he grumbled, "Next time I do this I'll bring my third hand."

"Saw, please."

Again the scrub nurse was ready, placing the handle of the bone saw in Lucy's outstretched palm. To the anesthetist Lucy said, "What problem is that?"

Positioning the saw blade as high as she could, Lucy began to move it in short, even strokes. There was the dull, penetrating sound of bone scrunching as the saw teeth bit inward. The anesthetist said, "Paying for it all."

Lucy laughed. "We'll have to keep you busier—schedule more surgery." She had sawed halfway through the bone now; it was proving tougher than some, but of course young bones were naturally hard. Suddenly the thought occurred to her: this is a moment of tragedy, and yet here we are, casually talking, even jesting, about commonplace things. In a second or two, no more, this leg would be severed and a young girl—little more than a child—would have lost, for always, a part of her life. Never again would she run freely, wholly like other people, or dance, or swim, or ride horseback, or, uninhibited, make love. Some of these things she would eventually do, and others with effort and mechanical aid; but nothing again could ever be quite the same—never so gay or free or careless as with the fullness of youth and the body whole. This was the nub of the tragedy: it had happened too soon.

Lucy paused. Her sensitive fingers told her that the saw cut was almost complete. Then, abruptly, there was a crunching sound, followed by a sharp crack; at the last moment, under the weight of the almost separated limb, the final fragment of bone had snapped. The limb was free and it fell to the table. For the first time raising her voice, Lucy said, "Catch it! Quickly!"

What is the effect of letting the leg drop?

But the warning was too late. As the intern grabbed and missed, the leg slipped from the operating table and thudded to the floor.

"Leave it there!" Lucy spoke sharply as, forgetful of the fact that he would render himself unsterile, the intern bent to retrieve the limb. Embarrassed, he straightened up.

The circulating nurse moved in, collected the leg, and began to wrap it in gauze and paper. Later, along with more packages containing other surgical specimens, it would be collected by a messenger and taken to Pathology.

"Hold the stump clear of the table, please." Lucy gestured to the intern, and he moved around her to comply. The scrub nurse had a rasp ready, and Lucy took it, feeling for the rough edges of bone that the break had left and applying the rasp to them. Again for the students she said, "Always remember to get the bone end clean, making sure that no little spikes stick out, because if they do, they're likely to overgrow and become extremely painful." Without looking up, she asked, "How are we doing for time?"

The anesthetist answered, "It's been seventy minutes."

Lucy returned the rasp. "All right," she said; "now we can begin to sew up." With the end in sight she found herself thinking gratefully of the coffee which would be waiting in the surgeons' room down the hall.

The process concludes.

Reading and Interpreting

1. This is a fictional account. How much of your interest is in the process recorded? What else in the account interests you?

2. Describe the attitude of Lucy Grainger toward her patient and toward the operation.

Writing Techniques

1. Assume you were to extract from the selection the portions that could be condensed into a medical handbook as an entry under "How to Amputate a Limb at the Femur." How would the whole be changed?

2. How is Corey's selection on how to frame an A-frame like this piece in its method?

3. The process is developed as a continuous narrative, but is the narrative divided in any way into steps in the process? Point out any divisions.

Word Study

Following are some of the words that may have been strange to you: *femur, anesthetist, pneumatic tourniquet, prepped, hexachlorophene, zephiran, fascia, posterially, scalpel, quadriceps.* Some of these terms are part of the general vocabulary, although you may not be sure of the difference between *anesthetist* and *anesthesiologist,* and *prepped* could be called slang. But most of these are *technical terms.* Are such terms a needless affectation? Or do they have some reason for existence in our kind of society? What did you do about them when you read this piece? What should a layman do about them?

Suggestions for Writing

Write an explanation of a process, dramatizing it by developing a narrative in which you or somebody else does something. Get any help you can from Hailey's method or from Corey's.

Definition: A Way of Looking Closer

Everybody knows about definitions as ways to tell you how to use words. Not everybody thinks of them as devices for developing writing. In a fifteenth-century glossary *pension* is defined as "dette [debt] to be payed." When Dr. Samuel Johnson got around to defining the word some three hundred years later he expanded the statement as follows: "An allowance made to any one without an equivalent. In England, it is generally understood to mean pay given to a state hireling for treason to his country."

The first part of Johnson's entry is definition as we commonly think of it. The word had somewhat changed its meaning by his time, and he is explaining more precisely how it is used. But the second part is rather different. Apparently the good doctor did not like the way a corrupt government was bribing people and the second sentence becomes a sort of one-line editorial. The definition becomes development.

In the selections below you will find both uses of definition. Noah Webster and Joseph Worcester, early American dictionary makers, are trying to tell their fellow countrymen how to use the word *style*. Henry David Thoreau, on the other hand, while using the posture of defining style, is considering the problem of how to write. So are more recent rhetoricians like Gorrell and Gibson. The selection from *Cloak and Cipher* **54e** about codes and other sorts of secret writings, is an intermediate mixture. The authors are defining a term in code-making, but the definition provides occasion for a discussion, even a few illustrative examples, including a story.

You may want to notice the last piece, especially. Jacob Bronowski calls it "The Reach of Imagination," and this title describes very well what he has to say. He is trying to show us what the imagination is by showing us how far it can go as well as what it can do. This may remind us that etymologically *definition,* from Latin *de finibus,* "concerning borders," implies setting up the limits of meaning as the borders of a country mark out the limits of a nation.

That is one thing definition can do; it can tell us something of what a word is not, what it does not mean. What else can it do? How can it tell us what the meaning of a word is? In the selections following, what do you find the various writers using definition for? Are any of the earlier pieces in this book in any sense definition? How about number **11,** about the prospective automated battlefield? Is there any definition in the piece called "Le Pirate," **9**? What about the article by Helen Epstein, about the right to die **40**? Can even a mixture of narrative and description become definition of a sort? What about number **12,** "Portrait of a Mugger"? Is any of the "Declaration of Independence" definition? We have seen Lerner **48** using definition as the basis of classification.

Earlier we noticed that description could be used for an entire essay, but more commonly it was seeded into other sorts of writing, especially into narrative. Would you say that definition may serve something of the same sort of function in exposition and argument, that it readily becomes part of such writing even when a whole essay is not developed by definition? In this connection you may want to notice what we have observed before—for example in Section X—that most pieces of writing, even most paragraphs, are developed with more than one strategy.

DICTIONARY DEFINITIONS   **54**

a. Noah Webster, *lawyer, teacher, journalist, was also America's first great lexicographer and wrote the most revealing definitions that English had as yet enjoyed;* **b. Joseph E. Worcester,** *also lexicographer, improved on Webster in many ways, but for whatever reason his countrymen have paid him little honor;* **c.** The Century Dictionary and Cyclopedia, *1889–97, set a new standard for making word books for English; the English* Oxford *was still being edited;* **d.** Webster's Third New International Dictionary *has continued efforts to describe how and what words mean;* **e. Dan Tyler Moore** *and* **Martha Waller** *are authorities on the complexities of codes and ciphers; this excerpt is from* Cloak and Cipher.

a. Noah Webster, *An American Dictionary of the English Language**

STYLE, *n.* . . . . 1. Manner of writing with regard to language, or the choice and arrangement of words; as, a harsh style; a dry style; a tumid or bombastic style; a loose style; a terse style; a laconic or verbose style; a flowing style; a lofty style; an elegant style; an epistolary style. The character of style depends chiefly on a happy selection and arrangement of words.

> Proper words in proper places, make the true definition of style.
>
> *Swift*

> Let some lord but own the happy lines,
> How the wit brightens and the style refines!
>
> *Pope*

2. Manner of speaking appropriate to particular characters; or in general, the character of the language used.

> No style is held for base, where love well named is.
>
> *Sidney*

> According to the usual style of dedications.
>
> *Middleton*

So we say, a person addresses another in a style of haughtiness, in a style of rebuke.

b. Joseph E. Worcester, *A Dictionary of the English Language*†

STYLE, *n.* . . . . 3. The distinctive manner of writing which belongs to each author, and also to each body of writers, allied as belonging to the same school, country, or age; manner of writing or of composition; diction; phraseology.

> The style of Dryden is capricious and varied; that of Pope is cautious and uniform.
>
> *—Johnson*

> Johnson's style, unfortunately, is particularly easy of imitation, even by writers utterly destitute of his vigor of thought: and such imitators are intolerable.
>
> *Abp. Whately*

Syn. . . . from its etymology, would naturally be applied only to written composition; and diction (L. *dictio*) to what is spoken. They are both, however, applied to the manner both of writing and speak-

* First octavo (New Haven, 1841), 2 v.

† Boston, 1860.

ing; yet, more commonly, to what is written. Style expresses much more than diction. The terms phrase and phraseology are applied as often to what is spoken as to what is written. Phrase respects single words or a single expression; phraseology, a succession of words, or a series of expressions.

c. The Century Dictionary and Cyclopedia: An Encyclopedic Lexicon of the English Language*

STYLE, *n.* . . . 3. Mode of expression in writing or speaking; characteristic diction; a particular method of expressing thought by selection or collocation of words, distinct in some respect from other methods, as determined by nationality, period, literary form, individuality, etc.; in an absolute sense, appropriate or suitable diction; conformity to an approved literary standard: as, the style of Shakespeare or of Dickens; antiquated or modern style; didactic, poetic, or forensic style; a pedantic style; a nervous style; a cynical style.

> Stile is a constant & continuall phrase or tenour of speaking and writing, extending to the whole tale or processe of the poeme or historie, and not properly to any peece or member of a tale.
> Puttenham, *Arte of English Poesie,* p. 123

> Proper words in proper places make the true definition of a style.
> *Swift*

> Jeffreys spoke against the motion in the coarse and savage style of which he was a master.   Macaulay, *Hist. Eng.,* vi

> If thought is the gold, style is the stamp which makes it current, and says under what king it was issued.
> Dr. J. Brown, *Spare Hours,* 3d ser., p. 277

d. Webster's Third New International Dictionary†

STYLE, *n.* . . . 2a: mode of expressing thought in oral or written language: as (1): a manner of expression characteristic of an individual, a period, a school, or other identifiable group (as a nation) ⟨ a classic [style]; a flowery 18th century prose [style] ⟩ (2): the aspects of literary composition that are concerned with mode and form of ex-

* New York, 1889–97.
†Springfield, Mass., 1961.

pression as distinguished from content or message ⟨ his [style] is so graceful that one regrets he has nothing to say ⟩ (3): the; manner, tone, or orientation assumed in discourse ⟨ spoke in the [style] of a master to slaves ⟩ ⟨ took a very lofty [style] with us ⟩ b: the custom followed (as in a business, editorial, or printing office) in spelling, punctuation, and typographic arrangement and display.

e. Dan Tyler Moore and Martha Waller

IN secret writing, whenever letters retain their own identities (A being really A, B being B, et cetera) but are separated from each other, transposed, or mixed up in their order, the cipher is called a "transposition." When writing was first invented, there was no need for ciphers, since the letters of hieroglyphs were so mysterious that only a handful of people could read them. But twenty-three hundred years ago, when the Persian Empire was in a temporary period of peace with Greece, there were plenty of people who could read Greek, so the Spartans invented the first system of transposition to safeguard their secret communications.

Definition by example.

A slave who had journeyed hundreds of miles through enemy territory from Sparta to Byzantium arrived in Sestos, where the Spartan leader, Lysander, was encamped. He had been stopped and searched many times, but was allowed to proceed with his harmless letter to the Spartan ruler.

When he arrived, Lysander showed no interest in the letter. Ordering everyone from the room, he asked the astonished slave for his colorfully-decorated belt. He thrust one end of the belt into a hole in his Commander's baton, then twisted the belt around the baton in a tight spiral so that the edges touched.

An incident to develop a definition.

The jumble of letters on the belt, which looked like a religious charm, sprang into words and sentences when read down the length of the baton. To his horror, Lysander learned that his "friends," the Persians, were really his enemies, and that they were hatching a plot against him in Sparta preparatory to taking over the city. Lysander rushed his army back to Sparta by forced marches and smashed the plot. The *scytale* (rhymes with Italy), the oldest-known type of transposition cipher, had saved Greece from the barbarians.

There are many other ways in which letters can be scrambled or transposed to form secret writing. Even simpler than the *scytale* is writing in reverse. Thus I LOVE YOU becomes UOY EVOL I. Reversed writing has the advantage of speed. Some people find that they can write almost as rapidly in this cipher as they can in plain language. One helpful trick is to use a mirror for writing or reading in reverse; the eye works from left to right and the mirror reverses the image. Care must be taken that the letters themselves are not reversed along with the order. Я in place of R would give away the game at once. Like the *scytale*, reversed writing is of very low security

Another quick method of jumbling the letters of a message is to split them apart like this:

I O E O

L V Y U

On one line, I LOVE YOU then becomes IOEOLVYU. This is known as the "rail-fence" cipher. Simple as this system is, it was used as late as the American Civil War.

Reading and Interpreting

1. What differences are there in the definitions of style? How clearly do they define?

2. In what sense is selection **e** a definition?

Writing Techniques

1. There are many methods of defining; the most common, sometimes called logical or formal, puts something into a class and then distinguishes it from other members of the class. Which definitions use this pattern?

2. Since most of these definitions are from dictionaries, they raise questions about the uses of dictionaries. What are dictionaries good for? What can they not do? What makes one dictionary better than another?

3. How does the method of selection **e** differ from that of the dictionaries? How adequate is it as a definition?

Suggestions for Writing

Try writing a definition of a slang word, one that is not defined in current dictionaries or that you know to be used in senses different from the dictionary definitions.

a. Henry David Thoreau *(1817–1862), who thought of himself as a naturalist, has become a bastion of American literature, notably for* Wal - den, *his* Journals, *and a few essays; The definition is from his* Literary Remains: Notes for Lecture XIV; **b. Robert M. Gorrell,** *Vice-President for Academic Affairs at the University of Nevada, and one of the editors of this book, has written widely on language and its use; the selection is the introduction to "Very Like a Whale: A Report on Rhetoric";* **c. Walker Gibson,** *professor at the University of Massachusetts, is a poet and has written on writing and related subjects, as in* Tough, Sweet and Stuffy *(1966), from which this selection comes.*

a.   Henry David Thoreau

ENOUGH has been said in these days of the charm of fluent writing. We hear it complained of some works of genius that they have fine thoughts, but are irregular and have no flow. But even the mountain peaks in the horizon are, to the eye of science, parts of one range. We should consider that the flow of thought is more like a tidal wave than a prone river, and is the result of a celestial influence, not of any declivity in its channel. The river flows because it runs down hill, and flows the faster, the faster it descends. The reader who expects to float downstream for the whole voyage may well complain of nauseating swells and choppings of the sea when his frail shore craft gets amidst the billows of the ocean stream, which flows as much to sun and moon as lesser streams to it. But if we would appreciate the flow that is in these books, we must expect to feel it rise from the page like an exhalation, and wash away our critical brains like burr millstones, flowing to higher levels above and behind ourselves. There is many a book which ripples on like a freshet, and flows a glibly as a mill-stream sucking under a causeway; and when their authors are in the full tide of their discourse, Pythagoras and Plato and Jamblichus halt beside them. Their long stringy, slimy sentences are of that consistency that they naturally flow and run together. They read as if written for military men, for men of business, there is such a dispatch in them. Compared with these, the grave thinkers and philosophers seem not to have got their swaddling-clothes off; they are slower than a Roman army in its march, the rear

Definition by figurative comparison?

camping to-night where the van camped last night. The wise Jamblichus eddies and gleams like a watery slough.

> "How many thousands never heard the name
>   Of Sidney, or of Spenser, or their books?
> And yet brave fellows, and presume of fame,
>   And seem to bear down all the world with looks."
> Samuel Daniel

The ready writer seizes the pen and shouts "Forward! Alamo and
Fanning!" and after rolls the tide of war. The very walls and fences
seem to travel. But the most rapid trot is no flow after all; and thither,
reader, you and I, at least, will not follow.

A perfectly healthy sentence, it is true, is extremely rare. For the
most part we miss the hue and fragrance of the thought; as if we
could be satisfied with the dews of the morning or evening without
their colors, or the heavens without the azure. The most attractive
sentences are, perhaps, not the wisest, but the surest and roundest.
They are spoken firmly and conclusively, as if the speaker had a right
to know what he says, and if not wise, they have at least been well
learned. Sir Walter Raleigh might well be studied, if only for the ex-
cellence of his style, for he is remarkable in the midst of so many
masters. There is a natural emphasis in his style, like a man's tread,
and a breathing space between the sentences, which the best of modern writing does not furnish. His chapters are like French parks, or
say rather like a Western forest, where the larger growth keeps down
the underwood, and one may ride on horseback through the openings. All the distinguished writers of that period possess a greater
vigor and naturalness than the more modern—for it is allowed to
slander our own time—and when we read a quotation from one of
them in the midst of a modern author, we seem to have come suddenly upon a greener ground, a greater depth and strength of soil. It
is as if a green bough were laid across the page, and we are refreshed
as by the sight of fresh grass in midwinter or early spring. You have
constantly the warrant of life and experience in what you read. The
little that is said is eked out by implication of the much that was
done. The sentences are verdurous and blooming as evergreen and
flowers, because they are rooted in fact and experience, but our false
and florid sentences have only the tints of flowers without their sap
or roots. All men are really most attracted by the beauty of plain
speech, and they even write in a florid style in imitation of this. They
prefer to be misunderstood rather than to come short of its exuber-
ance. Hussein Effendi praised the epistolary style of Ibrahim Pasha to
the French traveller Botta, because of "the difficulty of understanding
it; there was," he said, "but one person at Jidda who was capable of

Complex development—reasons, examples, analogy.

The simile continues.

He uses metaphors also.

understanding and explaining the Pasha's correspondence." A man's whole life is taxed for the least thing well done. It is its net result. Every sentence is the result of a long probation. Where shall we look for standard English but to the words of a standard man? The word which is best said came nearest to not being spoken at all, for it is cousin to a deed which the speaker could have better done. Nay, almost it must have taken the place of a deed by some urgent necessity, even by some misfortune, so that the truest writer will be some captive knight, after all. And perhaps the fates had such a design, when, having stored Raleigh so richly with the substance of life and experience, they made him a fast prisoner and compelled him to make his words his deeds, and transfer to his expression the emphasis and sincerity of his action.

Has the paragraph defined a healthy sentence?

Men have a respect for scholarship and learning greatly out of proportion to the use they commonly serve. We are amused to read how Ben Jonson engaged that the dull masks with which the royal family and nobility were to be entertained should be "grounded upon antiquity and solid learning." Can there be any greater reproach than an idle learning? Learn to split wood, at least. The necessity of labor and conversation with many men and things, to the scholar is rarely well remembered; steady labor with the hands, which engrosses the attention also, is unquestionably the best method of removing palaver and sentimentality out of one's style, both of speaking and writing. If he has worked hard from morning till night, though he may have grieved that he could not be watching the train of his thoughts during that time, yet the few hasty lines which at evening record his day's experience will be more musical and true than his freest but idle fancy could have furnished. Surely the writer is to address a world of laborers, and such therefore must be his own discipline. He will not idly dance at his work who has wood to cut and cord before nightfall in the short days of winter; but every stroke will be husbanded, and ring soberly through the wood; and so will the strokes of that scholar's pen, which at evening record the story of the day, ring soberly, yet cheerily, on the ear of the reader, long after the echoes of his axe have died away. The scholar may be sure that he writes the tougher truth for the calluses on his palms. They give firmness to the sentence. Indeed, the mind never makes a great and successful effort, without a corresponding energy of the body. We are often struck by the force and precision of style to which hard-working men, unpracticed in writing, easily attain when required to make the effort. As if plainness and vigor and sincerity, the ornaments of style, were better learned on the farm and in the workshop than in the schools. The sentences written by such rude hands are nervous and tough, like hardened thongs, the sinews of the deer, or the roots of the pine. As for the graces of expression, a

A different approach to definition. How would you describe it?

These sentences read like epigrams. Do they supply much evidence?

great thought is never found in a mean dress; but though it proceed from the lips of the Wolofs, the nine Muses and the Three Graces will have conspired to clothe it in fit phrase. Its education has always been liberal, and its implied wit can endow a college. The world, which the Greeks called Beauty, has been made such by being gradually divested of every ornament which was not fitted to endure. The Sibyl, "speaking with inspired mouth, smileless, inornate, and unperfumed, pierces through centuries by the power of the god." The scholar might frequently emulate the propriety and emphasis of the farmer's call to his team, and confess that if that were written it would surpass his labored sentences. Whose are the truly *labored* sentences? From the weak and flimsy periods of the politician and literary man, we are glad to turn even to the description of work, the simple record of the month's labor in the farmer's almanac, to restore our tone and spirits. A sentence should read as if its author, had he held a plough instead of a pen, could have drawn a furrow deep and straight to the end. The scholar requires hard and serious labor to give an impetus of his thought. He will learn to grasp the pen firmly so, and wield it gracefully and effectively, as an axe or a sword. When we consider the weak and nerveless periods of some literary men, who perchance in feet and inches come up to the standard of their race, and are not deficient in girth also, we are amazed at the immense sacrifice of thews and sinews. What! these proportions — these bones — and this their work! Hands which could have felled an ox have hewed this fragile matter which would not have tasked a lady's fingers! Can this be a stalwart man's work, who has a marrow in his back and a tendon Achilles in his heel? They who set up the blocks of Stonehenge did somewhat, if they only laid out their strength for once, and stretched themselves.

> Is Thoreau using *labored* in two senses? What is the value of this in a definition of style?

b. Robert M. Gorrell

HAMLET. *Do you see yonder cloud that's almost in shape of a camel?*
POLONIUS. *By the mass, and 'tis like a camel indeed.*
HAMLET. *Methinks it is like a weasel.*
POLONIUS. *It is backed like a weasel.*
HAMLET. *Or like a whale?*
POLONIUS. *Very like a whale.*

Rhetoric is very like an umbrella. Under its expansive shade cluster, more or less comfortably, a variety of subjects — semantics, logic, usage, style. Rhetoric is very like an arch. It spans a wide area, bridging psychology and linguistics and sociology and philosophy. Rhetoric is very like a dynamo. It is the machinery for generating the ideas and languages of communications. Rhetoric is something very like a whale, with its mouth open, sweeping the ocean. Rhetoric is also very like a jellyfish.

c. Walker Gibson

WHEN a writer selects a style, however unconsciously, and so presents himself to a reader, he chooses certain words and not others, and he prefers certain organizations of words to other possible organizations. I take it that every choice he makes is significant in dramatizing a personality or voice, with a particular center of concern and a particular relation to the person he is addressing. Such self-dramatizations in language are what I mean by style. The Tough Talker, in these terms, is a man dramatized as centrally concerned with himself—his style is *I-talk*. The Sweet Talker goes out of his way to be nice to us—his style is *you-talk*. The Stuffy Talker expresses no concern either for himself or his reader—his style is *it-talk*. These are three extreme possibilities: the way we write at any given moment can be seen as an adjustment or compromise among these three styles of identifying ourselves and defining our relation with others.

Reading and Interpreting

1. How is Thoreau's comment early in his third paragraph—"Learn to split wood, at least"—related to his ideas on style?

2. Recall the comments of Laird 45 and Orwell 46 on the use of language. Would they agree or disagree with Thoreau? Explain.

3. Gibson's and Gorrell's statements are both introductory paragraphs, amplified in detail in the articles following them. In what ways do they suggest approaches to writing different from that of Thoreau?

Writing Techniques

1. Etymologically, *definition* would mean something like "setting limits or borderlines to things." Do these selections define in that sense?

2. Thoreau's paragraphs are long and complex. Try analyzing his third paragraph. Does it develop in sequences of topics and subtopics? A modern writer would have broken this into several paragraphs, say three to six. Try doing so, providing a topic sentence for each of the chunks you treat as a paragraph.

3. Thoreau makes frequent use of figurative language to clarify, as in his comment on "the flow of thought" in the opening paragraph. Find at least two more examples of figurative comparisons of this sort and comment on their effectiveness as definitions.

TONGUES   **56**
John Ciardi

John Ciardi, *best known as a contemporary poet, writes an occasional column for the* Saturday Review *of which this selection is an example; see also selection* **21.**

THE mystery of language is that it uses man as much as man uses it.

The evolutionary process that took a drop of sea water, put a membrane around it, moved the resultant thing onto the shore, and eventually made a man of what followed, filled him with little hair-trigger mechanisms he knows little about. Why and by what means do crabs, for example, taken from the sea and studied far inland, continue to show bodily changes that are exactly synchronized to the *synchronized* rise and fall of the tides a thousand miles away? Why do pilots suffer serious maladjustments after jetting across time zones and back *maladjustments* again? The crab seems to keep some inner clock despite displacement: The pilot seems to be dependent on some clock outside himself and pays a penalty for moving across the earth at super- *superanimal* animal speeds.

Birds do migrate enormous distances, but my ignorant guess is that they stay more or less within the same time zone. They move North and South. Is there some mechanism in creatures that confines them to time zones and punishes them for hurdling across longitudes? Do pilots who fly North-South routes show the same symptoms of ma- *malaise* laise that afflict pilots on East-West routes? Herds of animals do move East and West at times but so slowly that they have time to adjust. The penalty seems to be imposed on those who leap longitudes at a rate beyond evolutionary adaptation.

What makes the difference? I do not know where an answer to such a question might begin. I know only that there is a question here when we learn how to ask it.

Man's language habits and their effects upon him will never be well understood until we learn to ask questions we have not yet come to. Something in the respiratory system developed the ability to make sounds, and that ability became a survival mechanism. Screams and shouts warned the pack of danger. Some sounds served to iden- tify members of the pack to one another. Other softer sounds con- veyed an intention to mate and so to continue the species. But what is happening when an infant practices sound making for its own sake? Infant, man, or woman, some people are obviously proud of their way of making sounds. "He likes the sound of his own voice," we say. But how did the mechanism of sound making become a source of self-delight and even of pomposity? *conveyed*

The infant begins outside the language code. It hears its adults use language. It starts with an innate ability to scream discomfort signals. In the normal rearing pattern such signals usually result in a cuddle, food to ease hunger, and a change of clothing to ease dis- comfort. *innate discomfort*

Even when it is comfortable, the infant discovers that its bab- bling attracts mother and results in a cuddle and a soft, pleasant babble from her. Such early training in cause and effect may in itself be enough to explain why so many of us like the sound of our own voices. We were taught early that we could babble our way to love. *discovers*

How would we feel about the sound of our own voices if our first howls had been generally ignored or if the answer to our infant babbling had regularly been a smack in the face?

With any sort of luck, it does, thank heaven, go another way. As the child develops the ability to put his bubbles, hisses, tongue twists, and gargles together and to make approximate words of them in the adult language code, it begins to say ma-ma and da-dee. It is still no great shakes as an orator, but in any reasonably happy family such efforts are likely to produce extravagant love attentions. It is a soggy little ego we start from. To be cuddled and feasted with praise for having managed a first few syllables of language is bound to be addictive. Baby is on its way to becoming a self-pleased chatterbox, perhaps to the point of irritating its parents, who then start an inhi- bition by telling it to shut up. *approximate* *extravagant*

Some foundation of future character is being laid in such ex- changes. Psychiatry has tended to look to early sexuality as the weight-bearing wall of future character. It is at least worth asking if the development of early language habits may not be as important as sex. *exchanges*

However it goes with the individual, it is certain that man has put an enormous part of his psychic energy into shaping language, and that language has, in turn, powerfully affected his behavior. In most primitive languages, for example, and surviving as late as classical Greek *barbaros,* the same word does for both "stranger" and *surviving* "enemy." If I have separate words for these two ideas, I can look at an unknown person without an alarm signal. If I have one word for them, I will be less ready to let the man pass unmolested. I am already in Oedipus' chariot en route to Thebes and half-cocked to kill my unknown father when his chariot blocks mine on the road. The language my fathers made, makes me my father's killer.

unmolested

In the same way language can set a man's total profession of himself. "Faith," I once heard a preacher explain, "moves all we do. Columbus had faith in his theory that the world was round. He had faith in his floating needle. In my own small way I cannot drive across town without faith that approaching trucks will keep to their own side of the road. If I must have faith in order to drive to the grocery store, how can I fail to have faith in God's goodness?"

profession

The preacher had more faith than semantics. He could foresee salvation. He could not see that language had tricked him into using the same word to mean at least four different things. Columbus had faith-A (a willingness to risk his life to prove a theory) and faith-B (a reliance on the practical observation that his primitive compass pointed North). The preacher as motorist had faith-C (the assumption that no approaching truck would hit him because no previous approaching truck had done so). Since one word could be made to do for these three different categories, they all came to the same thing in his mind, and the three unrelated categories, joined in one language ambiguity, served him as proof (faith-D) that the universe took a personal interest in him.

approaching

So are we all confused by tongues. Yet in a deeper sense it is these very ambiguities that give language the power of ritual over us. Language, as Wallace Stevens said in an interview with a *Times* reporter, is a sanction, and the more important to us as traditional sanctions lose their force.

confused

Stanley Burnshaw's *Seamless Web,* a book that may well open a new era of literary criticism, argues that language works upon all the bodily functions. It stirs those evolutionary hair triggers built into us. Man exists at a depth beyond the reasons he is able to give for himself. Language stirs depths beyond the reasons he invents from it.

Reading and Interpreting

1. Ciardi's column raises at least as many questions as it answers. Can you approximate answers to any of his questions?

2. What is the evidence Ciardi presents to support the idea that language uses man?

3. How do the questions about a sense of time in the second and third paragraphs relate to the main idea of the entire column?

Writing Techniques

1. Is Ciardi's piece a definition in any sense? If so, what does it define?

2. Could the third and fourth paragraphs from the end have been written as one paragraph? Why are they written as two?

Word Study

1. The words listed in the margins of the selection all have been formed some time in the past by adding a prefix to a root word. Consider the meaning of each of the words in its context (*synchronized, maladjustments, superanimal, malaise, conveyed, innate, discomfort, discovers, approximate, extravagant, exchanges, surviving, unmolested, profession, approaching, confused*), trying to identify the prefix in each word and to define the meaning of the prefix. Then look up each word in a dictionary, paying particular attention to its origin, and write a definition of each prefix. Does one prefix sometimes have different meanings?

2. Write three words in addition to the one in the text that uses each prefix.

Suggestions for Writing

Almost any word can profitably be used as the basis for a paper exploiting definition, if the term means something to you, even a term as inclusive as *education* or as personal as *my blue jeans.* Write a paper focusing on your understanding of some term, not necessarily trying for a complete, formal definition, but presenting an interpretation of what the term signifies or suggests.

THE REACH OF IMAGINATION
Jacob Bronowski

57

Jacob Bronowski, *Pole by birth and a biologist and mathematician by training, has written many influential books, of which* The Ascent of Man *(1973) has attracted the most popular attention. The following article is taken from the* American Scholar.

FOR three thousand years, poets have been enchanted and moved and perplexed by the power of their own imagination. In a short and summary essay I can hope at most to lift one small corner of that mystery; and yet it is a critical corner. I shall ask, What goes on in the mind when we imagine? You will hear from me that one answer to this question is fairly specific: which is to say, that we can describe the working of the imagination. And when we describe it as I shall do, it becomes plain that imagination is a specifically *human* gift. To imagine is the characteristic act, not of the poet's mind, or the painter's, or the scientist's, but of the mind of man.

My stress here on the word *human* implies that there is a clear difference in this between the actions of men and those of other animals. Let me then start with a classical experiment with animals and children which Walter Hunter thought out in Chicago about 1910. That was the time when scientists were agog with the success of Ivan Pavlov in forming and changing the reflex actions of dogs, which Pavlov had first announced in 1903. Pavlov had been given a Nobel prize the next year, in 1904; although in fairness I should say that the award did not cite his work on the conditioned reflex, but on the digestive gland.

The implication of "human."

Hunter duly trained some dogs and other animals on Pavlov's lines. They were taught that when a light came on over one of three tunnels out of their cage, that tunnel would be open; they could escape down it, and were rewarded with food if they did. But once he had fixed that conditioned reflex, Hunter added to it a deeper idea: he gave the mechanical experiment a new dimension, literally—the dimension of time. Now he no longer let the dog go to the lighted tunnel at once; instead, he put out the light, and then kept the dog waiting a little while before he let him go. In this way Hunter timed how long an animal can remember where he has last seen the signal light to his escape route.

The results were and are staggering. A dog or a rat forgets which one of three tunnels has been lit up within a matter of seconds—in Hunter's experiment, ten seconds at most. If you want such an animal to do much better than this, you must make the task much simpler: you must face him with only two tunnels to choose from. Even so, the best that Hunter could do was to have a dog remember for five minutes which one of two tunnels had been lit up.

I am not quoting these times as if they were exact and universal: they surely are not. Hunter's experiment, more than fifty years old now, had many faults of detail. For example, there were too few animals, they were oddly picked, and they did not all behave consistently. It may be unfair to test a dog for what he *saw*, when he commonly follows his nose rather than his eyes. It may be unfair to test any animal in the unnatural setting of a laboratory cage. And there are higher animals, such as chimpanzees and other primates, which certainly have longer memories than the animals that Hunter tried.

As a scientist Bronowski is careful to qualify.

Yet when all these provisos have been made (and met, by more modern experiments) the facts are still startling and characteristic. An animal cannot recall a signal from the past for even a short fraction of the time that a man can—for even a short fraction of the time that a child can. Hunter made comparable tests with six-year-old children, and found, of course, that they were incomparably better than the best of his animals. There is a striking and basic difference between a man's ability to imagine something that he saw or experienced, and an animal's failure.

Animals make up for this by other and extraordinary gifts. The salmon and the carrier pigeon can find their way home as we cannot: they have, as it were, a practical memory that man cannot match. But their actions always depend on some form of habit: on instinct or on learning, which reproduce by rote a train of known responses. They do not depend, as human memory does, on calling to mind the recollection of absent things.

Where is it that the animal falls short? We get a clue to the answer, I think, when Hunter tells us how the animals in his experiment tried to fix their recollection. They most often pointed themselves at the light before it went out, as some gun dogs point rigidly at the game they scent—and get the name *pointer* from the posture. The animal makes ready to act by building the signal into its action. There is a primitive imagery in its stance, it seems to me; it is as if the animal were trying to fix the light on its mind by fixing it in its body. And indeed, how else can a dog mark and (as it were) name one of three tunnels, when he has no such words as *left* and *right*, and no such numbers as *one, two, three*? The directed gesture of attention and readiness is perhaps the only symbolic device that the dog commands to hold on to the past, and thereby to guide himself into the future.

I used the verb *to imagine* a moment ago, and now I have some ground for giving it a meaning. To *imagine* means to make images and to move them about inside one's head in new arrangements. When you and I recall the past, we imagine it in this direct and homely sense. The tool that puts the human mind ahead of the animal is imagery. For us, memory does not demand the preoccupation that it demands in animals, and it lasts immensely longer, because we fix it in images or other substitute symbols. With the same symbolic vocabulary we spell out the future—not one but many futures, which we weigh one against another.

I am using the word *image* in a wide meaning, which does not restrict it to the mind's eye as a visual organ. An image in my usage is what Charles Peirce called a *sign*, without regard for its sensory quality. Peirce distinguished between different forms of signs, but there is no reason to make his distinction here, for the imagination works equally with them all, and that is why I call them all images.

Is a legal term like *provisos* appropriate here?

A question here makes a good topic sentence.

Language and minds.

Definitions to restrict.

Indeed, the most important images for human beings are simply words, which are abstract symbols. Animals do not have words, in our sense: there is no specific center for language in the brain of any animal, as there is in the human being. In this respect at least we know that the human imagination depends on a configuration in the brain that has only evolved in the last one or two million years. In the same period, evolution has greatly enlarged the front lobes in the human brain, which govern the sense of the past and the future; and it is a fair guess that they are probably the seat of our other images. (Part of the evidence for this guess is that damage to the front lobes in primates reduces them to the state of Hunter's animals.) If the guess turns out to be right, we shall know why man has come to look like a highbrow or an egghead: because otherwise there would not be room in his head for his imagination.

The images play out for us events which are not present to our senses, and thereby guard the past and create the future—a future that does not yet exist, and may never come to exist in that form. By contrast, the lack of symbolic ideas, or their rudimentary poverty, cuts off an animal from the past and the future alike, and imprisons him in the present. Of all the distinctions between man and animal, the characteristic gift which makes us human is the power to work with symbolic images: the gift of imagination.

This is really a remarkable finding. When Philip Sidney in 1580 defended poets (and all unconventional thinkers) from the Puritan charge that they were liars, he said that a maker must imagine things that are not. Halfway between Sidney and us, William Blake said, "What is now proved was once only imagined." About the same time, in 1796, Samuel Taylor Coleridge for the first time distinguished between the passive fancy and the active imagination, "the living Power and prime Agent of all human Perception." Now we see that they were right, and precisely right: the human gift is the gift of imagination—and that is not just a literary phrase.

Nor is it just a literary gift; it is, I repeat, characteristically human. Almost everything that we do that is worth doing is done in the first place in the mind's eye. The richness of human life is that we have many lives; we live the events that do not happen (and some that cannot) as vividly as those that do; and if thereby we die a thousand deaths, that is the price we pay for living a thousand lives. (A cat, of course, has only nine.) Literature is alive to us because we live its images, but so is any play of the mind—so is chess: the lines of play that we foresee and try in our heads and dismiss are as much a part of the game as the moves that we make. John Keats said that the unheard melodies are sweeter, and all chess players sadly recall that the combinations that they planned and which never came to be played were the best.

I make this point to remind you, insistently, that imagination is

Transition to a new topic.

Development by contrast.

A shift in direction or a return?

the manipulation of images in one's head; and that the rational manipulation belongs to that, as well as the literary and artistic manipulation. When a child begins to play games with things that stand for other things, with chairs or chessmen, he enters the gateway to reason and imagination together. For the human reason discovers new relations between things not by deduction, but by that unpredictable blend of speculation and insight that scientists call induction, which—like other forms of imagination—cannot be formalized. We see it at work when Walter Hunter inquires into a child's memory, as much as when Blake and Coleridge do. Only a restless and original mind would have asked Hunter's questions and could have conceived his experiments, in a science that was dominated by Pavlov's reflex arcs and was heading toward the behaviorism of John Watson.

> Imagination defined. Development by definition?

Let me find a spectacular example for you from history. What is the most famous experiment that you had described to you as a child? I will hazard that it is the experiment that Galileo is said to have made in Sidney's age, in Pisa about 1590, by dropping two unequal balls from the Leaning Tower. There, we say, is a man in the modern mold, a man after our own hearts: he insisted on questioning the authority of Aristotle and St. Thomas Aquinas, and seeing with his own eyes whether (as they said) the heavy ball would reach the ground before the light one. Seeing is believing.

Yet seeing is also imagining. Galileo did challenge the authority of Aristotle, and he did look at his mechanics. But the eye that Galileo used was the mind's eye. He did not drop balls from the Leaning Tower of Pisa—and if he had, he would have got a very doubtful answer. Instead, Galileo made an imaginary experiment in his head, which I will describe as he did years later in the book he wrote after the Holy Office silenced him: the *Discorsi . . . intorno a due nuove scienze,* which was smuggled out to be printed in the Netherlands in 1638.

> ◄Analyze this as a topic sentence.

Suppose, said Galileo, that you drop two unequal balls from the tower at the same time. And suppose that Aristotle is right—suppose that the heavy ball falls faster, so that it steadily gains on the light ball, and hits the ground first. Very well. Now imagine the same experiment done again, with only one difference: this time the two unequal balls are joined by a string between them. The heavy ball will again move ahead, but now the light ball holds it back and acts as a drag or brake. So the light ball will be speeded up and the heavy ball will be slowed down; they must reach the ground together because they are tied together, but they cannot reach the ground as quickly as the heavy ball alone. Yet the string between them has turned the two balls into a single mass which is heavier than either ball—and surely (according to Aristotle) this mass should therefore move faster than either ball? Galileo's imaginary experiment has uncovered a con-

> Development by example? Again, is it also definition?

tradiction; he says trenchantly, "You see how, from your assumption that a heavier body falls more rapidly than a lighter one, I infer that a (still) heavier body falls more slowly." There is only one way out of the contradiction: the heavy ball and the light ball must fall at the same rate, so that they go on falling at the same rate when they are tied together.

This argument is not conclusive, for nature might be more subtle (when the two balls are joined) than Galileo has allowed. And yet it is something more important: it is suggestive, it is stimulating, it opens a new view—in a word, it is imaginative. It cannot be settled without an actual experiment, because nothing that we imagine can become knowledge until we have translated it into, and backed it by, real experience. The test of imagination is experience. But then, that is as true of literature and the arts as it is of science. In science, the imaginary experiment is tested by confronting it with physical experience; and in literature, the imaginative conception is tested by confronting it with human experience. The superficial speculation in science is dismissed because it is found to falsify nature; and the shallow work of art is discarded because it is found to be untrue to our own nature. So when Ella Wheeler Wilcox died in 1919, more people were reading her verses than Shakespeare's; yet in a few years her work was dead. It has been buried by its poverty of emotion and its trivialness of thought: which is to say that it had been proved to be as false to the nature of man as, say, Jean Baptiste Lamarck and Trofim Lysenko were false to the nature of inheritance. The strength of the imagination, its enriching power and excitement, lies in its interplay with reality—physical and emotional.

I doubt if there is much to choose here between science and the arts: the imagination is not much more free, and not much less free, in one than in the other. All great scientists have used their imagination freely, and let it ride them to outrageous conclusions without crying "Halt!" Albert Einstein fiddled with imaginary experiments from boyhood, and was wonderfully ignorant of the facts that they were supposed to bear on. When he wrote the first of his beautiful papers on the random movement of atoms, he did not know that the Brownian motion which it predicted could be seen in any laboratory. He was sixteen when he invented the paradox that he resolved ten years later, in 1905, in the theory of relativity, and it bulked much larger in his mind than the experiment of Albert Michelson and Edward Morley, which had upset every other physicist since 1881. All his life Einstein loved to make up teasing puzzles like Galileo's, about falling lifts and the detection of gravity; and they carry the nub of the problems of general relativity on which he was working.

Indeed, it could not be otherwise. The power that man has over nature and himself, and that a dog lacks, lies in his command of

Further significance of the Galileo illustration.

Is this a major transition?

imaginary experience. He alone has the symbols which fix the past and play with the future, possible and impossible. In the Renaissance, the symbolism of memory was thought to be mystical, and devices that were invented as mnemonics (by Giordano Bruno, for example, and by Robert Fludd) were interpreted as magic signs. The symbol is the tool which gives man his power, and it is the same tool whether the symbols are images or words, mathematical signs or mesons. And the symbols have a reach and a roundness that goes beyond their literal and practical meaning. They are the rich concepts under which the mind gathers many particulars into one name, and many instances into one general induction. When a man says *left* and *right,* he is outdistancing the dog not only in looking for a light; he is setting in train all shifts of meaning, the overtones and the ambiguities, between *gauche* and *adroit* and *dexterous,* between *sinister* and the sense of right. When a man counts *one, two, three,* he is not only doing mathematics; he is on the path to the mysticism of numbers in Pythagoras and Vitruvius and Kepler, to the Trinity and the signs of the Zodiac.

Summary and restatement.

I have described imagination as the ability to make images and to move them about inside one's head in new arrangements. This is the faculty that is specifically human, and it is the common root from which science and literature both spring and grow and flourish together. For they do flourish (and languish) together; the great ages of science are the great ages of all the arts, because in them powerful minds have taken fire from one another, breathless and higgledy-piggledy, without asking too nicely whether they ought to tie their imagination to falling balls or a haunted island. Galileo and Shakespeare, who were born in the same year, grew into greatness in the same age; when Galileo was looking through his telescope at the moon, Shakespeare was writing *The Tempest* and all Europe was in ferment, from Johannes Kepler to Peter Paul Rubens, and from the first table of logarithms by John Napier to the Authorized Version of the Bible.

Let me end with a last and spirited example of the common inspiration of literature and science, because it is as much alive today as it was three hundred years ago. What I have in mind is man's ageless fantasy, to fly to the moon. I do not display this to you as a high scientific enterprise; on the contrary, I think we have more important discoveries to make here on earth than wait for us, beckoning, at the horned surface of the moon. Yet I cannot belittle the fascination which that ice-blue journey has had for the imagination of men, long before it drew us to our television screens to watch the tumbling astronauts. Plutarch and Lucian, Ariosto and Ben Jonson wrote about it, before the days of Jules Verne and H. G. Wells and science fiction. The seventeenth century was heady with new dreams and fables

He goes on using examples.

about voyages to the moon. Kepler wrote one full of deep scientific ideas, which (alas) simply got his mother accused of witchcraft. In England, Francis Godwin wrote a wild and splendid work, *The Man in the Moone,* and the astronomer John Wilkins wrote a wild and learned one, *The Discovery of a New World.* They did not draw a line between science and fancy; for example, they all tried to guess just where in the journey the earth's gravity would stop. Only Kepler understood that gravity has no boundary, and put a law to it—which happened to be the wrong law.

All this was a few years before Issac Newton was born, and it was all in his head that day in 1666 when he sat in his mother's garden, a young man of twenty-three, and thought about the reach of gravity. This was how he came to conceive his brilliant image, that the moon is like a ball which has been thrown so hard that it falls exactly as fast as the horizon, all the way round the earth. The image will do for any satellite, and Newton modestly calculated how long therefore an astronaut would take to fall round the earth once. He made it ninety minutes, and we have all seen now that he was right; but Newton had no way to check that. Instead he went on to calculate how long in that case the distant moon would take to round the earth, if indeed it behaves like a thrown ball that falls in the earth's gravity, and if gravity obeyed a law of inverse squares. He found that the answer would be twenty-eight days.

In that telling figure, the imagination that day chimed with nature, and made a harmony. We shall hear an echo of that harmony on the day when we land on the moon, because it will be not a technical but an imaginative triumph, that reaches back to the beginning of modern science and literature both. All great acts of imagination are like this, in the arts and in science, and convince us because they fill out reality with a deeper sense of rightness. We start with the simplest vocabulary of images, with *left* and *right* and *one, two, three,* and before we know how it happened the words and the numbers have conspired to make a match with nature: we catch in them the pattern of mind and matter as one.

> What is the role of this paragraph for the whole definition?

Reading and Interpreting

1. Does Bronowski answer his question, "What goes on in the mind when we imagine?"?

2. How does Bronowski define *image?* What is the importance of his definition for his essay?

3. What seems to be Bronowski's view of science? Does it differ from other attitudes toward science you have heard?

Writing Techniques

1. What uses of definition does Bronowski make in his essay? Identify parts of it that are most clearly definition.

2. Part of Bronowski's definition of the imagination is developed by examples. What other techniques does he use?

Word Study

Following the pattern of the Word Study exercise for selection **56,** pick ten words from Bronowski's essay that have been formed by prefixes. Then write a definition of each prefix in the words you select.

Suggestions for Writing

With Bronowski in mind, try defining a concept or a word, for example, one like *professionalism*. A doctor, a rock singer, and a basketball player might give quite different definitions.

Comparison, Contrast, Analogy

In the previous section you probably read the quotation in which Hamlet—a witty young man who had by the way recently been a student—needles a pompous old busybody into saying that a cloud looks at once like a camel, a weasel, and "very like a whale." Hamlet is having fun, partly because he considers the busybody both vicious and stupid. In the passage you read, Gorrell goes on to have more fun with more outrageous likenesses, that rhetoric can also be at once very like a whale and a jellyfish.

Taken more seriously, or at least more literally, this laying of one thing beside another is a good way to make people see, and consequently it provides a good way to develop writing. By comparing things we may see both of the compared entities more clearly.

Roughly speaking, this sort of development is called *comparison*, but more strictly speaking, only things that are essentially alike can be compared. We can compare two sprinters: we can say that Sprinter A can run the 100-yard dash in 9.5 seconds, but the best Sprinter B has ever done is 9.6 seconds. We can also use comparison to show unexpected similarities in things not essentially alike. We might say that although New York and Los Angeles are superficially very different in architecture and general plan, actually they are more similar than many people suppose, both being centers of entertainment, business and finance, shipping and international trade.

As you will observe, the title of this section includes both the words *comparison* and *contrast,* as though these were two distinct operations. We have included the two terms in deference to common practice. People frequently assume that they are quite different, comparison showing only how things are alike and contrast showing only how things are different. Actually, they are parts of the same process, as we saw when we considered Sprinter A and Sprinter B; we compared them as runners, but we contrasted their speeds. Comparison implies contrast; if two human beings were precisely alike in everything, they would be identical, and that, so far as we know or can imagine, has never happened. The idea of comparison includes the idea of difference.

Analogy is sometimes called an extended comparison, or an extended metaphor, but it differs from comparison as a device for development. Comparison and contrast point out similarities and differences of similar things — two cities, two games, two magazines for women as in the selection by Harrington, or two views of life as in Arnold. Analogy is a device for explaining one thing in terms of another, usually for explaining something complex or unfamiliar by talking about something simpler and more familiar. You can talk to a child about a planet by using a tennis ball. Thomas Henry Huxley, in a famous analogy, describes life as a game of chess.

Thus the two, comparison-contrast and analogy, are at once similar and different, so different that they have uses at odds with one another. What is each good for? You have probably been warned that you should not try to use analogy as evidence. Why not? How is each used in the following selections? You will find a sharp example of comparison-contrast in the piece called "Two Letters to an American." The selections from Edward Bellamy and Stephen Leacock use analogy to explain complexities simply — to describe a society as people pulling and riding on a stagecoach, to explain atomic theory by looking at an Irishman whirling a shillelagh.

CAN MAN SURVIVE?   **58**
William Safire

William Safire *is one of* The New York Times *editorial writers whose comments are widely syndicated; a piece like this is likely to have been printed in many papers.*

"IS there hope for man?"

That stark question is posed by political economist Robert Heilbroner in a short new book," An Inquiry Into the Human Prospect," and his answer troubles some of the people in guilt-edged Washington who consider themselves, in Heilbroner's phrase, "the sentries of our society."

The author assesses the "civilizational malaise," or dread of the future, that appears to grip us, and finds that such anxiety is well-founded. World population growth and food shortages, in his view, will lead to "iron" governments in have-not nations and ultimately to nuclear war; if this does not obliterate us, environmental pollution is ready to replace the bang with the whimper.

In the face of these external challenges to mankind, Heilbroner suggests — "whether we are unable to sustain growth or unable to tolerate it" — both the capitalist and the socialist worlds will have to deny even lip service to individual liberty and humanism. Instead they will have to learn to live with harsh hierarchies of power capable of responding to demands of population control, war control and environmental control.

Heilbroner admits with some pain that his prescription "plays directly into the bands of those who applaud the 'orderliness' of authoritarian or dictatorial governments." But the freedom of man must be sacrificed on the altar of the survival of mankind.

"If then," he concludes, "by the question 'Is there hope for man?' we ask whether it is possible to meet the challenges of the future without the payment of a fearful price, the answer must be: No, there is no such hope."

Unlike previous catastrophists such as Thomas Malthus and Oswald Spengler, Heilbroner writes lucidly. For a mythic symbol he rejects Prometheus, who stole fire from the gods to give to man and who stands for daring and creativity, replacing him with fellow-titan Atlas, who carried the heavens on his shoulders, to suggest that the future spirit of mankind must be one of resignation to the bearing of an intolerable burden."

Fortunately for the affirmative Net Net Net Net Net
Fortunately for the affirmative Net Net Net Net Net among us, another human prospector has come on stream at the same time, with a book the same length and price (about 140 pages, $5.95) and a wholly different vision. He is Daniel Boorstin, senior historian at the Smithsonian Institution, who recently was awarded the Pulitzer Prize for the final volume of his monumental triology, "The Americans," and who now offers "Democracy and Its Discontents: Reflections on Everyday America."

"Perhaps it would be more comfortable," writes Boorstin, "to live in an age when the dominant purposes were in full flood when the hope for fulfillment had not been overshadowed by the frustrations of fulfillment." But today, in the "omnipresent present," Americans are worried and puzzled about "self-liquidating ideals."

A self-liquidating ideal is one that crosses itself off the national agenda as it is accomplished but leaves behind more frustration than satisfaction. For example, we have set aside huge areas in national parks to preserve the wilderness for people to enjoy—but as more people trek to the parks to enjoy them, the democratized wilderness loses its virginity.

As achievements accrue, Boorstin points out, dissatisfaction is guaranteed. Heilbroner sees this, too, as the explanation why social harmony does not follow economic growth: "Poverty is a relative and not an absolute condition," he writes, "so that despite growth, a feeling of disprivilege remains . . ."

Every solution breeds a new problem, Prometheus, Boorstin and Atlas Heilbroner would agree, but from this statement they march in opposite directions. Heilbroner envisions such immense problems that the only political solution is anti-democratic.

Boorstin thinks a "belief in solutions" is fallacious, caused by the example of technology in solving technical problems. Democracy is not the solution to anything, but is the process of solving the problems its solutions create—as he puts it, "getting there is all the fun."

"The most distinctive feature of our system is not a system, but a quest," Boorstin holds, "not a neat arrangement of men and institutions, but a flux. What other society has ever committed itself to so tantalizing, so fulfilling, so frustrating a community enterprise?"

The debate is worthwhile: Heilbroner is positive in his negation and Boorstin is profoundly serious in his affirmation. Which one will history prove to be realist?

To me, the creativity of Prometheus better symbolizes the human prospect than the resignation of Atlas. As long as the Boorstins can place our discontent in historic perspective, and the Heilbroners can shake us with purposeful foreboding, there is "hope for man."

Reading and Interpreting

1. Summarize the two positions described in this book review, the Atlas position and the Prometheus position. Which seems to you the sounder?

2. Do the views from the two books seem to you to offer too pessimistic a view of the future of mankind?

Writing Techniques

1. The selection is a clear example of one method of using comparison and contrast for development. Describe the pattern the review follows.

2. What sort of conclusion occurs in the last two paragraphs? Does it provide a resolution to the differences?

Suggestions for Writing

Especially in the years since World War II and atomic fission, human beings have raised questions about their survival. Twenty years ago Americans were digging and equipping air raid shelters, which are all but forgotten today. Are people now assuming that humanity will survive indefinitely? Or have they decided to ignore the question? Try writing a paper in which you narrow the general subject of the future of man to a topic that interests you — one of the dangers to man's future, or one practical change we should consider, or one attitude that would make people happier.

TWO LETTERS TO AN AMERICAN   **59**
C. A. Doxiadis

C. A. Doxiadis *is a Greek concerned with urban planning; but planning implies a future, and Doxiadis sees the now in the light of the future of the world. Of the three letters originally published in* Daedalus *only two have been reprinted here.*

DEAR AMERICAN:

I hate you.

You have asked me to justify this statement which has shocked you so much. All right, I will give you my opinion in as polite a way as I can.

I hate you for economic reasons. You are the richest nation on earth and you don't care about the others, or at least about the poorest ones. The proof is that you do not pay any taxes which can be of benefit to our global community. You told me once that you are seriously discussing — but have not yet approved — paying 1 percent of

Opening sentences identify topics.

your income for this purpose; but even this proves why I hate you. Though the richest citizens pay a higher percentage than the next income group, you discuss paying merely the same percentage as that proposed for western Europeans, who have much lower incomes than you do.

I hate you because you have more concessions outside your country than any other nation. You exploit our resources and you pay very little for doing so. Once this was limited to exploiting natural resources, but now you exploit every sector of our economies. Your large corporations invade our countries and underbid our own firms on small jobs, causing them to lose money until they are driven out of business and you have a monopoly. You have told me that such an invasion speeds technological progress in our countries, but I don't think this is worth losing our own enterprises. I don't believe that teaching a young girl how to make love means that one is entitled to monopolize her for the rest of her life and eliminate her chances for a good marriage. Teaching is one thing and exploiting is another.

Do you think of yourself as an exploiter?

You rape not only with technology, but also with money. You organize great financial concerns and you eliminate traditional family industries. We had fifty-five companies producing beautiful champagne in Catalonia, but all have been bought by you. Now there are only three or four and they are yours. You said that one of them is controlled by a French concern. When I said that it also was under your control, you laughed and called me naïve.

I hate you for social reasons. The greatest income gaps in the world are between your rich and your poor. You have told me in some countries there are still feudal lords exploiting peasants, but in those countries there is real hope for revolution, while in your country, despite the rhetoric of your so-called political extremists, there is no such hope.

I hate you because you are a racist and a segregationist. You have told me that in India there are millions of people completely ignored by their countrymen, that blacks are against Indians and Pakistanis in East Africa, and that blacks are even more violently against other blacks in countries like Burundi, where great racial and tribal massacres have taken place. This is true, but you are rich and educated and have the means to overcome these problems first.

What is the effect of the repeated "I hate you"?

I hate you because you began the revolutionary youth movement, which has now come to influence my children, who turn against me. You told me that I am a liberal when I speak against you and a conservative when I speak of my family, but that is my business. "Don't try to tell me what I should do," I said — and you smiled.

I hate you because you do not have basic good manners. Again and again I have seen you, inside a confined public space like an airplane, slamming cards on the small tables and laughing loudly. This is pollution. When I told you that this is like the adolescent revving the motor of his car just to show off his presence, you got angry and said that I must be an Italian peasant woman or a Levantine merchant who always speaks and does not allow anyone to rest and sleep. All right, it is clear you cannot stand me and I cannot stand you. By the way, don't speak to me again about pollution (which is such a fashionable subject with you) and asphyxiate me with the smoke from your cigar.

Has a smoker a right to object to pollution?

I hate you for political reasons. You say you are a liberal, but you oppose all liberal nations. You carry out wars against people. You feign abhorrence of the Russian actions in Hungary and Czechoslovakia, but these actions did not kill so many people as have been killed in Vietnam. When you lose in Vietnam, you are going to abandon all the middle-class people in Asia who have helped you, and some day you are going to withdraw only to the countries from which you receive oil and other resources. I am inconsistent, you said, but I am not, although it is my right. If you are going to exploit people, you at least ought to support them for good. Otherwise, the middle class and your friends are going to hate you as a traitor.

You probably doubt this.

Your press is autocratic. Do not mention again with a smile the Chinese and Russian cases. They fight for the people; yours fights for the capital. You have two strong political parties but no good Communist or anarchist party. You promote a few leaders and their wives, and thus you help a Greek shipowner to make front-page news and defeat my Norwegian compatriots who are his competitors. What about the people who have not married into your family?

I hate you for military reasons. You are so strong that I cannot hope to defeat you, you and your ubiquitous CIA. Don't remind me again of the time you were able to prove that one of my best liberal friends was a Russian agent. That was only an accident.

I hate you for technological reasons. You are ahead of all of us and you are exploiting us. Yes, you have told me repeatedly of Dutch and, lately, Japanese companies. I particularly remember what you said about Japanese "tourists" posing a friend in front of a shop window in the Champs-Elysées in order to photograph the new exhibits. You are right: everybody is stealing ideas and goods. We always have some people in our meetings who run back to publish as their own any new idea we exhibit. You, however, also steal our people, making it harder for us to produce new ideas.

You might notice the author's use of concrete detail.

I hate you for cultural reasons. You have created the Hollywood culture which is imposed upon us. When I told you this you laughed and said that you do not like Hollywood and it has lost its values, but you still control the film distribution. You are pushing us toward a dangerous standardization in all our expressions. To hear taxi-drivers and shop assistants in my country answer with "okay" is disgusting. "Okay" is the least of the cultural standardizations you have brought us. You have said that you do not force such things on us, but it is a virus of your making.

If you do not believe what I say about cultural standardization, you should see the reactions in airplanes when the passengers have to hear repeated asinine announcements in several languages, supposedly expressing the crew's wish that everybody enjoy the flight, describing the airplane, and giving the names of the officers and stewardesses, who smile their corporation smile and display, they think, enough of their bodies to titillate. On a Christmas day flight from Athens to New York people had to hear wishes for a Merry Christmas eight times in English alone. Even Christians got angry, let alone the Jews, Moslems, and Hindus who were on board. The formula even required a captain on another flight to describe the "beautiful city" of Buffalo, New York, which was hidden beneath the clouds. Nobody listens to this drivel, though we are forced to hear it. When I hear the same things in your big hotels and restaurants, I will go underground. You asked me why I blame you for all these things which are becoming common to other nations' airlines. You started it, and you are its most avid practitioner.

Is this our fault?

Speaking of your hotels, don't think that they are not also denying our rights. A big American hotel corporation, in order to show off, managed to break the regulations in Athens and double the height allowed for its hotel. Thus Athens had two tall monuments— the Acropolis and the hotel. This which you began was continued by the Greeks, who added their own office building, the "tower of Athens." Now the city has several such monuments being built. You have brought free license to rape. Today "American meat" is produced in the north of Greece to supply the big hotel with "American" food.

Development by example?

I hate you because no matter what we think about you, you are ahead of us, exploiting us and blocking our own chances, while not doing anything for us.

You still haven't figured out who I am. I am the poor citizen of every country on this earth. I am the poor black of America, the leftist of every country, the small businessman of the areas you have invaded, the political leader you ignore, the university professor or civil servant who never received an invitation from an American university or annual convention, the technician whose ideas you have stolen, the Spanish peasant who sees everybody profit from American tourists but himself, the European artist whose works you don't buy because you say that in pop art you are ahead, the intellectual who believes that you are wrong, the student who has not been admitted to your universities, and . . . and . . . so many more.

Is this a good way to start a conclusion?

I am a simple, complex man. I hate you.

DEAR AMERICAN:

I love you.

I have told you so many times. I have kissed you, bowed to you in my traditional way, and you were amazed. You asked me, my very dear friend, to tell you why I love you so much and why I tell you so repeatedly. Here is my reply which is objective, as you requested, dear friend, but also warm, for I cannot be neutral in my great affection for you.

I love you because you fed me and my family when we were starving. You supplied UNRRA immediately after the war. As soon as my country was liberated from the Nazis, great trucks entered our warehouses and everybody ran there to get food—the foundation of survival. I loved you then so much that when the government of Greece sent one of its young civil servants, a girl architect, to the island of Chios in order to define the damages and needs and then to assign to every village the proper amount of supplies, everybody came out of a village with flags and flowers to welcome and kiss her. She was the beloved American "Madame UNRRA."

I love you because you had the imagination and courage to conceive and carry out the Marshall Plan for aid to the war-stricken countries. It gave me a good loan to rebuild my industry. Your people were very generous and agreed that I could pay back in local currency that passed through many inflation crises. It would have been wonderful, had it not been for that damned countryman of mine who insisted that we pay back in dollars so that the benefits would reach not only the industrialists but also spread to the people. You were pure, for you had not lived through an inflation, and you defended the right approach: lend dollars and accept repayment in local currency.

I love you because you continue applying your principles of aiding other nations. You contribute a great deal to international lending agencies like the International Bank for Reconstruction and Development and the Interamerican Bank, and you put some of your best people at the top of them. Thank you, thank you very much.

I love you for social reasons also. You are the one big country that receives people and ideas from everywhere without prejudice. This does not happen in western and northern Europe, where you must be well established in order to be accepted. Not all, but most of your newspapers are open to the views of outsiders, and even a simple family from a small American Midwestern town will invite me into their home.

I love you because, as I have learned from all people, you do not make any distinction among races and social classes. My Jewish friends, whose community has the highest percentage of well-educated people, tell me that they do not have difficulty in rising to

What about the "I love you" sequence?

Compare with the second paragraph of the first letter.

What does this imply about the author as a fair-minded critic?

powerful positions. You have said that I forget the blacks, Puerto Ricans, Mexicans, and Jews whom many clubs will not accept nor corporations hire; but I still see greater chances for me, as a member of a minority group, to join an American club or work for an American corporation. Even in countries like Australia, absorbing and depending on immigrants, people laughed when I assumed that a person with two university degrees from two European countries could be recognized as a professional. He would not be allowed to pass their examinations, they said, and he would have to take courses in their universities for four years.

I love you because you have a strong labor class and no aristocracy. You said that I forget the elite of big cities like New York, an elite whose youth seems not to be living in our time. You mentioned the episode on a big Atlantic ship, where aristocratic young American men entered the tourist class restaurant at night wearing evening clothes to impress the young Mediterranean girls and the girls abandoned them in protest. I remember all your remarks, but when I visit your country I do not see the aristocrats. You smile and you say how could I, they have never set foot on any street, while I am accustomed to walking.

I love you because you can find an ignored scholar like Marshall McLuhan, praise him very much, and make him a symbol. You said that this is done because his theories strengthen the mass communication media, which has the power to elevate or sink anyone, including intellectuals. I accept your remark, but this is also a reason why I love you. It is better to praise somebody in a free economy, even if in the interest of capitalist forces, than to let the power reside in a government-controlled press. I prefer Madison Avenue to Goebbels.

I love you for military reasons. Without your military, Europe would have been under the Nazis, and you would have been a weak power in contrast to the unified continents of Europe-Asia-Africa, with Berlin the capital. Many people would have been believing, as do Fascists, that George Orwell was not trying to warn us, but to show us the future we all need. By now the "Three Continents" would have been preparing to celebrate the realization of 1984.

He will not scrawl "Yankees go home."

I love you because without your initiative to create organizations like NATO, the "Three Continents" would have been under Stalin and the preparations for the celebration of 1984 would have been decided at the Kremlin. Thank you, my dear American. Keep your fleet in the Mediterranean and the Persian Gulf. I must confess that I do not like the pollution it leaves behind, but I still prefer its pollution to the sole presence of the Russian fleet. I prefer two flags in the Mediterranean, and between the two I prefer the one with three interwoven colors; it is more democratic. The problem is not new; it is an age-old one. The Mediterranean has been either a challenge to many peoples—the Phoenicians, Greeks, Arabs—or it has been controlled by one, such as the Romans, who imposed their Pax Romana but also had people like Nero at the top.

He is tolerant. Is he too tolerant?

I love you for political reasons also. You have a wonderful congress which speaks much about democracy and always defends the liberal regimes. You said then: "But what happens? At the end the Pentagon decides." I answered: my dear much beloved American. This is what always happens. We speak of all freedoms and we permit only those that are not detrimental to our real interests. It appears to be a bitter truth, but it is better at least to speak for democracy and defend it occasionally than never to support it at all. I remember my old friend Pericles speaking beautifully about democracy in Athens but not always applying his principles in the Athenian League, which had all types of member states subservient to Athens. This is life.

I love you because your country offers the greatest number of choices. For me this is the most practical definition of democracy because, to tell the truth, I am fed up with declarations for democracy. Reality demands that we believe not in what is said, but in what is practiced. I remember a three-hour meeting at a big corporation in Chicago where people were speaking about political democracy at coffee break, but nobody even smiled when I presented some jokes because the boss was stern. When the boss started laughing, the whole audience found that I was indeed joking and exploded with laughter. This is not an indication of democracy in practice, but it is nevertheless a good lesson for other corporations that are more human. If we have no extreme cases, we do not appreciate the values of the balanced ones, which serve as a democratic example.

What about analysis in this essay?

I love your political system in spite of what you so often have told me about mafias in city halls and police departments. It is still a better system than the autocratic regimes of left and right or the aristocratic traditions which permit in positions of power only those people whose forebears were financially successful.

I love you for scientific and technical reasons. Your medicine, for example, helps me more than the medicine of any other country. Yes, you did inherit many ideas and people from Europe, as you so often say, but your present-day contribution is great. It is great in individual fields, but also because you collect huge amounts of information and classify it and make it available to all of us through your National Institutes of Health.

I love you for the great progress you are making in so many fields of knowledge. You are contributing immeasurably to the advancement of Man. I remember how angry you were when I first mentioned this, and how you started speaking against physics because it led to the atomic bomb, but you forget that nobody now blames the inventors of dynamite in the nineteenth century. When we look from a distance, we know, for example, that Constantinople eventually would have fallen to the Ottoman Turks, even if they had not been using the most advanced cannons of the time. The barbarian invasions of Europe were no better than the wars fought with the aid of gunpowder, and they may well have been much worse.

Are there subdivisions? Does one start here?

I love you also for your support of culture. You are helping many artists by buying their works or inviting them to perform in your country. You always remind me that you stole them from Europe and the Indian subcontinent, but you must remember that many of them would have had a difficult time in their own countries, where for economic or political reasons they would never have risen to prominence. Do not forget, my dear friend, that you give people more opportunities and allow them freedom to express themselves. Even when they cannot leave their countries, you often support them there through your foundations.

And here we come to your greatest contribution: education at the university level. No other country has encouraged so many young men and women to teach in their own ways. No other country has helped so many people to be trained in so many fields, old and new. When, far in the future, the history of education will be written, you will be recognized as the nation that began the change from the education of a few to the education of all. You have told me that the Russians educate many more people, but are they doing so in as many fields? Are they really educating or merely training in highly specialized fields? In any case, I doubt if they would have opened their schools to more students if you had not broken the aristocratic traditions in education and helped us all.

The climax apparently.

You need a conclusion, you said, about my motives for this love affair. Here it is: I cannot forget that you have helped and inspired me in so many ways—from the purely economic and military to the cultural ones. I admit it to few people, even only rarely to myself, but I always hope that in a moment of crisis in my personal life, profession, social class, nation, or global region, that you are going to do it again. I hope you will always be great and strong so that I can come and place my head on your knees, my very, very, beloved American.

Seemingly, the conclusion does not come at the end. Or is this a second conclusion?

And now—I breathe because I have been crying from pleasure feeling your hand on my head—I can tell you who I am. I am the Frenchman who was starving for the first time in his life and received food from you. I am the inhabitant of Rio de Janeiro who had water piped to his home because of your aid. I am the Southeast Asian farmer (not Vietnamese) who learned to use a better strain of rice to increase his food and income. I am a Vietnamese bourgeois from the south and (do not reveal it) from the north also. I am a European laborer who hopes to be admitted to your country next year, a democrat from Argentina or Spain or Greece who still hopes that you will intervene, a Polish nationalist who hopes that our love affair may some day enable him to divorce Russia (age-old unhappy affair), an African scientist who expects to get his Ph.D. in an American university, an author, a poet, an archaeologist who received your support. I am a young man from everywhere who hopes to enter one of your universities and learn, learn, learn, gain prestige in my own country, and, when angry, be free to form a new group—left side of my face bearded, right side shaved—and express all my age-old grievances against you and see my photograph on the front page of your newspapers.

Compare this with the conclusion to the first letter.

I am a complex, simple man. I hope that all my dreams will come true and in the meantime I always, assuming at least some dreams come true, will love you my very beloved American.

Reading and Interpreting

1. Which of the two letters seems to you to make the better case?

2. Paragraph 7 in each letter deals with the same subject—racism. How many other paragraphs are similarly parallel in subject matter? How can the writer hate and love for the same general reasons?

Writing Techniques

1. Like Safire, Doxiadis organizes his essay by giving all of one side and then all of the other. He could, however, have first broken his subject into parts and then contrasted each of these. What are the advantages and limitations of each method?

2. How does Doxiadis use repetition as a device for clarifying his organization for the reader? Compare the introductions, conclusions, and topic sentences in the two letters.

3. What is the effect of dealing with general topics in the same order in the two letters?

Suggestions for Writing

Try using the method of this selection to write two letters of your own—"I hate you" and "I love you"—on another country, if you happen to have lived in one or have studied about it. Or choose a city, the faculty, the police, a shopping center, or anything for which you can collect particular instances to support your two views.

TWO POEMS

a. Richard Wilbur *has taught at Harvard and Wesleyan Universities and his poems have won the Pulitzer Prize and the National Book Award;* **b. William Shakespeare's** *sonnets are among the most admired poetry in the language.*

a. *Mind,* **Richard Wilbur**

Mind in its purest play is like some bat
That beats about in caverns all alone,
Contriving by a kind of senseless wit
Not to conclude against a wall of stone.

It has no need to falter or explore;
Darkly it knows what obstacles are there,
And so may weave and flitter, dip and soar
In perfect courses through the blackest air.

And has this simile a like perfection?
The mind is like a bat. Precisely. Save
That in the very happiest intellection
A graceful error may correct the cave.

b. *Sonnet 18,* **William Shakespeare**

Shall I compare thee to a summer's day?
Thou art more lovely and more temperate:
Rough winds do shake the darling buds of May,
And summer's lease hath all too short a date:
Sometime too hot the eye of heaven shines,
And often is his gold complexion dimm'd;
And every fair from fair sometime declines,
By chance or nature's changing course untrimm'd:
But thy eternal summer shall not fade
Nor lose possession of that fair thou ow'st,
Nor shall Death brag thou wand'rest in his shade,
When in eternal lines to time thou grow'st;
    So long as men can breathe or eyes can see,
    So long lives this and this gives life to thee.

Reading and Interpreting

1. Explain the exception in the last two lines of Wilbur's poem.

2. What is the main idea of Shakespeare's sonnet? How directly does the comparison develop it?

Writing Techniques

1. Comparison and contrast are especially useful devices for poets, sometimes illustrating minor points in a poem and sometimes, as here, directing the entire development. How do the uses of comparison differ in the two poems?

2. Shakespeare develops his poem by making comparison on a series of specific topics. List the topics on which he compares the person addressed to a summer's day.

Suggestions for Writing

Extended metaphors like those in the two poems are not easily contrived, but as an exercise you might try a paragraph developing a comparison of this sort—in a poem if you wish.

TWO FACES OF THE SAME EVE   **61**
Stephanie Harrington

Stephanie Harrington *is a free-lance writer and movie critic; this piece was published in the* New York Times Magazine.

To the Editor:
  I am a survivor. (What woman isn't?) Of a suffocating marriage, two destructive affairs, even thoughts of suicide. (I suppose that sounds melodramatic—arsenic after black lace.) I was brought up to believe that a   *arsenic* *woman could live only through a man. And social and economic realities make it hard to do anything else. But your magazine let me know that I*   *magazine* *wasn't alone, that I am not crazy, that there are women all across the country who are determined to start considering their own needs and to accomplish something* for themselves by themselves. *The support I find in your magazine has given me the courage to finally reorder my priorities.*
  Right on!
                                             EMMA BOVARY
                                             Yonville Parish

But . . . a letter to the editor of what? Of *Ms.,* the political self-help magazine whose publisher says, "I think of us as a kind of connective tissue for women all across this country who felt isolated until we came along and let them know they were not alone, that they certainly weren't crazy and that they shouldn't feel guilty"? Or of *Cosmopolitan,* the psychosexual self-help magazine, whose articles editor says, "There are a lot of women out there who need help and they are $100 and 50 miles away from a psychiatrist, and what we are trying to do is absolve them of guilt by letting them know they're not alone"?

psychiatrist

Ms. or *Cosmopolitan?* But isn't the idea that the same woman could feel solidarity with *both Ms.* and *Cosmopolitan* a little like saying liberty or death is an echo, not a choice? After all, there is *Ms.,* the feminist monthly, grabbing women by the consciousness in every issue and asking them, "Can you learn to love yourselves and change the system?" And *Cosmopolitan,* in the 10th year of its fleshly and highly profitable incarnation as the masscult update of the "Kama Sutra" as interpreted by Baby Snooks. *Cosmopolitan,* the magazine that goes on and on asking women in italicized Cosmospeak: "Don't you just *love* loving men, and don't you feel just *miserable* when you *don't have* a man to love, and wouldn't you love to learn how to love them *better,* and without fear or guilt and—*best of all*—to get the *right* one to love *you?"*

The contrast takes shape.

incarnation

But if the idea of *Cosmopolitan* as an alternative to *Ms.* seems only as serious as the idea that Helen Gurley Brown, the prototypical Cosmo Girl, will one day emerge from a phone booth and stand revealed as Rosa Luxemburg, the fact is that both magazines rode in on a tide of "revolution"—cultural revolutions set in motion by a technology that has reduced the amount of time women have to spend on household chores and by a rising living standard that has sent more women out to work to supplement family incomes.

Cosmopolitan has been the working "girl's" chronicle of the sexual revolution that took off in the nineteen-sixties; *Ms.* is the journalistic clearing-house for the current phase of the feminist revolt, which had its political seeds in the civil-rights and student movements of the nineteen-sixties. Both magazines are trying to be supportive of women who, to varying degrees, feel alienated from some or all traditional feminine roles and are attempting, some radically, some moderately, to live outside the old assumptions. But one revolution does not always wait on another. So the reformists of Cosmo Consciousness and the relatively radical cadres of *Ms.* Consciousness, who insist that the sexual revolution freed women "only from the right to say no to sexual intercourse," are working out their life-styles side by side, occasionally coming together on issues like economic equality and emancipation from housework.

Comparison of the two magazines.

cadres

So there is the Cosmo Girl, ready for an article like "How to Make a Man's Pay," but not beyond day-dreaming over "The Poor Girl's Guide to America's Rich Young Men"; there she is, considering the questions of "Women, Men and Kinky Sex" and whether "One Man [Is] Truly Enough," knowing that, out there in Peoria, she is on the front lines, that the keypunch operator sitting next to her isn't even *ready* for *Cosmopolitan*. And at that very same moment, the magazine that is the Cosmo Girl's guide to revolution, is, to feminists, a journal of reaction.

Helen Gurley Brown, however, did have her day on the barri- *barricades*
cades. Even if she did not start the sexual revolution, as she insists in
her own defense against those who greeted *Cosmopolitan* as the Gos- A major
pel according to Jezebel, she was its one-woman Committee of Corre- subdivision?
spondence. In the process of, as she says, "simply reporting what *is*,
and trying to be helpful if someone is troubled by what is," she tried
to separate guilt from sex, and that made her as suspect as fluoride or *fluoride*
the New Deal to fundamentalist believers in clean thoughts and the
American Way. She was denounced by Jerry Lewis and shouted
down on television talk shows. "*Cosmopolitan*," *Ms.* editor Gloria
Steinem observes, "was a step forward from the formula of the traditional magazines that if you got divorced or had affairs before marriage, you would come to a bad end. . . . If one magazine says
women are sexual, it's an improvement. In the land of the blind the
one-eyed is king." (*Sic:* queen?)

And Steinem ought to know, having been, between 1963 and A deft limited
1970, a contributing editor to *Glamour, The Ladies' Home Journal,* transition.
McCall's and *Seventeen.* She also wrote for the now defunct *Show*
magazine (making her first big splash by working as a Playboy
Bunny and writing an exposé for *Show* called "A Bunny's Tale"), *Esquire,* and *The New York Times Magazine.* But, as she has complained,
and at least one male editor has conceded, until she became a contributing editor to *New York* magazine, she could not get the political
assignments she wanted and male writers usually got. The general
rule that women either wrote for women's publications or were assigned to "women's stories" was important in the founding of *Ms.*

And, if Steinem and Brown are not like Bogey and Claude Rains Is this a
in the final fade-out of "Casablanca," walking arm in arm into the subdivision
mists of the antisexist resistance, Brown has had still another revolu- within a
tionary thrust—her assumption that the American Dream is not an subdivision?
exclusively male fantasy, that women, too, could take up the challenge of Horatio Alger. It is an assumption drawn from her own
life—the saga of a scared little girl from Green Forest, Ark., who *saga*
overcame a fatherless, financially insecure Depression childhood,
helped care for a sister crippled by polio, worked as a secretary for 18
years, pushed her natural resources to their limits (she had her acne

scars sanded off, her nose fixed, her hairline adjusted, she dieted, exercised and gulped vitamins), and was, at long last, made an advertising copywriter because her boss was impressed by her "entertaining letters." And, at the desperate age of 37, this tiny, whispery woman whose apparent fragility belies a survivor's determination, made the big M—marriage to movie executive David Brown (who produced "The Sting"). At his urging she wrote "Sex and the Single Girl," the how-to book on the pursuit of, uh . . . relationships, that catapulted her into the wonderful world of celebrity.

"My own credo," Brown has said, "has been to marshal everything I had" and keep "on struggling and working and . . . one thing led to another. . . . " Helen Gurley Brown's credo. America's credo! Hard work, self-reliance, courage, stick-to-it-iveness. And Brown really *believes* that we can *all* climb, climb up Sunshine Mountain. So every month in *Cosmopolitan,* her faith in the *possibilities* inherent in the sensual union of the Greatest Happiness Principle and the Protestant Ethic are packaged in the inspirational rhetoric of Coué, Norman Vincent Peale, Dale Carnegie, Dr. David Reuben, Adam Smith, and Betty and Veronica. If feminist protests have led her to wonder if it's a disservice to promote the bosomy, artificial Cosmo cover girl as a physical ideal, to push "young women to be something they may not be able to become," she has concluded that just trying "makes you feel good." And every month she exhorts her girls to *apply* themselves to their sexual activity with persistence and optimism, to follow a regimen of physical fitness and good grooming, to employ Yankee ingenuity and the ethics of an account executive. While *Ms.,* adorned with coverpersons like George McGovern, Bella Abzug, Helen Gahagan Douglas and Wonder Woman, discusses the need to redefine sex roles and to overhaul our economic system to ensure equal opportunity for *all* women, Brown instructs her readers on how each of them can try to carve for *herself* a bigger, juicier piece of the existing social and economic pie.

Yet, between the cleavage on the cover and the ads for Frederick's of Hollywood underwear in the back, *Cosmopolitan* has run articles on Bella Abzug, Margaret Meade and Bernadette Devlin. And this does not contradict *Cosmopolitan*'s editorial thrust because these women, whatever their politics (a subject that does not engage Brown), have been *successful.* Brown wants her girls to *achieve.* Isn't it progress if a magazine that encouraged upward mobility with "The Complete Husband-Hunting Wardrobe" and "The Case for A Less-Than-Red-Hot Marriage Versus Not Marrying At All" is now also insisting that a woman can be "a sex object *and* president of General Motors"?

This is not to say that man-trapping is not still the primary preoccupation of the Cosmo Girl—just that the approach is not quite so

Why does the tone change here?

Are other types of development being used within contrast?

Why not omit this paragraph?

crass. "Today," Brown explains, "our major articles have to do with women understanding their own psyches, and men's, so men and women can live together." And with articles advising women on how to deal with shyness, anger, frigidity, masochism or the fear of commitment, articles telling women they are not alone in their anxieties, *Cosmopolitan* reflected very early the growing national sense of togetherness in neurosis. It was a media pioneer in the pop therapy of discovering, through the public sharing of private hang-ups, that the problems we had clung to as our own were pretty common after all. In her efforts, then, to enhance the male-female connection, Brown anticipated consciousness-raising—the psycho-political tool with which feminists hope to loosen that connection.

So, *Cosmopolitan* contains as much feminism as it can incorporate into its own message—just enough to keep up with events without losing readers. The rock of Helen Gurley Brown's faith, the revealed truth for everyone at *Cosmopolitan*, from the publisher to the elevator man, is that Helen Gurley Brown knows whom she is trying to reach—herself 20 years ago. Which is to say, demographically, a single, man-hunting career woman between the ages of 18 and 34 who lives in a metropolitan area outside New York. And 60 per cent of *Cosmopolitan*'s readers are 18 to 34 (70 per cent of *Ms.* readers are), 78 per cent of them do live in metropolitan areas (66.6 per cent of *Ms.* readers do) and 61.3 per cent do work (74.6 per cent of *Ms.* readers work). But only 37.8 per cent of *Cosmopolitan*'s nearly two million readers are single, while 49.8 per cent of *Ms.*'s 400,000 readers are. More than twice as many *Ms.* readers as *Cosmopolitan* readers attended college, and more than a third of *Ms.* readers hold advanced degrees. *Ms.* readers, nearly half of whom personally earn $10,000 or more, are more affluent than those of *Cosmopolitan*. And only 5.5 per cent of *Ms.* readers also read *Cosmopolitan*.

After all, a woman who is a college graduate and earning $14,000 a year is not apt to take kindly to being called "little love" or "little Cosmo girl," as Brown addresses her readers. Nor is she likely to respond to the rococo girlishness of *Cosmopolitan*'s style, which is passed on to writers in a 16-page, mimeographed pamphlet, "Editing (and Writing) Rules for *Cosmopolitan*," which offers observations like "the theme [of an article] will *probably* have something to do with the title," and suggestions that "profound statements must be attributed to somebody appropriate (even if the writer has to invent the authority)," and a warning to "avoid attacking advertisers . . . and where convenient mention advertised brands rather than nonadvertised competition."

And a woman with a graduate degree, whose taste in magazines runs to *Time, Newsweek, Psychology Today, Saturday Review World* and

What does this do to the direction of the piece?

Notice specific detail.

Is this a different sort of evidence?

A long topic sentence. Would a short one be clearer?

Intellectual Digest (the top five choices of *Ms.* readers — not one of their top 10 is another woman's magazine), is not likely to buy a magazine whose editor insists that ideas be made "baby simple" and is, as she emphasizes, "dedicated to not doing merely *critical* reviews [of books, movies, etc.] because . . . the best thing we can do for girls *and* the books is . . . to *recommend* books that would bring a girl pleasure."

Ms., on the other hand, does not provide the promise of sweet   Contrast again.
delights the Cosmo girl craves. After all, a woman who likes her celebrity interviews to star Elizabeth Taylor or Robert Redford, or Robert Redford or Elizabeth Taylor, is not going to feel any urgency about "Barbara Mikulski and The Blue-Collar Worker" or thrill to *Ms.*'s wall-to-wall reports on the progress of the Equal Rights Amendment.

In its "Gazette News," in which readers share experiences and exchange information on mutual-help projects; in articles on women in higher education, in law and medicine, in the space program, in offices and in factories, and in articles on the almost total exclusion of women from finance, *Ms.* has provided valuable information on the status of women and ways to improve it. Some of it is digestible, but much of the prose is as riveting as the telephone directory — the gray, not the yellow pages.

There are, however, enough women on both levels of consciousness to support both magazines in profitable co-existence. . . .

[After more discussion of both magazines, the article concludes that Brown "is selling half a feminist magazine, garbled though it is, to women who might otherwise buy none."]

Reading and Interpreting

1. Does this article have a main thesis? Is its main point embodied in the final paragraph of this excerpt? Is it mainly about the two magazines, about Helen Gurley Brown, the editor of *Cosmopolitan,* or about the status of women in our society?

2. What are some of Harrington's criticisms of the policies of *Cosmopolitan?*

Writing Techniques

1. The introduction is an imaginary letter from Emma Bovary, the central character in Flaubert's novel *Madame Bovary,* who commits suicide after a dull marriage and unsuccessful love affairs. How does the introduction lead to the contrast central to the essay?

2. Describe the way comparison and contrast are organized in this essay. Is the method more like that of Safire or that of Doxiadis?

3. How does analysis contribute to the organization of the essay?

Word Study

The English language has been distinguished from its earliest history for the ease with which it borrows from other languages. The following words in Harrington's article came into English from other languages: *arsenic, magazine, psychiatrist, incarnation, cadres, barricades, fluoride, saga.* Look up each one in an etymological dictionary or a historical dictionary such as the *Oxford English Dictionary,* and indicate the language in which each originated. Then select three of the words and write a paragraph on each, constructing as much as you can of its history.

Suggestions for Writing

1. Write a paper comparing two magazines or newspapers you read, selecting topics treated by both and then considering ways in which the periodicals agree or differ in their attitudes on them.

2. Use Harrington's essay to suggest some topics you might want to develop on women and their problems in our day.

THE THIRD MOST POWERFUL MAN IN THE WORLD   **62**
Norman Cousins

Norman Cousins, *more than any other person, has made the* Saturday Review, *of which he is editor, a crystalizer of American thought, not only about literature and the arts, but notably about international affairs and the part that the United States should play in them. The following is one of his editorials.*

NEXT to Gerald Ford and Leonid Brezhnev, the most powerful man in the world is not Mao Tse-tung or the head of any other government. The third most powerful man in the world is a commander of a Trident submarine.

A single Trident submarine today carries more destructive force than all the military establishments of Great Britain, Italy, Spain, Brazil, Argentina, West Germany, Japan, the Philippines, India, and Pakistan put together.

A Trident has built into it an undersea launching platform for the thermonuclear bombs, some of which contain more explosive force than a thousand atomic bombs of the kind that destroyed Hiroshima in 1945.

thermonuclear

Theoretically, the American people ought to feel completely secure in the fact of such power being deployed in their behalf. The Trident has almost unlimited mobility; it can launch an attack on any country of its choosing, yet it is practically immune to counter-attack by being able to hide in the seas.

But there are problems. A Trident has both the advantages and the disadvantages of being an autonomous war machine. The men who operate it are in a position, theoretically at least, to make their own decisions about the use of the total power at their command. Suppose one of them decides, out of what he believes to be a higher patriotism, to activate a thermonuclear bomb. Trident commanders are human beings subject to all the stresses and quirks of human personality that make other mortals fallible and unpredictable. We can be certain that every test for stability and reliability has been applied in the selection of Trident officers. But psychologists cannot guarantee that any individual will not be seized at some point by a totally irrational idea or by an aberration. All we know for sure is that the Trident officers have in their hands more power than had been accumulated by human beings in recorded history up through 1945.

autonomous

aberration

Meanwhile, the Soviet Union may not have submarines with Trident capability, but what they have is ominous enough — snorkel-type subs with launching platforms for intermediate-range missiles. This relative lack of range does not prevent the Soviet submarines from getting close enough to our shores to make every major American city a potential target. And the same questions must be raised about the danger that a Soviet submarine commander might take it into his head to trigger a holocaust.

ominous

potential

Military and political annals are replete with examples of men — from the lowliest orderlies to generals and rulers — who took it upon themselves to use available force for an insane purpose. As recently as the Vietnam War, there was the example of the bombing of Hanoi without the express order of the President. Some years ago a French colonel flying over Algeria dropped bombs without authorization on a populous target.

holocaust

The main threat to human life in this world has invariably been represented by the irresponsible use of force. Even well-intentioned men have lost their sensibilities when they have had unchecked power at their disposal. Nothing was of greater concern to the American Founding Fathers than the ease with which men in authority collect power and then abuse it. If John Adams and Alexander Hamilton were alive today, what would they say about the fact that submarines of the United States and Soviet Union are roaming the oceans and that their commanders have the ready means to annihilate an entire population and start civilization on a downward spiral? *annihilate*

The Trident submarine is a logical development in an illogical situation. Given the existence of an explosive that can incinerate a million human beings, it is logical in military terms to try to devise highly mobile delivery systems that enjoy a wide margin for error and that cannot be easily hunted down and destroyed. *incinerate*

But there is a higher logic that needs to be asserted today. That logic must begin with a full understanding of what nuclear war is all about. Historically, the main purpose of a nation's foreign policy is to protect the lives, values, and property of its citizens. If this purpose becomes impossible because of the nature of nuclear explosives, then much of the official policy on national security is not security at all but an illogical venture in mass suicide. The hard truth is that the only security for the American people today, or for any people, is to be found through the control of force rather than the pursuit of force. In turn, such control of force must be connected to the existence of a world order capable of administering justice and dealing with basic causes for war.

This is a good time for anyone who is running for the Presidency to talk sense about the connection between world peace and a workable world order. And unless a Presidential candidate understands the global nature of most of our other problems, he disqualifies himself to deal with the major issue of our time.

Is it too much to hope that the Presidential candidates will address themselves to the question of a world made safe and fit for human habitation? This is the main test. Everything else is peripheral. *peripheral*

Reading and Interpreting

This editorial was written during the presidential campaign of 1976. Does it still have pertinence? Do the reasons for choosing a President carry over into the responsibility of a candidate once he is elected?

Writing Techniques

Presumably this piece is basically argument. Which of the strategies described in this and earlier chapters are here used for development? Does Cousins use any strategies that have not been considered? How does he use comparison and contrast to support his argument?

Word Study

From the context write a brief definition of each of the words in the margins (*thermonuclear, autonomous, aberration, ominous, potential, holocaust, annihilate, incinerate, peripheral*). Then look up each word, paying particular attention to its origin, and revise your definitions as appropriate.

Suggestions for Writing

If you voted for an administration now in control at the federal, state, or other level, can you now recall why you cast your ballot as you did? Has the administration lived up to its promises, or to your expectations? Write an editorial on the responsibilities of public officers and in fulfilling or failing to fulfill these obligations, using the evidence you have observed.

HEBRAISM AND HELLENISM
Matthew Arnold

63

Matthew Arnold *(1822–1888), poet, teacher, and critic, is known especially as a champion of "sweetness and light" during the nineteenth-century scientific revolution. The selection is from* Culture and Anarchy.

LET me go back for a moment to Bishop Wilson, who says: "First, never go against the best light you have; secondly, take care that your light be not darkness." We show, as a nation, laudable energy and persistence in walking according to the best light we have, but are not quite careful enough, perhaps, to see that our light be not darkness. This is only another version of the old story that energy is our strong point and favorable characteristic, rather than intelligence. But we may give to this idea a more general form still, in which it will have a yet larger range of application. We may regard this energy driving at practice, this paramount sense of the obligation of

Two forces to be compared.

duty, self-control, and work, this earnestness is going manfully with the best light we have, as one force. And we may regard the intelligence driving at those ideas which are, after all, the basis of right practice, the ardent sense for all the new and changing combinations of them which man's development brings with it, the indomitable impulse to know and adjust them perfectly, as another force. And these two forces we may regard as in some sense rivals—rivals not by the necessity of their own nature, but as exhibited in man and his history,—and rivals dividing the empire of the world between them. And to give these forces names from the two races of men who have supplied the most signal and splendid manifestations of them, we may call them respectively the forces of Hebraism and Hellenism. Hebraism and Hellenism,—between these two points of influence moves our world. At one time it feels more powerfully the attraction of one of them, at another time of the other; and it ought to be, though it never is, evenly and happily balanced between them.

Terms to distinguish the forces.

   The final aim of both Hellenism and Hebraism, as of all great spiritual disciplines, is no doubt the same: man's perfection or salvation. The very language which they both of them use in schooling us to reach this aim is often identical. Even when their language indicates by variation—sometimes a broad variation, often a but slight and subtle variation—the different courses of thought which are uppermost in each discipline, even then the unity of the final end and aim is still apparent. To employ the actual words of that discipline with which we ourselves are all of us most familiar, and the words of which, therefore, come most home to us, that final end and aim is "that we might be partakers of the divine nature." These are the words of a Hebrew apostle, but of Hellenism and Hebraism alike this is, I say, the aim. When the two are confronted, as they very often are confronted, it is nearly always with what I may call a rhetorical purpose; the speaker's whole design is to exalt and enthrone one of the two, and he uses the other only as a foil and to enable him the better to give effect to his purpose. Obviously, with us, it is usually Hellenism which is thus reduced to minister to the triumph of Hebraism. There is a sermon on Greece and the Greek spirit by a man never to be mentioned without interest and respect, Frederick Robertson, in which this rhetorical use of Greece and the Greek spirit, and the inadequate exhibition of them necessarily consequent upon this, is almost ludicrous, and would be censurable it it were not to be explained by the exigencies of a sermon. On the other hand, Heinrich Heine, and other writers of his sort gave us the spectacle of the tables completely turned, and of Hebraism brought in just as a foil and contrast to Hellenism, and to make the superiority of Hellenism more manifest. In both these cases there is injustice and misrepresentation. The aim and end of both Hebraism and Hellenism is,

Similarities in aim—confusion?

Examples to illustrate.

as I have said, one and the same, and this aim and end is august and
admirable.

Still, they pursue this aim by very different courses. The uppermost idea with Hellenism is to see things as they really are; the uppermost idea with Hebraism is conduct and obedience. Nothing can do
away with this ineffaceable difference. The Greek quarrel with the body
and its desires is, that they hinder right thinking; the Hebrew quarrel
with them is, that they hinder right acting. "He that keepth the law,
happy is he"; "Blessed is the man that feareth the Eternal, that deligh-
teth greatly in his commandments"; — that is the Hebrew notion of felicity; and, pursued with passion and tenacity, this notion would not let
the Hebrew rest till, as is well known, he had at last got out of the law a
network of prescriptions to enwrap his whole life, to govern every moment of it, every impulse, every action. The Greek notion of felicity, on
the other hand, is perfectly conveyed in these words of a great French
moralist: *"C'est le bonheur des hommes,"* — when? when they abhor that
which is evil? — no; when they exercise themselves in the law of the
Lord day and night? — no; when they die daily? — no; when they walk
about the New Jerusalem with palms in their hands — no; but when they
think aright, when their thought hits: *"quand ils pensent juste."* At the
bottom of both the Greek and the Hebrew notion is the desire, native in
man, for reason and the will of God, the feeling after the universal order, — in a word, the love of God. But, while Hebraism seizes upon certain plain, capital intimations of the universal order, and rivets itself,
one may say, with unequalled grandeur of earnestness and intensity on
the study and observance of them, the bent of Hellenism is to follow,
with flexible activity, the whole play of the universal order, to be appre-
hensive of missing any part of it, of sacrificing one part to another, to
slip away from resting in this or that intimation of it, however capital.
An unclouded clearness of mind, an unimpeded play of thought, is
what this bent drives at. The governing idea of Hellenism is *spontaneity
of consciousness;* that of Hebraism, *strictness of conscience.* . . .

*Contrast in
pursuit of aim.*

*Topic-by-topic
contrast.*

Reading and Interpreting

1. In you own words identify Arnold's distinction between
Hebraism and Hellenism.

2. Can Arnold's distinctions be applied to society today? Which
of the two ways of pursuing "man's perfections or salvation" would
apply best to our society?

Writing Techniques

1. Although this excerpt from Arnold's longer essay is developed mainly by comparison and contrast, the organization differs
from that of Safire and Doxiadis. What is the basic difference?

2. The final paragraph presents two views on a series of topics. What are the topics?

Word Study

The following words from the first paragraph of Arnold's essay have been formed by adding common suffixes to the base words: *laudable, persistence, characteristic, earnestness, combinations, indomitable, dividing, respectively, influence, powerfully.* Try to identify each suffix and to determine its use, in signaling the meaning or the function of a word. Then look up each suffix in a dictionary and write a brief definition of it.

Suggestions for Writing

Write a paper developed by comparison and contrast using the kind of organizations Arnold employs—that is, comparing on one topic after another rather than presenting one view entirely and then the other. You may wish to rewrite an earlier comparison paper shifting it to this pattern.

TWO ANALOGIES

64

Analogies frequently make up parts of paragraphs, but occasionally they are extended, as in the following: **a. Edward Bellamy,** *in* Looking Backward *(1888), endeavored to view the world in the year 2000;* **b. Stephen Leacock,** *professor at McGill University, Canada, was one of the most delectable humorists of his day; he also popularized knowledge, as in the posthumous excerpt below, from* Last Leaves *(1945).*

a. Edward Bellamy

BY way of attempting to give the reader some general impression of the way people lived together in those days, and especially of the relations of the rich and poor to one another, perhaps I cannot do better than to compare society as it then was to a prodigious coach which the masses of humanity were harnessed to and dragged toilsomely along a very hilly and sandy road. The driver was hungry, and permitted no lagging, though the pace was necessarily very slow. Despite the difficulty of drawing the coach at all along so hard a road, the top was covered with passengers who never got down, even at the steepest ascents. These seats on top were very breezy and comfortable. Well up out of the dust, their occupants could enjoy the scenery at their leisure, or critically discuss the merits of the straining team. Naturally such places were in great demand and the competition for them was keen, everyone seeking as the first end in life to secure a seat on the coach for himself and to leave it to his child after him. By the rule of the coach a man could leave his seat to whom he wished, but on the other hand there were many accidents by which it might at any time be wholly lost. For all they were so easy, the seats were very insecure, and at every sudden jolt of the coach persons were slipping out of them and falling to the ground, where they were instantly compelled to take hold of the rope and help drag the coach on which they had before ridden so pleasantly. It was naturally regarded as a terrible misfortune to lose one's seat, and the apprehension that this might happen to them or their friends was a constant cloud upon the happiness of those who rode.

But did they think only of themselves? you ask. Was not their very luxury rendered intolerable to them by comparison with the lot of their brothers and sisters in the harness, and the knowledge that their own weight added to their toil? Had they no compassion for fellow beings from whom fortune only distinguished them? Oh, yes; commiseration was frequently expressed by those who rode for those who had to pull the coach, especially when the vehicle came to a bad place in the road, as it was constantly doing, or to a particularly steep hill. At such times, the desperate straining of the team, their agonized leaping and plunging under the pitiless lashing of hunger, the many who fainted at the rope and were trampled in the mire, made a very distressing spectacle, which often called forth highly creditable displays of feeling on the top of the coach. At such times the passengers would call down encouragingly to the toilers of the rope, exhorting them to patience, and holding out hopes of possible compensation in another world for the hardness of their lot, while others contributed to buy salves and liniments for the crippled and injured. It was agreed that it was a great pity that the coach should be so hard to pull, and there was a sense of general relief when the specially bad piece of road was gotten over. This relief was not, indeed, wholly on account of the team, for there was always some danger at these bad places of a general overturn in which all would lose their seats.

b.   Stephen Leacock

TILL these researches began, people commonly thought of atoms as something like birdseed — little round, solid particles, ever so little, billions to an inch. They were small. But they were there.

You could weigh them. You could apply to them all the laws of Isaac Newton about weight and velocity and mass and gravitation—in other words, the whole of first-year physics.

Let us try to show what Rutherford did to the atom. Imagine to yourself an Irishman whirling a shillelagh around his head with the rapidity and dexterity known only in Tipperary or Donegal. If you come anywhere near, you'll get hit with the shillelagh. Now make it go faster; faster still; get it going so fast that you can't tell which is Irishman and which is shillelagh. The whole combination has turned into a green blur. If you shoot a bullet at it, it will probably go through, as there is mostly nothing there. Yet if you go up against it, it won't hit you now, because the shillelagh is going so fast that you will seem to come against a solid surface. Now make the Irishman smaller and the shillelagh longer. In fact, you don't need the Irishman at all; just his force, his Irish determination, so to speak. Just keep that, the *disturbance*. And you don't need the shillelagh either, just the *field of force* that it sweeps. There! Now put in two Irishmen and two shillelaghs and reduce them in the same way to one solid body— at least it seems solid but you can shoot bullets through it anywhere now. What you have now is a hydrogen atom—one proton and one electron flying around as a *disturbance* in space. Put in more Irishmen and more shillelaghs—or, rather, more protons and electrons—and you get other kinds of atoms. Put in a whole lot—eleven protons, eleven electrons; that is a sodium atom. Bunch the atoms together into combinations called molecules, themselves flying around—and there you are! That's solid matter, and nothing in it at all except disturbance. You're standing on it right now: the molecules are beating against your feet. But there is nothing there, and nothing in your feet. This may help you to understand how "waves," ripples of disturbance—for instance, the disturbance you call radio—go right through all matter, indeed right through *you*, as if you weren't there. You see, you aren't.

The peculiar thing about this atomic theory was that whatever the atoms were, birdseed or disturbance, it made no difference in the way they acted. They followed all the laws of mechanics and motion, or they seemed to. There was no need to change any idea of space or time because of them. Matter was their forte, like wax figures with Artemus Ward.

Reading and Interpreting

1. Bellamy's book pretends to be looking back from the year 2000, so that in this excerpt he is describing the society of his own day. What is the pattern of the society he is describing in his anal-

ogy? Who are the riders on top of the coach? Who are the "toilers of the rope"? What are jolts and accidents?

2. Describe the theory of the atom as Leacock explains it. Is his description accurate in terms of modern physics?

Writing Techniques

1. How do these analogies differ from comparisons like that by Harrington of two women's magazines?

2. Both Bellamy and Leacock are trying to explain complex ideas by describing familiar, concrete objects. What are the advantages and disadvantages of this method?

3. Can you recall any earlier uses of analogy in this book? Would the poems by Wilbur and Shakespeare be candidates?

Suggestions for Writing

1. Developing an analogy is not easy, but try to explain something complex in an extended analogy: learning to write is like learning to swim, a political convention is like a rock concert, war is like a football game, a university is like. . . .

2. Using Bellamy's idea, adapt the stagecoach analogy to some other period in society or some other view of society.

Serious Fun

A laugh is man's indestructible weapon. It is powerful, and it cannot
be eliminated. However, it is hard to use, and most people never
manage to control it much. Usually it can be best answered, if at all,
with another laugh, which may be hard to come by; even the so-called
"last laugh" may be less potent than the first one. Society uses
laughter as a means of social control, where it works so well that
some cultures have needed no police and little by way of a judicial
system; they use public opinion, especially as expressed in laughter.

Humor has become one of the strategies a writer can use, and
some have, to telling effect. Mark Twain would never have attracted
the attention he did as a novelist had he not been a humorist. To a
lesser degree, the same is true of the playwright George Bernard
Shaw, and currently popular novelists like Vonnegut and Heller have
gained their following partly through humor. Humor may be
misused: Justice is sometimes laughed out of the court, and women's
suffrage was delayed in this country, while many men and some
women laughed at it. But although humor, like all other means of
using language, can be diverted to wrong ends, that misuse is no
denial of its power.

Humor in writing varies highly, with both the humorist and
the intended victim. There are so many kinds that we cannot illustrate

them all here. Furthermore, one sort of laughter tends to blend into another, so that they become hard to distinguish and define. One of the most common, on a personal level, is mimicry, which as a formal device becomes *parody.*

For a simple example, look at "Catch Her in the Oatmeal." Anybody who knows J. D. Salinger's *Catcher in the Rye* will recognize that Dan Greenburg's title is a series of plays on words, enhanced by the ludicrous picture we get of "her" wallowing in some gooey gruel—not, one would suppose, the most sensual site for seduction. Thus, when you start the piece you are ready to laugh.

This parody should not, of course, be thought of as an attack on Salinger by Greenburg. He probably considered *Catcher* a very good novel; after all, he dignified it by writing a piece on it for an important magazine. His parody should be considered as serious criticism as well as fun.

And here you might well ask yourself some questions. What is Greenburg implying about Salinger as a novelist and about *Catcher* as a novel? What are the advantages or the limitations of a "review" like this—for we must consider it as a review, not only as a witty joke. What are the limitations of this parody, and perhaps of parody generally? Does it include anything but a sort of lofty mimicry? Certainly wit contributes, but does anything else?

We noted above that we may be laughing for more than one reason, that the various sorts of humor can blend into one another. For an example, look at "The Poll's the Thing." The title echoes Hamlet's much-quoted conclusion, "The play's the thing." Thus we are ready for fun, and we are given a hint that the fun will involve Shakespeare and maybe poll-takers. The resulting piece is not only a parody; it also becomes a *satire,* which is defined in one dictionary as "a literary work in which vices, follies, stupidities, abuses, etc. are held up to ridicule and contempt." What is being satirized in this parody? What comments do the authors seem to want to make?

There are other devices relying on humor, such as *exaggeration.* You should be able to find some examples of that in the selections below. *Wit* and *ridicule* we have already hinted at. And the pieces printed in this section are not the only ones in the book that make at least some use of humor. There is humor of a sort in "Diary for TuTu." And a favorite device for humor is saying just the opposite of what you mean, a favorite trick of Swift's. In fact, there are so many contradictions in "A Modest Proposal," and such outrageous ones, that you might have thought that satire funny, except that laughing would have been as out of place as snickering at a funeral.

The following selections suggest two levels of popular humor: **a.** "Tall tales" are said to be characteristic of frontier American humor; this one, "The Split Dog," was printed in *Fisher's River Scenes and Characters* (1859); **b. Don Marquis** wrote a newspaper column, considerably more sophisticated than most, for the now defunct New York *Sun*. Marquis once wrote his autobiography.

> Born July 29, 1878, at Walnut, Bureau Co., Ill. a member of the Republican party.
>
> My father was a physician, and I had all the diseases of the time free of charge.
>
> Nothing further happened to me until, in the summer of 1896, I left the Republican party to follow the Peerless leader [William Jennings Bryan] to defeat.
>
> In 1900 I returned to the Republican party to accept a position in the Census Bureau. . . . I left the Republican party again and accepted a position as reporter on a Washington paper. . . .
>
> There is little more to tell . . . [except to] add a careful pen picture of myself. . . .
>
> Height, 5 feet 10½ inches; hair, dove colored; scar on little finger of left hand; has assured carriage, walking boldly into good hotels and mixing with patrons on terms of equality; weight 200 pounds; face slightly asymmetrical, but not definitely criminal type. . . . dislikes prunes, tramp poets, and imitations of Kipling; trousers cut loose over hips and seat; would likely come along quietly if arrested.

The bit below, if we may believe Marquis, was written by archy, a loquacious cockroach who sometime during the night would crawl onto the columnist's typewriter and leave a note, doing so by hopping from key to key. Since archy could not hold the shift key down and jump on another key at the same time, he had to get on without capitals and most punctuation.

a.   *A Tall Tale, "The Split Dog"*

HAD me a little dog once was the best rabbit dog you ever saw. Well, he was runnin' a rabbit one day, and some fool had left a scythe lyin' in the grass with the blade straight up. That poor little dog ran smack into it and it split him open from the tip of his nose right straight on down his tail.

Well I saw him fall apart and I ran and slapped him back together. I had jerked off my shirt, so I wrapped him up in that right quick and ran to the house. Set him in a box and poured turpentine all over the shirt. I kept him near the stove. Set him out in the sun part of the time. Oh, I could see him still breathin' a little, and I hoped I wouldn't lose him. And after about three weeks I could see him tryin' to wiggle now and then. Let him stay bandaged another three weeks—and then one morning I heard him bark. So I started unwrappin' him and in a few minutes out he jumped, spry as ever.

But—don't you know—in my excitement, blame if I hadn't put him together wrong-way-to. He had two legs up and two legs down.

Anyhow, it turned out he was twice as good a rabbit dog after that. He'd run on two legs till he got tired, and then flip over and just keep right on.

Aa Lord! That little dog could run goin' and comin', and bark at both ends.

b.   Don Marquis

archy visits washington

> washington d c july
> 23 well boss here
> i am in washington
> watching my step for fear
> some one will push me
> into the food bill up
> to date i am the only thing
> in this country that
> has not been added to it by
> the time this is
> published nothing that
> i have said may be
> true however which is a
> thing that is constantly happening
> to thousands of
> great journalists now in
> washington it is so hot here that
> i get stuck in the asphalt
> every day on my
> way from the senate press
> gallery back to
> shoemakers where the
> affairs of the nation

are habitually settled by
the old settlers it
is so hot that you can
fry fish on the
sidewalk in any part of
town and many people
are here with fish to fry
including now
and then a german
carp i am lodging on
top of the washington
monument where i can
overlook things
you can t keep a good bug
from the top of
the column all the time i
am taking my meals with
the specimens in the
smithsonian institution when i
see any one coming i hold
my breath and look like another
specimen but in the
capitol building there
is no attention paid to me
because there are so
many other insects
around it gives you a
great idea of the
american people when you
see some of the
things they elect after july
27 address me care
st elizabeth hospital
for the insane i am going out
there for a visit with
some of your other
contributors

                                    archy

Reading and Interpreting

What serious criticisms of government in Washington are included in Marquis's column?

Writing Techniques

1. What is the basis for the humor in the tall tale of the split dog? Would the story have been funnier if it had been more plausible?

2. What does Marquis gain by the device of making his speaker a cockroach?

Suggestions for Writing

Tall tales are still a part of American folk humor—the fish that got away or the stories from the annual national liar's contest. Write a tall tale that you have heard, or make one up.

THERE'S A DUMB BASEBALL FAN BORN EVERY MINUTE   **66**
Russell Baker

Russell Baker *is best known for his humorous editorials that appear under the head "Sunday Observer" in* the New York Times Magazine *and are nationally syndicated. One is reprinted below.*

AS a baseball fan, I realize I am supposed to be dumb, and I try hard. Half the sports writers assume I am an idiot, the players hold me in contempt, those company finks who describe games on television assume I am too stupid to tell a real reporter from a swill, and the club owner—well, the club owners deserve a book on the subject of how to get rich by never underestimating the stupidity of the fans.

In Washington not long ago there was a club owner who regularly sold me cold hotdogs for 50 cents apiece. Did I throw the mustard pot at his limousine? Did I stop buying his frigid hotdogs? You bet your collection of World Series peanut shells I didn't. I knew that as a fan I was expected to be dumb enough not to make a scene.

In New York the club owners have just tapped the municipal treasury for $100 million and change to improve the Yankee Stadium. That's money the city could be using to increase the frequency of dog-dung removal from the sidewalk in front of my house, but I'm not kicking. I'm a fan. I am eager to rush up to the Bronx and lay out more cash to get into the stadium I'm paying the city to provide for the club owners.

If enough of us fans don't pay to get in, the club owners might move the team to Ashtabula. Then where would we be? And what is a fan's life without a home team to run up his taxes, sell him cold hotdogs and treat him like a prize ass?

So, as a fan I struggle to be as dumb as possible. There are limits, however, to what can be swallowed, and the hypocrisy of the whole baseball racket as displayed this past week puts a heavy burden on my powers to go on playing the sap.

For one thing, I am unable to shudder with dismay because Charles O. Finley sold three human beings he owned in Oakland to buyers in Boston and New York. My first reaction to the news that he had cleared a cool $3.5 million in the flesh market was a satisfied confirmation of my suspicion that Finley is the smartest operator in baseball.

Because of recent legal changes in the law governing club owners' ownership of people, Finley was about to lose the chance to market those three bodies for any price at all. By getting them sold before his title to them became void, he turned a total loss into a tidy sum of cash. Smart dealer, that Charlie O. Or so I thought.

It was the wrong thing for a fan to think. The next day's paper laid out the proper line in angry columns by sports writers and purple comment from other club owners and fans alike. Finley's sale was bad for baseball.

These are terrible words, the worst that tongue can utter among the faithful. I have never risen to them with true believer's zeal. It seems to me that almost everything that has happened in baseball lately, except last fall's World Series, has been disastrous for baseball. It is hard to get upset by something that is merely bad for baseball.

Nevertheless, the incantation had been uttered and, being a true fan, I put on my dunce cap and tried to follow the argument. It required mind-buckling labors at nincompoopery. First there was this uproar about its being disgraceful to sell players for cash, like so much baled cotton.

No fan with his half-a-brain could accept this. The great Babe Ruth himself was sold for a mere sheaf of bucks, by the Boston Red Sox to the Yankees. Did these whiners mean that the Babe's going to the Bronx and building the House that Ruth Built was bad for baseball? Connie Mack had trafficked widely in bodies almost as glorious, and was in the Hall of Fame. The Hall of Fame was bad for baseball?

Well, there was the complaint that rich teams which could afford to buy would end up owning all the talent and make it impossible for other teams ever to win championships. This was an unpersuasive argument for a fan who had paid 50 cents per stomach spasm to eat cold hotdogs in the realm of the Washington Senators, who hadn't won a championship since the bank holiday.

In some towns, the best the fans could hope for was a perpetual loser because, if your team started winning, the club owner promptly moved it to another town. Calvin Griffith did this with the Senators and Walter O'Malley with the old Brooklyn Dodgers. As a fan, you are resigned to the truth that money brings perpetual winners to some town and that occasional winners in other towns means you will shortly see your team moved across the continent.

Finally, fans were asked to believe that sordid cash transactions would leave them cynical and embittered, that we would now look upon baseball as a crass commercial operation instead of the national pastime. I choked laughing on this one. Players are abandoning the home team franchise from town to town like carnivals in search of unjaded suckers, and they are afraid we might get the impression that somebody in baseball is interested in money.

This is the ultimate insult to a fan's intelligence. I am willing to work hard at being dumb enough to suit this gang of sharpsters, so long as they play the game occasionally between multimillion-dollar heists, but, even as a fan, I can't be stupid enough to weep at the discovery that they aren't the kind of folks who would rather be running a church supper.

Reading and Interpreting

1. Explain the title of Baker's piece. Is he writing as a "dumb" baseball fan?

2. Baker focuses his article on a 1976 incident that has probably been forgotten, but what general comment about baseball — or all professional sports in America — is he making?

Writing Techniques

Pick out at least three sentences in which Baker uses irony to make his point.

Suggestions for Writing

Write what might be copy for a newspaper column about some current sports event, trying to say or imply something about what the event really means.

THE POLL'S THE THING
Robert Lasson and David Eynon

This appeared in the theater section of The New York Times. *If it needs explanation, it is not so funny as it is supposed to be.*

VIRGIN-QUEEN OPINION POLLS, LTD.
12 Grypers Lane
London, England

March 8, 1587

To: David Herrick Producer, Globe Theater, Southwark.

Herewith, presented for the inspection of your good self, the tabulation of our audience opinion survey at the opening night of your recent production, "Hamlet."

LIKE IMMENSELY	3%
LIKE VERY MUCH	4%
LIKED	7%
DIDN'T DISLIKE	21%
DID DISLIKE	38%
DISLIKED INTENSELY	30%
ASKED FOR MONEY BACK	7%

Introduction.

As is our custom, we are appending several representative comments, verbatim, to wit:

POLLSTER: Good evening, sir. I wonder if we might have your occupation and your opinion of tonight's play?

GROUNDLING: Yers, I'm a groundling—and I don't 'old with all that hanky-pank in 'igh places. Sets a bad example for the tykes, seein' Kings and Queens and such, carryin' on like that.

POLLSTER: You feel that too much violence on the stage leads to—

GROUNDLING: Wouldn't surprise me if they was pourin' poison in people's ears all over Southwark, this time next week!

POLLSTER: And if the poisoning incident were deleted, would you feel—

GROUNDLING: Wouldn't have no play then, would you, gov?

POLLSTER: Could we have your occupation, miss, and your impression of tonight's play?

ORANGE GIRL: I'm an Orange Gel, like . . . I sell oranges. (*Seductively*) Know what I mean?

POLLSTER: And the play?

ORANGE GIRL: What play?

POLLSTER: Why, er, "Hamlet." The new drama that opened this evening.

ORANGE GIRL: New one, was it? No better than last week's. What they need is some dancin' and a few ditties. Somethin' you could whistle, like, on your way back to Lunnun. Know what I mean?

POLLSTER: More dancing and singing?

ORANGE GIRL: Would you like an orange, luv—know what I mean?

POLLSTER: Ahem, well, I have a number of interviews to conduct. Tell me, did you feel that the vacillation of the main character sufficiently motivated the rising action to the denouement?

ORANGE GIRL: 'Ere, I'm a *nice* gel, I am. None of them dirty French questions, now. I got oranges to sell—know what I mean?

POLLSTER: Good evening, sir. Could I have your occupation and your reaction to tonight's play.

MARLOWE: Yeah, I'm a play doctor. I'm Abe Marlowe.

POLLSTER: What did you think of the play?

MARLOWE: You're in trouble, sweetie.

POLLSTER: How do you mean?

MARLOWE: Look, what kind of playwright kills off the ingenue in the fourth act? That stuff may go in Stratford, but not in London, Jack.

POLLSTER: You feel that Ophelia's death—

MARLOWE: Look, it's bad enough to show a teenager going psychotic right on the stage, but this antihero stuff . . . well, you can't . . . look, a writer can't parade his private sickness on a stage and expect sophisticated Elizabethans to pay money to watch it.

POLLSTER: Do you feel the producers should call you in to do some doctoring?

MARLOWE: That's their business. But if this bit runs a week, may I be stabbed to death this very night!

POLLSTER: Good evening, sir, might I have your occupation and your impression of tonight's drama?

KING JEROME: My name is Jerome the Listless. I am a king by trade.

POLLSTER: Ah! How's business, Your Majesty?

KING JEROME: Regal.

POLLSTER: I suppose you found a lot to empathize with in tonight's show?

KING JEROME: Not really. *C'est amusant*, but really on the wild side. The royal succession just does not function in this manner. Be-

A simple organization on the basis of different interviews.

What did happen to Christopher Marlowe?

sides, what sort of a king naps in an orchard. I ask you? Denmark? In the winter time? *Ce n'est pas logique. Si ce n'est pas logique, ce n'est pas français.*

POLLSTER: The situation of the play is stretched beyond credence?

Does this
satirize the
pollster?

KING JEROME: It is certainly stretched beyond *my* principality.

POLLSTER: Your Highness, was there anything about the evening that you *did* enjoy?

KING JEROME: Well, yes . . . there was an orange girl . . . did you happen to notice which way . . . (*Looks off, sees girl, waves, walks off intently.*)

POLLSTER: Good evening, sir, could you tell me your occupation and how you enjoyed tonight's performance?

MANUFACTURER: I'm in rags.

POLLSTER: I beg your—

MANUFACTURER: The cloak and doublet game. A manufacturer.

POLLSTER: And what did you think of our play, sir?

MANUFACTURER: Is this the time to attack a minority group? I mean, with the Armada practically at our throats?

POLLSTER: A minority group? I don't understand, sir—

MANUFACTURER: Who do you think Rosencrantz and Guildenstern are supposed to be, Welshmen?

POLLSTER: I'm sure it never occurred to the author that—

MANUFACTURER: Now last week, *that* was a play! The one about the colored general. So why couldn't Guildenstern be a general? A colonel, at least?

POLLSTER: I'll be glad to pass your suggestions along to the playwright, sir. And thank you for—

MANUFACTURER: Tell him to write something with a *businessman* in it . . . maybe a man with a daughter to marry off . . . he could be a foreigner, even.

POLLSTER: Thank you, sir.

POLLSTER: Good evening, sir, might I have your occupation and your reaction to tonight's preview?

BACON: Gladly. My name is Sir Francis Bacon. I'm a lawyer.

POLLSTER: Ah, then you should have some very incisive thoughts on tonight's play.

Look for
Shakespearean
quotations in
Bacon's answers.

BACON: Let's just say . . . all the perfumes of Araby will not sweeten this turkey!

POLLSTER: You feel it was—

BACON: A disgrace to the boards. Screaming. Shouting. Posturing. Five acts full of sound and fury, signifying nothing.

POLLSTER: But the motivation of the main character, Sir Francis?

BACON: It certainly didn't hold a mirror up to nature for *me*. A writer should stick to what he knows!

POLLSTER: Perhaps, given more time . . . experience.

BACON: Let me say this: This man will be a playwright when Birnam Wood comes to Dunsinane. Good evening.

Mr. Herrick, this research clearly shows that many people do not comprehend the premise of the play. There is considerable negative reaction to the love story. (Could you cut out the teen-agers and put in a few more orange girls?)

We much regret that we cannot present, in good faith, the encouraging figures we turned up last week for the dancing bear. But there is considerable profit in knowing definitely that this author does not write works of more than passing interest, no matter what his past successes may have led you to believe.

Yours for good theater,

GILES BULLSTABLE, *Senior Prognosticator*

> Conclusion returns to the pollster's report to Herrick.

Reading and Interpreting

1. What is the satire making fun of? Poll-taking, theatre-goers, *Hamlet,* or some combination?

2. Does the piece imply any serious criticism?

3. How important to appreciating the piece is some knowledge of *Hamlet?*

Writing Techniques

1. If you find the piece funny, can you say why? What are some of the characteristics of the writing that make the humor work?

2. How would you describe the tone of the piece? Would it work as well if it did not pretend to be serious?

Suggestions for Writing

Humorous writing is not easy, but you might try something like this piece with a different topic. For example, a poll taken by Martians on American higher education or American love of basketball, or an imaginary interview with a candidate for office, or for a beauty contest.

COMPULSION

Peter De Vries

Peter De Vries *is one of America's most distinguished writers of humor. To enjoy him fully requires a lively and well-stored mind. Pieces like this generally appeared in the* New Yorker. *This selection is included in* Without a Stitch in Time.

"THE things my wife buys at auctions are keeping us baroque," I said. There was a perceptible movement of cocktail guests away from me, and a round or resentful murmurs varying according to the amount of my talk each person had, in the past hour, been within earshot of. I had in that period stated to a small group discussing modern tonality that not since Debussy had dissonance, in my opinion, lent enchantment; asked a woman who was planning to winter in Tijuana, "Tijuana go there for the climate or just to gamble?"; and dilated on music in the heir as potential compositional talent in one's offspring.

An incident as introduction.

The guests were a cross-section (by now, I might add, a *very* cross section) of Westport town life. Psychiatry was represented by a sprucely tweeded man in his fifties named Granberry, who looped an arm through mine, drew me aside, and said, "I think I can help you."

"Help me?" I said, plucking a canape from a passing tray.

"It's obviously a compulsion with you," Granberry went on. "You know what compulsions are. Hand washing, crack avoiding, counting—"

"I know what compulsions are," I said, and went on to note that an acquaintance of mine at this very party couldn't eat salmon caviar because of a need to tally the roe as they exploded against the roof of his mouth.

"All right," Granberry said. "Your trouble is, you can't pass a word up. You're a compulsive punner. Your mutilating conversation springs from whatever subterranean conflict hinders you from participating in it maturely."

"Don't you fellows ever have a fear you're not being followed?" I said.

Granberry's manner became arch. "Mind telling me your earliest recollection?" he asked, with a small, pursed smile that gave him rather the look of a winsome weasel.

"Not in the least," I said. "It's about an alarm clock I had in my bedroom when I was a kid. A clock I always think of as the potato clock."

"Potato clock?" Granberry repeated, with a puzzled frown. "Why potato clock?"

"Because I had to get up potato clock every morning."

"You're a sick man," Granberry said, "or you're pulling my leg with an old vaudeville joke." He pursued the more succulent of the alternatives. "There is something we call *Klang* associations. It's a sort of chain punning, and is characteristic of certain encysted types. Your pattern is a complex and refined variation of these word salads."

"It is also," I answered coolly, "if I am not mistaken, the method by which James Joyce constructed *Finnegans Wake.*"

I turned and walked off.

For some days, however, I was unable to get Granberry's impromptu observations out of my mind. I sedulously derided his phrase "mutilating conversation" in talking the encounter over with my wife, aware that I was doing so because that quill had gone home. One aspect, in particular, of my habit tended to bear Granberry out—the fact that these rejoinders of mine did not arise principally out of a wish to play the wag, and not infrequently fell as drearily on my own ears as on those of my hearers. Perhaps I was indeed driven by some subcutaneous need to sabotage dialogue. Since Granberry had put his finger on that much, why not, I thought, let him try to uncover the cause of my compulsion, which was really so much sand in the gears of my social relations and repeatedly cost me my wife's good graces? So I took up the genial challenge, "Come see me sometime," which Granberry had flung over his shoulder—or, rather, over mine—as I walked away from him, and made an appointment for the first of what was to be a series of interviews, in his midtown office.

> The narrative divides into parts.

Granberry's headway with me may be inferred from the way matters stood at the end of one month. As my fourth weekly consultation drew to its close, he leaned across his desk and asked, "Do you feel, now, that you're acquiring a better grasp of your symptoms?"

"Symptoms I do," I answered, "and then again, symptoms I don't."

"*Don't be discouraged,*" Granberry said, with a smile that tendered me every good wish. "*I'm* not."

> Does this suggest the psychiatrist as "straight man"?

Granberry remained, throughout the proceedings, the soul of patient industry, never doubting that we were burrowing steadily toward the root of my *volonté.* His confidence buoyed me. Then, suddenly, my responses became completely phonetic. When, in some illustrative reference of Granberry's to his own formative years, he mentioned that he was born in Oklahoma, I threw out "Oklahoma tell your mother she wants you."

I wet my lips nervously and slid up in my chair. "Good God," I said, "I was never *that* bad before. What's happened? Now I even dream in puns. Like last night I dreamed of a female deer chasing a male deer in the mating season."

"?"

"A doe trying to make a fast buck."

"!"

I was vexed to see Granberry, while I was visualizing ostracism from all but the most undiscriminating circles, rise and rub his hands.

"We're muddling the disease, so to speak — the way medication sometimes stirs up an infection before it can get to correcting it," he said. "Your white count, as it were, is way up."

"Well, let's get it down," I said.

But up it stayed. I now not only refrained from mingling in society — I didn't dare leave the house (except, of course, to visit Granberry). During this period, only my wife knew that I was "worse." I wouldn't care to give any detailed evidence of my white count other than the above ramshackle instances. Granberry, on the other hand, had never been so optimistic; he said that nothing proved so much as the intensification of my condition how close we were to uncovering the traumatic incident that undoubtedly lay at the heart of it. But weeks went by and still no traumatic incident.

So finally, resentful of Granberry and the pass to which he had brought me, I made up a traumatic incident that I felt would, preparatory to my bailing out on the whole business, caricature both him and the calling he professed.

I sprang it on him midway of an interview.

"Say," I said, pausing in a train of reflections on my early school days, "I just remembered something. Something that comes back to me now, after all these years."

"What's that?" Granberry said alertly.

"I was in fifth or sixth grade," I said. "We were being asked to use words in a sentence. When it came my turn, the teacher gave me the word 'ominous.' 'Let's hear you use "ominous" in a sentence,' she said. I got up and stood in the aisle." I hesitated in my narrative, as though the strain of resurrection were a taxing one.

"Go on," Granberry said.

"I groped desperately for a way to use the word assigned me," I resumed. "As I did so, I heard the kid in the seat behind me — a kid who was always razzing me in the schoolyard — I heard him whisper something to somebody and snicker. Burning with anger, I turned and said, 'If he doesn't shut his mouth, ominous sock him one!' "

Granberry set down a letter knife he had been bending back

> Exaggeration is a device for humor.

and forth in his hands. He coughed into his fist and rose.

"It's impossible, you see, to cheat," he said. "I mean a hoax is just as significant as a bona fide memory. More so, in what it reveals of you, because it's an act of *conscious* selection, whereas memory is an *un*conscious one."

Embarrassed for me, he walked to the window and tugged at the cord of a Venetian blind. "I can never seem to adjust this thing," he said. "Why, I have no choice but to take your little charade at face value. And I think that what it consitutes is nothing less than an X-ray of your personality."

Does this characterize Granberry?

The thought seemed to steep him momentarily in a gloom as great as my own; Granberry, that is, had the same sense as I of being stuck with this very corny case history.

"Couldn't it be part of the white count?" I asked, trying to renege.

Granberry shook his head. "It would still be just as revelatory," he said.

Returning to the chair behind his desk, he plunged into an interpretation of the data I had given him.

"It confirms and crystallizes what I have felt about you all along," he said. "You are fundamentally afraid of people. I said from the start, this habit of yours was a way of mutilating conversation, and now we know why you mutilate it. You do so in order to escape the risks of engaging in it on an adult level, because you're afraid you won't stand up to the test of social comparisons it constitutes. Everybody you meet is that boy in the schoolyard—oh, I don't doubt that there *was* one, or many—and you ought to recognize that, in trying to grasp why you deflate people." He paused, then went astringently but sympathetically on. "Freud has explained that humor is a denial of anxiety, so you must understand that these puns of yours arise from one of the most intense forms of belligerence—the belligerence of the insecure."

He let this sink in a moment, "Let that do for today," he concluded. "Think over what I've said, and we'll talk about it some more next time."

There weren't many more next times. At first I was piqued, but soon I came to feel that Granberry was probably right. With this new insight into myself, I determined to control my tendency, and, slowly, I succeeded. Success came somewhat faster once Granberry had stressed this important point: "Always bear in mind that the other fellow is just as afraid of you as you are of him."

At length, my habit cleared up. When, for example, some friends of my wife's and mine named Pritchett phoned to invite us to come listen to a record they had just acquired, adding that it was "the new long-playing *Godunov*," I did not reply, as once I might

Even a funny piece has organization.

have, "That's Godunov for me." Nor, when a dinner companion exclaimed that she had glimpsed three wedges of southbound geese over her rooftop in one day, did I succumb to the temptation to murmur, "Migratious!"

Granberry dismissed me as arrested. "I think it'll stick," he said. "Your adjustment should last indefinitely. Unless, of course, you have some experience sufficiently unsettling to jar loose your old resentment and antagonism. But I think that unlikely. I can't imagine what it could be."

Nor could I. Matters seemed to have been resolved.

Then, one Saturday morning a month or so after Granberry and I had shaken hands and bade one another farewell, I was drinking midmorning coffee at home with my wife when I saw the mailman drive up.

"I'll get it," I said, and rose and went to the mailbox.

There were three pieces of mail—one, I saw by the return address on the envelope, from Granberry's office. I had not opened it by the time I rejoined my wife.

"This is from Granberry," I said, giving her the two others, which were addressed to her. "Probably his bill."

"Well, whatever it is, it's worth it," she said, abstractedly perusing the other things. "There's nothing whatever left of that awful habit of yours. Not one iota."

I opened the envelope and peered inside. I uttered a cry of genuine shock.

"How do you like that!" I exclaimed. "Fifteen calls and iota bandit seven hundred and fifty dollars!"

Is he cured?

Reading and Interpreting

1. Explain the puns in the first paragraph?
2. What is the attitude of the piece toward Granberry?
3. What is the effect of the conclusion?

Writing Techniques

1. Puns are frequently regarded as the lowest form of wit; people conventionally groan at them. Are some of De Vries's puns funnier than others? What seems to be the attitude of the piece toward the puns; that is, is the reader supposed to think of them as "good" puns?

2. Does some of the humor come from satire on Granberry and psychiatry?

3. Does some of the humor depend on exaggeration? Cite examples of exaggeration.

4. The narrator of the piece pretends to regret his compulsion to pun. How does the reader react to this pretense? How seriously do you take the narrator's efforts to cure himself?

CATCH HER IN THE OATMEAL
[In the manner of J. D. Salinger]
Dan Greenburg

69

Dan Greenburg *is a free-lance writer and editor, and the author of several books, including* How to Be a Jewish Mother. *The parody reprinted here was one of his many contributions to* Esquire.

IF you actually want to hear about it, what I'd better do is I'd better warn you right now that you aren't going to believe it. I mean it's a true *story* and all, but it still sounds sort of phony.

Anyway, my name is Goldie Lox. It's sort of a boring name, but my parents said that when I was born I had this very blonde hair and all. Actually, I was born bald. I mean how many babies get born with blonde hair? None. I mean I've *seen* them and they're all wrinkled and red and slimy and everything. And bald. And then all the phonies have to come around and tell you he's as cute as a bug's ear. A bug's ear, boy, that really kills me. You ever *seen* a bug's ear? What's cute about a bug's *ear*, for Chrissake! Nothing, that's what.

So, like I was saying, I always seem to be getting into these very stupid situations. Like this time I was telling you about. Anyway, I was walking through the forest and all when I see this very interesting house. A *house*. You wouldn't think anybody would be living way the hell out in the goddam *forest*, but they were. No one was home or anything and the door was open, so I walked in. I figured what I'd do is I'd probably horse around until the guys that lived there came home and maybe asked me to stay for dinner or something. Some people think they *have* to ask you to stay for dinner even if they *hate* you. Also I didn't exactly feel like going home and getting asked a lot of lousy questions. I mean that's *all* I ever seem to do.

Anyway, while I was waiting I sort of sampled some of this stuff they had on the table that tasted like oatmeal. *Oatmeal*. It would have made you puke, I mean it. Then something very spooky started

phony
Lox

horse around

lousy

happening. I started getting dizzier than hell. I figured I'd feel better if I could just rest for a while. Sometimes if you eat something like lousy oatmeal you can feel better if you just rest for a while, so I sat down. That's when the goddam *chair* breaks in half. No kidding, you start feeling lousy and some stupid *chair* is going to break on you every time. I'm not kidding. Anyway I finally found the crummy bedroom and I lay down on this very tiny bed. I was really depressed.

crummy

I don't know how long I was asleep or anything, but all of a sudden I hear this very strange voice say, "Someone's been sleeping in *my* sack, for Chrissake, and there she is!" So I open my eyes and here at the foot of the bed are these three crummy *bears*. *Bears!* I swear to God. By that time I was *really* feeling depressed. There's nothing more depressing than waking up and finding three *bears* talking about you, I mean.

sack

So I didn't stay around and shoot the breeze with them or anything. If you want to know the truth, I sort of ran out of there like a madman or something. I do that quite a little when I'm depressed like that.

On the way home, though, I got to figuring. What probably happened is these bears wandered in when they smelled this oatmeal and all. Probably bears *like* oatmeal, *I* don't know. And the voice I heard when I woke up was probably something I dreamt.

So that's the story.

I wrote it all up once as a theme in school, but my crummy teacher said it was too *whimsical*. Whimsical. That killed me. You got to meet her sometime, boy. She's a real queen.

queen

Reading and Interpreting

1. Parody is similar to caricature in that it works mainly by exaggerating characteristics of a style or prevalent points of view in order to criticize them. Reading Salinger's *Catcher in the Rye* will help you see more of the fun in this parody, but even without reading it you can see much of what the parodist is making fun of. What does Greenburg seem to be criticizing?

2. Why does a parodist select a familiar story as a vehicle? What does this selection suggest about the work being parodied?

Writing Techniques

1. List characteristics of writing style that seem to be exaggerated in the parody.

2. Is the parody funny? If so, what is the basis of the humor?

Word Study

Part of the parody involves the vocabulary of Goldie Lox (what is the meaning of *lox?*). Try to define the following of her favorite words as she uses them: *phony, horse around, lousy, crummy, sack, queen.*

Suggestions for Writing

Parodies are not easy, but trying them can be fun. Try a parody on something that you think needs criticizing: a government bulletin, a sentimental story, a television soap opera, a popular song, a sports column.

FAMILY LIFE IN AMERICA
Robert Benchley

70

Robert Benchley—*as an actor, screen writer, drama critic, and in various other capacities—was another of those wits who helped to change the course of American humor, notably through the* New Yorker.

Part 1

THE naturalistic literature of this country has reached such a state that no family of characters is considered true to life which does not include at least two hypochondriacs, one sadist, and one old man who spills food down the front of his vest. If this school progresses, the following is what we may expect in our national literature in a year or so.

The living room in the Twilly's house was so damp that thick, soppy moss grew all over the walls. It dripped on the picture of Grandfather Twilly that hung over the melodeon, making streaks down the dirty glass like sweat on the old man's face. It was a mean face. Grandfather Twilly had been a mean man and had little spots of soup on the lapel of his coat. All his children were mean and had soup spots on their clothes.

Grandma Twilly sat in the rocker over by the window, and as she rocked the chair snapped. It sounded like Grandma Twilly's knees snapping as they did whenever she stooped over to pull the wings off a fly. She was a mean old thing. Her knuckles were grimy and she chewed crumbs that she found in the bottom of her reticule. You would have hated her. She hated herself. But most of all she hated Grandfather Twilly.

"I certainly hope you're frying good," she muttered as she looked up at his picture.

"Hasn't the undertaker come yet, Ma?" asked young Mrs. Wilbur Twilly petulantly. She was boiling water on the oil-heater and every now and again would spill a little of the steaming liquid on the baby who was playing on the floor. She hated the baby because it looked like her father. The hot water raised little white blisters on the baby's red neck and Mabel Twilly felt short, sharp twinges of pleasure at the sight. It was the only pleasure she had had for four months.

"Why don't you kill yourself, Ma?" she continued. "You're only in the way here and you know it. It's just because you're a mean old woman and want to make trouble for us that you hang on."

Grandma Twilly shot a dirty look at her daughter-in-law. She had always hated her. Stringy hair, Mabel had. Dank, stringy hair. Grandma Twilly thought how it would look hanging at an Indian's belt. But all that she did was to place her tongue against her two front teeth and make a noise like the bathroom faucet.

Wilbur Twilly was reading the paper by the oil lamp. Wilbur had watery blue eyes and cigar ashes all over his knees. The third and fourth buttons of his vest were undone. It was too hideous.

He was conscious of his family seated in chairs about him. His mother, chewing crumbs. His wife Mabel, with her stringy hair, reading. His sister Bernice, with projecting front teeth, who sat thinking of the man who came every day to take away the waste paper. Bernice was wondering how long it would be before her family would discover that she had been married to this man for three years.

How Wilbur hated them all. It didn't seem as if he could stand it any longer. He wanted to scream and stick pins into every one of them and then rush out and see the girl who worked in his office snapping rubber bands all day. He hated her too, but she wore side-combs.

Part 2

The street was covered with slimy mud. It oozed out from under Bernice's rubbers in unpleasant bubbles until it seemed to her as if she must kill herself. Hot air coming out from a steam laundry. Hot, stifling air. Bernice didn't work in the laundry but she wished that she did so that the hot air would kill her. She wanted to be stifled. She needed torture to be happy. She also needed a swift clout on the side of the face.

A drunken man lurched out from a doorway and flung his arms about her. It was only her husband. She loved her husband. She loved him so much that, as she pushed him away into the gutter, she stuck her little finger into his eye. She also untied his necktie. It was a bow necktie, with white, dirty spots on it and it was wet with gin. It didn't seem as if Bernice could stand it any longer. All the repressions of nineteen sordid years behind protruding teeth surged through her untidy soul. She wanted love. But it was not her husband that she loved so fiercely. It was old Grandfather Twilly. And he was too dead.

Part 3

In the dining room of the Twilly's house everything was very quiet. Even the vinegar cruet which was covered with fly specks. Grandma Twilly lay with her head in the baked potatoes, poisoned by Mabel, who, in her turn, had been poisoned by her husband and sprawled in an odd posture over the china closet. Wilbur and his sister Bernice had just finished choking each other to death and between them completely covered the carpet in that corner of the room where the worn spot showed the bare boards beneath, like ribs on a chicken carcass.

Only the baby survived. She had a mean face and had great spillings of Imperial Granum down her bib. As she looked about her at her family, a great hate surged through her tiny body and her eyes snapped viciously. She wanted to get down from her highchair and show them all how much she hated them.

Bernice's husband, the man who came after the waste paper, staggered into the room. The tips were off both his shoe-lacings. The baby experienced a voluptuous sense of futility at the sight of the tipless lacings and leered suggestively at her uncle-in-law.

"We must get the roof fixed," said the man, very quietly. "It lets the sun in."

Reading and Interpreting

1. What is Benchley criticizing in his piece?

2. In what way is Benchley's comment like parody?

Writing Techniques

1. Benchley changes the point of view from which his story is told from time to time. What is the effect of these changes?

2. How does the humor here differ from that of De Vries or of Lasson and Eynon's poll-taker?

Suggestions for Writing

1. Humor, as we have observed, is not easily imitated. But you might try a story of a different American family, perhaps the kind presented in current television comedy series or in a television series dealing with cute children. It is important not to try too hard to be funny but to let details speak for themselves.

2. For a more ambitious paper you might try writing about some aspect of American humor or about the humor of a group of people you know. American humor was once thought to have a special character, growing partly out of the raw life of the frontier. What is American humor like today — on television, in films, in night clubs, on records?

A PRIVATE AUDIENCE — OR MAYBE TWO? **71**
Richard Condon

This is a chapter in The Vertical Smile *(1971), one of several novels that are establishing* Condon *among the most respected young writers in America. To read the passage you should know that Os (Osgood Noon), seventy and sexy, had hesitated to go to bed with Ada (Clarke) for fear of a fatal heart attack. A lonesome widow (who insists she is not a nymphomaniac), Ada finally got him into bed by promising him an unheard of Sunday appointment with a renowned heart specialist, the great Dr. Weiler. Os is skeptical, but Ada is used to having her way and says, "You let me handle Weiler."*

MIRACULOUSLY, Ada was able to get a private audience with Dr. Abraham Weiler whose fame had been secured when he had been invited to conduct a routine check-up on the heart of Dr. Christiaan Barnard. Weiler not only did not make house calls (after all even an interne wouldn't make a house call), but he would not permit patients to make office calls and he rarely visited a hospital. He remained far back in the AMA incense, available for consultation, usually only by telescreen telephone, only to Heads of Departments of Cardiology of leading (non-integrated) universities. It was at Weiler's desk that the chain of fee-splitting stopped. He was too big a man to split fees. He took the whole fee. When feeder physicians referred data to him they were paid with the honor of his receiving it, if he would consent to receive it. They had to pay his fees plus the fees which the patient would have to pay them and, further, had to submit to sodium pentathol tests, then to a lie detector when stating the amount of the fees they would charge the patients. Weiler personified the meaning of the evolved Hippocratic Oath and owned two ski lifts at Megeve.

The great doctor was extremely grave with Os and extremely affable with Ada in his waiting room. Os was left with many copies of the *Literary Digest* and *Liberty* magazines while Ada and the doctor spent an immeasurably long time consulting behind a locked door within the Surgery about Os' symptoms and background. For whatever reason, the doctor had not only locked the door, but had bolted it in two places, loudly.

When Os was, at last, called in, Ada was busy at a mirror fussing with her hair and Dr. Weiler seemed strangely out-of-breath for a heart man. Os was feeling very edgy. He felt like those Aztecs must have felt when they climbed the three hundred and sixty-five steps of the pyramid at Teotihuacan toward the old gentleman with the red-black matted hair and the crimson-spattered feather apron who waited with a stone knife at the top. Weiler was a great doctor but this was *Os'* heart they would be talking about while Weiler seemed to be having even worse trouble with his own.

The distinguished doctor was staring fixedly at Os with popping eyes while he gulped air and clawed with his right hand at his chest. The doctor was behaving like a man who had been forced to race up all the stairs of a skyscraper while carrying two anvils. He motioned weakly for Os to sit in the facing chair. While he fought to recover into a less shocking breathing cycle he shuffled X-rays, EKG's, medical reports and letters concerning Os which had been rushed to his desk by Os' various doctors in the hope that Dr. Weiler would remember them and perhaps even nod to them at the next tax-deductible medical convention at Las Vegas. At last he regained control of his speech and his wizardry became immediately apparent.

"I have digested these data, Mr. Noon," he said slowly, "and regardless of any other opinion you may have been given, you may now be sure that you have a transient left-bundle branch block which indicates ischemia of a transient sort. You have, therefore, a coronary insufficiency with angina pectoris."

"Well—yes," Os said. They had all told him that.

"The episodes of precordial distress which occurred during intercourse two years ago, according to A. Edward Masters' diagnostic report, are typical of angina and I am pleased with you that you are not overweight and do not smoke."

Weiler seemed to look right through all the O's in Os' name and into his soul piercingly, an illusion lent to physicians by extreme myopia and developed for the profession under grant by the late Lionel Barrymore.

"I understand, doctor," Os said.

"None*less*—it is essential that we lessen your anxieties and

Obviously the details require some interpretation.

What seems to be on the great doctor's mind?

reduce your tensions which are so constantly a-building—and I refer to certain personal, circumstantial and situational matters of which you are well aware."

"I worked like Old Ned to lose sixty pounds over the past two years."

"However, I do not feel that the use of chemical tranquilizers is advisable in your case." The doctor yawned suddenly. "What is bothering you?" he asked abruptly.

Os glanced across at Ada for a second, clearing his throat. "Uh—well—the fact is I am fearful that I might drop dead during sexual intercourse and what with my total recall of almost every miniskirt I had ever seen before *Women's Wear Daily* took that away from us, to say nothing of the prevalence of highly spiced foods—this keeps me continually anxious and tense."

Weiler leaned forward in his great throne of a chair. "I pre*scribe* intercourse for you," he said dramatically. "I prescribe it as a *must* for you." His own right hand gripped his chest more tightly. "But intercourse under experienced, expert care. Do you wish me to recommend a reliable practitioner?"

Os darted a glance at Ada again. She was seated with her gorgeous legs crossed. She smiled at him lasciviously and shook her head almost imperceptibly. Os turned back to the doctor. "No, thank you," he said. "That will not be necessary."

Reading and Interpreting

1. What impressions do you get of Dr. Weiler? Of Os?

2. Fiction is frequently used for satire, as Swift did in *Gulliver's Travels* or Voltaire in *Candide*. What is being satirized here?

Writing Techniques

1. Compare Condon's narrative with Benchley's. How do they differ in the development of satire?

2. How much of Condon's humor depends on exaggeration? Is the episode absurd or plausible?

Index of Authors